# Sanctity, Gender and Authority in Medieval Caucasia

**Edinburgh Byzantine Studies**

*Innovative approaches to the medieval Eastern Roman empire and its neighbours*

Edinburgh Byzantine Studies promotes new, theory-driven approaches to the empire commonly called Byzantium. The series looks at the literary, historical, material and visual remains of this long-living political order and its neighbours, often from a multi-disciplinary and/or cross-cultural vantage point. Its innovative readings highlight the connectivity of Byzantine culture as well as of Byzantine Studies.

**Series Editors**
Louise Blanke, The University of Edinburgh
Ivan Drpić, University of Pennsylvania
Niels Gaul, The University of Edinburgh
Alexander Riehle, Harvard University
Yannis Stouraitis, The University of Edinburgh
Alicia Walker, Bryn Mawr College

**Books available in the series**
*Imperial Visions of Late Byzantium: Manuel II Palaiologos and Rhetoric in Purple*
Florin Leonte

*Identities and Ideologies in the Medieval East Roman World*
Edited by Yannis Stouraitis

*The Monotheisation of Pontic-Caspian Eurasia: Eighth to Thirteenth Centuries*
Alex M. Feldman

*Social Stratification in Late Byzantium*
Christos Malatras

*Sanctity, Gender and Authority in Medieval Caucasia*
Nikoloz Aleksidze

*Greek Captives and Mediterranean Slavery, 1260–1460*
Alasdair Grant

Visit the Edinburgh Byzantine Studies website at edinburghuniversitypress.com/series-edinburgh-byzantine-studies.html

# Sanctity, Gender and Authority in Medieval Caucasia

Nikoloz Aleksidze

EDINBURGH
University Press

Edinburgh University Press is one of the leading university presses in the UK. We publish academic books and journals in our selected subject areas across the humanities and social sciences, combining cutting-edge scholarship with high editorial and production values to produce academic works of lasting importance. For more information visit our website: edinburghuniversitypress.com

© Nikoloz Aleksidze, 2024, 2025

Grateful acknowledgement is made to the sources listed in the List of Illustrations for permission to reproduce material previously published elsewhere. Every effort has been made to trace the copyright holders, but if any have been inadvertently overlooked, the publisher will be pleased to make the necessary arrangements at the first opportunity.

Edinburgh University Press Ltd
13 Infirmary Street
Edinburgh EH1 1LT

First published in hardback by Edinburgh University Press 2024

Typeset in 10.5/13 Warnock Pro by
IDSUK (DataConnection) Ltd

A CIP record for this book is available from the British Library

ISBN 978 1 4744 9861 6 (hardback)
ISBN 978 1 4744 9862 3 (paperback)
ISBN 978 1 4744 9863 0 (webready PDF)
ISBN 978 1 4744 9864 7 (epub)

The right of Nikoloz Aleksidze to be identified as the author of this work has been asserted in accordance with the Copyright, Designs and Patents Act 1988, and the Copyright and Related Rights Regulations 2003 (SI No. 2498).

# Contents

| | |
|---|---|
| List of Illustrations | viii |
| Acknowledgements | x |
| A Note on Translations, Transliterations and References | xii |
| | |
| Introduction: The Cult of Saints and Body Politic | 1 |
|    'The Lot of the Mother of God' | 1 |
|    'Martyrs for Faith and the Fatherland' | 3 |
|    Tbilisi's Saintly Topography | 7 |
|    Why This Book? | 9 |
|    The Saintly and the Feminine | 12 |
|    Sources | 13 |
|    Value | 14 |
|    Ambiguity | 16 |
|    Exception | 20 |
|    Text Structure | 21 |

**Part I**

| | |
|---|---|
| Introduction to Part I: Late Antique Foundations | 27 |
| | |
| 1  Saints at the Foundations | 35 |
|    1.1 Saints and History: Eastern Roman Models | 35 |
|    1.2 Materiality of History: Armenian Vision | 40 |
|    1.3 Relics and Kingship | 48 |
|    1.4 The *farrah* of the Kings | 54 |
|    1.5 Hidden Treasure and Its Discoverers | 58 |
|    1.6 The Treasure of a Christian King | 63 |
| | |
| 2  An Exceptional Saint for Exceptional Times: The Cult of St Nino | 68 |
|    2.1 The *k'adagi* | 68 |
|    2.2 'The Captive Who Captivates' | 74 |

|  |  |  |
|---|---|---|
|  | 2.3 The 'Conversion' | 80 |
|  | 2.4 A 'New' History | 84 |
|  | 2.5 From Multiplicity to Unity | 88 |
|  | 2.6 From North to South | 92 |
| 3 | The Politics of Female Relics | 102 |
|  | 3.1 The Proto-Martyr | 102 |
|  | 3.2 The Story | 104 |
|  | 3.3 Reciprocity | 107 |
|  | 3.4 The Political Life of Shushanik's Body | 110 |
|  | 3.5 Shushanik Revisited | 116 |
|  | 3.6 The Debt | 119 |

Conclusion to Part I: Relics, Gender and Politics in
Late Antique Caucasia                                                123

## Part II

Introduction to Part II: The Saintly World of the Bagratids   131

| | | |
|---|---|---|
| 4 | Masculinising Saints: The Bagratids | 139 |
|  | 4.1 In the Presence of Martyrs | 139 |
|  | 4.2 The New Kartli | 141 |
|  | 4.3 The 'Grand Narrative' | 147 |
|  | 4.4 An Old King for Modern Anxieties | 151 |
|  | 4.5 St George | 155 |
|  | 4.6 The Counterpart | 161 |
| 5 | The Lot(s) of the Mother of God | 166 |
|  | 5.1 *Sak'art'velo*: A Project | 166 |
|  | 5.2 The Family | 170 |
|  | 5.3 Protector of Strangers | 173 |
|  | 5.4 The Acquri Icon of the Mother of God | 179 |
|  | 5.5 Women at the Margins | 187 |
| 6 | The Queen's Three Bodies | 189 |
|  | 6.1 The Two Queens | 189 |
|  | 6.2 Theotokos's Kin | 192 |
|  | 6.3 The Two Crowns | 196 |
|  | 6.4 A State of Exception | 207 |
|  | 6.5 The Liminal Figure | 214 |

Conclusion to Part II: The Legacy and Myth of Queen Tamar   223

## Part III

Introduction to Part III: The Rhetoric of Gender and Sanctity from
    Imperialism to Nationalism    229

7   The Saints of the Empire    233
    7.1 The Political Body of Queen Ketevan    233
    7.2 Imperial Taking    236
    7.3 Imperial Giving    242
    7.4 The Sacred and the Erotic    249

8   The Saints of the Nation    258
    8.1 'The Glory of Georgia'    258
    8.2 Gender Problematised (Again)    261
    8.3 Roads Old and New    266
    8.4 A New Nino    275

9   The Sacred, the Feminine and the National    281
    9.1 Guardians of the Borders: Saints and the Nation State    281
    9.2 Blasphemy    289
    9.3 *Cilxvedri*    294
    9.4 The Witches of Independent Georgia    301

Conclusion to Part III: The Modern Lives of Old Saints    307

Final Remarks    312

Bibliography    317
    Medieval Narrative Sources in Georgian    317
    Early Modern Georgian Literature    319
    Medieval Narrative Sources in Armenian    320
    Late Antique, Byzantine and Medieval Sources    320
    Early Modern Russian and Western Sources    321
    Collections of Medieval and Early Modern Documents    321
    Nineteenth- and Twentieth-Century Sources    322
    Anthologies of Poetry    322
    Online Databases    322
    Studies    322

Index    336

# Illustrations

**Figures**

2.1 Copy of the lost bas-relief of St Nino from the Church of Oshki, tenth century. Photo: Maka Chkhaidze. 72
2.2 Nineteenth-century Russian photograph of a fortress in the Darial Gorge. Source: Library of Congress. 97
2.3 Jvari' or the Holy Cross church, erected in the late sixth-century on the site of one of Nino's crosses, overlooking Mtskheta, with the Svetitskhoveli Cathedral in the background. Photo: Zurab Ttsertsvadze. 99
2.4 The Trinity Church of Gergeti, fourteenth century, with Mt Kazbegi in the background. Khevi, Georgia. Photo: Badri Vadachkoria. 101
4.1 Coronation of King Demetre I (left) and Coronation of St Katherine next to St Barbara (right). Church of the Saviour (Mac'xvariši), twelfth century. Nakipari, Upper Svaneti. Photo: Zurab Tsertsvadze. 140
4.2 Chancel of Urt'xva, early eleventh century, Shida Kartli, Georgia. Source: Ekaterine Gedevanishvili. 157
4.3 The Icon of St George in Nakipari, Upper Svaneti, eleventh century. Photo: Zurab Tsertsvadze. 158
5.1 Crest of the Bagrationi Family (one version). Source: Artanuji Publishers. 166
5.2 Apse of the Church of the Mother of God of Gelati. Source: Artanuji Publishers. 171
5.3 The Khakhuli Tryptich, twelfth century. Source: Artanuji Publishers. 172
6.1 Queen Tamar and Giorgi III. Church of Dormition of Vardzia, thirteenth century. Source: Artanuji Publishers. 205

| | | |
|---|---|---|
| 7.1 | The Cross of St Nino, in a seventeenth-century metalwork. Source: Artanuji Publishers. | 245 |
| 8.1 | Michael Sabinin, *The Glory of the Georgian Church*. Source: Artanuji Publishers. | 258 |
| 8.2 | The Royal Panel of Betania with Laša-Giorgi, Tamar and Giorgi III, thirteenth century. Author: Zurab Tsertsvadze. | 264 |
| 8.3 | Russian topographic map of the Georgian Military Highway. Source: Library of Congress. | 267 |
| 9.1 | Lia Ukleba, 'Mary with a Toy Gun'. Source: Lia Ukleba. | 289 |
| 9.2 | An iconic photo of a woman (Nana Makharadze) carrying a black flag the day after the 9 April massacres. Iury Mechitov's photograph has since become the symbol of 9 April and of the eve of Georgia's independence. Notably, for decades, most people were convinced that the woman held the Georgian flag due to the bright white background. Author and source: Iury Mechitov. | 303 |

## Maps

| | | |
|---|---|---|
| I.1 | Map of Iberia in the sixth century. The map roughly depicts the borders of the Caucasian kingdoms in the sixth century. Source: D. Muskhelishvili, Historical Atlas of Georgia. | 29 |
| II.1 | Georgian kingdoms and principalities in the second half of the tenth century. Source: D. Muskhelishvili, Historical Atlas of Georgia. | 132 |
| 6.1 | The Georgan Kingdom during the reign of Queen Tamar. Source: D. Muskhelishvili, Historical Atlas of Georgia. | 189 |
| III.1 | Georgian kingdoms and principalities as annexed by the Russian Empire in the early nineteenth century. Source: D. Muskhelishvili, Historical Atlas of Georgia. | 231 |

## Tables

| | | |
|---|---|---|
| 1.1 | Structural similarities between *The Life of Vač'agan* and *The Life of P'arnavaz* | 55 |
| 2.1 | Structural symmetry of the *Mok'c'evay k'art'lisay* | 82 |

# Acknowledgements

The present book was in gestation for at least seven years, and has been made possible thanks to several generous scholarships, research grants, leaves and individuals. Its idea was conceived sometime in 2014 or 2015, during our weekly Thursday meetings at Trinity College, Oxford in Bryan Ward-Perkins's office. Bryan then directed a four-year research project funded by the Advanced European Research Grant, *The Cult of Saints in Late Antiquity: From Its Origins to circa AD 700, across the Entire Christian World*. My role in the project was to collect, classify and study late antique and early medieval Georgian and Armenian cult-related data. The present book, at least in part, is the result of observations gathered in our meetings where we had a unique opportunity to introduce, discuss and debate the regional and linguistic peculiarities of sainthood that we have encountered across late antique Christian communities from the British Isles to Iran.

I would, therefore, like to extend my exceptional gratitude to the PI, Dr Bryan Ward-Perkins for bringing me back to Oxford and letting me spend several peaceful years exploring the wonderful (and occasionally morbid) world of relics and sanctity. Bryan's incessant curiosity, cheerfulness and the ability to be excited about an obscure piece of cult-related data, while transferring the same excitement to you, is perhaps the reason this work has eventually seen the light of day. I am also grateful to Robert Wiśniewski, the project's co-director, and to fellow research associates in Oxford for generously sharing their expertise in respective fields and creating a congenial atmosphere. Pembroke College, Oxford has generously hosted me as a Junior Research Fellow for another four years, after my graduation from the same college in 2013.

Then, in 2021, in the challenging times of Covid, I had a rare opportunity as a Summer Fellow at the Dumbarton Oaks Research Library and Collection. Finally, in the Fall of 2021, I had an opportunity to spend a term in Budapest, as a visiting fellow at the Central European University's

Institute for Advanced Study, in a wonderful guesthouse just under the Buda Castle.

The manuscript was finalised during Nutsa's and my stay at Washington University in St Louis, where, while Nutsa was busy writing her own book, I had an opportunity to quietly sit and complete this work while occasionally having enlightening chats with Jim Wertsch and Pascal Boyer at Whispers Café or at 'JHOP' (early morning pancakes at Jim's place).

Throughout all these years, I was selflessly supported by my friends and colleagues, who have read the manuscript, criticised it and have generously supplied me with ideas (and images): Giorgi Cheishvili, György Geréby, Hubertus Jahn, Buba Kudava, Shalva Lezhava, Nicholas Matheou and Zurab Ttsertsvadze. But I am especially grateful to two brilliant scholars: art historian Ekaterine Gedevanishvili and philologist Dali Chitunashvili, with whom I have spent many days staring at frescoes in Svaneti or at manuscript pages at the National Centre of Manuscripts.

As always, this book too would have been impossible without Nutsa's intellectual and emotional input, and her power to inspire.

# A Note on Translations, Transliterations and References

Throughout the book all the primary sources are either quoted from the existing English translations or, unless otherwise specified, are my own. Whenever necessary, existing translations are corrected throughout. Since most of the quoted sources are available online, the original texts will not be provided. Most of the medieval Georgian sources and some Armenian ones are digitised and available at titus.uni-frankfurt.de. The database meticulously follows the pagination of the standard academic editions. Therefore, wherever necessary, instead of quoting the full original Georgian texts, precise references will be provided to the database along with a URL link for those who wish to consult the original texts. The original Georgian, Armenian, Russian or Greek texts are provided only (a) where the translation is my own, (b) when there is a philological argument to be made, (c) when there is a need to correct the existing translation or (d) where the translation is uncertain.

The transliteration system for the Georgian and Russian languages follows the Library of Congress romanisation rule. The Armenian system follows the established rule adopted by the *Revue des Études Arméniennes*. However, to avoid over-usage of diacritic marks, transliteration is used sparingly, mostly for terms and concepts. While some medieval and early modern proper and place names are transliterated according to these rules, such personal and place names that are still in use are not transliterated and follow the modern spelling. Thus, for example, Shushanik (not Shushanik), Tbilisi (not T'bilisi or Tp'ilisi), Chavchavadze (not Č'avč'avadze), Rustaveli (not Rust'aveli), Mtskheta (not Mc'xet'a), Apkhazeti (not Ap'xazet'i) and so on. However, since, for example, in Armenian philology, scholars insist on transliteration, the established forms will be used, such as Movsēs Xorenac'i and not Moses Khorenatsi. Proper names that are international and do not exhibit a particularly wide variety of spelling will be used in their international form, for example David, and not Davit', Constantine and not Konstantine, Alexander and not Alek'sandre. However, elsewhere the markedly English forms are avoided: for example King Giorgi and not King George, Archimandrite Grigol/Patriarch Grigor and not Gregory, Step'ane/Step'anos and not Stephen, Nikoloz and not Nicholas, Movsēs and not Moses and so on (the only exception is perhaps Gregory the Illuminator). In the Bibliography and references, original titles written in non-Latin alphabets will be transliterated according to the above rules.

In memory of my father, Zaza Aleksidze (1935–2023),
who couldn't wait to see this book.

# Introduction
# The Cult of Saints and Body Politic

## 'The Lot of the Mother of God'

In 2002, the Katholikos-Patriarch of All Georgia, Ilia II inaugurated a foundation that he named the 'Society of Iveria'. The society had one purpose: to fundraise for the building of a gigantic church on one of the several hills surrounding Tbilisi. Ten years later, in 2012, the church was officially opened and dedicated to the icon of the Mother of God of Iveria, that is the Theotokos of the Gate (*Portaitissa*), a medieval icon housed at the Iveron Monastery on Mt Athos. The committee of the church's *ktetors* (founders), as they called it, included some of the most influential members of Georgian elites. In 2011, President Saakashvili chaired the opening of the church. The declared purpose of the church was to prepare a seat for the miraculous appearance of the Icon of the Mother of God *Portaitissa* housed on Mt Athos. The church, which is as of now still unfinished, now stands as a *hetoimasia* of sorts, a Marian 'empty throne', expecting the miraculous return of 'Georgia's main woman' to Georgia. The home page of the society website reads,

> The allotment to the All-Holy Mother of God has been since antiquity bequeathed to the Georgian nation as a great responsibility to remain true to the Orthodox faith. The history of the Georgian nation is that of love of the truth and its heroic defence. As per Church tradition, following Christ's ascension, the apostles threw dice to determine who would preach in which land. The celestial queen was allotted the land of Iveria, that is Georgia. But, on the Lord's order, the Mother of God stayed in Jerusalem, whereas instead Apostle Andrew was sent to Georgia with the Theotokos's icon 'not-made-by-hand', which later became known as the Mother of God of Acquri. The Lord also said that the icon would act on the Theotokos's behalf as a protector of our nation until the end

of times. Over time, the Mother of God, as proof of her benevolence, gifted the Iverians with yet another great holy relic – the icon of the Mother of God, which miraculously escaped the persecution of icons in the Byzantine Empire and arrived at Mt Athos, at the Monastery of the Iverians. The icon was called the Mother of God of Iveria and was assigned the same mission as the *acheiropoieton* Icon of Acquri – to protect Orthodoxy, this time however, on Mt Athos, until the end of times. The honour to retrieve the icon from the sea was given by the Theotokos to a pious monk called Gabriel who lived in the Monastery of the Iverians.[1]

The website then narrates the role of the Iveron Monastery in the history of Georgian identity, scholarship, and statehood, and is called a symbol of Georgia's 'civilisational choice', that is the Byzantine commonwealth. Unfortunately, continues the website, over time, the Greeks snatched the monastery away from the Georgians. The Patriarch's initiative was, therefore, to make a new abode for the Mother of God, which would symbolise the responsibility that the nation allotted to the Mother of God has taken.

There was a sequence of rather surreal events leading to the selection of this particular spot for the church: For several years, a certain woman had experienced visions in which she was visited by the Mother of God *Portaitissa*. Being aware that the Western world would soon be engulfed in a doomsday war, the *Portaitissa* looked for a safe place to live. According to this person, the *Portaitissa* had chosen Georgia, and specifically this hill, as her last station to make sure that the Georgian nation remained immune to imminent disasters.

This person's claim might have been one of many apocalyptic fears experienced near the millennium's edge, but the Patriarch took an interest in her words and often met and conversed with her. With this foundation, the patriarch wished to erect a lasting monument to the oldest and most persistent myths of Georgian Christianity, that Georgia is the lot or the portion of the Mother of God, infinitely reproduced in early and late medieval Georgian chronicles, hagiographies, early modern letters, documents and all genres of literature and public discourses. As a result of the Patriarch's efforts, instead of being confined to the obscurity of mediaeval annals, nowadays the concept of the Lot of the Mother of God remains a central trope of Georgian political and religious discourses,

---

[1] http://iveriisa.ge/pages/5/ (01.03.23).

which may be encountered in unexpected contexts. The political implications of the 'Lot of the Mother of God', although constantly changing, remain remarkably stable.

## 'Martyrs for Faith and the Fatherland'

On 23 April 2015, as part of the commemoration of the centenary of the Armenian Genocide, the Armenian Apostolic Church proclaimed the victims of the Ottoman atrocities as saints of the church. To celebrate the occasion, the Katholikos of All Armenians Karekin II commissioned an icon depicting the multitudes slaughtered by the Ottomans. The icon conveys a collective and abstract image of Armenia. It illustrates the social diversity of the Armenian victims by highlighting the individual features of the men, women and children. A description on an official poster copy of the icon reads,

> It is a unique work of iconography, depicting the first 'new' saints to be recognised by the Armenian Church in several centuries: the martyrs who (in the words of the official prayer of intercession) gave 'their lives during the Armenian Genocide for faith and the homeland'. The Holy Martyrs are portrayed in the dress typical of the Ottoman Empire in 1915, and represent all ranks of Western Armenian society: ... all of whom perished in the brutal crime of 1915.[2]

The canonisation of the Genocide victims was the first such act in Armenia in centuries. The Armenian Church has long lost the tradition of beatification together with a sound theology of sainthood. By representing an imagined community of saints, this icon simultaneously addresses the modern concept of nationhood and its ethno-symbolism, meanwhile reaching out to the foundations of Armenian Christianity and identity. It covers all central components of Armenian national identity – its history, the monuments destroyed in historic Armenia, the social diversity of the victims, as well as other nuances of Armenian identity in the Ottoman Empire. Thus, the object of veneration on the icon is double: individual saints (as since canonisation every victim has become a saint of the Armenian Church) and the mystical body of the nation, as symbolised by the static host of the saints engulfed in the dynamics of history. Thus, on the one hand, the icon depicts an imagined community of saints, and on the other, a singular image of

---

[2] I am grateful to Dr Hratch Chilingirian for kindly providing the image.

the sacred body of the nation. A formula has been coined to describe the icon: 'Commemoration of the Holy Martyrs, who were killed during the Armenian Genocide for their faith and their fatherland.'[3] Here, the preposition 'for' carries a double meaning – it can be understood both as an active participation – for example 'for the sake of their faith', or as a passive victimhood of being killed 'on account of their faith'. While in its latter meaning, the formula reinforces the post-Genocide victimised identity, in its former sense, it reaches deeper into history, reminding modern Armenians of the first such collective martyrdom that took place in the fifth century in the wars against the Sasanians.

Since the romantic nationalist reimagination of Vardan Mamikonean's anti-Persian war as a 'War of Liberation', the deeds of Vardan, the *Vardanank'* have become a prototype of Armenia's eternal struggle for self-definition in an eternally hostile surrounding.[4] Back in the fifth century, the historians of Vardan had applied the earlier Hebrew Maccabean brothers' narrative template to interpret the Armenian resistance and sacrifice, just like fifteen hundred years later, these fifth-century metaphors of martyrdom were applied to the narrative of the Armenian Genocide. If the pattern set by the Maccabees is followed faithfully, being killed for one's ethnic or religious identity, even without active martyrdom, becomes a sufficient cause for canonisation. Therefore, on the one hand, the medieval religious concepts of sanctity are adapted to novel, 'national' requirements, while on the other, the modern image of the nation is retrojected to medieval history, as an interpretive schema, through which the medieval narratives of sanctity are to be read and interpreted. The icon, while canonically problematic, effectively encapsulates two dimensions of victimhood: the implicit formula of 'martyrdom for faith and the fatherland' ascribed to Late Antique historians is merged with the legal definition of Genocide – 'the intent to destroy, in whole or in part, a national, ethnical, racial or religious group, as such'.[5] Through this profound and, arguably, conscious theological ambiguity, this icon reaches the foundation era of Armenian identity, and depicts the Armenian nation in its totality, as a historically fluid, yet remarkably stable religious and political subject.

---

[3] The expression can be found all over the web, especially after 2015. See, e.g., https://armenianprelacy.org/2021/04/22/feast-of-the-holy-martyrs-of-the-armenian-genocide/ (03.06.23).

[4] Derenik Demirchian's novel *Vardanank'* was most influential in this respect.

[5] See Article 2 of the Convention on the Prevention and Punishment of the Crime of Genocide. http://www.ohchr.org/EN/ProfessionalInterest/Pages/CrimeOfGenocide.aspx (03.06.23).

Indeed, not everyone was happy with the icon. The canonicity of the icon was doubted and worries were expressed that the beatification of the victims could shift the Armenian identity discourse from victim-centred to, as it were, triumphant, which could theoretically undermine the Armenian post-Genocide identity narrative. Abel Manoukian's justification of the canonisation illustrates the resulting tension between the theology of sainthood and the urgent requirements of a modern nation: 'In these instances, we see the scriptural principle of "necessity abolishes the law" in operation. Contrary to the defined rules of the Catholic Church, *oikonomia*, the well-known principle embedded in the Church's tradition, is used when the Church administers or responds to the needs of the faithful.'[6] Such a temporary suspension of the law is facilitated by the existing paradigm of the Armenian martyrs of Avarayr and by the medieval concept of 'Baptism in Blood'. Although 'necessity abolishes the law' is a misinterpretation of Hebrews 7:12, the resulting Latin maxim, *necessitas legem non habet*, here comes into operation also in matters of sainthood. In this sense, the necessity, or rather emergency, is the immediate requirement of the nation state. In other words, while the canonisation of the genocide victims may be problematic from the canonical point of view, the necessities of the nation allow a temporary suspension of the law.[7]

These two vignettes from recent Georgian and Armenian history are certainly different. They, however, share a common feature: the medieval conceptions of sanctity and cults of saints are embedded in modern ethno-religious and political discourses. And on the other hand, medieval conceptual networks are interpreted through the lens of the modern nation state. Even in utterly secular contexts, the old tropes of sanctity can be and are injected, and exhibit surprising longevity in many areas of public discourses and policies. It is essentially this continuous adaptation of the cult of saints, and the rereadings of earlier cult-related narratives in changing political circumstances, rhetoric and discourses that constitute the core interest of the present book.

Saints, their lives and their representations found extraordinary vitality in the lives of the modern Georgian people. The fascination with the cult of the saints and its inclusion in national narratives was ignited well before de-Sovietisation, due to the tremendous effort of Patriarch Ilia II and his personal obsessions with saints. Since the collapse of the Soviet Union, a

---

[6] Manoukian, *New Saints*.
[7] Cf. for example with György Geréby's discussion in 'Angels of the Nation', 823, on nationalistic rhetoric in the liturgy of the Hungarian church, where 'nobody asks for formal legitimacy since the presence of the "national" goes without saying'.

virtual archaeology of saints has been launched by the church, with a zeal to uncover Georgia's holy men and women hidden under the debris of time, or whose memory was suppressed by the atheistic Soviet regime. Almost every year, on the decree of the Holy Synod, an individual joins the ranks of the saints. Some of them are historic figures whose sanctity has only now been acknowledged by the Church, whereas others are recently deceased men and women. While many of these recovered saints have been confined to ecclesiastic commemorations, never leaving the church's horizon, others became included in national commemorative practices. Along with officially sanctioned cults, other influential cults have also emerged, celebrated illicitly but widely, and flourishing under the selectively blind eye of the Church. Every once in a while, national broadcasts feature relics of saints that are paraded, stolen, gifted, loaned and commodified in ways that are not too dissimilar to the ways they were used during the middle ages.

The endurance and perpetual 'rediscovery' of the cult of saints in Armenian and especially Georgian public discourses is largely determined by the centrality that the medieval literary canon occupies in education. Late antique and early medieval saintly stories, hagiographies or historical accounts centred around the lives and deeds of holy men and women, constitute the axis of elementary and secondary education in Georgia. The earliest samples of Georgian writing that emerged in the fifth century are all *Martyrdoms*, and some of the finest samples of medieval literary Georgian language are the lives of the saints. These early hagiographies are taught to ninth-graders in the original old Georgian. Only after a proper induction to hagiography are the students introduced to secular literature. The first and only medieval non-hagiographic compulsory reading for pupils is the twelfth-century *Knight in the Panther Skin*. In other words, since the establishment and standardisation of school curricula in the nineteenth century, which have not experienced significant changes throughout the Soviet and post-Soviet years, Georgian children follow a similar path as the history of Georgian literature, internalising saints' lives as the foundation of national identity. The fifth-century *Martyrdom of Queen Shushanik* is taught as the earliest and finest piece of Georgian literature, while the *Conversion of Kartli* and the *Life of Nino* are often referenced as trustworthy accounts of Georgia's Christianisation in the early fourth century; the eighth-century *Martyrdom of Abo of Tbilisi* is taught as a parable of Georgia as the last refuge of Orthodoxy in the Christian East under the Arabs. Whereas since the discovery and edition of the ninth-century *Life of Grigol of Xanc't'a*, the life of this powerful abbot has been generally interpreted as a testament to a very modern understanding of Georgian national unity. Therefore, the characters, tropes, symbols and linguistic idiosyncrasies cherry-picked from these texts remain engrained in cultural memory, national narrative, political thinking, both domestic and foreign, and public discourse in general.

## Tbilisi's Saintly Topography

Saints also prosper outside of narratives, being ubiquitously present in the daily lives of the Georgian people. While representations of saints and their monuments are common in all European cities, in Georgia's capital they seem to enjoy intense political lives, nurtured by current religious and political anxieties. Here, the 'sites of memory', even if not directly saintly, are often in one way or another, connected with or interpreted through the lens of historical saintly discourses. If one strolls down Rustaveli Avenue towards Freedom Square, one shall first stop in front of the Parliament building at a monument dedicated to the massacres of 9 April 1989, when the Soviet troops killed twenty-one peaceful protesters. In Georgian nation-building, 9 April was a momentous day, and, as argued near the end of this book, the imagery cast by this event and the interpretive prism through which the events of April 1989 were interpreted were deeply rooted in the textual imagery of the Late Antique *Conversion of Kartli*. It was this Late Antique narrative that forged the imagery from which the tropes of 'beginnings' and 'transitions' were adopted in national narratives, by often placing (holy) women at the core of these transitional events.

Further down the avenue, the nineteenth-century square is topped by an imposing statue of St George, erected there in 2004 as a commemoration of the Rose Revolution, which culminated on 23 November 2003, on St George's day. According to its commissioner, President Saakashvili, the golden statue symbolised Georgia's inevitable vanquishing of its foe, the empire of evil, that is Russia. The problem, however, as many have pointed out, is that the replica of the statue designed by a Russian-Georgian artist could be found in several cities across Russia. Since 2003, Saakashvili has often brought up St George as Georgia's protector against Russia – the implicit dragon. Less than a year after the Rose Revolution, on another feast of St George, although the one in Spring, Saakashvili's government took control over the separatist Achara region ousting its long-time quasi-feudal ruler. In subsequent Rose Revolution mythology, therefore, both of these events were associated with St George and his feast, and the quintessential warrior saint's statue in Tbilisi's centre served as a material commemoration of these two transitional events in Georgia's recent history. This political valence of the cult of St George was both Saakashvili's invention, but also rooted in history. The spurious phonetic association of George with

Georgia, the emergence of this cult in the middle of Byzantine-Georgian warfare in the eleventh century, its appropriation by the ruling Bagratid Dynasty during Georgia's unification, and finally George's discovery as a hyper-masculine counterpart to the feminine members of Georgia's saintly pantheon – many of these medieval tropes that we shall encounter below have been embedded in the innumerable ancient and modern representations of this warrior saint.

From atop a cliff, St George is overlooked by a tall and serene statue of *K'art'vlis Deda* (Mother of a Georgian). The statue was erected in 1958 to celebrate the 1,500-year anniversary of the foundation of Tbilisi and was replaced by a new version in the early 1990s. While similar monuments with identical names can be found across former Eastern Bloc states ('Mother of the Nation' stands in Kyiv, 'Motherland Calls' overlooks Volgograd, 'Mother Albania' stands in Tirana and 'Mother Armenia' towers over Yerevan), most of them were dedicated to the victory in World War II, except the one in Yerevan. The Georgian 'Mother' shares common features with these monuments, yet is also unique in that it was intentionally designed to project ambiguity. The 'Mother' holds an unsheathed sword in her right hand and a bowl of wine in her left hand. The statue was supposed to symbolise Georgia's history par excellence – the centuries-old balance of war and hospitality, and crucially, to celebrate the striking prevalence of female figures in its religious history such as St Nino, St Shushanik, Queen Tamar, Queen Ketevan and many other women who have become principal protagonists of the grand narrative of Georgia's religious history. Yet, as we shall see below, throughout history, many of these figures, in various guises, just as the monument itself, have projected ambivalence, with their cults also being engulfed with uncertainties. In this, the *K'art'vlis Deda* monument encapsulates what Mary Douglas calls 'purity and danger', in that it simultaneously articulates two exclusive yet complimentary features – menace and hospitality.[8] This ambiguity, as it shall be argued below, became a hallmark of medieval and modern Georgian representations of female sanctity, women who are both holy and unholy, pure and impure, feminine and masculine, whose sanctity was both legal and dissident, who both acted as charismatic founders of the realm and were challenged as the reasons for its downfall – in other words, stuck in the grey zone of adulation and misogyny.

If one takes a sharp left towards Pushkin Square, one will arrive at Georgia's Museum of Fine Arts, a nineteenth-century pseudo-classical

---

[8] Douglas, *Purity and Danger, passim.*

INTRODUCTION: THE CULT OF SAINTS AND BODY POLITIC        9

building with a porch and a colonnade. To the left, a curious bricolage of icons, lit candles and other church inventory can be observed. The porch has been redesigned as a temporary chapel where a group of people regularly gather with a single aim: to pray for the miraculous delivery of two of Georgia's holiest icons from the museum and their translation to the Church: the icon of Anč'i of the Saviour and the Acquri Icon of the Mother of God. Monk Gabriel, a recently deceased ascetic (and eccentric) monk and saint, is depicted on a large banner on the left, with his quote: 'If the nation does not deliver the Anč'i icon from the Museum, if the Acquri icon of the Mother of God does not reveal itself, and if the Icon of Iveria [the *Portaitissa*] does not arrive [in Georgia], how shall Georgia prosper [*gabrcqindeba*]?!'[9]

Tbilisi's saintly topography is, therefore, more than a mere commemoration of the holy men and women. It embodies the very modern anxieties over identity, national belonging, international aspirations and domestic policies. Aspects of modern identity discourses, such as Euro-Atlanticism vs Eurasianism, Georgia's European integration and its challenge by Soviet legacy, liberal and conservative worldviews, all of these dilemmas of a contemporary nation state can be identified and deciphered as encapsulated in the memory and physical presence of saints and their relics.

## Why This Book?

It is perhaps one of the paradoxes of modernity that despite a general decline of religiousness across the Western world, a reverse surge can be observed in the academic interest in the cult of saints. Many books, articles, book series and several important research projects investigating one or another aspect of sainthood have appeared over the last few decades. Since the seminal studies by Peter Brown on holy men, sainthood and the body in Late Antiquity, almost no aspect of the cult of saints has been left without scrutiny, be it the complicated history of the origin and development of the cult of saints, the geographic and cultural peculiarities of cultic practices, the intricate interplay of sanctity and power discourse, sanctity and gender, sanctity and economy, and many others. The study of the cult of saints, if initially rooted in research into hagiography, has long left the boundaries of saintly narratives, and the varieties of cult practices are now identified in archaeological evidence, and in the analyses of cult-related objects in line with the general 'materiality turn' in social

---

[9] A picture of the banner can be easily found with a simple Google search of 'Atskuri icon'.

sciences and the humanities.¹⁰ Many other interpretive theories have been applied to the cult of saints, from Marxism to critical theory, anarchism, phenomenology, deconstruction, modern hermeneutics and many others that scrutinise the cult of saints as a means for a better understanding of the human condition. Since Simone de Beauvoir's interest in the cult of the Theotokos, and the internal contradiction that Beauvoir has observed in the 'supreme victory of masculinity' in the cult of Christianity's 'most important' woman, the gendered and power-related aspect of the cult of saints has also been widely addressed. Indeed, this modern intellectual fascination with sainthood can be explained perhaps precisely by the general spiritual detachment from this curious aspect of our cultural history and human experience.

In the study of sainthood, the Caucasian, that is Georgian, Armenian and Caucasian Albanian sources, remain peripheral due to their relative linguistic inaccessibility. Despite the wealth of sources related to the cult of saints, as of now there exists no monographic study of the history of the cult of saints in Georgia, or even Caucasia, apart from research in hagiography or the representations of sainthood in visual art.[11] The first systematic interest in the early cult of saints in Caucasia was expressed by the European Research Council-funded project the *Cult of Saints in Late Antiquity*, based at the Faculty of History at Oxford and supervised by Brian Ward-Perkins. The project mapped

> the cult of saints as a system of beliefs and practices in its earliest and most fluid form, from its origins until around AD 700 (by which date most cult practices were firmly established): the evolution from honouring the memory of martyrs, to their veneration as intercessors and miracle-workers; the different ways that saints were honoured and their help solicited; the devotion for relics, sacred sites, and images; the miracles expected from the saints.[12]

My responsibility within the project was to analyse Late Antique Armenian and Georgian sources related to the cult of saints. I had a somewhat tangential interest in the cult of saints before the project, but in time, and as a result of our weekly conversations at Trinity College, Bryan Ward-Perkins's

---

[10] Most recently, Robert Wiśniewski, who has extensively studied the material aspect of the cult saints, has dedicated his monograph, *The Beginning of the Cult of Relics*, to this particular aspect of sainthood.

[11] David Marshal Lang's *The Lives and Legends of the Georgian Saints* may be an exception, yet it is more of an anthology of Georgian vitae than a proper study.

[12] https://cultofsaints.history.ox.ac.uk/ (03.06.23).

office, I became fascinated by the cult of saints and its ability to absorb and transform other cultural phenomena.[13] We have come to realise that the cult of saints in Late Antique Caucasia had a distinct word to say in the history of Christianity, perhaps contrary to original expectations. This conceptual uniqueness was the thoroughly political nature of the earliest Caucasian cult-related narratives, and the deep embeddedness of the cult of saints in identity and political rhetoric in early medieval Armenians, Georgian and also Caucasian Albanian sources, whose trace is faint, yet important in the history of Christendom. Arguably, this trait was largely determined by the diversity of cultural and religious practices in Caucasia. Located on a virtual crossroad of civilisations, the Late Antique Caucasian kingdoms and cultures were exposed to and have internalised religious traditions and conceptual systems from across Eurasia: from Christianity to Islam and Judaism, and from local mountainous religious practices to Zoroastrianism. As such, writers of the period often had to manoeuvre between various and often competing understandings of sacredness, the materiality of religion or commemorative practices. All these tendencies, whether in their symbolic form, rhetorical or political manifestation, contributed to the creation of the extraordinary cultural landscape of Late Antique and medieval Caucasia, reflected also in the nature and relevance of the cult of saints.[14]

Among many shades of sanctity, the present book focuses on its one aspect, and its manifestations in changing political contexts. What follows below can be read as an exercise in a hermeneutical unfolding of a conceptual system created at the intersection of three phenomena – sanctity, gender and politics – and the transformations that this conceptual system has experienced in changing political circumstances.

---

[13] The electronic searchable corpus of the early evidence for the cult of Christian saints can be consulted online at http://csla.history.ox.ac.uk (04.04.23).

[14] For an overview see e.g. Aleksidze, 'Caucasia', 135–57. Another reason for writing this book is my earlier work, *The Narrative of the Caucasian Schism: Memory and Forgetting in Medieval Caucasia*, based on a DPhil dissertation defended at Oxford in 2013. The study explores the debates that broke out between the Chalcedonian Georgians and non-Chalcedonian Armenians in the seventh century, and the reimaginations of this conflict in the later middle ages. One chapter of the book explores the cult of the fifth-century Armenian martyr-queen St Shushanik, and her commemoration as a crucial part of the memory wars between the Armenians and Georgians in the middle ages over the interpretation of the foundations of the Christian cultures in Caucasia and the nature of orthodoxy and dissent. While at that time, the book was not focused on saints and my familiarity with the cult of saints in general and in the Caucasus in particular, was limited, the present book acts as a certain spin-off over the political rhetoric and sainthood in medieval and modern Caucasia.

## The Saintly and the Feminine

Apart from a tendency to politicise the cult of the saints in identity and political rhetoric, medieval Georgian religious rhetoric has another additional characteristic commonly spotted by anyone with even a superficial knowledge of its religious history – a dramatic prominence of female saintly figures. The introducer of Christianity in Georgia, St Nino, was a woman, and so were the pseudo-epigraphic authors of her mission. The first piece of original Georgian writing is a martyrdom account of a holy queen, St Shushanik. Meanwhile, the cults of Armenia's great virgin-martyrs, Hṙip'simē and Gayanē, enjoyed a considerable influence in Georgia. The late twelfth-century holy queen Tamar (1184–1213) was established as a figure of unmatched centrality in Georgian historiography, religious traditions and folklore. Since the seventeenth century, Saint Ketevan (1560–1624), mother of King Teimuraz I, has been hailed as the last of the great Georgian martyrs, brutally killed by the Safavids on account of her Christianity, thus ending this long and turbulent chapter of history.

Due to the continuous readings and rereadings of the foundational texts that constituted the core of the medieval corpus, some of the influential medieval, early modern and indeed modern authors perceived the entanglement of sanctity, gender and politics as an essentially Georgian conundrum.[15] Indeed, to the best of my knowledge, no other medieval Christian literary tradition has been as concerned with the interrelation of the feminine, the sacred and the political, as the Georgian. Apart from several medieval discourses that directly address this question, it will be demonstrated below that this conceptual problem implicitly transpires in much of Georgian writing. While this fixation on the feminine was originally determined by the gender of Georgia's illuminatrix, the reflections on the interaction of the feminine, the political and the religious became particularly passionate during and after the reign of Queen Tamar. The disproportionately strong veneration of female saints was further reinforced by the extraordinary cult of the Mother of God and by the persistence of the political concept of Georgia as the Theotokos's allotment.

Surely, female saints show no quantitative dominance, and the sheer number of male martyr saints in Georgian liturgical calendars is overwhelming. Nevertheless, male saint names of Georgian origin make an extremely rare appearance in the onomasticon. Eustathios (the name of

---

[15] The history of women in Georgia has been a subject of interest for over a century. For one of the earliest studies, see Bakradze, *K'art'veli k'alebi*. For the most recent monograph on the subject, see Vashalomidze, *Die Stellung der Frau, passim*.

the great sixth-century saint) has never become even remotely popular (although, admittedly, my great-grandfather was Eustathios), and no Abos, Razhdens or any other names have become widely disseminated. While names such as Giorgi, David, Demetre and Alexander constitute the core of the Georgian male onomasticon, they have little to do with the cult of saints in Georgia. Conversely, three of women's most popular names, Nino, Tamar and Ketevan with their innumerable variations (Nini, Ninutsa, Keti, Keta, Keto, Ketato, Tamta, Tamuna, Tako and many more), are all those of the three great female saints. Recently, even the names of many female characters of the *Conversion of Kartli* have started to appear, and even the somewhat peripheral Shushanik (a markedly Armenian name) has become more common than the names of the above-listed male saints. The fact that Georgia's foundational narrative focuses on Nino and her all-female companions, that the first original Georgian hagiographic account and also the last great one, narrate the martyrdom of holy queens, and that the greatest monarch in Georgian cultural memory was a woman, contributed to a strong intertwining of holy female bodies and body politic.

## Sources

The chapters below trace the readings and rereadings of the foundational cult narratives throughout several consecutive periods of Georgian history, and identify recurrent political conceptualisations of sainthood in some of the following rhetorical contexts: the foundations of orthodoxies (and heterodoxies) in the Caucasian region in the Late Antique and early medieval era (roughly from the fifth to the seventh centuries); the formation and consolidation of the Bagratid powers and rhetoric in the eleventh-century Byzantine commonwealth, followed by the era of Queen Tamar and the subsequent formation of her living memory and cult (tenth–thirteenth centuries); the establishment of first Muscovite–Georgian diplomatic ties in the sixteenth and especially seventeenth centuries; nineteenth-century Russian Imperialist and opposing nationalist rhetoric; followed by a brief sketch of the Soviet and post-Soviet rediscoveries of the cult of saints and its political implications.

The sources discussed throughout the book are, therefore, chosen by the degree of their dissemination, rewritings and rereadings in each of these drastically different contexts. Of all the earliest primary sources quoted, none are unproblematic from the point of view of dating, attribution and authenticity. Although a consensus exists over the dating of some of the early Armenian and Georgian narratives, nevertheless, the expediency of the cult of saints in political and identity rhetoric was far too crucial for these texts to have remained sterile from severe ideological interpolations. This is particularly true of narratives related to the founding saints of the Christian Caucasian cultures, such as St Gregory in Armenia and St Nino in Georgia. While, for example, the *Life of Gregory the Illuminator* is dated to the fifth century, individual parts of the narrative, especially related to the various aspects of St Gregory's cult, are far less convincingly assigned to the same early period. This is even truer for the cult of St Nino, whose numerous *vitae* reveal stronger divergence and ambiguities. While the earliest account of her life may be a seventh-century or earlier composition, the evidence for such dating is more circumstantial than secure. The cult of a saint was a living, breathing phenomenon and subject to constant revision and adaptation. With the development of established monasticism, and court and dynastic rhetoric, such texts were rewritten and adapted to urgent rhetorical necessities. This and the previous century have seen volumes arguing for and against the virtual existence of, for example, St Nino, the ethnic identity of St Shushanik's original *Martyrdom*, or the validity of Armenian claims regarding the work of Gregory the Illuminator and the founder of Armenian literacy, St Maštocʽ. None of these questions is addressed in this book. Instead, a certain phenomenological perspective shall be adopted, whereby I shall focus on the readers' and interpreters' experiences and interpretations rather than on source criticism of these early medieval compositions.

The principal argument of the book is that due to the nature of the medieval Georgian experience with the cult of saints, a unique relationship among the religious, the political and the feminine representations of sanctity has been formed. Consequently, some of the questions asked are: What was the nature of this relationship? How are the material remains and memories of a saint politicised? What kind of phenomena are generated with the politicisation of specifically female saintly remains and their memories? It is my hope that this conceptual crossroad explored in a small area of the Christian world can potentially serve as a theoretical interpretive tool, and will open research avenues also in other geographic as well as cultural milieux.

## Value

I intend to make use of and enrich some of the well-established theoretical concepts from historiography, anthropology and political science as I read and interpret sources to answer some of the questions outlined above, some of which will remain grounded within their traditional framework, while others may be modified to better explain our sources.

Since relics and the politicisation of saintly remains will be a recurring theme, it is the theory of value that will often be addressed, along with associated concepts, such as gift-giving, exchange, commodity, 'inalienable possessions' and so on.[16] My interpretation of 'value' is mostly informed by anthropological theory and the more recent materiality turn in the humanities. Here I have adopted Georg Simmel's and Arjun Appadurai's theories of value as something that arises from exchange. Appadurai has famously coined the term 'regimes of value' to describe the convertibility of the value of things among different cultures.[17] In other words, as Patrick Geary writes, 'the value of the relics rests on the communal acceptance of a set of shared beliefs that determine its authenticity and efficacy in a particular social and cultural environment.'[18] My interest lies in the transformation and transitivity of value and the strategies by which the relics and memories of the saints are endowed with political value. In the case studies below, the sacred remains and objects associated with saints travel precisely among these 'regimes of value'. Roman, Byzantine and Russian Imperial rhetoric generated their own 'regimes of value' within which these sacred objects and cult narratives moved and operated. Valences of the cults also changed as 'regimes of value' changed, while at the same time maintaining striking constancy.

When it comes to the discovery and ownership of relics, they often indeed 'resist their ownership', to paraphrase Simmel's famously laconic definition of value, with their value resting in their distribution or investment in body politic.[19] Therefore, the relics of saints, often conceptualised as the treasure in early medieval narratives, have the power to create a discursive tension between private and political, and herald a transition from the former to the latter. When endowed with political value, the relics become inalienable to the charismatic person who has discovered or inherited them, while being given away and invested into body politic. In exchange, this person assumes a political body, as demonstrated early in the book with several examples. Relics can also act as symbols of political sovereignty. In the early modern period, for example, the relics as material confirmations of Georgia's religious and political sovereignty were perceived as Georgia's inalienable possessions, yet they were both taken by the Russian Empire and gifted back, 'in exchange' for political annexation. Therefore, some of the

---

[16] For a critical overview of the theories of value, see Graeber, *Anthropological Theory of Value*.
[17] Appadurai, 'Commodities and Politics of Value', 3–63.
[18] Geary, 'Sacred Commodities', 175.
[19] Simmel, *Philosophy of Money*, 67.

aspects of the commodification of the sacred explored below will be those of 'giving, while retaining', or inversely, taking while giving. As summarised by Annette Weiner,

> the paradox inherent in the processes of keeping-while-giving creates an illusion of conservatism, of refashioning the same things, of status quo. Although possessions, through their iconographies and histories, are the material expressions of 'keeping', the most that such possessions accomplish is to bring a vision of permanence into a social world that is always in the process of change. The effort to make memory persist, as irrational as the combat against loss can be, is fundamental to change. The problems inherent in 'keeping' nurture the seeds of change.[20]

The additional question of the present book is, therefore, how is this value transformed with the gender of the relics of a saint? Does the femininity of a saint affect the value as endowed in her memory or material presence? The preliminary answer is indeed, the value of a material or mnemonic relic is often transformed when the gender aspect is introduced into them. More often than not, this value becomes that of mediation, of situatedness in the ambiguous zone of in-between, whether of two realms, two times or two existential conditions. Therefore, the second major interpretive framework of the present study is that of ambiguity.

## Ambiguity

The Late Antique Georgian corpus that can be conventionally titled the *Conversion of Kartli*, although the narrative of Georgia's conversion has appeared in many other shapes and forms, introduced a specific method of conceptualising female sanctity. Nino, the protagonist of the narrative, while in subsequent centuries celebrated and praised in all possible ways, was, as a woman, also a conceptual problem. The fluctuation of Nino's cult continued further in subsequent centuries: if, for example, during the rise of the military Bagratids, some resentment transpires towards her, Nino then becomes central to Queen Tamar's living and posthumous cult. It is argued below that the ambiguity generated by Nino's cult was translated into her liminality. Nino and other female saints, especially the martyred queen Shushanik, became liminal figures of sorts, as they were closely and strongly associated with temporal and geographic in-betweenness. In medieval Georgian historical and religious thinking, Nino, together with the objects associated with her, was the marker of

[20] Weiner, *Inalienable Possessions*, 8.

the end of the old and the beginning of the new, thus standing in the centre of the ambiguous space in-between. A similarly liminal nature was inherited by her cross, which marks the North–South divide of the Caucasian mountain range, or the political boundaries in the middle of the kingdom.[21] Similarly, St Shushanik became a symbol of the fuzzy space between the Armenian and Georgian realms, as well as between the past and the present in the shared history of these two peoples. The *Conversion of Kartli* is also the first text that elaborates on political and religious geography by problematising the idea of the 'North', and the movement between the northern and southern realms, which has become an enduring metaphysical and political concept in medieval and modern Georgian identity discourses. Even the holy queen Tamar and the martyred queen Ketevan were conceptualised by the authors of their cults as metaphors of temporal and existential transitions. Over time, all these religious and political ideas – the past and the present, the north and south, power and sanctity, the political and the natural – have become embedded in the ambiguous bodies of the female saints.

The central interpretive framework for the reading of these sources is the concept of ambiguity of the feminine. In *Purity and Danger*, a classic study of ambiguity in animate and inanimate objects, Mary Douglas studies creatures that fall in between the categories we use to structure our world.[22] These creatures, things or, in our case, people, are seen in traditional societies as particularly powerful, sacred and dangerous. Douglas's original thesis has been adopted in religious history as well. Mary Beard, for example, points to the gender ambiguity of Vestal Virgins exactly from the vantage point espoused in the present book:

> thus the ambiguity of their sexual status, the way they share the characteristics of virgins, matrons and even men need be regarded no longer as an awkward aspect somehow to be accommodated in any explanation of their position, but as a crucial element in designating their sacredness... just as the perception of the pangolin as interstitial (falling between mammal and fish) must be closely related to its sacred role, so the highly ambiguous status of the Vestal Virgins must be seen as playing an important part in their symbolic position. The fact that, through various aspects of their dress, their cult obligations and their privileges, they may be perceived as falling between several categories of sexuality, marks them out as sacred.[23]

---

[21] Eastmond, 'Art on the Edge', 64–92.
[22] Douglas, *Purity and Danger, passim*.
[23] Beard, 'Sexual Status', 21.

Further Beard elaborates,

> the greater number of strictly defined physical stages in the life of a woman, compared with those in a man's career, itself encourages the kind of subtle play of ambiguity that we see in the case of the Vestals. One need only think of the barriers crossed by a woman in the course of her life (menarche, first intercourse, first parturition, menopause) and the way these, in many societies, are visibly signalled by costume or involve different forms of title and address, to understand the greater versatility in the figure of the woman for the creation of a sacred status through a confusion of standard categories.[24]

The perception of holy women as transgressors was particularly persistent in early Christianity, as observed in female saintly accounts. In her study of the *Martyrdom of Vibia Perpetua*, Elisabeth Castelli argues that Christian women,

> through rigorous bodily pieties, constructed their special relationship to holiness, relationships that came to be described as the transformation of gender. These women's refusal to participate in conventional sexual roles ascribed to them by late antique culture (not as an attempt to undercut the patriarchal social order, but in order to achieve spiritual perfection) was perceived ambivalently. On the one hand, their holiness was marked by the abandonment of socially sanctioned gender roles; on the other hand, the same abandonment was seen as dangerous to the natural and hierarchical order of social relations.[25]

These ambiguous figures often assume the function of mediation between two structures, and, while situated in between these structures, are sacralised further. By drawing on Claude Levi-Strauss's classic studies, Edmund Leach writes,

> In every myth system we will find a persistent sequence of binary discriminations as between human/superhuman, mortal/immortal, male/female, legitimate/ illegitimate, good/bad ... followed by a 'mediation' of the paired categories thus distinguished. 'Mediation' (in this sense) is always achieved by introducing a third category which is 'abnormal' or 'anomalous' in terms of ordinary, rational categories. Thus, myths are full of fabulous monsters, incarnate gods, virgin mothers. This middle

---

[24] Ibid., 21–2.
[25] Castelli, 'I Will Make Mary Male', 46.

ground is abnormal, non-natural, holy. It is typically the focus of all taboo and ritual observance.[26]

The ambiguity of the feminine was a hallmark of the earliest of Christian discourses. The greatest of such 'ambiguous' figures was the Theotokos who, as a mother and a virgin, as the bearer of God, and as the link between humanity and divinity, was perceived as the ultimate mediatrix. Yet, in all her exceptionality, in certain traditions, especially the Gnostic Gospels, Mary too had to 'shed' her femininity and 'become male'. In the Gnostic *Gospel of Thomas*, Christ's disciples wish to cast Mary (probably Magdalene) away due to her gender. Christ, however, objected: 'Behold, I myself shall lead her so as to make her male, that she too may become a living spirit like you males. For every woman who makes herself male will enter the kingdom of heaven.'[27] Transgressing one's feminine self, was, therefore, a crucial step towards holiness. In her study of the cult of the holy women, Maria Galatariotou discusses the ambiguity and exceptionality as the essence of the cult of the Mother of God. Galatariotou argues that

> It was precisely Mary's sex – and the ambiguities with which it had been endowed – that was the most decisively important ingredient in her makeup as 'The Great Mediator'. Mary partakes of more than one of the categories with which the Christian mind had structured its universe: on a sexual level, she is-both a virgin (a sexually unspecified creature, a less-than-female woman) and a mother (a sexually unambiguous, fertile woman); on the level of social kinship, she is both the mother of a son and the bride of that same son: both, further, a bride of the son and of the father. The creation of not only one ambiguity but of an entire structure of such; the tension caused by any attempt to understand Mary's persona according to any accepted social categories, . . . all combine to make Mary an extremely powerful symbol. . . . Power acting through culture, Church and State control and ideology, ruled out the first possibility and forced the second: Mary was declared the *Panagia*, the All-Holy.[28]

The female protagonists of the present book are such liminal characters who, through their perpetual ambiguity, project 'purity and danger'. By virtue of their ambiguous femininity, they act as intermediaries between two times, two realms, between sacred and the profane, between civilisation and wilderness, the Golden Age and the catastrophe. It is the ambiguity

---

[26] Leach, *Genesis as Myth*, 11.
[27] Cf. as quoted in Castelli, 'I Will Make Mary Male', 31.
[28] Galatariotou, 'Holy Women', 90.

conceived in a female saint's body and its political manifestations that are the primary interest of the present book.

## Exception

Finally, the most commonly used theoretical concept throughout the book is that of exception. 'The state of exception', as coined by Karl Schmitt, was reworked by Giorgio Agamben as a 'no-man's-land between public law and political fact'.[29] My usage of exception or 'state of exception' is perhaps the least similar to Karl Schmitt's original concept of political theology. However, it can still help us interpret some of the sources as well as understand how the theology of sainthood is readapted in changing structures, from medieval ideas of kingship to the modern nation state. Exception, as a concept, warrants three questions: Who decides on the exception? How is an exception justified? And what are the implications of an exception for whatever is left beyond the exceptional?

There are two contexts in which 'exception' is used below. The first refers to the unique and irreplicable merging of the political and the feminine, especially in the sacred image of Queen Tamar that became a central interpretive framework of female sanctity in medieval and early modern narratives and surviving folklore. As the creators of Tamar's cult argued, this unique suspension of the order of things, in this case of gender roles, occurred first in the event of the *Conversion* – in Nino's mandate to preach and convert, and second in Tamar's exclusive and inalienable mandate to rule in her name. In these two extraordinary instances of history, the advantages of the feminine nature in religion and politics were conceptualised as a total and inimitable exception. Such conceptualisation of the exception allowed a simultaneous retaining of the traditional association of femininity with destruction and catastrophe, retained in the stories of other non-exceptional women of history.

My second reading of the 'state of exception' is tied with the modern theology of sainthood and nationhood. As in the case of the Martyrs of the Genocide, in modern Armenian and Georgian discourses of sanctity, we often encounter justifications for canonisation that acknowledge the noncanonical nature of such canonisations, yet justify them by the (urgent) requirements of the nation state. It was arguably this idea of emergency that shaped the twentieth-century and contemporary political theology of sainthood and nationhood of Georgian and Armenian ecclesiastic and political elites. This situation of exception was utilised as

---

[29] Agamben, *State of Exception*, 1–2.

a principal argument by the initiators of the canonisation of the victims of the Genocide in Armenia, as well as of a range of figures of importance yet dubious saintly careers in Georgia by Patriarch Ilia II.

## Text Structure

The book is conventionally divided into three parts and nine chapters that analyse the conceptual entanglement of the holy, the feminine and the political. Each subsequent chapter illustrates cascading readings and recycling of earlier texts in new historical realities.

The first chapter, in a sense, sets the tone for the remainder of the study. Earliest Caucasian cult-related narratives are introduced with a focus on their relevance for political and identity discourses. It focuses on how the relics of the saints were incorporated into the rhetoric of royal legitimation in Armenia, Georgia and Caucasian Albania, and how the political value of these relics was generated and propagated. In this opening chapter, the Armenian sources have some predominance, since, arguably, the early Armenian rhetoric of cult-related narratives exercised influence also beyond Armenia, in Georgian and Caucasian Albanian writing and their conceptualisations of sainthood.

The second chapter carries on the discussion of Georgian foundational narratives with a focus on the *Conversion of Kartli*. It was in this Late Antique composition where, for the first time in Georgian writing, the feminine identity of a saint was problematised, and gave rise to the ambiguous cult of St Nino. After a certain gap, in the middle ages, the *Life of Nino* became the most influential narrative in medieval and modern Georgian corpora and affected the interpretation of other cults and political discourses. While the *Life* has been edited and rewritten numerous times since its creation, the living cult of St Nino enjoyed much less popularity than her narrative, resurfacing only in isolated instances. Arguably, the *Conversion* corpus crafted the image of Nino as an absolute exception, whose centrality, despite her gender, was determined by the extraordinary and transitional times in the universal history of salvation, an aspect of Nino's cult that was also retained in the folk reimaginations of this person. Nino was seen as a great mediator between historical times and Kartli's geo-political loci. Her *vita* conceptualises her both as the mediator between the past and the present, paganism and Christianity, and between the enlightened South and the obscure North, by spearheading Iberia's transition between these structures and anti-structures.

The third chapter offers a case study of the cult-related traditions of the fifth-century martyr, Queen Shushanik. The chapter draws on Claude

Levi-Strauss and Marcel Mauss's classical structuralist anthropological theories of 'gift-giving' and 'women as gifts'. Shushanik's cult was discovered during the religious controversies that began in the seventh-century Caucasus between the Armenians and the Georgians, with much of the rhetoric of these debates unfolding around the commemoration of Shushanik and the site of her relics. It is argued that the political value of the memory and the relics of the holy queen were determined by the gender role of this person, and by her conceptualisation as a gift and a bride given by the Armenians to the Georgians, a gift that was 'unreciprocated'. Meanwhile, while St Shushanik's femininity played a crucial role in the political value of her relics, as a female saint who marked the fuzzy space between the Georgian and the Armenian physical and mnemonic realms, she symbolised the strategically liminal region in Caucasia, a crucial military target of all major regional powers.

Part II is entirely dedicated to the formation of the Bagratid royal ideology in their dealings with the Byzantines, and the effect of their new religious and political aspirations on the political conceptualisations of sainthood and sanctity. In the eleventh century, along with the creation of a sizable religious and hagiographic corpus, the compilation of *K'art'lis C'xovreba* (The Georgian Chronicles) was initiated – a historiographic project that was supposed to create a new standard narrative of Georgia's history as seen from the era of Georgia's political unification. This period was marked by the relative abandonment of old saints and a marked masculinisation of the Georgian saintly pantheon, a topic addressed in Chapter 4. In this period, warrior saints saturated the Georgian saintly landscape, among whom St George was certainly the most prominent. The abandonment of the ancient Jerusalemite rite and the adoption of the Constantinopolitan tradition, along with the political and ideological unification of Georgia under the Bagratids and their opposition to the Byzantines, led to the quest for the 'new' definitions of Georgia and Georgianness, a project centered around the cult of old and new saints.

Chapter 5 is entirely dedicated to the most enduring concept of the medieval and indeed modern Georgian political theologies, the tradition of Georgia as the 'Lot of the Mother of God'. This belief emerged in the Middle Byzantine period first as a Bagratid claim and as a part of the identity discourses of the Georgian Athonite Fathers. In both instances, the cult of the Theotokos was forged as the marker of Georgian linguistic, ethnic and political identity as opposed to the Byzantines. The Lot of the Mother of God also became the galvanising concept of Georgia's political and cultural unity, while, in time, and since Georgia's disintegration, the same concept also became part of the separatist rhetorical arsenal of

Georgia's former constituent regions and later independent kingdoms and principalities.

The sixth chapter is entirely focused on the making of the cult of Queen Tamar, whose reign, as I argue, was transitional in the gender and political discourses of sanctity. The zeal of Tamar's writers to legitimise her inalienable and personal mandate to kingship created tropes and metaphors which contributed to the eventual sacralisation of this person of history and lore. Tamar's emerging cult also absorbed earlier cults, especially of St Nino and the Theotokos, and the three cults were merged as the justifiers of the 'exceptionality' of Tamar and her mandate. Yet, Tamar's as well as the cults of other female saints, remained ambiguous, caught between adulation and the traditional misogyny of the premodern societies.

The third section of the present book is mostly dedicated to the reception of the classical texts discussed in the two previous chapters – the *Conversion* cycle and the *K'art'lis C'xovreba* corpus. Chapter 7 takes the reader to the post-Byzantine and post-unity eras of Georgia's history. Georgia was disunited into four political entities and all four were caught among the three large geopolitical players – the Safavid Iran, the Ottomans and the emerging Muscovy/Russia. The central figure of this chapter and section is Queen Ketevan, the last great martyr-saint of Georgian tradition, brutally executed by the Safavids on account of her Christianity and her son's political activism. In the seventeenth century, Russians 'discovered' Georgia as a holy land of sorts, and were increasingly interested and focused on the holy relics that the Georgian principalities possessed. The Russian travellers, diplomats and ruling elites also noticed and internalised what they saw as the femininity of Georgia's religious tradition, having incorporated this vision in their imperialist and colonial representations of Georgia as a feminine 'other'.

In Chapter 8 the nineteenth-century nationalist responses to the imperial rhetoric are explored with a focus on the rediscovery of the medieval Georgian saintly narratives, cults and tropes. Georgia's national elites attempted to nationalise Georgia's saintly imagery, especially that of St Nino, which they saw as hijacked by imperial rhetoric. With the new nationalist rereading of the *Conversion of Kartli*, the early medieval trope of the menacing North was reapplied to the Russian Empire, as an alien and uncivilised land. In this process of crafting a new national symbolism of sovereignty, while deconstructing the imperial rhetoric of Georgia, the old Nino tropes were a crucial discovery.

The ninth and final chapter is a brief study of contemporary religious and political discourse and its entanglement with the notions of the feminine and the sacred. It focuses on how the readings of medieval texts and reinterpretations of the nineteenth-century constructions contributed to a unique ethno-religious discourse formed during the pontificate of the Katholikos-Patriarch Ilia II in Georgia, which involved the politics and gender of saints. Arguably, the interpretations of the foundational narratives and medieval political theologies were subsumed in contemporary opposition between the liberal pro-Western and (latent) pro-Russian rhetoric, and other issues constituting the core of modern national anxieties.

# Part I

# Introduction to Part I
# Late Antique Foundations

Caucasia, as a historical concept, may appear somewhat vague, especially Late Antique Caucasia. Recently, 'Caucasia' has been introduced as opposed to the more common 'Caucasus', to avoid the very concrete geographic boundaries of the latter term, which is limited to the southern and northern slopes of the Caucasus mountain range that runs from the northwest of the Black Sea towards south-east, all the way to the Caspian. As opposed to 'Caucasus', 'Caucasia' has been more commonly used as a political term with reference to the kingdoms, principalities and other state entities that had historically existed between the South Caucasus and the eastern Anatolian mountains; have had close cultural, linguistic and political ties with each other; were at various times partitioned between Roman and Persian powers; and shared other aspects of common regional history.

In Late Antiquity, by Christian Caucasia scholars refer to four state entities: Armenia, Iberia/Kartli, Lazika/Egrisi and Caucasian Albania, not to be confused with Albania of the Balkans. Yet, even this classification is somewhat nominal, since due to their location on a virtual border between the Roman and Sasanian commonwealths, and their continuous involvement in the conflict between the two superpowers, their boundaries changed dramatically. Armenia, for example, due to its location on a historic borderland of the Anatolian and Eurasian empires, was subject to several partitions. Therefore, over time, Armenia as a term referred to both the Late Antique Kingdom of Armenia, as well as to the central and eastern Anatolian Roman territories. The Sasanians occupied Armenia in 252 when the Kingdom was still ruled by the old Arsacid Dynasty. Their rule, however, ended in 387, when Armenia was partitioned once again, and the last Arsacid king was deposed in 428. Kingship in Eastern Armenia, also known as Persarmenia, ended, before the Bagratids came to power and established a new monarchy in the ninth century. It was under the Arsacid King T'rdat III (Tiridates) (c. 250–330) that in 301 (or sometime in the early fourth century), as claimed by the Armenian tradition that originates from the fifth-century Agathangelos, the kingdom was Christianised by Gregory the Illuminator who was of a noble Parthian descent. Gregory also founded a dynasty of patriarchs that presided over the Armenian church until the death of his descendant Sahak I (d. 437).

With Armenia's partition in 387, the western part of historic Armenia became incorporated into the Roman and then Byzantine Empires until it fell to the Seljuks in the eleventh century. Although it has partially retained Armenian ethnic and linguistic identity, western Armenia was predominantly Chalcedonian and part of Byzantine Armenia. The same year, the Sasanians annexed the eastern part and abolished kingship, instead a Persian *marzban* (frontier governor) was appointed. Nevertheless, along with the marzban, Armenia was ruled by several powerful local dynasties, the hereditary naxarars, who largely defined the political and ideological landscape of Armenia. The Mamikonean House was one of the strongest in the fifth century who commissioned much of Armenia's literary production of the period. In the fifth century, as claimed by Koriwn's *Life of Maštoc'*, a learned monk Maštoc' created Armenian letters and translated the Scripture and other Christian writings. This was a momentous event in Armenia's history, since with the creation of native letters, literary production erupted in Armenian. Apart from translations of biblical, liturgical and theological books, original histories, martyrdom accounts and theological treatises were created.

The history of Eastern Armenia (also known as Persarmenia) of the fifth century was defined by the Shah's anti-Christian policies and by the Armenian resistance, which resulted in a series of anti-Iranian insurrections over the course of the second half of the fifth century. The rebellion was spearheaded by the Mamikoneans, in particular by Vardan Mamikonean who died at the catastrophic Battle of Avarayr of 451. Yet, eventually on the terms of the 484 Treaty of Navarsak, the Armenians still succeeded in regaining religious autonomy from the Shah. Since then, Armenia has remained an Iranian vassal, and, following the rejection of Constantinopolitan Chalcedonianism by the Church of Persarmenia, also an ally against Byzantium. In 645, the Arab Caliphate invaded and occupied Armenia, establishing the province of Arminiya which included the lands of Armenia, Iberia and Caucasian Albania.

Iberia, or Kartli in Georgian, laid to the north of Armenia, with the Caucasus mountains and strategic mountain passes bordering it to the north (see Map I.1). However, just like Armenia, Iberia's political boundaries were extremely volatile and prone to constant change. Due to Iberia's location and its control of the north Caucasian mountain passes, as well as access

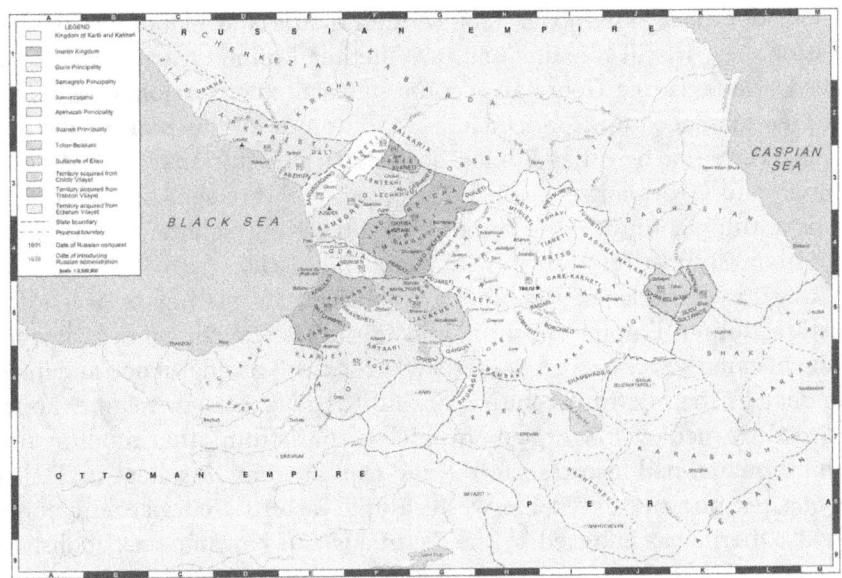

Map I.1 Map of Iberia in the sixth century. The map roughly depicts the borders of the Caucasian kingdoms in the sixth century. Source: D. Muskhelishvili, Historical Atlas of Georgia.

to the eastern Black Sea coast, it constantly oscillated between Roman and Persian powers. With the Treaty of Nisibis in 298, Iberia became a Roman vassal, and it was supposedly soon afterward that Mirian/Mihran III, Kartli's first king from the Chosroid Dynasty, adopted Christianity, perhaps immediately following Constantine in 325 or somewhat later in 337. Although, by tradition, Christianity was established in Armenia, Albania and Iberia in the fourth century, judging by the archaeological evidence, Christian communities had been present in the region long before the king's conversion. Christian burials appear in the centre of Iberia well before Christianisation, and as some scholars argue, compared to the population of Iberia, the Iberian king was a somewhat late convert to Christianity.[1]

The earliest report of Iberia's Christianisation belongs to historian Tyrannius Rufinus, who claims to have met an Iberian prince Bakourius in Jerusalem and who related to him the story of Iberia's conversion by a captive woman.[2] Rufinus's story is confirmed or expanded by the seventh-century Georgian *Conversion of Kartli* (*Mok'c'evay k'art'lisay*)

---

[1] Braund, *Georgia in Antiquity*, 238–239.
[2] Rufinus, *History*, 10.11, tr. Amidon, 396–400.

which identifies St Nino as Kartli's illuminator and elaborates on her mission. Yet, it still remains unclear whether Rufinus was indeed influenced by an existing Georgian account of Kartli's conversion, or whether the Georgian account is indeed an elaboration of Rufinus's original story, copied verbatim by other Roman ecclesiastical historians. According to Roman and Georgian sources, the first bishops were sent to Iberia from Constantinople, until in the late fifth century, King Vakhtang I Gorgasali (c. 449–502) substituted them with a local hierarchy.

Despite Christianisation, Iberia continued oscillating between the Eastern Roman Empire and Iran, and in the late fourth century, it once again became a Persian vassal. Iberia was relatively strengthened and independent in the late fifth century, during King Vakhtang's reign, who, as claimed by medieval Georgian chronicles, apart from other monumental achievements, had also transferred the capital from Mtskheta to Tbilisi, having temporarily unted the western and eastern Georgian kingdoms. In 480, Iberia was annexed by the Sasanians and kingship was abolished, instead, just like in Armenia, a *marzban* was installed, a common antagonist in Georgian martyrological accounts. In the late sixth century, Iberia was once again partitioned between Rome and Persia, and the boundary now ran between Mtskheta and Tbilisi, two adjacent cities. Iberia was ruled by hereditary princes, known as the Guaramids or the Bagratids, who adopted Byzantine honorary titles. A decisive moment in Iberia's history arrived when the Emperor Heraclius marched on the Persian part of Iberia in 627, having incorporated all of Iberia into the Byzantine commonwealth, which remained as such until the arrival of the Arabs.

Finally, the kingdom east of Iberia and Armenia was known as Albania, a kingdom and people who were over time completely lost to history.[3] In 252, Albania, along with Iberia and eastern Armenia, appears to be a Persian vassal, and due to its easternmost location in Caucasia, has remained as such. Albania was ruled by a local Arsacid Dynasty, yet in the early sixth century, they became extinct and kingship was abolished. The boundaries of Albania are vague. It occupied the territory of modern Azerbaijan, although not entirely. The history of the Christianisation of Albania is even more obscure than the Armenian and Iberian, since Albania was a very parochial polity and far less centralised than either Iberia or Armenia. According to medieval Armenian accounts, Christianity in Albania was established by Gregory the Illuminator with Gregory's grandson Grigoris being its first patriarch and martyr. Due to its unfortunate geographic location, by the

---

[3] For a comprehensive history of Caucasian Albania, see the recent volume: Gippert and Dum-Tragut, *Caucasian Albania*.

ninth century, Albania seized to exist as a polity and was partly absorbed by the Armenian and Georgian principalities, and partly replaced by the Muslim entities that had gradually emerged in the region. Most of the history of Caucasian Albania has survived in an Armenian corpus known as the *History of Albania* attributed to a certain Movsēs Dasxuranc'i or Movsēs Kałankatwac'i, who lived either in the seventh or the tenth century.

Although Caucasia was mostly Christian, Zoroastrian practices, cults and traditions have survived long after Christianisation, which among others also influenced the local peculiarities of cult practices. There seems to have been some sort of religious unity in Caucasia until the late sixth century. The decisions and repercussions of the 451 council of Chalcedon reached Caucasia slowly, but when they did, Chalcedon caused a major conflict, resulting in a schism of the early seventh century between the Iberian and Armenian churches. By the early seventh century, the Church of Iberia became decidedly Chalcedonian with its centre in Mtskheta, whereas the Armenian Church, centred in Dwin, adopted anti-Chalcedonianism, although until the eighth century there were further uncertainties in this regard. Although the reasons for the schism were theological, the political factors were decisive, since Iberia leaned towards Byzantium, whereas Armenia was a Persian ally. Albania was largely indecisive, but most of its church became antichalcedonian and subordinate to the Armenian Church, which became one of the reasons for its subsequent annihilation. Other parts of the Albanian Church were absorbed by the Chalcedonian Georgian Church.

The emergence and early history of the cult of saints in Caucasia, therefore, happed in the following cultural contexts: Christianisation and establishment of Christianity, formation of liturgical and monastic traditions, wars with the Sasanians and the Sasanian religious policies, and finally the ecclesiastic schism between the Armenian and Iberian churches. Martyrdom accounts proliferated under the Arabs. However, by then all the models and tropes of sanctity had been already formed in Caucasia.

The cult of saints was established in Caucasia simultaneously with the creation of the first pieces of literature. By then, Christians in all regions actively believed that saints can serve as intermediaries between the earthly and the divine realms since the fourth century. Almost immediately, as Peter Brown described, in the Roman world 'the Christian cult of saints rapidly came to involve the digging up, the moving, the dismemberment – quite apart from much avid touching and kissing – of the bones of the dead, and, frequently, the placing of these in areas from which the dead had once been excluded.'[4]

---

[4] Brown, *Cult of Saints*, 4.

The dead began to occupy public spaces, and prominently so. Material relics, as well as the memory and stories associated with these relics, were endowed with value, and as such became objects of commodity. Value, to use Georg Simmel's famously laconic explanation, is that quality of an object that 'resists our desire to own them.'[5] Once relics were endowed with this quality, those in power desired and made a tremendous effort to own them by searching, purchasing, stealing, showcasing, distributing or doing anything with them that one does with a scarce commodity.[6] As soon as these objects were associated with power, and this happened almost instantaneously, their religious value was transformed into political value. Such relics were gifted, donated and generally used in the process of government.[7] The emperors, their family members, bishops and the ruling elites zealously collected the relics of the saints to legitimise personal or dynastic rule, especially when the legitimacy of their rule was contested.[8]

In the later part of the sixth century, the religious aspect of imperial legitimisation was particularly bolstered. As Averil Cameron suggests, 'the late sixth century was crucial. It was a time when the Byzantine emperors in the capital presided over a process of cultural integration by which the élite and its ruler came to be fully identified. In this society such integration could only be expressed in religious terms.'[9] The usage of the saints, whether dead or alive, in imperial ceremonial increased dramatically, and the emperors zealously tied their legitimacy to various saints and relics, especially those associated with the Theotokos. Along with the dead saints, living holy men and women were also used to legitimise an emperor's mandate.

Relics, as implied by the word itself, also had a mnemonic function. Arguably, before the relics of the saints were fully incorporated into the arsenal of royal power, in fifth- and sixth-century imperial discourses, they sustained historic continuity in Christendom, and acted as a material attestation to the universal salvation history from the Old Testament to the New, the era of the foundations to contemporary times, from paganism to Christianity and so on, all of these embodied in the charismatic figure of the Emperor.

---

[5] Simmel, *Philosophy of Money*, 67.
[6] Geary, *Furta Sacra*.
[7] Rollason, 'Relic-Cults', 91.
[8] For Western examples, see, e.g., Julia Smith's discussion on the role of saints and their relics in legitimising the reign of Pippin and Charlemagne. Smith, 'Rulers and Relics', 78–80.
[9] Cameron, 'Images of Authority', 4.

While the belief that saints and their relics could exercise political influence was shared by all the regions of the Christian world, in practice the wider regions revealed a considerable degree of diversity. Compared to eastern Christendom, initially Western rulers were much more reluctant to carry around the bodily remains of saints, and were far less fascinated by the material aspect of sainthood. Yet, by the eighth century the Carolingians had fully integrated relics into their power struggles, and two centuries later, relics were spread all over Europe.

The cult of saints and of relics had a particularly important role to play in early Caucasian historical and identity rhetoric. In this, I believe, the Caucasian sources stand apart from the rest of Christendom. With the Christianisation of the south-Caucasian lands in the fourth century, the cult of the saints too was introduced and established in Georgian, Armenian and Albanian religious writings. The discussions on the cult of saints went hand in hand with the articulation of identity and political rhetoric by Late Antique and early medieval Armenian and Georgian authors. Whether in their zeal to define the religious limits of Georgianness or Armenianness or in the discourse of royal and dynastic legitimacy, the cult of saints and saints' relics played a central role. Therefore, in early medieval Armenian, Georgian and Albanian historical narratives, the religious and political manifestations of a saint's body were readily associated.

Finally, and crucially, Late Antique and early medieval Georgian saintly narratives introduced an additional trope to the political conceptualisation of sainthood and relics of saints. The fact that Georgia's greatest saint and its converter to Christianity was a woman generated a series of conceptual problems in subsequent political and saintly narratives. Yet, on the other hand, it allowed for a unique conceptualisation of the feminine which strongly affected medieval and indeed modern Georgian discourses of sanctity, identity and history. Therefore, in this first section we shall have a look at this foundational era of Christian Caucasian cultures, and we shall extract symbols and tropes of sanctity that reverberated on numerous occasions in subsequent eras and historical contexts.

# 1

# Saints at the Foundations

## 1.1 Saints and History: Eastern Roman Models

In what is perhaps the earliest association of the relics of the saints with political foundations, Paulinus, bishop of Nola (d. 431), credits the Emperor Constantine, albeit wrongly, with the translation of the relics of the Apostles to Constantinople. According to Paulinus, himself a dedicated relic collector, Constantine's zeal was to emulate Romulus as the founder of the new Rome, along with protecting the walls of Constantinople:

> Indeed, when Constantine was founding the city named after himself and was the first of the Roman kings to bear the Christian name, the godsent idea came to him that since he was embarking on the splendid enterprise of building a city that would rival Rome, he should also emulate Romulus' city with a further endowment, by gladly defending his walls with the bodies of the apostles. He then removed Andrew from the Achaeans and Timothy from Asia. And so, Constantinople now stands with twin towers, vying with the eminence of great Rome, or rather resembling the defenses of Rome in that God has counterbalanced Peter and Paul with a protection so great, since Constantinople has gained the disciple of Paul and the brother of Peter.[1]

Despite the graves of old and new saints reportedly attracting attention since the beginning of the fourth century, the first literary references to the revelation of the saints' relics appear only in the second half of the same century.[2] During the fourth century and into the fifth, the relics acquired

---

[1] Paulinus of Nola, *Carmen* 19.329–42, ed. Dolveck; tr. Mango, 'Constantine's Mausoleum', 53.
[2] Wiśniewski, *Beginnings of the Cult of Relics*, 101–20.

a new, political value in the Eastern Roman Empire. Since then, the political value of saints' relics has become a recurring theme in the discourse of power, sovereignty and legitimacy. Emperors and bishops, and Paulinus among them, passionately competed to collect the relics 'of the very special dead' for their foundations.³ It was most likely the Emperor Constantius (317–61), who imported and deposited the relics of the apostles Andrew, Luke and Timothy in the Mausoleum of his father, Constantine.⁴ Constantius has, in Jaś Elsner's words, inaugurated a 'meditation on the nature of history and the past embodied in the juxtaposition of objects from different periods on a new, composite monument'.⁵ As argued by Elsner, Constantine or Constantius adapted the imperial culture of the collection of *spolia* (e.g. the Arch of Constantine in Rome) to the cult of the relics, specifically to Constantine's Mausoleum, where Constantine allegedly wished to be buried *ad sanctos* among the relics of the Holy Apostles:

> The mausoleum took the antiquarianism of material objects and applied it (by 360 at the very least) to the excavation and display of the saintly bodies. Both monuments were concerned with the collecting and display of originals – whether original sculptures or authentic bones ... Very rapidly, both the culling of *spolia* and the cult of relics would become a culture of fragments as (in both cases) demand swiftly came to exceed supply.⁶

In other words, the eastern Roman emperors endowed the saints' relics with values of history, memory and legitimacy.

Later, according to Procopius of Caesarea, the apostles' relics were revealed to Justinian in 536 during the rebuilding of Constantinople after the devastating fire of 532. Procopius interprets this event as Justinian's confirmation as Constantinople's second founder.⁷ In both Paulinus's and Procopius's vision, therefore, the relics of the saints serve both as foundational elements of the new city, while also acting as symbolic bridges between the two times of religious and political history, united in the Emperor's charismatic figure.

---

³ Brown, *Cult of the Saints*, 69; Elsner, 'Culture of Spolia', 158; Cronnier, *Les inventions des reliques*, especially, 333–55; Klein, 'Sacred Relics and Imperial Ceremonies', 79–99.
⁴ *Chronicon Paschale*, ed. Dindorf, 542, tr. Whitby and Whitby, 33. CSLA.E07986 (D. Lambert).
⁵ Elsner, 'Culture of Spolia', 153.
⁶ Ibid., 162.
⁷ Procopius, *De aedificiis*, I, 4, ed. Haury; CSLA.E04334 (J. Doroszewska); Cronnier, *Les inventions des reliques*, 116–21; Wortley, 'Earliest Relic-Importations', 207–25; Bozóky, *La politique des reliques*, 94–97.

In Procopius's narrative, there is understandably a desire to emulate Empress Helena's discovery of the True Cross and Holy Nails in the Holy Land by incorporating material relics related to the foundations of Christianity into the discourse of power. According to Ambrose of Milan, the grace bestowed upon Helena and her son, Constantine, heralded the foundation of the new Christian Empire:

> Mary was visited to set Eve free; Helena was visited so that emperors should be redeemed. That is why she sent to her son Constantine a diadem brilliant with jewels, which were embedded in the more precious jewel of divine redemption [holy nails] bound in the iron of the cross; that is why she also sent the bridle. Constantine used both, and passed on the faith to subsequent rulers. Thus, the holy object on the bridle is the foundation of the belief of emperors.[8]

By the physical incorporation of the relics into the Imperial diadem, a model was given to subsequent generations of writers on how to integrate Christian materiality into the discourse of power. Theodoret interprets the inclusion of the holy nails in the horse's bridle as a fulfilment of the prophecy of Zechariah 14:20: 'There shall be upon the bridles of the horses Holiness unto the Lord Almighty.'[9] Ambrose concludes: 'Moreover, by the generosity of Christ our princes are to have the privilege that what has been said of the Lord can be said of the Roman emperor: You have placed on his head a crown of precious stones.'[10] Ambrose places in a single composite item an assemblage of the symbols of Orthodox faith, material wealth, and political power, a trope, which, as we shall see, will become common in early medieval Caucasian discourses of power. Through the power of this assemblage, the Emperor, as a political figure, embodied the entirety of Christian history of salvation. Eventually, majestic royal processions with holy relics mounted on horses and chariots, practised, among others, in Caucasia, may have been seen as an emulation of Constantine's original model.

The handling of relics by an emperor as a foundational activity, and as a sign of divine grace, became a particularly fashionable motif among the writers of the Theodosian Dynasty. Sozomen interpreted the discovery

---

[8] Ambrose of Milan, *Political Letters and Speeches*, tr. Liebeschuetz, 200. The same, although slightly modified, information is repeated in Theodoret, *HE* 1.17. Socrates and Sozomen claim that the bridle and helmet were made by Constantine. Socrates, *HE* 1.17; Sozomen, *HE* 2.7.
[9] Theodoret, *HE* 1.17.
[10] Ambrose of Milan, *Political Letters and Speeches*, tr. Liebeschuetz, 200.

and transfer of the head of John the Baptist to the Hebdomon near Constantinople in 392 as a sign of divine benevolence towards the Emperor Theodosius I (379–95).[11] The miraculous manifestation of the relics signals the legitimacy of Theodosius's and his house's rule, first through its founder, and then through the Empress Pulcheria, the lawful continuator of the dynasty. Pulcheria was reportedly particularly innovative in her treatment of saints' relics. In Constantinople she dedicated a church to St Lawrence, a Roman martyr of the third century, and another church to the prophet Isaiah. And although they were built to receive the relics of these two figures, eventually they were translated in the vicinity of her palace.[12] By integrating the relics into the symbolism of power of her dynasty, Pulcheria also forged her personal and intimate relationship with these remains. Kenneth Holum compares Pulcheria's treatment of the relics with the famous representation of the translation of relics on the Trier Ivory: Pulcheria 'devoted her resources to housing relics and memorialising the saints, to structures that expressed in monumental architecture the same intimacy between herself and the holy dead which the Trier Ivory captured in miniature'.[13] While relics of individual saints, such as the most coveted head of John the Baptist, were certainly invaluable possessions, there was also a tendency to create assemblages of relics. Rather than being random collections, the assemblages often betrayed intricate symbolic links between their constituent individual relics. Pulcheria's choice of relics, of Isaiah and Lawrence, was a 'historicist' act that drew attention to the two eras of Christian history, those of biblical times and of the recent Christian martyrs. These two eras thus became united in the charismatic body of the Empress, a merging that assigned to her and her house centrality in salvation history.

John Chrysostom, one of the staunchest promoters of the cult of saints, recounts in his homily *After the Remains of the Martyrs*, Constantinople's first majestic procession with the relics of the saints organised by the Empress Aelia Eudoxia (d. 404). Eudoxia is generously compared to the biblical Miriam who led the Israelites in a dance after crossing the Red Sea. She is also compared to King David when he escorted the Ark of the Covenant from the house of Obededom the Gittite to Jerusalem (2 Samuel 6:12–15), and with Phoebe and Priscilla of the Acts of the Apostles (Acts 18:2, 26; Romans 16:1).[14] Like her symbolic biblical analogue, by accompanying the

---

[11] Sozomen, *HE* 7.21.4, ed. Bidez and Hansen; CSLA.E04052 (E. Rizos); Holum, *Theodosian Empresses*, 136–8.
[12] Holum, *Theodosian Empresses*, 137.
[13] Ibid., 136.
[14] CSLA.E02660 (E. Rizos).

relics of the saints, Eudoxia united the multilingual procession. Through the Empress's charismatic presence and the validation of saintly relics, diversity turned into an imperial unity, merging into a 'river of fire' that stretched from the imperial city to Drypia.[15] To summarise in Elsner's words, the imperial relics 'conflated past and present, and displayed the past only in so far as the past is validated by, fulfilled in and made meaningful through the present', 'they belonged to the past but were assimilated to present needs – in liturgy, in church building, in commemorative monuments. Like an Old Testament type, or one of Constantine's predecessors on his Arch, their resonance oscillated constantly between their original meaning and their new significance in whatever context they were deployed'.[16]

In the later part of the sixth century, the religious aspect of imperial legitimisation was particularly bolstered. As Averil Cameron suggests, 'the late sixth century was crucial. It was a time when the Byzantine emperors in the capital presided over a process of cultural integration by which the elite and its ruler came to be fully identified. In this society such integration could only be expressed in religious terms.'[17] The usage of the saints, whether dead or alive, in imperial ceremonial increased dramatically, and the emperors tied their legitimacy to various saints and relics, particularly those associated with the Theotokos. The Emperor Maurice was particularly dedicated to assembling relics of saints in Constantinople to legitimise his rule due to internal unrest in the empire. Along with the dead saints, living holy men and women were also used to legitimise an emperor's mandate to rule. In time, the relics acquired some of the following political values: 'firstly the collection and donation of relics by the kings in order to increase their prestige and to symbolise their political status; secondly the use of relics in the processes of government; and thirdly royal patronage of particular relic-cults as an expedient to political influence'.[18]

While the relics in themselves were valuable, their added value was their ability to travel from one 'regime of value' to another. In imperial rhetoric, this value was generated by immediate political or ideological requirements, manifested mainly in the recurring need to legitimise the often dubious imperial mandate. Nevertheless, although the fifth-century Roman historians occasionally discussed the association of saints' relics with history and political foundations, these remarks remained somewhat

---

[15] As observed by Diliana Angelova, 'Eudoxia, the new and greater Miriam, unites the multilingual procession as a single people'. Angelova, *Sacred Founders*, 215.
[16] Elsner, 'From the Culture of Spolia', 176–7.
[17] Cameron, 'Images of Authority', 4.
[18] Rollason, 'Relic-Cults', 91.

intuitive and do not present an elaborate theoretical discussion on the nature of the relationship between relics and power.

It was only in the eighth century that the production and circulation of the relics were fully incorporated in political and identity discourses, in particular in the Latin West.[19] In western European traditions, such a political commodification of saints and their relics became particularly sophisticated under the Carolingians, when monarchs became obsessed with acquiring, possessing, distributing, gifting and stealing the treasured relics. Since the ninth century, in western Europe, relics have been increasingly described in terms of royal treasure, since they constituted an important part of royal treasury, and were often used as gifts.[20] Julia Smith explains that, while it is impossible to build a coherent picture of the royal interest in relics prior to c. 750, later, the relics of saints 'which passed through royal hands' displayed 'inter-convertibility' simultaneously marking their spiritual and material values, and evinced an exceptional ability to transform from one value to another. 'An "inter-convertibility" of valences thus marked relics as a special type of royal treasure.'[21] Although this has been a practice already since the fourth century, now encased in precious reliquaries, the spiritual and monetary value of relics became literally interchangeable.

Arguably, in South Caucasian writing explicit discussions on such 'inter-convertibility' of the relics of the saints and their endowment with political and identity meanings have appeared quite early, since the origin of writing in Georgian, Armenian and Albanian languages. Their unique political locus, ethno-religious experience and political circumstances contributed to the close association of material relics with the rhetoric of history, power and legitimacy.

## 1.2 Materiality of History: Armenian Vision

Late Antique writers from South Caucasia, especially Armenian historians of the fifth century, contributed to the politicisation of sanctity and holy remains with an important conceptual innovation. With the creation of writing and development of literary traditions in the fifth century, the cult of saints and relics became an inalienable part of the religious and political imagery of the Armenian and Georgian writers. Effectively, early Christian South Caucasian identity discourses were largely shaped by the intertwining of historical thinking and discussions on sanctity and sacred

---

[19] Bozóky, *La politique des reliques*, 120–203.
[20] Geary, 'Sacred Commodities', 169–92.
[21] Smith, 'Rulers and Relics', 76.

remains. In some way or another, the stories of Christianisation, the creation of alphabets, wars against the Sasanians or doctrinal and dogmatic controversies were embedded in the memories or material remains of saints. Early Armenian, Georgian and Albanian authors fused the cult of relics with identity rhetoric, particularly in accounts of political foundations. This was in part determined by eastern Roman literary models, yet also by particularities of local cult practices.

The religious and political conceptualisation of the Armenian nation, as articulated by fifth- and early sixth-century historians (Agathangelos, the *Epic Histories*, Ełišē and Łazar P'arpec'i), was founded on a dialectical mediation between the past and the present, embodied in, among other aspects, the memory and bodily presence of old and new saints. Chroniclers of Armenia's Christianisation and of the struggle of the Armenian people to maintain religious autonomy perceived conversion to Christianity as a process that transcended a sudden change in religious preference, nor was conversion described solely with religious metaphors. Rather, early and medieval Armenian and Georgian chroniclers, hagiographers and hymnographers regarded conversion as the history of establishment of their 'nations' (*azg* in Armenian; *eri* in Georgian) as agents on the stage of universal salvation history. Due to Christianisation, an event of religious, political and apocalyptic significance, a new political and religious paradigm was formed – that of a distinct Christian nation, yet also an integral member of the Christian commonwealth. As such, the language of conversion was both theological and political, meditating on historic as well as political significance of this monumental event in history.

Over centuries of rewriting, these conversion-narratives were adapted and chiselled to meet the ideological and rhetorical demands of diverse eras. The cults of the founding fathers were constantly fluid, reimagined to legitimise ruling dynasties, who, in imitation of their imperial colleagues, sought to appropriate these cults for their political agendas. With the diversification of ideological agendas and expansion of territorial claims, these narratives were amplified beyond the limits of immediate conversion stories, reaching out to the foundations of Christianity. Apostolic origins of the churches were claimed and narrative bridges were constructed between disjointed events, involving a plethora of historical or quasi-historical figures. Thus, grand narratives of a 'long' conversion were created, whereby each new event confirmed some old story and vice versa.[22] With their miraculous discoveries, new relics pointed to more ancient relics, revealing some organic unity with

---

[22] Calzolari, 'Je ferai d'eux mon propre peuple', 179–97; Mahé, 'Entre Moïse et Mahomet', 121–53.

it, and creating a sense of unity and teleology in history. In these grand narratives, the original illuminators appear both at the sources of the cycles, but also represent the culmination of these stories, serving as a narrative axis around which other sub-narratives and pious cycles revolved. As a result, two or three centuries after Christianisation, a rich saintly topography was formed in Caucasia that on the one hand pointed to a historic unity, while also being infused with changing political values.

In this respect, Agathangelos's account (c. 450) of Armenia's Christianisation by Gregory the Illuminator was pioneering. It provided models for the conceptualisation of sainthood and saintly relics for subsequent generations of writers, Armenian as well as Georgian and Albanian. Agathangelos's *History of Armenia*, also known as the *Life of Gregory the Illuminator*, recounts the Christianisation of Arsacid Armenia and the conversion of king T'rdat in the early fourth century, followed by the establishment of the Armenian Church, patriarchal succession and other institutions that became essential to medieval Armenian identity. The *History* was supposedly written some time after Sasanian Iran had abolished native Arsacid kingship in eastern Armenia (423). In the absence of kingship, it was the father of the Armenian Church, Patriarch Gregory, whom Agathangelos, and since Agathangelos, all medieval Armenian authors, viewed as the founder of the new Christian Armenia, with its new institutions and ecclesiastic hierarchy.[23] The patriarchal succession remained hereditary within Gregory's house, even though native Armenian kingship had ceased to exist for a long time. In Agathangelos's time, 'the church was left as the sole focus and instrument of national solidarity', a phenomenon that set the Armenian writing apart from the neighbouring Georgian histories.[24] Consequently, political institutions gave way to a thoroughly religious conceptualisation of Armenia and Armenianness. Agathangelos describes St Gregory, the founder of this 'new Armenia', as a living martyr who endured years of torture and isolation in an underground pit under the pagan T'rdat, yet eventually converting the king through divine intercession and miracles. Immediately after the story of the conversion, by reporting Gregory's sermon and vision, Agathangelos reflects on the essence of the new Christian Armenian nation by meditating on the deeper meaning of its holy relics.

As Agathangelos's narrative unfolds, he juxtaposes the memories and material bodies of martyred saints, both living and long dead, an interplay

---

[23] For only a few examples, see medieval panegyrics dedicated to St Gregory, translated with commentary in Terian, *Patriotism and Piety*.

[24] Thomson (1976), *Agathangelos, History of the Armenians*, xci–xciii.

which contributes to the creation of Armenia as a reborn martyr-nation: Gregory's martyrdom and the conversion of the royal family were preceded and prepared by the first shedding of blood for Christ's sake on Armenian soil. The Roman nuns, Hṙip'simē, Gayanē and their companions, who had fled Diocletian's persecution, had then fallen into the hands of the still pagan king T'rdat, who brutally executed them for their faith. As noted by Valentina Calzolari, the drama of the virgins unfolds while Gregory is still locked for years in the pit on the Ararat Plain, thrown there by the same T'rdat. Yet, it is following the 'impregnation of the Armenian soil by the blood of the Virgins' that Gregory emerges from the pit, as a living relic of sorts, and manifests himself to the Armenian people for the king's and the people's salvation.[25] Once Gregory converts the realm, the reverse occurs, and the hidden relics of the virgins are revealed to the Armenians. The martyrdom of the virgins Hṙip'simē and Gayanē was an act of apostolic significance, signalling this final stage in the history of salvation. Yet, it was through Gregory's involvement since his emergence from the pit that the 'untamed' intercessory powers of the female Hṙip'simēan relics were harnessed, institutionalised and entrusted to the king and the political realm: 'Behold the thirty-seven Christian cups who came to serve you!', Gregory reportedly announces to T'rdat, referring to the number of women who had followed Hṙip'simē and Gayanē to Armenia.[26] Further, the author of Gregory's *Teaching* makes him address T'rdat:

> But now God has sent his Son to mankind who came and walked on earth and sent his disciples throughout the whole world. These blessed ones [Hṙip'simē and Gayanē], who have come as far as you, have shown you not only mere words, but also signs of their miracles through your punishments. Although yesterday you [T'rdat] killed them, they are God's and now are living and will live forever. By their intercession you will be reconciled with God according to the instructions of the companion apostle to those apostles of yours, the great Paul, who said: 'Through us be reconciled with God by the death of his Son [II Cor. 5:18].' For the Son of God died and lived, and likewise his beloved martyrs are alive and intercede for you.[27]

This passage represents one of the earliest examples of political intercession of saints' relics, in which the martyrs' remains legitimise and bless a

---

[25] The rather beautiful analogy belongs to Valentina Calzolari, in Calzolari, 'Le sang', 180.
[26] Thomson, *Teaching of St Gregory*, 128.
[27] Thomson, *Teaching of St Gregory*, 138.

monarch's rule. Gregory's sermon delivered on the occasion of the king's conversion, recounts the history of universal salvation from Creation to Incarnation leading to the formation of the Christian nations, and specifically the Armenian. These holy relics, according to Gregory, assign T'rdat and through him to Armenia, centrality in universal salvation history. The sermon is followed by Gregory's account of his vision, an important apocalyptic episode in the history of Late Antique Armenian writing, and crucial for subsequent Armenian identity discourse.[28] Here Gregory visualises Hŕip'simē and Gayanē as two pillars of the church and priesthood, that is himself and his house, as the third pillar, with the 'Armenian nation', embedded in the church and founded on the relics of these saints:

> And I looked up and saw three other bases: one in the place where saint Gayanē was martyred with her two companions, and one in the place where saint Hŕip'simē was martyred with her thirty-two companions, and one in the place of the wine-press. And these bases were red, the colour of blood, and the columns were of cloud and the capitals of fire. And on top of the three columns were crosses of light in the likeness of the Lord's cross. And the crosses of these columns were level with the capital of the column of light, for that one was higher than they. And from the four columns, above the crosses, marvellous vaults fitted into each other. And above this I saw a canopy of cloud, wonderfully and divinely constructed in the form of a dome. Under the canopy but above the vaults I saw these thirty-seven holy martyrs in shining light, with white garments, which I am not capable of describing.[29]

The three bases mark the sites of the main church and the three martyria built to house the relics of the thirty-seven martyred virgins. 'The arches represent the unity of the Christian Church, the canopy is a type of the celestial city, the throne represents the almighty nature of God, the torrent flowing forth is baptism, the plains turn blue because the earth will become like heaven, and the many altars indicate the expansion of the service of the Eucharist over the whole country.'[30] In its totality, as an assemblage, Gregory's narrative, together with his vision and his own martyrdom, serves as Armenia's rite of passage from a pagan and barbaric people to a Christian nation, towards becoming an integral part of the Christian Oecumene.[31]

---

[28] Thomson, 'Vision of St Gregory', 285–95; La Porta, 'Vision of St Grigor', 296–312; Aleksidze, 'Visions of Grigor and Sahak', 326–40.
[29] Agathangelos, *Patmowt'iwn*, ed. Thomson, 80; tr. Thomson, 213–74.
[30] Thomson, 'Vision of St Gregory', 287.
[31] On Gregory, as a living martyr, see, e.g. Terian, *Patriotism and Piety*, 81–2 n. 7.

Sergio La Porta further argues that Gregory's vision, and his theologisation on Christian symbolism and the relics, is essentially a symbolic and physical superimposition of a Christian superstructure over an earlier Zoroastrian structure: it usurps an apocalyptic vision from its Iranian context; it reapplies traditional Zoroastrian imagery for Christian purposes and alludes to a concrete displacement of a fire temple by the cathedral church. 'These three modes of expression are critical in the definition of religious identity and through their conversion the vision provides a new paradigm for an Armenian Christian self-definition that accords with their new faith.'[32]

Immediately after recounting his vision, Gregory and everyone present start building Armenia's first church. For this new foundation, Gregory imports the relics of two martyr saints, John the Baptist and Athenogenes of Pedachthoe, a martyr killed during Diocletian's persecutions, and adds them to those of the Hr̄ip'simēan virgins.[33] While Agathangelos explains in detail the value of the Hr̄ip'simēan relics, the reason for bringing in specifically these additional relics is not explicitly stated. Yet, similarly to the biblical relics of the imperial collectors, they embody the author's experience of Christian history, and serve as a material confirmation of the sermon and Gregory's vision: John serves as a symbol of universal salvation history, of mediation between the two covenants, and transition to Christianity. It is revealed in the sermon that John has inherited and transmitted the priesthood, the kingship and the prophecy, thus linking the Old and the New Testaments: 'So all the grace of the tradition of the prophecy of the race of Israel, which the keeper of the tradition of the blessing of the covenants, and the anointing bore, the priesthood, with the kingship, was entrusted [to John] through the tribe of Levi.'[34] Besides, John the Baptist is the earliest martyr for faith, and the proto-martyr par excellence. By contrast, paired with John, Athenogenes is introduced as a recent martyr, a victim of Diocletian's persecutions and, crucially, a martyr of Caesarea, where Gregory was consecrated and where the Armenian apostolic church by tradition identifies its origin and legitimacy. Therefore, the relics of the two 'foreign' saints underline Armenia's double belonging since its conversion: to universal

---

[32] La Porta adds an archaeological argument, suggesting that the original church was built on a Zoroastrian fire temple, which indeed had four bases for columns, as described in the vision, and a water basin with conduits that recalls the image in the vision of the water spreading through the columns and filling the land. La Porta, 'Vision of St Grigor', 307.

[33] For a summary and study of Athenogenes's martyrdom account, written between the fourth and the sixth centuries, see CSLA.E02993 (E. Rizos). Athenogenes was very closely associated with Gregory of Neocaesarea. CSLA.E01103 (E. Rizos).

[34] Thomson, *Teaching of St Gregory*, 94–5.

history and the recent history of Christianity and its hierarchy.³⁵ While John and Athenogenes are saints and martyrs of the universal church, Hŕip'simē and Gayanē are 'nationalised' martyrs who had shed their blood on Armenian soil. Thus, an assembly of relics with Gregory's own martyred body in its centre is created. In conjunction with properly 'Armenian' relics of the Hŕip'simēan virgins, this assembly embodies the history of Christianity and marks Armenia's newly acquired centrality within this history. Through the interaction of different stages of history – biblical, Christian and 'national', which for early Armenian historians constituted the basis of Armenianness and its integrity – the essence of the Armenian Church, and of the Armenian body politic, is announced.

The political and 'national' valence of the relics of the saints is amplified by the literary models that Agathangelos utilises. Robert Thomson explains that Agathangelos, as well as other early Armenian historians, extracted tropes from Jewish history in their zeal to establish the cult of the national saints as symbols of opposition against the Sasanians. It was the 'fortunes of the Maccabees that struck a particularly responsive chord in the Armenian mind, and here we have not only interesting examples of literary influence, we also have the influence of ideology.'³⁶ For example, St Hŕip'simē's willingness to offer her tongue to be pulled out is compared to the third Maccabean brother's sacrifice. The same simile is used when T'rdat brought stones to build the martyrs' tombs. As a third example, Thomson points out that the Armenians could not make offerings to the martyrs' tombs nor could Gregory raise altars until a properly constituted priesthood was established in the country.³⁷

In time, Agathangelos's metaphysical reflections on history and identity were amplified with other, somewhat cruder attempts to sustain historic continuity. In the eighth century, Movsēs Xorenac'i, who wrote for his Bagratid patrons, appeared as the most dedicated historian to the project of bridging different historic eras to sustain an uninterrupted charismatic continuity of the tradition by narratively linking the biographies and bodies of the foundational saints of different eras. A particularly striking example is his story of Gregory's conception on the grave of the Apostle Thaddaeus – the original missionary to Armenia. As a result, Gregory 'received the grace of that same apostle, and having been begotten beside his grave he completed what was lacking in his spiritual labours.'³⁸ By

---

³⁵ CSLA.E00102 (N. Aleksidze).
³⁶ Thomson, 'Maccabees', 330.
³⁷ Thomson, 'Maccabees', 333–4. For the reception of the Maccabean martyr in the early Christian tradition, see Ziadé, *Les martyrs Maccabées, passim*.
³⁸ Movsēs Xorenac'i, *Patmowt'iwn*, ed. Thomson, 211–12; tr. Thomson, 217.

being conceived on the grave of Apostle Thaddaeus, 'one of the seventy-two disciples', who, according to later Armenian tradition, had originally preached Christianity in Armenia, Gregory the Illuminator became an embodied bridge between Christianity as a universal phenomenon, as preached by the original Apostles, and the unique ethno-religious experience of Armenian Christianity. While Gregory remained in the centre of Armenia's salvation history, his mission was validated through his charismatic association with the Apostle Thaddaeus. In reverse, in Xorenac'i's rhetoric, the apostolic foundation of the Armenian Church and the apostles' first mission to Armenia are retrospectively confirmed as historic fact through their association with St Gregory. In this way, Gregory's mythological biography encapsulates the entirety of Armenia's salvation history, heralding the birth of new Armenia:

> Its leader is no longer that Proteus who in the past sat enveloping the infinite world with its five peaks, but Mark with the preaching of the gospel. No longer do there exist tombs of heroes descended from the dragons, but the splendid martyria of the saints. No longer on the twenty-fifth of Tubi is celebrated the superstitious festival of crowning beasts of burden, the worshipping of snakes, and the distribution of cakes; but on the eleventh of the same month of Tubi is celebrated the feast of the Epiphany of the Lord, the praising of the victorious martyrs, the welcoming of strangers, and the giving of presents to the poor. No more do they sacrifice to the evil demon Serapis, but they offer the sacrifice of Christ's blood. They no longer seek oracles from Proteus, god of the underworld, but they study the power of various sciences from the new Plato.[39]

In Armenian cultural memory, the persona of Gregory the Illuminator encapsulated not only Armenia's past but also the future. He foresaw the nationalisation of the Armenian Church and the condemnation of the Council of Chalcedon – a radical step taken by the Armenian Church in its formative period in the sixth and seventh centuries.[40] Later chroniclers praise Gregory's immediate successors, all those holy fathers who led Armenia towards becoming a distinct nation, guaranteeing that through their distinct non-Chalcedonian orthodoxy, unique language and writing, or victimised identity, the nation would remain on the stage of history and

---

[39] Movsēs Xorenac'i, *Patmowt'iwn*, 3.62, ed. Thomson, 345–6; tr. Thomson, 201–3.
[40] Medieval Georgian writers used the vision of St Gregory in their polemic against non-Chalcedonian Armenians, claiming the vision foretold Armenian apostasy from Orthodoxy. On this prophecy, see Arseni Sap'areli's (tenth-century) reference, in Aleksidze and Mahé, 'Arsène Sapareli', 59–132; Aleksidze, 'Visions of Grigor and Sahak', 326–40.

remain prominently indeed.[41] Therefore, although the act of conversion was indeed tied to specific individuals of the early fourth century, St Gregory in the Armenian tradition and St Nino in the Georgian counterpart, the conversion was conceptualised both as an act and a process, a happening and a becoming, a sequence of events that extended far beyond the lifetime of these two great saints. For the Armenians this was 'the invention of the Armenian alphabet; the stand the Armenians took against Sasanian attempts to reconvert them to Zoroastrianism; the rejection of the Council of Chalcedon and the breach with Byzantium; and finally, the "classical" definition of the Armenian Church's doctrinal position and its organisation under Catholicos Yovhannēs Awjnec'i (John of Odzun) in the early eighth century'.[42] For medieval writers all these events set Armenia apart as an identifiable nation.

## 1.3 Relics and Kingship

The foundational and political values associated with saints' relics, as well as their appropriation in the rhetoric of history, were perhaps anachronistic to the early fourth century, when the events of Agathangelos's *History* unfolded. By the second half of the following century, however, when Agathangelos's account was supposedly written down, the eastern Roman Empire had a history of translating relics from one place to another for the purposes of political legitimacy. Whether or not we are dealing with literary parallels with the late fourth- and fifth-century Constantinopolitan experience of the political translation of relics, Agathangelos's account exercised a fundamental impact on subsequent Armenian writing by providing blueprints for the conceptualisation of the metaphysical image of the Armenian nation. By conceptualising the relics of the saints, Agathangelos fostered a resounding understanding of Christian history, also reflected in Albanian and Georgian narratives, and has set the stage for the further appraisal of the political role that the saints' relics had to play.

In the neighbouring Caucasian Albanian historical writing, almost entirely collected in the *History of Caucasian Albanians*, Agathangelos's

---

[41] Katholikos Yovhannēs Ōjnec'i (717–728) viewed Armenia's salvation history as a long story of nationalisation epitomised in the series of Church councils, through which Armenia acquired a unique ethno-religious identity and defined the limits of Armenianness. In this history of conversion, which mirrors universal salvation history, Vardapet Maštoc', who returns with biblical translations executed in the newly created Armenian letters, is perceived as a new Moses descending from Mt Sinai. Zekiyan, 'Die Christianisierung', 189–99.

[42] Van Lint, 'Formation of Armenian Identity', 269–70.

tropes were applied to the rhetoric of charismatic kingship and the monarch's divine mandate to rule. The *History of Caucasian Albanians* is a corpus of chronicles and episodes from the history of Albania written at various times between the sixth and the eleventh centuries. Its authorship or compilation is commonly attributed to a certain Movsēs Kałankatwac'i or to Movsēs Dasxuranc'i, who arguably lived in the tenth century, although some scholars prefer a seventh-century date. Although the corpus recounts the history of Caucasian Albania, it has survived in Armenian, or, and more likely, was originally written in Armenian, and was as such heavily indebted to Armenian literary sources. The *History* is not a single or even a coherent history, and is rather an amalgam of disjointed episodes from the history of Caucasian Albania, often revealing awkward attempts to sustain continuity. The earliest strata of Book One are conventionally dated to as early as the second half of the sixth or the seventh century, while the rest is markedly late, with the final parts written in the eleventh century. The opening chapters focus on the reign of Arsacid Vač'agan III the Pious (d. c. 510), the last king who restored Christianity in Albania and thereby founded, although for a very short while, a new political and religious order.[43] Vač'agan's episode stands out, lacking any context or knowledge that kingship in Albania ended with his death. Instead, after its conclusion, the narrative goes back in time to an entirely independent story. Consequently, there is a general, albeit cautious, consensus that the *Life of Vač'agan* was created as an independent text, perhaps soon after the king's death in the sixth century.[44] The *Life of Vač'agan* is a unique example of Late Antique Christian writing, as it illustrates a rite of passage to legitimate kingship through an exercise in historical anamnesis and a dramatic involvement of the relics of the saints.[45]

The *Life of Vač'agan* adopts Agathangelos's rhetoric of saints' relics and adapts it to Albanian political history. Yet, it also introduces a new political valence of relics, absent in early Armenian accounts, that is their power to provide the king with a charismatic mandate and to guide him in his

---

[43] Hakobyan, 'King Vač'agan', 239–48.
[44] The dating, although convincing, is still to be taken with a degree of caution, therefore I will not speculate about the historical context of its creation. For arguments, see Mahé, 'Vac'agan III', 13–126; Zuckerman, 'Khazars and Byzantium', 399–432; Hakobyan, 'King Vač'agan', 239–48. See also, Akopyan, 'Roman ob albanskom tsare', 159–71.
[45] The identity of the author, as well as the original language of its compositions, ethnic and cultural belonging of the *History*'s protagonists are controversial between Armenian and Azerbaijani scholars, and will not be addressed in this study, since they are irrelevant to the present discussion. The arguments sway from the essentialisation of medieval Albanian identity to its complete rejection.

passage to legitimate kingship. Vač'agan's story is also reminiscent of traditional accounts of initiation to kingship, found in Iranian as well as oral Caucasian traditions. As an amalgam of Roman, Iranian and Caucasian imagery, Vač'agan's quest, discovery and procession with the relics of the saints is one of the most elaborate and complex narratives of its age, to my knowledge having no analogue in Late Antique Christian writing.

The final destination of the royal processions and the quest, accompanied by dreams, visions and apparitions, is the discovery of the relics of Albania's legendary founding patriarch and first martyr saint, Grigoris (the grandson of Gregory the Illuminator).[46] Grigoris is conceived both as the instrument of Albania's Christianisation and as Albania's very own martyr, echoing Agathangelos's conceptualisation of the relics of Hṙip'simē and Gayanē as the pillars of the Armenian Church and nation.[47] By reporting a ritualised royal procession with the saints' relics and extensively deliberating on their metaphysical and political power, the anonymous author's intention was to define Albania's and its king's unique place in universal salvation history.

In the narrative, the first relics to reveal themselves, much earlier than Vač'agan was even born, were those of Apostle Eliseus. In the *History of Albanians*, Eliseus appears as the apostle who preached Christianity in Albania and was martyred on this account on the same land. The revelation of Eliseus's relics act as a premonition to the age of great discoveries of relics, and, together with the relics, of history, memory and Albanian identity by king Vač'agan:

> When a long time had passed, he appeared to a certain pious man in a vision, and they went in a body to the site of the ditch and saw a great heap of bones, and all were uncertain [as to which were those of St Eliseus]. They removed them and piled them up, however, and kept watch over them that night in prayer. In the morning there was a great earthquake, and those who stood there fell to the ground. A violent wind blew from the desert and scattered over the fields the bones of those who were not saints, so that only the bones of the apostles remained. From these a certain Step'annos, the pious priest of the village of Urekan, took the skull and then hurried away on his horse. The crowds followed him, for a dark cloud had descended and frightened them, and they returned to their homes. And St. Eliseus appeared to them in a vision, and they

---

[46] For the earliest reference to Grigoris and his martyrdom, see *Epic Histories*, tr. Garsoïan, 72–3.
[47] *Epic Histories*, tr. Garsoïan, 376–8. See, also, CSLA.E00135 (N. Aleksidze).

fetched and buried his remains where his skull had been laid by the holy priest Step'annos, namely in the village of Urekan. From there they were transferred to the holy monastery of Nersmihr which is now called Jrvstik, to the glory of our Almighty Lord. After many years had passed, the pious Vač'agan, king of Albania, erected a column in the ditch of the martyr and it was consecrated, the king's chamberlain becoming a stylite upon the column.[48]

Vač'agan's *Life* establishes a complex chain of associations among the bodily remains of saintly figures of different eras and integrates it into the narrative of Albanian history and identity. The king's quest is directed to the quintessentially 'Albanian' martyr-saint, and is narrated as a journey chaperoned by the relics of the two earlier martyr saints. In emulation of Agathangelos, these relics belong to Zechariah, a biblical martyr and father of John the Baptist, and to Pantaleon, who, like Athenogenes, was martyred in Nicomedia during Diocletian's persecutions.[49] Grigoris was believed to have brought these relics to Albania when he had established Christianity in the country, but they have since been lost. Together with the relics of Grigoris, these relics too were awaiting a charismatic royal figure to reveal themselves. Upon Vač'agan's accession to the throne, as a manifestation of his divinely sanctioned mandate and as a premonition of a new era in Albania's political history, the relics of Zechariah and Pantaleon began to miraculously manifest themselves through healings, conversions and other wonders.[50]

Vač'agan's career, condensed almost entirely in his quest for the relics, is an exercise in historical anamnesis that restores the chain of memory between Vač'agan's times and those of the foundations. The relics of Grigoris on the

---

[48] Movsēs Kałankatwac'i, *Patmowt'iwn*, ed. Ēmin, 17–18; tr. Dowsett, 6. For a brief, yet rare, discussion on medieval Albanian identity-narratives, see Yuzbachian, 'Einige Bemerkungen', 181–9.

[49] Procopius of Caesarea reports that the Emperor Justinian rebuilt a martyr shrine dedicated to Pantaleon/Panteleemon on the shores of Bosphorus, near Constantinople. Procopius, *De Aedificiis* 1.9.11, 13; CSLA.E04413 (J. Doroszewska). For additional bibliography on the saint and his *Martyrdom*, see CSLA.E07104 (C. Papavarnavas). As for Zechariah, the only other early reference to the translation of his relics is attested in the *Chronicon Paschale*. In 415 the Emperor Arcadius translated the relics of Joseph, the son of Iakob and of Zechariah to the Great Church of Constantinople. See, also, Bozóky, *La politique des reliques*, 877–93.

[50] Dowsett, *History of the Caucasian Albanians*, 18–24. The peripeteias accompanying the quest for the relics are typical to Late Antique relic narratives. Multiple visions, one leading to another, often constitute the core of the story of revelation of the relics. Cronnier, *Les inventions de reliques*, 189–209.

one hand, and those of Zechariah and Pantaleon on the other, complement each other and engage in a political and theological dialectic of the universal and the 'national'. Zechariah's and Pantaleon's relics operate as clues and guides that lead the king to the most coveted relics of Grigoris. In addition to Agathangelos's pattern, according to which the relics of the saints of the universal church endorse and sanctify those of Armenia's own martyrs, the author of Vač'agan's story introduces further dynamism into the narrative: Vač'agan sent letters to all bishops and priests asking them to aid him in his quest for 'the hidden treasure'. He located and retrieved the relics of Gregory the Illuminator, Hřip'simē and Gayanē in Artsakh that had been sent to Albania and sealed by the Armenian katholikos Yovhannēs Mandakuni (478–90). He personally met the relics of these great Armenian saints placed them with the relics of Zechariah and Pantaleon. And so 'they took along with them the five holy martyrs of Christ, that is, the great Gregory, the venerable Zechariah, the most blessed Pantaleon, and the most renowned and victorious combatants Hřip'simē and Gayanē to intercede with great and all-powerful God so that through them his request would be fulfilled'.[51]

As argued by J.-P. Mahé, the author of the account was an Armenophile Albanian, whose literary language was Armenian, in which he composed the narrative.[52] As such, the author ties Albania with the Armenian realm, and presents Albania's history as part of Armenian history. In the end, the coveted relics of Grigoris, like his grandfather Gregory's in the Armenian tradition, are conceptualised as a material encapsulation of the universal salvation history, of recent Christian history, as well as the Armenian cultural orbit, thereby symbolising the *raison d'être* of the Albanian polity.

Vač'agan's quest is in effect a ritual assumption by a local ruler of the monarch's political body achieved through an intimate relationship with the relics of historic saints. The king's ritual transitioning from a private person to a public figure through the handling of saints' relics introduces in Caucasian writing a distinction between private and public, or political, ownership of relics. Reflections on the 'public' as opposed to private ownership of saints' relics appears sporadically in Late Antique Christian discourses. Some relics, while previously kept in private possession, reportedly often refuse to remain as such, or to be made available to private individuals. For example, in *Oration 24*, Gregory of Nazianzus recounts the story of the discovery of the relics of Cyprian in the house of a pious woman. The relics, however, were destined to be made public. Gregory explains that 'since the God of the martyrs did not suffer to turn a blessing belonging to all into a private possession, or to curtail the common good

---

[51] Movsēs Kałankatwac'i, *Patmowt'iwn*, ed. Ēmin, 75–6; tr. Dowsett, 39.
[52] Mahé, 'Vač'agan III', 118.

by his special favour to her, he made the body manifest by a revelation.'[53] As another example, the fourth-century Syriac *Martyrdom of Pinhas* recounts a miracle performed by the martyr's relics, where the relics punished their illicit owner, since they belonged to an ecclesiastical community. In the *Martyrdom of Mar Pinḥas*, as in Babik's case, the ambiguity is retained with reference to the relics, specifically Pinhas's finger joint, which is consistently rendered as a pearl.[54]

Relics often manifest and make themselves available to charismatic persons, such as monarchs or other founding figures who embody institutions or body politic. It is common for such relics to exhibit recalcitrance, resist private ownership and to insist on their desire to be institutionalised. The most notable example from Late Antiquity is Sozomen's report of the discovery of the relics of the Forty Martyrs of Sebaste and their manifestation to the Empress Pulcheria. Sozomen emphasises that the relics were destined to reveal themselves to an imperial figure only. As a confirmation of their belonging, in a vision that Pulcheria saw, the martyrs were dressed in imperial chlamys.[55] In time, in Late Antique and early medieval saintly narratives, also outside Caucasia, the discovery of hidden relics became almost invariably political in nature, in that the relics were supposed to benefit the community, monastic or political, rather than individuals. In Caucasian writing, what we see is the king's, as a public figure's, exclusive charismatic mandate to discover, own and distribute relics, thereby defining the limits of his realm.[56] Arguably, the materiality of the relics introduced with the

---

[53] CSLA.E00966 (E. Rizos).

[54] McCollum, *Story of Mar Pinḥas*, 27, CSLA.E00251 (S. Minov).

[55] Sozomen, *HE* 9.2. 6–7, ed. Bidez and Hansen; tr. Rizos: 'It seems that God willed that the aforesaid site should be so perfectly obliterated, and that such a long period of time should elapse, because He wished to render more extraordinary and spectacular the finding of the martyrs and His favour for the finder. And the latter was the sister of our reigning sovereign, the empress Pulcheria. The divine Thyrsos appeared to her three times, and disclosed to her who were buried in the ground, commanding that they be moved by his side, in order that they share the same position and veneration. But also, the Forty themselves appeared to her, wearing splendid chlamyses'. CSLA.E04058 (E. Rizos). Cronnier, *Les inventions*, 152–6.

[56] Cf. with Proclus of Constantinople's rhetoric regarding Stephen the First-Martyr's new political purpose in Constantinople since the transfer of his relics by the Empress: 'Back then, he defended the words of the Cross, and now Stephen is the Church's victory crown, for he was the first to trample down the sting of death! Stephen is in the palace, for our empress and virgin has received him in her lodgings! Stephen is with our officials, for he has turned the servant of his host into an emperor's father! Stephen is in charity, for he has become the rich and trusted steward of widows and orphans! Stephen stands against the Jews, for he has denounced their synagogue which was polluted by idols! Stephen stands against heretics, for he shuts the mouths of God's adversaries by crying: "Great is our Lord!"' CSLA.E05403 (E. Rizos).

advent of Christianity in Caucasia has merged with the already-existing narrative topos of 'royal treasure', as a mark of royal charisma. Over time, the two, saintly relics and royal treasure, began to be used interchangeably as signs of investiture, so much so that oftentimes it becomes impossible to distinguish whether one refers to holy relics or material treasure.

## 1.4 The *farrah* of the Kings

As a story of a royal rite of passage, the *Life of Vačagan* bears structural resemblance to the early medieval Georgian epic of King P'arnavaz, part of the opening section of the eighth-century *Life of the Georgian Kings*.[57] The *Life of P'arnavaz* chronicles the foundational event in Iberia's history – the establishment of kingship, political order and institutions that its early medieval author(s) considered fundamental to Georgian religious and political identities. In the third century BC, P'arnavaz was reputed to have created Georgia's administrative units, established a royal and centralised cult, shaped a distinct Georgian writing and mandated Georgian as the sole official language of the kingdom. These achievements, however, were the culmination of P'arnavaz's career, preceded by his journey towards legitimate kingship. According to its authors, the formation of Iberia was a transition from wilderness to polity, from barbarian lawlessness to a state, all of which was embodied in the initiation of P'arnavaz to kingship. Throughout this rite of passage, P'arnavaz, an outstanding hunter (a quality essential for an Iranian king), from a private yet charismatic individual, transubstantiates

[57] The *Life of the Georgian Kings* is a universal history which begins with the story of Noah's grandsons and the eponymous founders of the Caucasian peoples, followed by a description of the foundation of the Georgian kingdom, the lives and deeds of its kings, and culminating in Kartli's Christianisation. Arguably, the *Life of the Georgian Kings* is modelled after Iranian quasi-historical epic narratives. Rapp, *Sasanian World*, 187–261. The *Life* was incorporated into *K'art'lis C'xovreba* (*Life of Georgia*), an eleventh-century compilation of historical narratives, so that the account leads towards the Christianisation of the kingdom, although, most likely, this was not the intention of the original, and the thoroughly Christian elements were a later development. It has been argued that the early medieval Georgian historical corpus has not survived in its original form, and what we currently have is a result of extensive reworking, both textual and ideological, with attempts to override the Iranian components within the narratives, and adapt Sasanian accounts to the ideological demands of the age. See Rapp, *Sasanian World*, 204–5. While a relatively old scholarly consensus dated the text to the eleventh century and attributed the entirety of the *K'art'lis C'xovreba* to Bishop Leonti of Ruisi, more recently other scholars have argued that the *Life of the Georgian Kings* and the *Life of King Vakhtang Gorgasali* must have been shaped before the rise of the Bagratids, and thus dated to c. 800. Rapp, *Medieval Georgian Historiography, passim*.

into a public figure and acquires a political body.⁵⁸ Material objects – relics and treasure – their discovery, ownership and distribution, are at the centre of Vač'agan's and P'arnavaz's journey to kingship.

Taking the reader on a journey of dreams, visions, and apparitions that initiated their legendary founders into legitimate kingship, both *Lives* describe the foundation of the Iberian and Albanian polities. On this path, the transitional stages emphasised in Vač'agan's story are almost identical in P'arnavaz's legend. Similarly to P'arnavaz's Iberia, Vač'agan's Albania experienced a transformation from the lawlessness of the forests to the order of a Christian kingdom.⁵⁹ Like P'arnavaz, Vač'agan is credited with reforms that became fundamental to Albanian identity: he restored and fortified orthodox Christianity by suppressing religious dissent and heresies, united Albania in faith, promulgated laws, and essentially defined the essence of the Albanian body politic. Arguably, the structural similarities of the two narratives suggest a deeper and shared understanding of the transitional stages of royal investiture:

Table 1.1 Structural similarities between *The Life of Vač'agan* and *The Life of P'arnavaz*

| *The Life of Vač'agan* | *The Life of P'arnavaz* |
|---|---|
| a. Vač'agan's story opens with his declaration as the rightful heir to the throne, as opposed to his immediate predecessor, as he is the brother of Vač'ē of Albania. | a. P'arnavaz is declared as the descendant of Kartli's original rulers, the *mamasaxlisis*, as opposed to Azon, his predecessor. |
| b. Vač'agan is acknowledged as a suzerain by Albanian lords and chieftains. | b. P'arnavaz sees a dream where the light, the *farrah*, descends on him. |
| c. Vač'agan's right to kingship is confirmed by the 'oecumenical' king – the Shah. | c. P'arnavaz discovers the treasure. |
| d. Vač'agan sees dreams and discovers the saints' relics. | d. P'arnavaz is acknowledged as a legitimate king by a powerful western Georgian ruler and others. |
| e. Vač'agan is baptised and receives the divine light. | e. P'arnavaz's right to kingship is confirmed by the 'oecumenical' king – Antiochos. |
| f. Vač'agan promulgates canons and establishes church institutions.⁶⁰ | f. P'arnavaz unites Kartli and establishes political institutions.⁶¹ |

---

⁵⁸ For an analysis, albeit different from the one provided here, of P'arnavaz's road to kingship, see Rapp, 'Images of Royal Authority', 155–72.
⁵⁹ This lawlessness is marked by bizarre sects spread in Albania, particularly that of the 'thumb-cutters' whom Vač'agan discovered in a forest and duly eliminated.
⁶⁰ Movsēs Kałankatwac'i, *Patmowt'iwn*, 60–82; tr. Dowsett, 29–42.
⁶¹ The episodes are found in *C'xovreba k'art'velt'a mep'et'a*, ed. Kaukhchishvili, 20–6, tr. Thomson, 34–8.

The story of Vač'agan, as a foundation narrative, is a synthesis of Christian and Iranian narratives of royal investiture, which is even more transparent in the Georgian *Life of P'arnavaz*.[62] Although the author or the editor of the *Life of P'arnavaz* is a dedicated Christian, the protagonist of the narrative is a pre-Christian king. Yet the author does not dismiss, and even embraces, P'arnavaz's very Zoroastrian charismatic kingship. Although Christianity introduced radically different concepts of sanctity, pre-Christian and Zoroastrian beliefs were far from eradicated in Christian Caucasia. Throughout Late Antiquity and the early medieval period, Caucasia was a ground of both conflict and cohabitation, as well as syncretism between Christian and Zoroastrian worldviews. Despite the thoroughly Christian nature of early medieval literary production, and their Hellenising projects, Caucasian cultures remained integral parts of the Iranian commonwealth, with Iranian and Zoroastrian imagery persisting in the language, symbolism, folklore and political imagery of the local people.[63]

Like Constantine and subsequent Emperors, who engaged with their non-Christian past, Caucasian writers had to manoeuvre between their Iranian and Christian identities. Christian and Iranian imagery of holiness was syncretised in Late Antique Caucasian writing by Christian appropriation and transformation of the Iranian symbolism of royal investiture. Often, Iranian symbols of *farrah* (glory, fortune, honour), *p'ark'* in Armenian, were replaced with Christian symbolic language, such as the glory of the martyrs or Christian kings. Yet, as Nina Garsoïan argues, Christian Armenians were aware of the original 'political' meaning of the word, and material remains that embodied political power and charisma could still evince *farrah* despite their non-Christian belonging.[64] Even such a staunch defender of Christianity and advocate of anti-Iranian rhetoric as the fifth-century author of the *Epic Histories*, recounts with reverence the ancient Armenian practice of veneration of the bodily remains of the Arsacid

---

[62] Aleksidze, 'Martyrs, Hunters and Kings', 249–69.
[63] For some important titles, see Greenwood, 'Sasanian Reflections'; Russell, *Zoroastrianism in Armenia*; Rapp, *Sasanian World*. Sergio La Porta has argued that in Agathangelos's original story of Gregory the Illuminator, his apocalyptic vision and miracles, 'the overwhelming presence of light and fire imagery ... is a continuation and reinterpretation of the imagery of fire and light of Armenia's pre-Christian and Zoroastrian beliefs'; La Porta, 'Vision of St Grigor', 307.
[64] Garsoïan, *Epic Histories*, 552. The appropriation of this and other Iranian political concepts in Caucasia is discussed in detail in Garsoïan, 'Prolegomena', 177–234. For the definition of *farrah* as used in the present book, see Gnoli, 'Farrah'. For another discussion of the Armenian adaptation of this concept, see Ajello, 'Armeno *p'ark'*', 25–33.

kings. In one of the episodes, in 364, the Sasanian King Shapur II invaded Armenia, and ordered his generals to remove the bones of the Armenian kings from their tombs and to carry them to Iran. 'For they said, according to their heathen beliefs: "This is the reason that we are taking the bones of the Armenian kings to our realm: that the glory of the kings and the fortune and valour of this realm might go from here with the bones of the kings and enter into our realm."[65] Armenians, however, refused to tolerate this offence. They put together all their forces, and reclaimed the relics of their kings, burying them in a safe and inaccessible gorge near Mt Aragats. Only after this did they start rebuilding the looted land.

Although the author does add a disclaimer that these were heathen beliefs, Garsoïan points out that this passage still provides evidence that the 'Iranian Zoroastrian belief that the supernatural qualities of legitimate kings – their glory, "fortune", and "valour" – clung to them even after death and protected their realm were still current in Christian Armenia.'[66] Even if the author of the *Epic Histories* did not believe in the supernatural powers of the relics of old kings, he still linked the return of the bones with the establishment of peace and prosperity in Armenia. The belief in the 'glory' and 'valour' embedded in the buried bones of the ancient kings, and in their intercessory powers, was also known to Agathangelos who does not provide a sound rebuttal of this practice.[67] One may even observe an

---

[65] *Epic Histories*, ed. Garsoïan, 158; tr. Garsoïan, 158.
[66] Garsoïan, *Epic Histories*, 294 n. 12.
[67] Early medieval Georgian monarchs and their historians adopted the concept of *farrah*, the glory of the Iranian kings with equal success. The exact term, however, has not clung to the Georgian language and was substituted by an autochthonous *dideba* (glory). Nevertheless, the word was retained in the names of some prominent pre-Bagratid kings: P'arnavaz, P'arnajom, P'arsman and others. See Rapp, *Sasanian World*, 227–32. Early medieval Georgian historians, such as the authors of the *Life of the Georgian Kings* and of the *Life of Vakhtang Gorgasali*, were certainly aware of the strong Iranian component in the identity of the first kings and that *farrah* was embedded in their names. See Rapp, 'Images of Royal Authority', 161–2. Rapp suggests that the relative absence of sacred and religious dimensions of kingship in pre-Bagratid historical writing can be explained by the excising of the Iranian component by Georgian editors. Another solution is that Late Antique Georgian kingship was not replete with sacral imagery, and that the Kartvelian kings may have been seen as a part of the universal monarchy ruled by the great Iranian king, theerefore special religious connections were reserved for him. 'Perhaps local royal imagery had such sacred connections, but if the texts as we now have them are based on considerably older oral traditions, as they probably are, then it is altogether possible that these oral traditions lacked detailed information about the divine bases of Kartvelian rulership as they presented a popular and not royal perspective'. Rapp, 'Images of Royal Authority', 172.

evolution in the interpretation of this episode from the fifth-century *Epic Histories* to Movsēs Xorenac'i, as by the eighth century, the latter already seems to be baffled by this practice.[68] The Iranian substratum, embedded in the Armenian tradition, prompted Xorenac'i to forge or popularise an alternate history for his patron Bagratid house, by creating, or at least developing, the myth of their Jewish ancestry and identity, and thereby claiming their direct participation in Christian history. For this purpose, Xorenac'i forges a story, whereby the direct ancestors of the Bagratids were Jewish martyrs for the Law, and have thus preserved the charisma of the kings.[69] Therefore, arguably, in Caucasian traditions, the political value of bodily remains and their power to bring prosperity to their owners was an established phenomenon, despite the general distaste in Zoroastrian cultures towards material remains.[70]

## 1.5 Hidden Treasure and Its Discoverers

Holiness, therefore, at least in the earliest Caucasian historical narratives, transcended strictly Christian requirements, and was independently associated with the charisma embedded in a historic dynasty, sacred kingship and material objects associated with this kingship. The bones of the old kings, as well as Vač'agan's relics and P'arnavaz treasure, were a public good,

---

[68] Other parallel narratives entirely omit the story, just as it is omitted in the Greek version of Agathangelos. Garsoïan, *Epic Histories*, 294 n. 12. 'This term (*k'ajut'iwn*) is occasionally used merely for intensification with the sense of "very, mighty, powerful" ... or for Christ ... or the saints ... who are God's champions. The most common usage in [the fifth-century *Epic Histories*], however, is to denote the supernatural valour that is one of the main characteristics distinguishing the legitimate ruler of Iran in the Zoroastrian tradition. This quality was bestowed on them by the god Vərəθrayna (Arm. Vahagn), who was himself "created victorious" (*pērōzgar*), as is explicitly stated by [the Armenian] Aa [witness of Agat'angełos] ... This heroic epithet also became part of the Sasanian royal title, according to [Movsēs Xorenac'i] ... [The Epic Histories] normally reserves this title for the hereditary ruling dynasty of the Aršakuni in Greater Armenia ... , thus showing that he was still acquainted with its transcendental implications, as does his transfer of the epithet to the Mamikonean family.' Ibid., 534–5.

[69] Thomson, 'Maccabees', 329–41.

[70] Among others, the Iranian substratum was also palpable in the conceptualisation and physical veneration of the relics, as well as in the necessity to regulate this practice even several centuries after Christianisation. This necessity apparently arose from an incompatibility between the traditionally Zoroastrian understanding of matter and Christian demands. Aram Mardirossian suggests that Yovhannēs Mayragomec'i's (seventh-century) prohibition of the burial of the relics of the saints 'where the liturgy is celebrated' is a residue of the traditional belief that no material remain can ever be sacred, even those of the martyrs. Mardirossian, *Livre des canons*, 455–61.

and as such were inalienable belongings of the body politic. P'arnavaz's endowment with *farrah* and the miraculous discovery of the wondrous treasure, related in a particularly solemn tone, is the central episode in the future king's rite of passage:

> Then P'arnavaz saw a dream: he was in an uninhabited house and was wishing to depart, yet could not leave. Then a ray of sunlight entered the window and seized him around the waist; it drew him up and brought him out the window. When he had come out into the country-side, he saw the sun bending down. He stretched out his hand, wiped the dew on the sun's face, and anointed his own face. P'arnavaz awoke, was astonished, and said: 'The dream means that I should go to Ispahan, and there I shall find good (fortune).' On that day P'arnavaz went out and hunted alone; he chased a deer in the plain of Dighom. The deer fled into the rough ground of Tbilisi. P'arnavaz followed; he shot an arrow and hit the deer. The deer went on a little, and fell at the foot of a cliff. P'arnavaz went up to the deer. Now the day, (already) evening, was declining. So he sat down by the deer in order to spend the night; in the morning he would go off. Now at the foot of the cliff was a cave, the entrance of which had been blocked up long since by stones; the ravages of time had caused dilapidation in the edifice. Then a heavy rain began to fall. So P'arnavaz took up an axe and broke away the entrance to the cave in order to keep himself dry from the rain inside. He entered the cave and saw there unparalleled treasures, gold and silver and incomparable dishes of gold and silver. Then P'arnavaz was astonished and filled with joy. He remembered the dream, and closed up the entrance to the cave in the same fashion. He hastened off and informed his mother and two sisters. That same night the three of them returned with donkeys and carts, and began to collect the treasure and to bury it in an appropriate (place). When day dawned, they again closed up the entrance to the cave in the same way. In this fashion they collected the treasure for five nights, and planned their opportunity.[71]

P'arnavaz's dream is a typical revelation of royal *farrah* of Iranian royal investiture narratives, an essential attribute of legitimate kings. As a material confirmation of the king's investiture, the dream and anointment is followed by the discovery of treasure.[72] Yet, arguably, it is what follows the discovery

---

[71] *C'xovreba k'art'velt'a mep'et'a*, ed. Kaukhchishvili, 21.12–22.9; https://titus.uni-frankfurt.de/texte/etcs/cauc/ageo/kcx1/kcx1.htm; tr. Thomson, 29–30.
[72] For multiple examples, see Soudavar, *Aura of the Kings*. For the association of *farrah* with royal hunting in Iranian tradition, see, e.g. Allsen, *Royal Hunt*.

of the treasure that essentially determines whether or not the prospective king has the charisma to be a legitimate monarch. After this momentous event, P'arnavaz exchanged the treasure for the right to kingship bestowed upon him by Antiochos, thus transforming the material treasure into political capital: 'P'arnavaz sent envoys to King Antiochos of Asurastan, and offered valuable gifts. He promised to serve him, and requested from him help against the Greeks. Antiochos accepted his gifts, called him his son, and presented him with a crown.'[73] Crucially, the same treasure was used to secure alliance with other neighbouring rulers and to thus unite the realm, as the authors of the *Life* perceived its unity, under a single crown.

The discovery or miraculous reception of treasure as a manifestation of royal charisma is attested in a wide range of cultures from antiquity to recent ethnographic records, from Polynesia to Iran.[74] These discoverers are usually hunters, quintessentially liminal figures operating in two realms. In Iranian imagery, 'by virtue of a successful hunt, the king acquires a radiant nimbus as a sign of his acquired *Farrah* (right).'[75] As explained by Thomas Allsen, special skill in hunting demonstrated one's charisma, or good fortune, which could be transferred to the political arena and interpreted as a heavenly mandate to rule. This kind of charisma was at the very heart of imperial ideology in the ancient Near East. 'In Middle Persian this glory is called *khvarenah*, in Turkic *qut*, and in Mongolian *suu*.'[76]

In Caucasia, the theme of hunting as a transitional event, as adopted from the Iranian traditions, is well attested in Late Antique narrative sources and art.[77] A hun takes the hunter across a threshold to a new world, where

---

[73] *C'xovreba k'art'velt'a mep'et'a*, ed. Kaukhchishvili, 23.11–15; https://titus.uni-frankfurt.de/texte/etcs/cauc/ageo/kcx1/kcx1.htm; tr. Thomson, 32.

[74] Perhaps the most famous example is Herodotus's account of Scythian ethnogenesis, which describes the children of Targitaos, the first Skythian king, receiving the divine treasure. It is by the agency of the valuable items that Herodotus appears to be fascinated: 'In the time of their reign, golden products fell from the sky: a plough and also a yoke, a battle axe, and a *phialē* fell to Scythia. Seeing these first, the oldest went close, planning to take them, but as he approached, the gold burst into flame. When he had departed, the second son approached the gold, and it flared up again. And when the flaming gold had repelled them, the fire was extinguished at the approach of the third and youngest son, and he carried it off as his own. The older brothers then accepted that the whole kingship be handed over to the youngest'. Herodotus, *Histories* 4.5. ed. Goodley, 202–3.

[75] Allsen, *Royal Hunt*, 160–86.

[76] Ibid., 162.

[77] Garsoïan, 'Prolegomena', 216–18. Garsoïan associates the concept of the hunt with Mithra: 'the hunt motif both in literature and iconography is a kaleidoscopic symbol reflecting both the present and eternity: the noble rank of the subject, his superior royal qualities, and his supernatural attributes shared with the divine Mithra and obtained through the valour of his companion Vərəθrayna.' Garsoïan, 'Locus of the Death', 29–35.

he may have extraordinary adventures, or encounters, and from where he returns with special knowledge and a life-changing experience.[78] Iberia's first Christian king Mirian too had his life-changing experience of conversion during a hunt. In heroic epic, such as the twelfth-century *Knight in the Panther Skin* and the supposedly eleventh-century *Amirandarejaniani*, which heavily draw upon Iranian epic, hunt is used as a literary device that initiates a transitional event in a hero's life, and to set the scene for an accidental, yet life-changing discovery – of a person, treasure or magic. It is, often, however, at the treasure's discretion to hand itself to the future king or to refuse to do so. In other words, it is in the power to 'resist ownership' that the true value of the discovered treasure is revealed. Louis Gernet calls such empowering valuable objects *agalmata*, specifically with reference to treasure that possesses both manifest and hidden powers. These *agalmata* exhibit a certain dangerous ambiguity that can decidedly affect the fate of their owner: 'The qualities of power and danger are attached to something that is valuable and precious possession. To know whether or not it will be wasted – or more precisely trampled on – is crucial.'[79] The intrinsic nature of this type of treasure is its ambiguity, a potentiality that can lead either to the owner's triumph, or his demise, or indeed both.

In this regard, while P'arnavaz's and Vač'agan's rites of passage are modelled after Iranian religious and epic traditions, their adventures are analogous to the foundation myths spread in Caucasian oral traditions. A hunter's unexpected discovery of a hidden treasure in eastern Georgian highland folklore is often commemorated through the foundational myths (*andrezi*) of a village, tribe, religious community or larger polity founded as a result of the discovery.[80] The hunter, who, as a liminal figure operating in two realms, the natural and the political, possesses the potential to actualise his political charisma through the discovery of treasure in the wilderness. This, however, happens extremely rarely. As anthropologist Zurab Kiknadze has pointed out, the treasure will never cede itself to a private person who does not represent the community, or body politic.

---

[78] Hanaway, 'Concept of the Hunt', 27–8.
[79] Gernet identifies this in an episode in *Agamemnon* which immediately precedes Agamemnon's death: 'Agamemnon accomplishes his own destruction by likening himself to the gods and by accepting the sinister consecration that contact with the purple cloth brings with it. And if, before admitting defeat, Agamemnon's last word can be taken as an expression of shame over the waste of such a thing of luxury, we can find in this scene, if we desire, witness of a bourgeois form of avarice.' See Gernet, *Anthropology of Ancient Greece*, 83.
[80] *Andrezi* is a dialectic variant of Georgian *anderdzi*, a word of Iranian origin, which stands for 'testament, will, tradition'.

The rarely successful encounter of the treasure with the hunter is a manifestation of the person's charisma, his mandate to rule or assume a priestly office. The hunter witnesses hierophany, a cross, or a divine dove, resulting in his transformation into a priest or a political founder, and a foundation of a religious or a political community on the same spot.[81] The accidentally discovered treasure must inevitably belong to the community, and must be put to political use. Therefore, in most cases, the Caucasian *andrezis* are pessimistic accounts that focus on failed, or indeed tragic, encounters between the hunter and the treasure, often resulting in forgetfulness or in extreme cases in a catastrophic resolution. Often, a hunter nearly discovers the treasure but it is the treasure that refuses to cede itself to him. One typical cycle of *andrezis* narrates a story of a farmer who was ploughing on top of the ruins of an ancient fortress, where unexpectedly unseen treasure manifested to him. On top of the treasure sat a golden ram. The farmer instantly lost his mind and completely forgot how he got to the cavity or where it was. In another story, a man discovered hidden treasure but fled in terror, not daring to take it. Eventually, it turned out that the treasure was destined for him but the hunter had missed his chance. Both the treasure and the cave had disappeared by the time he visited the place again. Other anecdotes, associated with foundation myths, narrate stories of priests and shepherds, who discover treasure but eventually lose their minds, and either perish or wander off in forgetfulness.[82]

The physical treasure is often replaced in Caucasian and eastern Anatolian folklore by a mysteriously lost grave of a legendary person, almost always Queen Tamar, Georgia's twelfth-century holy monarch. The place and circumstances of Tamar's burial have historically been shrouded in mystery and have generated folk traditions and foundation myths related to the notable absence or miraculous discovery of her remains. In a story recorded by John Oliver Wardrop in the late nineteenth century, the grave of the Queen is conceptualised identically to the treasure of the Caucasian *andrezis*: the inhabitants of Murġuli, in Artvin, claim that Tamar is buried there and that anyone who steps over her grave becomes mad. One evening a shepherd fell asleep on her grave and in the morning, he was mad. He wandered in the forests, yet wild beasts did him no harm. The people asked him where the grave was but he had forgotten. Once again, he was led by God's command to Tamar's tomb and prayed to the King (*sic.*) to cure him. He became well, but could not remember where the tomb was.[83]

---

[81] Kiknadze, *p'arnavazis sizmari*, 152–3.
[82] E.g., Kiknadze, 'andrezebi', 150, 217.
[83] Oxford, Bodleian Libraries, MS. Wardr.c.26.

The dire and often fatal outcomes of the encounter with treasure are mostly due to a lack of charisma on the part of the discoverer, a fatal character flaw that can be revealed only at the time of the encounter. Thus, as great and heroic as the persons who come across the treasure may be, unless they transcend their physical selves, and acquire political bodies, the consequences can be grim. An epic hero's accidental discovery of treasure transforms from a good omen into a curse in this instance. Even though he may indeed come across the treasure, he may not be its charismatic owner, since the treasure must exclusively belong to the king's political body and through him to the realm. Famously, the discovery of treasure by Siegfried triggers all the tragedies that befell him and nearly everyone in the *Nibelungenlied*. By contrast, in *The Knight in the Panther Skin*, the protagonist of the poem, General Tariel, the implied heir to the throne of India, accidentally stumbles on treasure during a hunt, which brings him good fortune, and makes the rescue of Princess Nestan-Darejan and their subsequent reign in the Kingdom of India possible.

One typical story that ties together legitimacy with the ownership of treasure, is that of T'orġva the hunter, an alleged member of the royal Bagratid Dynasty, yet an illegitimate pretender to the throne. Although T'orġva was a historic person and lived in the fourteenth century, for reasons lost to history, he was soon transposed into the realm of mythology. According to this oral tale, Georgia's king entrusted T'orġva with holding the Pankisi Valley, an artery connecting the north Caucasus with the south. T'orġva, however, rebelled and attempted to take over the valley. One day he was hunting a deer in the Pankisi forest, when he stumbled upon an ancient ruin. Upon entering, he discovered innumerable treasures protected by a sword-wielding giant and an eagle-like bird. Terrified, T'orġva fled, while the entrance into the ruin immediately vanished. The *andrezi* reflects historic T'orġva's illegitimate pretences to rule, as well as his lack of political charisma, and draws a moral conclusion: 'For this reason it is said among us, that if the treasure does not give itself to you, neither you nor your family will profit from it.'[84] This, and other similar accounts, whether successful or tragic, almost invariably juxtapose the private and the political, as well as legal and illegitimate, and accentuate the political destination and destiny of the discovered treasure.

## 1.6 The Treasure of a Christian King

There is an episode in the early medieval Caucasian corpus where one can identify a certain transitional situation, whereby the material treasure

---

[84] Kiknadze, 'andrezebi', 243. For additional comments on this event, see Kiknadze, *p'arnavazis sizmari*, 19–20.

is substituted by holy relics, while keeping all the features of the above-described oral or written accounts. This is the story of Babik, prince of Siwnikʽ, a province south-east of Lake Sevan, told in the opening chapter of Book Two of the *History of the Albanians*.[85] Babik is introduced as the son of Andok, the former ruler of Siwnikʽ, who fell out of favour with the Shah Shapur II (309–79). However, as a gratitude for Babik's victory against the king of the Huns, Shapur restored to the prince his father's domains and honours. Once Babik's legal rights have been restored, his divine legitimation followed. One day, in the first year of his reign, Babik went on a hunt to inspect the deserted lands. He climbed a hill and scared a stag that ran towards a mound over an old church. During the pursuit, Babik's horses hoof sunk into the mound. As Babik and his men were digging under the horse, they were struck with awe 'as they found the beautiful church full of divine treasure and sweetly smelling'. A service was celebrated immediately and great healings occurred. Unbelievers were converted, and the unbaptised were baptised.[86]

The treasure that Babik uncovered had been hidden during the war by his father, Andok. However, it remains unclear whether Babik stumbled into a material treasure or holy relics. Although the ensuing healings indicate that reference is made to the relics of saints, the saints whose relics were discovered are not identified. This is indeed unusual, since the relics of the saints were not normally mentioned in passing and anonymously. Their identity was of importance and their legitimising power in such narratives was embedded in their individual or collective identity. I would therefore suggest that this episode is an early medieval Christian reimagination of an old foundation story of the discovery of material treasure. The original story of Babik, at least its schema, had indeed referred to physical treasure as a manifestation of his royal investiture. In the *History*, the editors interpreted the material treasure as holy relics that conferred legitimacy. This could have been both a conscious rewriting or a simple confusion, since it has already been a common practice to refer to relics as 'treasure'.

That the original story most likely referred to material treasure is corroborated by roughly contemporaneous Georgian chronicles. Here, the motif of treasure hidden by ancestors and recovered as a sign of charismatic continuity and legal kingship is a recurring narrative device. In an undated insertion in Juanšer's *Life of Vakhtang* (possibly originally an eight-century composition), the hiding of the royal treasure signals the end of an era

---

[85] Unlike chapter 1 of the *History*, the second part is a later, probably an eighth- to tenth-century, creation.

[86] Movsēs Kałankatwacʽi, *Patmowtʽiwn*, ed. Ēmin, 124–5; tr. Dowsett, 65.

and the beginning of apocalyptic times, heralded by the rise of Islam. For Prince Archil (c. 750s), the treasure had historic and mnemonic function, since it was destined to reveal itself only upon the restoration of the dynasty. He tells his brother Mihr: 'And when the Greeks come the emperor will seek (vengeance) for our family and will give them (back) the kingdom and also that treasure.'[87] In fact, according to the *Martyrdom of King Archil*, he was martyred by the Arabs specifically because of his refusal to reveal the whereabouts of the treasure of kings Mirian and Vakhtang, and the Emperor Heraclius, and had thus saved the annihilated kingdom for posterity.

In the *Georgian Chronicles*, however, perhaps due to a literary continuity with P'arnavaz's epic, while stories similar to Babik's are common, the treasures remain material and have not transformed into saintly relics. By contrast, the second book of the *History of Albanians* maintains this structural continuity with Vač'agan's *Life* through the relics of saints. The relics as conceptualised in Vač'agan's story are essentially the Christianised treasure of P'arnavaz, and both are endowed with metaphysical as well as political value. In its entirety, Vač'agan's story is a Christianised rite of passage saturated with Iranian symbols of royal investiture. Ultimately, through the rites of passage of the two charismatic figures to legitimate kingship, Iberia's and Albania's *raison d'être* are defined. Both narratives illustrate four stages of initiation: legitimate descent, popular acclaim, imperial validation and the divine *farrah*, the latter confirmed through the discovery of the divine treasure by the two kings. P'arnavaz's dream and the descent of heavenly light are substituted by the light of Vač'agan's conversion and baptism. While the central transformative episode in Vač'agan's story is his discovery of the relics of ancient saints, P'arnavaz's deeds are launched by a discovery of material treasure. From a Christian perspective, P'arnavaz's treasure is purely material, and Vač'agan's discovery has a transcendental value, yet essentially both transcend their immediate physicality and acquire political values. While both 'treasures' were discovered by these Caucasian hunter-kings, immediately upon discovery, they relinquished and invested in the political realm. In Vač'agan's case this was achieved through spectacular processions with the relics, and their distribution across his reborn realm, which turned these relics into a material witness to the 'rediscovered' Christian kingdom of Albania.[88] This lengthy and earnest procession through every

---

[87] Juanšer, *c'xovreba*, ed. Kaukhchishvili, 236.18–20; https://titus.uni-frankfurt.de/texte/etcs/cauc/ageo/kcx1/kcx1.htm; tr. Thomson, 242–3.
[88] Compare Charlemagne's obsession with relics who always carried his relics with him wherever he went, thus sacralising his presence both in palaces and in tents. Smith, 'Rulers and Relics', 80.

village of Albania ends in the king's own village, which is the culmination of Vač'agan's quest. Then Vač'agan distributed the relics among the dioceses of Albania, leaving the largest part in Amaras, and storing the rest in special vessels. 'Moving off, the king went on foot, and the whole procession walked along with quiet, slow steps, flowing like a calm sea. The air exulted to harmonious sounds and glittering reflections. The angels themselves sang with them, and it was as if Earth had become very Heaven.'[89]

Immediately after the quest was finished and these relics revealed, Vač'agan promulgated church canons and established a 'national' religion across Albania, similar to P'arnavaz's final acts of creating native institutions. Finally, Vač'agan is compared to Constantine. Arguably, in addition to the *imitatio Constantini*, a duty of every good Christian ruler, Constantine is specifically referred to as the first such royal collector of relics who had a vision of connecting the past with the present through a conscious usage of *spolia* and relics. The discovery, accidental or intentional, of the relics of the saints became a fundamental concept both for the legitimisation of the royal rule and of the foundation of a polity.

With the discovery of the relics of the 'national' saint, made possible through the intercession and involvement of the relics of the Armenian saints, a martyr-saint of the universal church, and a biblical saint, Vač'agan secured for himself a place in universal history next to Constantine and T'rdat. His story culminates in the principal political message of the narrative:

> And thus the worthy king Vač'agan acquired the spiritual and transcendental booty which is the source of incorruptible and ineffable goodness; to no king before him, to none of his ancestors had such wonderful gifts been given. The camp, assembled in Christ, received a share, acquiring indescribable riches from the mercies of God through King Vač'agan, whom I do not consider less praiseworthy than Emperor Constantine, emperor of the west, or the Arsacid T'rdat who brought salvation to Greater Armenia. For us easterners, this blessed man became the door to the light of knowledge of God, the model of many virtues.[90]

Vač'agan's journey to kingship is indeed an extraordinary one due to the elaborate and complex involvement of saintly relics in the rhetoric of political power. Although both in Babik's brief story and Vač'agan's lengthy account, the relics of the saints essentially act as material treasures of a hunter king that make the hunter's political body manifest, and the relics of

---

[89] Movsēs Kałankatwac'i, *Patmowt'iwn*, ed. Ēmin, 90–1; tr. Dowsett, 46–7.
[90] Movsēs Kałankatwac'i, *Patmowt'iwn*, ed. Ēmin, 90; tr. Dowsett, 46–7.

Vač'agan are enriched with political, theological and historical symbolism. Unlike Babik's discovery, they are not mere remains of unidentified saints. Here the political relevance of the relics lies in their identity and historicity, as they link Albania's history with the universal salvation history and confirm the new king's right to rule this rebaptised realm.

In the following two chapters, we shall look at Late Antique and early medieval Georgian political and identity rhetoric of sanctity. The deliberations over the past and the present through the usage of saints and their relics are perhaps most dramatically articulated in the principal Late Antique Georgian foundation narrative – the *Conversion of Kartli* and the *Life of Nino*. This corpus adopted Agathangelos's idea of the past and the present, and created a uniquely persistent, yet problematic, imagery through a political conceptualisation of the persona of St Nino, Iberia's legendary enlightener. Like Agathangelos, the anonymous authors of the *Conversion of Kartli* and its derivatives were keen to conceptualise, visualise and theologise the rift between the old and the new realities, the past and the present, and to define the place of their kingdom and the church within these grant narratives through an appropriate theology of saints' relics. Through a conceptualisation of the place and role of female saints, the *Conversion of Kartli* formulated a unique relationship between sainthood and political theology. The 'triangulation' of the religious, the political and the feminine, as conceptualised by the *Conversion of Kartli* and related texts, demonstrated particular sturdiness in subsequent Georgian writing, and arguably created a uniquely Georgian experience of the interplay of power, sanctity and femininity.

# 2

# An Exceptional Saint for Exceptional Times: The Cult of St Nino

## 2.1 The *k'adagi*

The Caucasian highlands, especially the regions that at different times were under Georgian cultural influence, have preserved a certain hybrid form of folklorised Christianity. Earliest conversion narratives attest to the highlanders' resistance to Christianity's encroachment, proudly reporting about the force that had to be used to establish the new religion there. Hostility towards the centralising policies of the kingdom and the church lasted for centuries after Kartli's Christianisation. Over time, constant strife, as well as absorption of Christian beliefs and stories into local religious traditions across the Caucasus range, has produced hybrid forms of paganised quasi-Christianity, currently embedded in both the materiality as well as the oral traditions of the Caucasus. Despite centuries of contamination, the surviving lore remains a valuable source of information, as it offers a glimpse behind the glossed over rhetoric of medieval elites, and allows us to better comprehend some medieval narratives as they were distilled in popular imagination. Among others, a folk story, multiple versions of which have been recorded in central and south-eastern Caucasian highlands, addresses the question posed in the conclusion of the previous chapter. This otherwise typologically familiar story consists of miraculous discoveries of precious items by charismatic persons that led to the foundation of political or cultic entities. The protagonist of these narratives is, however, from the teller's perspective, an unlikely person – a woman. What follows are the basic elements of the story that can be extracted from its many variants.

Every summer, on top of Karatiststveri, the liminal mountain separating the valleys of Pshavi and Khevsureti, two regions of central Caucasian highlands, a shepherd boy and girl met. They were both virgins and loved each other as a brother and sister. One day they heard a horrible screech. A *xati* (icon) descended from heaven, carrying a bowl and a silver necklace, which took the shape of a cross. The children threw dice, and the girl received the necklace, whereas the boy got the bowl. They took the heavenly gifts to their village and hid them in safe places. That same night, however, an identical screech came out of their houses, forcing the children to tell their parents about their discovery. The parents then foolishly revealed the location of the secret places to the villagers. Unable to hide anymore, the girl had to flee. Eventually, she became a *k'adagi*, an itinerant preacher. But the villagers refused to accept the girl's new role and conspired to murder her. The girl, however, was possessed (captivated) by the *xati*, carried everywhere and protected by it. The *xati* and the girl flew to Tusheti (Georgian highland region north of the Caucasian watershed) and subjugated the local people by imposing a tax on them. They also travelled further north, beyond the Greater Caucasus, and converted the local tribes, the Didoans. The girl built a church, and established feasts: *At'engena* (feast of Athenogenes), Ascension and others. But, as the tellers insisted, she was not a priest, she did not perform a service, and remained an itinerant *k'adagi*. This girl was Khevsureti's first and perhaps last female *k'adagi*, while all the rest were men. Yet, she exhibited few or no female traits – she never menstruated and never married. Nothing but a plain bracelet on her arm betrayed her femininity.[1] Her name is mostly unknown, but in some versions, she is called Minani.

In this story, many of the elements of foundation narratives, which involve treasures or holy relics, are present: the miraculous discovery or reception of the objects by a charismatic figure, the objects' refusal to stay in private ownership and desire to be invested into a political community, the object's ability to differentiate between charismatic and non-charismatic figures, and the object's (inter-)convertibility between material and spiritual values. The only anomaly is the protagonist's gender, the female *k'adagi*, a word which, depending on the context, can stand for a charismatic preacher, a founder or a missionary. She was known as a *dačerili* (a captive) and was carried around by the *xati*. She did not have a will of her own, being fully possessed by the *xati*. While women traditionally were and still are strictly banned from Khevsureti's holy sites, this girl was the founder of some of the region's holiest places. Despite her manifest powers, her charismatic mandate to preach was unacceptable to the locals who persecuted her and sought her death. As such, she was an ambiguous person, full of internal contra-

---

[1] The story was recorded by ethnographer Tinatin Ochiauri in Khevsuretian dialect in 1944 in the village of Akušo. Ochiauri, *Mit'ologiuri gadmoc'emebi*, 161–2; Kiknadze, *Andrezebi*, 59–60; Vashalomidze, *Die Stellung der Frau*, 216–17.

dictions: she was a woman who founded holy sites that were prohibited to women. She lacked a woman's biological attributes, and as such was genderless, her femininity marked merely by her bracelet. In spite of her gender, she could preach and sanctify places, but she could not make an offering or officiate. The legend, confined to a few valleys of Georgia's highlands, bears an uncanny resemblance to the foundational story of the medieval Georgian religious and historiographic corpus, the *Conversion of Kartli*, an account of Iberia's conversion to Christianity through the efforts of a Roman girl – St Nino. Nino, like her folk alter-ego, was an ambiguous character, and her cult was an ambiguous cult, swaying from obscurity to centrality, from condemnation to celebration, and from marginalisation to nationalisation.

The question that much later, in the twelfth century, Katholikos Nikoloz Gulaberisże rhetorically asked was, Why a woman? Why was a woman tasked with such an important mission? Gulaberisże launched the most passionate and effective defence of Nino's gender, by building a series of elaborate arguments and angrily instructing everyone to henceforward 'close their mouths' on the matter of the gender of Georgia's apostle. Gulaberisże had his own political agenda, and a powerful patron to serve, but his irritation on this subject betrays the lingering of the same question throughout the previous centuries. The multiple editions of Nino's *Life* that appeared by the tenth century may make a false impression that her cult has thrived throughout since her introduction in hagiography. Before the late twelfth century, when a virtual exposition of her cult occurred, it was barely discernible outside of hagiographic narratives, whereas references to her relics, bodily or material, appear only in the eighteenth century.

Two centuries after the formation of the extended editions of the *Life of Nino* as we know it, in the eleventh century, Nikoloz I's distant predecessor, Katholikos Arseni composed a short account of the seventh-century Armeno–Georgian religious conflict. Arseni summarised the events that led to the schism, and even acknowledged the monumental role of St Gregory in Caucasia's conversion, yet had nothing to say about St Nino.[2] It is hard to imagine that in the eleventh century, a Georgian katholikos was unaware of the Nino tradition, yet, surprisingly, he did not deem it necessary to mention her in the context of Georgia's religious history together with Armenia's Gregory.

Nino's cult also differed geographically. While the Georgian authors in the Holy Land, the Mar Saba Monastery and Mt Sinai, have preserved and disseminated the extant traditions of St Nino, her cult is faint in the early centuries of Athonite monasticism. For instance, she is largely absent from

---

[2] Aleksidze and Mahé, 'Arsène Sapareli', 59–132.

the eleventh-century *Great Synaxarion* of Giorgi Mt'acmindeli (George the Hagiorite) (1009–65). Only two out of six manuscripts of the *Synaxarion*, the Jerusalemite (Jer.Geo.24–5) and the Sinaitic (O/Sin.Geo 4–61), both of Near Eastern origin, refer to her. The former merely mentions her in passing, whereas the latter includes her brief *Vita*. One manuscript (MS A-97 of the National Centre of Manuscripts of Georgia), copied in Tao-Klarjeti, lists Georgian and Armenian saints in its margins. Almost everyone known to the Georgian tradition is mentioned, aside from Nino – and this well after the appearance of the famous Shatberdi redaction of the *Life*.[3] A hymn to Nino is, however, included in the *Menologion* of Giorgi Mt'acmindeli.[4]

Yet, even the Sinai MS of the Synaxarion betrays a degree of uncertainty with regard to Nino's story: 'The same day [is commemorated] the death of the holy apostle Nino and enlightener of the Georgians, who undertook great labours and performed innumerable miracles and suffered multiple tortures from Mirian the *ungodly* king.'[5] The holy King Mirian, remembered as a pious ruler, and celebrated as a saint, is here dismissed as 'ungodly'. Even more surprisingly, the paragraph claims that Mirian had tortured Nino, which blatantly contradicts every surviving version of Nino's *Life*. It seems that the writer of this colophon did not have the opportunity to study Nino's *Life* and may have gathered information from an oral source or simply confused Mirian with the Armenian T'rdat who had indeed tortured and executed the Hrip'simēan virgins. Considering that this was written in Palestine, where in the tenth century at least two redactions of the *Conversion of Kartli* existed with a fully evolved Nino story, this sentence is indeed puzzling.

The instability of the Nino narrative is also corroborated by a paragraph in the *Acts of the Council of Ruisi and Urbnisi* (1103/4), which claims that after the original evangelisation by the Apostle Andrew, Georgians forgot the original teaching. Three hundred years later, the sun 'also looked at us through a certain captive woman, Nunna [*sic*.] of Cappadocia, certain books of church history found here also recount her story'.[6] Why would Nino be referred to in an obscure Greek form? Also, 'certain books recount her story' is not how one speaks about the founding figure of Georgian

---

[3] Aleksidze, *Narrative*, 135–41. Rapp and Crego, 'Conversion of K'art'li', 169–225.
[4] Published in Kavtaria (ed.), *Cminda Nino*, 387–98.
[5] *Synaxaria*, ed. Gabidzashvili and Abuladze, 351: ამასვე დღესა მიცვალებაი წმიდისა ნინო მოციქულისაჲ ქართველთა განმანათლებლისაჲ, რომელმან ფრიადნი მოლუაწებანი და ურიცხუნი სასწაულნი აღასრულნა და მრავალგზის წამებანი [დაითმინნა] მირიან უღმრთოისა ჴელმწიფისაგან.
[6] Published in Zhordania, *k'ronikebi*, 2, 58.

Figure 2.1  Copy of the lost bas-relief of St Nino from the Church of Oshki, tenth century. Photo: Maka Chkhaidze.

Christianity. Evidently, the authors are referring not to the canonical *vitae* of St Nino, but to Ephrem Mc'ire's (twelfth century) summary of Georgia's ecclesiastic history.

As if reflecting on this confusion, an editorial colophon to one of the versions of the *Life of Nino* expresses worry regarding the instability of Nino's cult: 'the Book of the *Conversion of Kartli*, through which God had revealed the light . . . we found as a talent hidden by the elders after a long time and many years'.[7] Although this claim may be a literary convention, it may suggest that the Nino tradition was far from standardised even by the turn of the millennium and was subject to 'discovery'. Nino's visual representation is even scarcer. She is almost entirely missing from pre-thirteenth-century art. The only image that survived until recently was a now lost tenth-century bas-relief of the church of Oshki (see Fig. 2.1). Prosopographical testimony is also telling. Until the nineteenth century, Nino was far from being the most popular name of choice for girls. Although there are Ninos attested in the late medieval period, Georgians started actively calling their daughters Nino only in the nineteenth century and often in its Russian form (Nina), much unlike Giorgi, the most popular name among Georgian elites since the tenth century.[8]

---

[7] Gigineishvili and Giunashvili (eds), *Šatberdis krebuli*, 20–1.
[8] This, however, does not mean that Nino was not used as a monastic name. There are many instances in late medieval and early modern documents where a nun called Nino is mentioned together with her former name. In general, and rather strikingly, properly Christian names started to appear in Georgia only by the end of the eighteenth century. Throughout the late middle ages, the predominant Georgian onomasticon was Persian, Turkish and Arabic.

It certainly would be wrong to claim that Nino was altogether forgotten and rehabilitated only much later, but her cult certainly fluctuated and varied from region to region, and context to context. Georgian communities in the Holy Land and Sinai, on Mt Athos and across Byzantium, the ecclesiastical and secular elites of Mtskheta, the Apkhaz kings and the Bagratids of Tao had their own rhetorical agendas, and while Nino was central in some, she was peripheral in others.[9] Indeed, in its totality, the medieval Nino tradition, both in hagiography and beyond, transpires as a recurring effort to uncover the details of her career and to instrumentalise her cult for political objectives.[10]

Arguably, as indicated by Nikoloz I, the principal reason for the instability of Nino's cult was her gender and social status, and the incongruence between this status and her monumental achievement. While this contrast was at the core of the political rhetoric of the seventh-century writers of the *Conversion of Kartli*, and then the twelfth-century makers of the cult of Queen Tamar, in other periods it had no rhetorical value – hence the silence. Gender was a contributing factor to the volatility of Nino's cult, but whenever Nino's cult re-emerged, whether in the seventh or the twelfth centuries, it was presented as a case of a total exception highlighting and highlighted by the exceptionality of the transformations that her mission had triggered. In the *Mok'c'evay* narrative, the exceptional switching of gender roles in Nino's persona heralded the radical detour in Kartli's (salvation) history. Consequently, as an exception par excellence, her cult, as crafted in the first conversion narratives, was interwoven with the rhetoric of history, body politic and political geography, an entanglement that has resurfaced not once in subsequent Georgian history.

The folk story of Minani encloses issues that were raised, problematised and perhaps silenced by the *Conversion of Kartli* and other medieval authors. Both Minani and Nino were interpreted as exceptions, as extraordinary figures who have suspended the custom and the law, and as women who were allowed to act as preachers as well as founders in those extraordinary times. Exception that suspends but does not abolish the normative, woven into the fabric of Nino's cult, and realised in the cult of Queen Tamar, became a definitive feature of Georgian political theology of sanctity. Due to its ambiguity, and the encapsulation of mutually exclusive qualities, the cult of Georgia's illuminatrix was politicised, her material

---

[9] On the evolution of the cult of Nino, see Tarchnišvili, 'Die Legende der heiligen Nino', 48–75; von Lilienfeld, 'Amt und geistliche Vollmacht', 224–49; Martin-Hisard, 'Jalons pour une histoire', 53–78.
[10] Aleksidze, 'Disputed Saints', 77–94.

relics were endowed with the value of political mediation, and her memory was integrated into medieval as well as modern political and national discourses. Nino, her gender and her significance, created a conceptual problem, and the many ways of disentangling this problem determined the nature of many of Georgia's subsequent saintly and political discourses.

## 2.2 'The Captive Who Captivates'

A striking feature (at least for its medieval readers) of the *Life of Nino* is the prominence of female figures, a quality that may have determined its precarious existence while also accounting for its endurance. The pseudepigraphic original recorders of Nino's sojourn to Georgia as well as the authors of the implications of this mission for larger Christian history were Salome of Ujarma, the wife of the future king Rev, King Mirian's son; and Sidonia, daughter of Priest Abiat'ar. Nino's other pseudo-chronicler is Perožavr, probably an ethnic Armenian woman from Siwnik'. All three women are now saints of the Georgian Church, and are commemorated on the day after the feast of St Nino. Other protagonists of the *Life* who lived immediately or centuries before Nino, and whose stories are told as flashbacks to current events, are almost all women. Apart from Queen Nana, Kartli's first royal figure to be converted to Christianity, one of the principal protagonists was Sarah Miap'or, an Armenian nun and Nino's teacher who had directed Nino towards Georgia and pointed to Kartli as the site where the Tunic of the Lord was buried. The earliest witness to Christ's passion in Kartli was the Jewish woman Sidonia (not to be confused with Nino's *Life*'s pseudo-narrator Sidonia) who embraced Christ's Tunic upon its translation in Mtskheta. The strong feminine presence in Nino narratives is overseen by the principal woman of the Christian tradition, the Mother of God in whose name Nino was authorised to preach in Georgia.[11]

Despite her association with the Mother of God, arguably, the femininity of Georgia's primary missionary posed a problem to medieval writers. Even within the numerous versions of Nino's *Vita*, her femininity is described with negative qualifiers. Nino describes herself in self-deprecating terms as an alien and ignorant woman, which in Georgian alliterates as *uc'xo, umec'ari*.[12]

---

[11] The female component is present also in the Armenian conversion narrative, and, as argued by Valentina Calzolari, was determined by the popularity of St Thecla in fifth-century Armenian writing. The Armenian version of the *Acts of Paul and Thecla* were known as *The Prodigies of Thecla*. Calzolari, 'Legend of St. Thecla', 283–304. Arguably St Hṙip'simē and her fight against her rapist are modelled after Thecla. See also Pogossian, 'Women at the Beginning', 355–80; Zakarian, *Women, Too, Were Blessed, passim*.

[12] On 'female weakness' in Late Antique Christianity, see Clark, 'Ideology, History', 166.

As she journeys through Georgia, she is plagued by fears, loneliness, alienation and a constant sense of insecurity regarding her abilities. The contrast between Nino's gender and the magnitude of her achievement is the principal dynamic force of the narrative. The descriptions of the semi-barbarian land, with its treacherous valleys, gloomy mountain peaks, wrapped in dreadful mist and ruled by hostile people of the North, contrast dramatically with the tender teenage girl who arrived from the South.[13] When Christ appeared to Nino telling her to preach in Georgia, her initial reaction was that she was an ignorant woman who could not meet the very male requirements of the mission. In response, she received a written 'manifesto' of female apostolicity:

Ten sayings were written there, as on the former tablets of stone:
a) Wherever they preach this gospel, there shall they speak of this woman;
b) Neither male nor female, but you are all one (Gal. 3:28);
c) Go ye and make disciples of all the heathen, and baptise them in the name of the Father, of the Son and of the Holy Spirit (Matt. 28:19);
d) A light to shine upon the heathen, and to give glory to the people of Israel (Luke 2:32);
e) Preach the good tidings of the kingdom of heaven in all the world (Matt 26:13; Mark 14:9);
f) Whoever receives you, receives Me, and whoever receives Me receives Him who sent me (Matt 10:40);
g) Now Mary was greatly beloved of the Lord, so that He always hearkened to her truth and wisdom;
h) Be not afraid of those who can destroy your bodies, but are not able to destroy your soul (Mark 16:9);
i) Jesus said to Mary Magdalene, 'Go, woman, and tell the news to My brethren;
j) Wherever you go, preach in the name of the Father, the Son, and the Holy Spirit.[14]

These 'ten commandments' were intended for the sceptical readers and listeners of the story, who may have felt uncomfortable with such an overwhelmingly feminine account which contrasted with the masculine Armenian history of Gregory and his patriarchal dynasty. Although the Hṙip'simēan virgins were in effect the founders of Christianity on the Armenian soil, St Gregory and his descendants were responsible for the

---

[13] Agathangelos similarly contrasts the purity of the martyred virgins with the impurity of paganism in Armenia. Calzolari, 'Le sang', 182–4. According to Calzolari, Hṙip'simē's defence of her own 'purity', that is, virginity, is equated to the defence of Christianity against paganism.
[14] *Mok'c'evay k'art'lisay*, ed. Abuladze, 116–17; tr. Lerner, 163.

institutionalisation of faith, an aspect of masculinisation absent in the original *Life of Nino*. While Nino was presented as a charismatic founder, unlike her contemporary Gregory the Illuminator, she was not an institutional founder, and for Georgian writers, her charismatic mission required male validation. It was perhaps Nino's problematic gender, along with the necessity to concoct foundational stories for various monastic centres, that explains the emergence of a supplementary cycle of 'conversion' narratives set two hundred years after the original Christianisation. Although this is never explicitly said, arguably the story of Ioane of Zedazeni and the Syrian Fathers was created and disseminated, among other reasons, specifically to 'masculinise' and institutionalise the original conversion.[15] It seems that unlike the Palestinian Nino, the legend of the Syrian Fathers was elaborated in Georgia proper, in the monasteries that claimed to be founded by one of these Fathers. All the numerous versions of Ioane's and his companions' *Lives* date their arrival precisely to two hundred years after Nino's mission, yet persistently call Kartli newly converted (*axalnerg*) with unstable Christianity.[16] Upon his arrival in Kartli, Ioane first pays a visit to its most holy site, the Living Pillar. Nino's miracle is narrated here in a short, yet exhilarated paragraph: 'That night, the reason for all the goodness of Kartli, our holy and blossoming mother Nino stood in tears and beseeched our mighty Lord, Christ. And immediately, the captive one captivated all the strength of the king and the craftsmanship of the masons. She lifted the pillar through her prayers and hung it on top of the foundation.'[17] Nino's charismatic power encoded in the 'captive who captivates' trope is contrasted with Ioane's institutionalising mission, a pairing that will later occur also between St George and St Nino for identical purposes. The liturgical version of the *Life of Ioane* adds an episode to the saint's life where an angel appears to Ioane, telling him, 'Saint Nino, who converted Kartli and Kakheti, was a woman and she worked hard and struggled greatly, yet much of Kartli's and Kakheti's villages were left unconverted. And now, because you long for alienation, take twelve companions, take them with you and go to Kartli and Kakheti and firmly preach the faith of Christ and enlighten them!'[18] Ioane was directed to

---

[15] See, also, Synek, 'Life of St Nino', 3–13.
[16] This trope appears practically in all *vitae* of the 'Syrian Fathers' cycle. See especially, *C'xorebay iovane zedaznelisay* 4.14, ed. Abuladze, 92.
[17] *C'xorebay iovane zedaznelisay* 3.36–38, ed. Abuladze, 199–200: https://titus.uni-frankfurt.de/texte/etcs/cauc/ageo/gh/gh1/gh1lex.htm.
[18] *Synaxaria*, ed. Abuladze and Gabidzashvili, 387: წმიდა ნინო, ოდეს ქართლი და კახეთი მოაქცია, დედაკაცი იყო და ფრიადი შრომა დადვა და მრავალნი ილუაზა, არამედ უმრავლესი თემი დაუშთა ქართლად და კახეთად მოუქცეველი. და წარვედ და მუნ ათორმეტნი მოყუასნი შენნი გამოირჩიე და თანა წარიტანენ და

a mountain that overlooks the hill of the Holy Cross in Mtskheta, where St Nino had erected her first cross. Here, on Zedazeni, even higher than Jvari, as if overseeing the original holy site, Ioane founded Kartli's first monastery. Essentially, Ioane's mission was to institutionalise Nino's charismatic yet volatile achievement by masculinising and stabilising it.

Since the late twelfth century, overt apologies of Nino's gender have appeared, but entirely novel historical realities, during the reign of Queen Tamar. But these apologies, too, ought not be read as eulogies to the female apostolic mission or as a call for female emancipation, but rather as further conceptualisations of an 'exception', of an extraordinary political and metaphysical state of affairs, where the normal course of history and law was suspended. It is in these radical times that gender roles too were temporarily inverted, the 'captive captivated' and a woman's apostolic mission was made possible. This idea of exceptionality and liminality associated with femininity, as generated by the *Conversion of Kartli*, was particularly fostered in the thirteenth century with the creation of the political cult of the Holy Queen Tamar, whose reign and subsequent cult experienced similar ambiguities and were in constant need of reaffirmation.

In the surviving literary evidence, the ambiguities of Nino's cult are only sporadically addressed, and are mostly revealed in silence rather than in explicit challenge. By contrast, in the oral narratives of the Caucasian highlands that have arguably adopted her image, and merged it with local cultic narratives, all the ambiguities generated by Nino's gender were preserved and problematised in ambiguous female figures, often itinerant preachers and founders. Understandably, it is near impossible to determine the approximate age of these stories. However, they seem to be sufficiently old to have been entirely removed from their literary sources and adapted to the local traditions and customs. These oral narratives have adopted the idea of 'emergency' and 'exceptionality' associated with femininity as coined by the *Conversion* discourse, and have fused it with the traditional foundation stories of holy sites or communities.

In literary Georgian, the word *k'adagi* stands for preacher or missionary. However, in Caucasian highlands the *k'adagis* are normally itinerant charismatic shamanic figures, who, unlike the *xevisberi* (local 'secular' priest) or *xuc'esi* (priest), are under no one's jurisdiction and are directly controlled or possessed (*dačerili*) by the divinity, the *xati* (icon) or the *jvari* (cross).[19]

მიხუედ ქართლად და კახეთად, ვინაჲთგან უცხოსა ქუეყანასა ყოვა გსურის და იღუაწე და ქადაგე სარწმუნოება მტკიცე ქრისტიანობისა და განანათლენი იგინი. The *Lives* of the rest of the Syrian Fathers, too, pinpoint Nino's miracle as a reference point to the mission of the Fathers.

[19] Ochiauri, *k'art'velta uzvelesi sarcmunoebis*, 20; Kiknadze, 'andrezuli variantebi', 62–71.

Georges Charachidzé defines the *k'adagi* as a possessed person who acts as an intermediary between gods and men, the celestial and earthly realms.[20] The earliest reference to these figures is found in Vakhushti Bagrationi's eighteenth-century *Description of Georgia*: '[The Pshavians] are by language and religion Georgians, yet they have faith in *k'adagis* who present themselves as ignorant and self-made, and preach out loud on behalf of St George, and whatever they say, people accept as the truth.'[21]

As observed by Zurab Kiknadze, similarly to Nino, the founder of the Karati cult is a captive, a person possessed by the *xati*. The girl of Karati myth is referred to as the 'icon's captive'. This narrative borrows the terminology from the oldest versions of the *Life of Nino*, which resonates with Rufinus's reference to the person as *captiva*. While following the model of Hŕip'simē and Gayanē, Nino was originally known as a captive, the same term acquired a different meaning in folklore. Also, echoing the seventh-century version of the *Conversion*, the account claims that this *xati* has converted the Didoans, or the non-Christian Caucasians, similarly to Nino's original mission to the north Caucasus. That the locals initially wanted to kill the *k'adagi*, due to her femininity and her transgression of gender roles, arguably reflects the ambiguity that Nino's cult had initially experienced.

Françoise Thélamon was the first scholar to argue that the Latin *captiva*, the only qualifier originally used by Rufinus with reference to Iberia's enlightener, is a misunderstanding of the Georgian *dačerili*, and that the original Nino tradition as known to Rufinus was a reimagination of traditional Georgian highland foundation myths. In an extensive study of pre-Christian religious practices in Caucasia, mostly based on antique sources, Thélamon argues that the Nino image was a literary elaboration on the existing institution of *k'adagi*. This is how, according to Thélamon, the 'strange particularity' of the Georgian conversion narrative, which focuses on a woman enlightener much unlike all the other comparable stories of the period, can be explained.[22] Despite its elegance, Thélamon's argument is difficult to defend, as it leads to a chicken and egg problem: Was Nino embraced due to the conceptual links with the already-existing *k'adagi* traditions, or were the ambiguous female *k'adagis* based on her folklorised

---

[20] Charachidzé, *Le système religieux*, 113–86.
[21] Vaxušti Batonišvili, *aġcera*, ed. Kaukhchishvili, 533: არიან ესენი სარწმუნოებითა და ენითა ქართულითა, გარნა აქუსთ სასოება ქადაგსა ზედა, რომელი წარმოდგების კაცი უცები და ვითარცა ხელქმნილი, და ლადადებს მრავალსა მაგიერად წმიდის გიორგისა, და რასა იგი იტყვს, სიტნავთ და ჯერ იჟენენ უმეტეს ჭეშმარიტებისასა. While most of the earliest ethnographic records on *k'adagis* date to the first half of the twentieth century, this is the earliest description of the shamanic role of *k'adagis*.
[22] Thélamon, *Païens et chrétiens*, 86–122; 'Amazones et Gargaréens', 34.

image? It is more likely that the process was indeed inverse, and the stories of the exceptional female *k'adagis* are folk reimaginings of the Nino narrative, especially considering the fact that Nino was frequently called *k'adagi* in hymnography. The Nino story and her cult required constant endorsement and promulgation, a project that was at various times undertaken by Georgia's literary elites. Perhaps it was through the effort of the medieval centralising state that Nino's cult was also introduced and disseminated in the highlands. If the folk narratives indeed give us a glimpse into the premodern state of affairs, the only reception or rather a spinoff of the Nino tradition that has retained all the accompanying ambiguities remains the story of Minani, Khevsureti's first *k'adagi* and related stories.

The only other quasi-historic female *k'adagi* is Sanata, also a founder or rather discoverer of a holy site, although admittedly their proper names are of smaller importance as they tend to vary dramatically. A Pshav foundation myth recounts how Sanata accidentally discovered the holy site of Queen Tamar, where the Gabidauri clan had made a home for themselves. Through Tamar's intercession, she forced the clan to leave the sacred ground, and relocate to a nearby place, Kholair. As observed by Zurab Kiknadze, unlike the founder of the Karati Jvari, Sanata was also a founder of the political order – of the clan of Khošari.[23] The case of Sanata is even more extraordinary, because unlike Minani, she lights candles, honours the Mother of God, thus performing an act of church service, which is absolutely unprecedented.[24] Pshav folk traditions are eager to explain that Sanata's licence to worship was determined by the emergency caused by warfare in the region. In this, Sanata reveals similarities with the Old Testament's judge and prophetess Deborah.[25]

What ties together Minani, Sanata and Nino is their transgression of their gender and gender norms, and their endowment with an exceptional mandate to found and administer holy sites that are otherwise inaccessible to women. In Pshav and Khevsur lore, the sporadic prominence of female characters is exclusively tied to exceptional historical and metaphysical

---

[23] Kiknadze, *jvari da saqmo*, 155–6.
[24] Sanata is a literary protagonist of Vazha-Pshavela's (1861–1915) poem, *Bakhtrioni*, which describes an extraordinary situation that followed the catastrophic battle of Bakhtrioni between the highlanders and the Persian army. The alleged beholder of these events recounts in awe how the service was officiated by a woman: საჯარეს დიაცს რა უნდა? / არ თუ ეშინის დავისა? / მარტოს აუნთავ სანთელები / და ხატიც უდიდებია; / მარტოს დაუკლავ საკლავი, / თვითონვე უტყავებია; / მარტოდ-მარტოკას დიაცსა / ხატ-ღმერთი უხსენებია! What is a woman doing in a public space! / Isn't she afraid of a conflict? / All alone, she has lit the candles, / And praised the icons. / All by herself – a woman, / Has prayed to the Xati and God.
[25] Kiknadze, *jvari da saqmo*, 140–3.

states of affair, when the law, in this case women's usual banishment from the vicinities of the holy sites, is suspended. They act as political and metaphysical mediators between the realms, and, crucially, have an exclusive ability to transgress the northern boundaries of the Caucasus mountains. As such, their achievements are aggrandised and their figures mythologised, simultaneously perpetuating their exceptionality and the normative misogyny within the same societies.

The *Conversion* and its hypothetical oral version, such as the undocumented story where Mirian had tortured Nino, could have been reimagined in Caucasian lore as a reaction to Nino's 'transgressive' behaviour. As a woman, she had no right to preach, yet with the Theotokos's intercession, an exception was allowed once and only once, never to be repeated. By the end of the twelfth century, when Nino's cult acquired new relevance, together with the adoption of the tropes of the *Conversion* narrative, her image was put in service of an equally ambiguous living and then posthumous cult of Queen Tamar. *Dedakaci Nino*'s (the woman Nino), as she was called, mandate to convert the Georgians was an irreplicable exception, as was Queen Tamar's mandate to reign. By contrast, the oral narratives did not theorise on femininity, having interpreted the foundation stories of the first *k'adagis* as an absolute and total exception generated by exceptional times.

Below I propose to read the early cult of Nino as a symbol of transition, mediation and in-betweenness. Nino is 'betwixt and between' structures and anti-structures, unfolded in the *Mok'c'evay k'art'lisay* as a rhetorical juxtaposition of paganism and Christianity, anarchy and kingship, periphery and centrality, multiplicity and unity, the North and the South. The *Conversion* is an account of a radical detour and transition between these contrasting existential loci, a transition encapsulated in the burying and unearthing of Kartli's foundational relics, as well as the switching of gender roles in Nino's charismatic persona.

## 2.3 The 'Conversion'

As a foundational text of Georgian historical and religious writing, the *Mok'c'evay k'art'lisay* is comparable to Agathangelos's contribution to Armenian identity discourses.[26] It recounts how in the early fourth century, after a number of life-changing miracles, Kartli's royal family, Queen Nana and King Mirian, were Christianised by a Roman refugee, St Nino. Through this

---

[26] The *Conversion of Kartli* has survived in four manuscripts. The earliest, MS Sin. Geo.N. 48 and MS Sin.Geo.N. 50 are dated to the second half of the tenth century. The third manuscript is part of the tenth-century Šatberdi codex copied in 978–9. The fourth redaction is part of the thirteenth-century Č'eliši codex: Aleksidze, 'New Recensions', 409–21; Rapp and Crego, 'The Conversion of K'art'li', 169–225.

pious story structured around the life and mission of Kartli's legendary illuminatrix, the *Mok'c'evay* reflects on the religious, political and geographic implications of Christianisation, coining tropes that became embodied in subsequent representations of its principal protagonist.

Although traditionally the title *Conversion of Kartli* referred to one specific composition, to our current, yet fragmented, knowledge that stems from the 1975 discovery of the manuscripts in St Catherine's Monastery of Mt Sinai, by the tenth century, the unifying name *The Books of the Conversion of Kartli* included at least two corpora: (a) the original *Conversion*, which consists of two independent narratives: a brief historical chronicle from Alexander the Great to the Emperor Heraclius, with a more detailed exposition of the conversion of the royal family; and (b) an extended *Life of Nino*. The former has a seventh-century date, whereas the date of the latter's completion in its current form is more vague with the ninth century as the latest date. The Sinaitic '*Conversion*' corpus also includes the *Martyrdom of Abibos Nekreseli*, one of the 'thirteen Syrian Fathers' – a group of Syrian ascetics and missionaries who reportedly arrived in Kartli in the sixth century, establishing monastic communities in its centre and along the peripheries.[27] Arguably, since medieval historians saw in the mission of the 'Syrian Fathers' Kartli's 'second conversion', other narratives from the 'Syrian Fathers' cycle were also considered a part of this 'long conversion'.[28] Judging by the surviving collection, by the turn of the millennium, for the authors of the Sinai codices, Kartli's conversion was a historical process that unfolded between Nino's mission and the arrival of the Syrian Fathers, and was enveloped by events of oecumenical magnitude.

*Mok'c'evay* is more than just an account of Kartli's Christianisation. It is essentially a history of the making of Kartli as a body politic. As a seventh-century composition, *Mok'c'evay* reacts to the millenarianistic sentiments prevalent in the age. Although nowhere explicitly stated, *Mok'c'evay* conceptualises the making of Kartli as a history of the sixth, the penultimate, millennium, the one preceding the *eschaton*. The millennium of Kartli's history, that is the beginning of its conversion, opens with Alexander the Great's invasion of the territory of Kartli, when he drove the 'seed of Lot into the land of Cedar', and concludes one thousand years later with an event of comparable apocalyptic importance – the invasion of the Emperor

---

[27] This structure was revealed after the discovery of the new recensions of the *Conversion of Kartli* and the *Lives of the Syrian Fathers* at St Catherine's Monastery. Aleksidze, 'New Recensions', 409–21; Aleksidze and Mahé, 'Manuscrits Géorgiens', 487–94.
[28] On the typological similarities between the two waves of Christianisation in Kartli and Aksum, see Haas, 'Mountain Constantines', 101–26.

Heraclius, immediately followed by the rise of Islam. The millennium is condensed and schematised, with the short account of Christianisation placed precisely in between these two monumental events. This teleological vision is enclosed in the structural symmetry of the *Chronicle*, where the events of Kartli's Christian history mirror its pre-Christian history, with Nino's mission acting as the breakpoint between the two:

Table 2.1 Structural symmetry of the *Mok'c'evay k'art'lisay*

| Pre-Christian history | Christianisation | Christian history |
|---|---|---|
| Alexander invades the South Caucasus, driving out the barbarian 'Bun-Turks' and the Huns beyond the Caucasus and thereby 'cleansing' the Georgian land. Alexander invites his general Azon from 'Arian Kartli' (alternatively Greece) and establishes the Kingdom of Kartli. An annotated list of the succession of the Iberian kings and of their major achievements follows, focusing on the establishment of new pagan cults and the introduction of the royal cult. The Emperor Constantine and Queen Helena are Christianised.[29] | At this point, the narrative breaks and a detailed story is told of Nino's arrival in Kartli, the erection of three crosses, and the first church in its capital city of Mtskheta. Christ's Tunic is discovered in Mtskheta. In this axial event of the narrative, directly associated with Constantine's conversion, Kartli's political and religious *raison d'être* is revealed.[30] | d1. King Mirian and his spouse Nana are converted, which mirrors and emulates the conversion of the Imperial family.[31] c1. A list of the Georgian kings follows, with notes on the churches that they have built. It focuses on the reign of the fifth-century king Vakhtang Gorgasali (the Wolf-Head) and the establishment of the office of Katholikos, an event that marks the beginning of the independent Georgian Church. b1. During the reign of Bakur, the Sasanians abolished kingship in Kartli and the capital was transferred from Mtskheta to Tbilisi, thus ending the kingship established by Alexander. a1. Finally, the Emperor Heraclius marches in Georgia and besieges Tbilisi. He leaves Tbilisi, sacks Baghdad, captures Persia's Khosrow Parviz (590–628) and retrieves the True Cross. In the seventh year he returns to Tbilisi and 'cleanses faith and leaves.' Babylon/Baghdad was sacked by the Arabs. Here the chronicle of the *Conversion* ends.[32] |

---

[29] *Mok'c'evay k'art'lisay*, ed. Abuladze, 81–4.
[30] Ibid., 84–91.
[31] Ibid., 322–4.
[32] Ibid., 92–7.

The authors of the *Chronicle*, who probably wrote soon after Heraclius, and by the dawn of Islam, evidently believed to be writing at the end of times, close to Christ's second coming, which explains their very structuralist and teleological perception of history. Their vision of Kartli's history is that of a sequence of events unfolding between two events of apocalyptic importance, the invasion of Alexander and his Christian analogue – Heraclius. In between lies Kartli's history from the creation of the kingdom to its ultimate dissolution, from the erection of pagan idols to their decisive annihilation by Nino and the construction of churches in their stead, between the conversion of the Roman imperial family and their Georgian counterparts. This millennium serves not only as a historical backdrop of Kartli's conversion to Christianity, but is itself conceptualised as a long history of how Kartli, as body politic, came into being. Consequently, I believe that *Mok'c'evay* has a double meaning – it refers to Kartli's Christianisation, but also to the creation of the body politic and to Kartli's transfer from the periphery to the centre of the history of salvation. Due to Nino's evangelism, Kartli was removed from the fringes of the universal history and was placed within its core, an act that retrospectively reflects Alexander's original removal of Kartli from the realm of the 'North', and prefigures Heraclius's 'cleansing' campaign.

Nino's cult, as it was chiselled in the *Conversion* narrative, was since its inception a political cult, a child of the apocalyptic anxieties of the seventh-century Byzantine commonwealth. Nino rose virtually in the centre of events of apocalyptic magnitude, and in subsequent literary and oral traditions, her memory and relics were associated with events of equally extraordinary and transitional importance. In addition, the glaring contrast between the magnitude of her achievement and her female 'feebleness' evolved into a fairly unique political conceptualisation of the female body in Georgian religious and political thought, as well as the oral traditions of the Caucasian highlands. Nino's mission virtually changed the course of Kartli's history, by giving to this new body politic a political and eschatological purpose in universal history, an act mimicked on a smaller scale by Minani. Nino's evangelism marks a great detour in Kartli's history, reflected also in the narrative's structure. The dramatic switching of gender roles announced by what can be called the 'ten commandments of female evangelism', which occurred in the virtual axis of history, heralded the switching in historical trajectory and opening of the final chapter of Kartli's history. Due to Nino, not only Kartli's future trajectory has changed, but also its past. As with the discovery of Kartli's relics, Nino 'unearthed' its new and authentic history.

## 2.4 A 'New' History

While the *Conversion of Kartli* is an extremely schematic chronicle, its brief hints are expanded in the *Life of Nino*, in the *K'art'lis C'xovreba*, as well as a part of hagiography, such as the Syrian Fathers' corpus. Like the *Histories* of Agathangelos, Xorenac'i and Vač'agan's historian, the sense of historicity and a quest for historic continuity permeate the Georgian conversion narrative. Although Kartli's pre-Christian history is recounted in the chronicle, its 'authentic' history that will define its future, is yet to be retrieved through Nino's intervention. This knowledge is enclosed in the material relics discovered and the historical anamnesis exercised by the protagonists of the narratives, which includes Roman Nino, the Georgian royal family and, crucially, several Mtskhetan Jewish narrators who are central to the entire conversion story. Kartli's alternative history, which reveals it as a Holy Land by proxy of sorts, is braced by the history of the Georgian Jews who had virtually translated the Holy Land to Kartli, a story which is also discovered together with Christianisation. The apocalyptic obsessions with the Jews dominated seventh-century Byzantine writing, but in the *Mok'c'evay* narrative they play a particularly outstanding role.[33] This 'new history' was encapsulated in two of the greatest relics of the Old and the New Testaments brought and hidden by the Jews in Mtskheta: the Prophet Elijah's sheepskin brought by the first Jews (who had allegedly escaped Nebuchadnezzar) and Christ's seamless Tunic also brought by the Jews. Yet both relics, as well as the stories of their translation, were hidden, known only to the Jewish community, and awaiting the kingdom's final Christianisation to be revealed.

In the *Life of Nino*, the translation of the Tunic to Mtskheta is recounted by Nino's Jewish pupil Sidonia, daughter of Abiat'ar: Just after the turn of the Christian era, the Jewish community of Mtskheta was made aware of Christ's birth and his earthly career. Although they had never seen him or witnessed his miracles, they became Christian. Two Jewish men, Elioz of Mtskheta and Longinoz of Karsani, went to meet Jesus. Unluckily, however, they arrived just in time to witness his crucifixion.[34] The *Life* then

---

[33] Korneli Kekelidze believed that the entire *Life of Nino* was written by a Jewish Christian neophyte in Mtskheta. Kekelidze, 'mok'c'evay k'art'lisay's šedgeniloba', 27–76. On the early Jewish diasporas in Kartli, see Mgaloblishvili and Gagoshidze, 'Jewish Diaspora', 39–59.

[34] Cf. one of the Armenian apocryphal versions of the Theotokos's Dormition where the Apostle Bartholomew arrives too late in Jerusalem and finds Mary gone. Peter and Paul console Bsrtholomew by giving him an icon of the Mother of God which was made after her dormition. Later, during Barthlomew's mission in Persia and Armenia, the icon performs many miracles. See Calzolari, *Les Apôtres Thaddée et Barthélemy*, 165.

bombastically announces that the sound of the nailing of the Messiah to the Cross was heard by Elioz's mother who had stayed behind in Mtskheta: 'When the executioner in Jerusalem struck the cross with the blacksmith's hammer on Golgotha, the sound spread hither to his [Elioz's] mother [in Kartli] and the woman cried out bitterly, "Farewell, kingdom of the Jews, for you murdered your Messiah and Saviour and became enemies of the Creator"', after which she died.[35] The hammer's sound that reached all the way to the north, from the Holy Land to Kartli, signalled the end of the old and the beginning of the new, and symbolised the translation of the Holy Land itself to Kartli.[36] Elioz and Longinoz received Christ's Tunic in a game of dice, and brought it to Mtskheta. Upon their arrival, Elioz's sister, later identified as Sidonia, embraced the Lord's Tunic and, overwhelmed with grief, died instantly. Kartli's king, Amazael, wished to take the Tunic but nobody could remove it from the girl's clutch. The girl and the Tunic were then buried in a place known only to local Jews. Sidonia concludes the story by revealing that upon the Tunic's burial the Jews also discovered that an older relic, the sheepskin of Elijah, brought by the first Jewish refugees, had also been buried nearby.

In all three Caucasian foundation stories, following the example set by Helena and Constantine, the official conversion of body politic heralds the revelation of an ancient, yet essentially new and authentic history, embodied in the newly discovered or acquired relics. Agathangelos braced the continuity of the universal, Christian and Armenian histories by the relics of John the Baptist, Athenogenes and the Hṙip'simēan Virgins. The authors of the *Life of Vačagan* created a similar assemblage of the relics of Zechariah, Pantaleon and Albania's first martyred patriarch Grigoris. In both instances, the revelation of the relics was accompanied by the discovery of hidden histories embedded in these relics. The *Conversion of Kartli* made similar associations, yet its project was even grander and more focused on bracing the continuity between the old and the new, as Mtskheta now allegedly hosted two of the most prestigious relics of the Old and the New Testaments.[37] Christ's Tunic, Elijah's sheepskin, as well as the remembrance of their translation in Mtskheta, together with the story of the first

---

[35] *Mokc'evay k'art'lisay*, ed. Abuladze, 129.1–4. მჭელობით, მეფობაო ჰურიათაო, რამეთუ მოჰკალით თავისა მაცხოვარი და მჴსნელი და იქმნენით ამიერითგან მტერ შემოქმედისა.

[36] Ibid., 124–30. On the symbolic 'translation' of Jerusalem to Mtskheta, see Mgaloblishvili, 'How Mtskheta Turned into Jerusalem', 59–66; van Esbroeck, 'La place de Jérusalem', 59–75.

[37] The mantle or the sheepskin of Elijah was also allegedly kept in the Nea Ekklesia built by Basil I in Constantinople as recounted in Constantine Porphyrogenitus, *The Book of Ceremonies*, 117.

Christians on Georgian land, were revealed to the king only when Nino manifested herself to the Georgians, by physically emerging from behind a bush. Unlike Vač'agan's linear narrative, where the quest for Albania's foundational relics is similarly shrouded in mystery, remembrance and discoveries, Nino's story has a more synoptic structure, where various people tell the same story but from different perspectives, thereby creating a sense of narrative suspension. After the recovery of the material relics and the revelation of the story of the Georgian Jews, Nino announces to the king Kartli's new centrality by contrasting this news with its former isolation:

> For it is in your days that God looked down upon this northern valley (*napralsa amas*) whose mountains were covered by the mist of sin, and fields by the haze of error, as [is covered] by night, and light by darkness. And in this land reigned the Ruler of the universe,[38] who cast human souls down to the underworld, and who was driven from the face of the earth by the breath of God's mouth and who, being accused, longs for dark places. Yet the noon [southern] light of the True Sun has glanced upon you, Christ the Lord in His glory. You tasted His new taste, for the Lord is sweet. God has crowned you with baptism, and under His wing you rest in coolness.[39]

In this apocalyptic announcement, the geographic, political and eschatological loci of Kartli are merged. Through Nino's effort, Kartli's peripheral nature – its location at the fringes of the Byzantine and Persian Empires, at the foothills of the Caucasian range, and in the immediate vicinity of the apocalyptic 'enemy', was changed into a strategic advantage. These historical deliberations over the past and the present, the North and the South, culminate in Sidonia's report of the miraculous erection of the Living Pillar in the capital city of Mtskheta: When the people of Kartli were gathered around the Living Pillar, the two mountains enveloping Mtskheta collapsed and the River Aragvi flooded the city, killing everyone in it. Yet, Nino reassured everyone that this was just a hallucination of sorts and that everything was in order. This was just the sign of the mountains of paganism collapsing, and the rivers washing away the sins of previous heathen practices. Then, before the 'cock crowed', a powerful army attacked the gates of Mtskheta. Innumerable armies of the Persians poured in slaughtering everyone. Then a cry was heard that 'Xuara, king of the Persians, and Xuaran-Xuara, king of

---

[38] Cf. Jn 12:31: ὁ ἄρχων τοῦ κόσμου τούτου.
[39] *Mok'c'evay k'art'lisay*, §2, ed. Abuladze, 101.2–16: https://titus.uni-frankfurt.de/texte/etcs/cauc/ageo/gh/gh1/gh1lex.htm; tr. Lerner, 153, modified by N. Aleksidze. This episode appears only in the Čeliši redaction.

kings, commands that every Jew be delivered from the edge of the sword.' And rumours were heard that King Mirian too was captured. Then Nino, once again, was the only one to know that all this was just a mass dream. She then thanked the Lord, 'for this was the sign of their annihilation and Kartli's salvation, and of the glory of this place'. Nino then boldly turned to the Persian kings: 'Who are the Persian kings Xuara and Xuaran-Xuara, you who yesterday came from Sebastan? How did you arrive so quickly? There is a host greater than you are. You have destroyed this city and slain winds and breezes. Go to the darkness of the north, to those mountains of Kedar.[40] Here He comes from whom you flee.' She made the sign of the cross, and suddenly all the multitude of people disappeared and there was a great calm.[41]

This vision is central to the *Life* but also strange, since it is difficult to tell what is happening. Also, it is not a vision but a collective hallucination of sorts. Possibly, this collective vision experienced by Mtskheta's citizens is an echo of the apocalyptic prophecy that, according to the Syriac *Alexander Legend*, Alexander inscribed on the gate which he had built to fend off the Huns from beyond the Caucasus, foretelling the breaching and destruction of the gates and the last war.[42] In the original prophecy, the 'northerners' destroyed the Roman and the Persian Empires, whereas in the Georgian version, it is Sasanian Persia that is seen as this northern enemy, enclosed in 'the darkness of the North'. Although relative to Kartli, Persians were no northerners, and in this vision Sidonia conceptualises Kartli and the Holy Land simultaneously, as a single metaphysical and geographic entity, placing the adversaries to the North, beyond the Caucasus. Sidonia's story is that of the end of the old and the beginning of something radically new, foretelling the new mystical and political function of Kartli: the repelling of the abstracted 'Persians'.

The vision can be interpreted also in the context of the seventh-century crisis in the Byzantine Empire. As a mid-seventh-century composition, most likely crystallised in Palestine, the *Conversion* is a reaction to the catastrophe of the fall of Jerusalem to the Persians and the slaughtering of the Christians. The authors of the *Conversion* lived around the time Antiochos Strategos's

---

[40] *Mok'c'evay k'art'lisay*, ed. Abuladze, 140.37–141.2. Since *Mok'c'evay*, the Hebrew word *Kedar* has been established in Georgian writing as a reference to Kartli, the 'northern realm'. The word, which appears in Psalms 120:5 ('Woe is me, that I sojourn in Mesech, that I dwell in the tents of Kedar!') was interpreted in Patristic writing as 'darkness', 'gloom' or the 'realm of darkness'.

[41] *Mok'c'evay k'art'lisay*, ed. Abuladze, 138–9; tr. Lerner, 177–8.

[42] Pseudo-Callisthenes, *History*, tr. Wallis Badge, 154–6.

*Sack of Jerusalem by the Persians* was written, most likely in the same monastery of Mar Saba in Palestine. Elioz's mother's woeful exclamation upon Christ's crucifixion is a premonition of Jerusalem's ultimate fall described in similarly grieving words by Antiochos.[43] But the authors of the *Conversion* also aimed at creating a narrative of superiority against their fellow Greek monks in the Holy Land. Similarly to Antiochos's rhetorical aim to desacralise Jews from the elect identity and transfer it to Christian Romans, a common tendency among seventh-century Byzantine authors, the principal message of the *Conversion* is the symbolic transfer of the Holy Land to Kartli. Thus, in the vision, when Nino hears that the Persian 'Xuara' had ordered to spare all the Jews, Nino realised that the invasion was just a mirage, and the attack did not take place in Mtskheta at all. Indeed, the Jews, according to the Greek writing of the seventh century, including Antiochos, were spared during the capture of Jerusalem by the Persians. Antiochos even blames the Jews for allying with the Persians against the Christians and capitalising on the Persian takeover.[44] Possibly, the mirage in Mtskheta is a 'prophecy' of the fall of Jerusalem and the salvation of Kartli, a dichotomy confirmed by the translation of the relics by the Jews.

In this context, the mirage that the Mtskhetans experienced can be interpreted as a response to the crisis of the seventh century: Although Jerusalem fell, Mtskheta withstood due to Nino's involvement. Since the seventh century, therefore, Georgian colonists in the Holy Land, where the *Conversion* tradition was seemingly the strongest, have internalised and 'nationalised' the obsessions of the Byzantine authors with apocalyptic geography and elect nationhood. As these accounts and stories evolved and revolved around the representations of St Nino, her image and subsequent cult was politicised and incorporated in political and identity discourses. In time, the idea of an elect nation received a decisive twist, and the feminine component of the conversion, instead of being shunned, was embraced and celebrated. In its totality, the *Conversion* was a project to retrieve the history of Kartli as a part of the universal salvation history, to create conceptual and historical bonds between Kartli and the Holy Land, and to prepare Kartli for the Eschaton.

## 2.5 From Multiplicity to Unity

Nino's cult as a marker of transition is revealed in several aspects in the *Conversion*, which generates dichotomies such as periphery vs centre, the North and the South, multiplicity vs unity, Roman and Persian and so on.

---

[43] Eshel, *Elect Nation*, 30–3.
[44] Antiochus Strategus, 'Capture of Jerusalem', tr. Conybeare, 508; Dagron and Déroche, *Juifs et chrétiens*, 22–8.

Arguably, the function of the cult of Nino is to mark this in-betweenness and the transition between the two structures.

The transition from multiplicity to unity is one of the central subjects of the *Conversion*. Unification was, according to both the *Mok'c'evay* and the *Georgian Chronicles*, the principal achievement of Alexander. Not only did Alexander purge Kartli from 'the multitude of mixed races' and their 'abominable' ways, but he also founded Kartli as a unitary kingdom, ordering Kartlians to 'serve the invisible god', 'a religion that he himself had thought up' 'and had imposed on every land during his reign'.[45] Originally, according to the *Lives of the Kings*, different races were mingled in Kartli, by following the Jewish immigration during Nebuchadnezzar, and the Georgian language, a mixture of these different languages, was created.[46] Still later P'arnavaz, who founded the kingdom, disposed of all the other languages, created the Georgian writing, and since then only Georgian was spoken in Kartli.[47]

Language, therefore, became central in the discourse of 'long conversion'. Mirian's forgetting of his native Persian language and complete Georgianisation was one such step towards his ultimate conversion. Over time, especially among the Georgian monastic communities in the Holy Land, where they constituted a minority, the Georgian language acquired apocalyptic significance. Thus, since the tenth century, language appears paired with St Nino in menologia and hymns dedicated to the illuminatrix: 'Glory to the wondrous miracle! For the Life-Giving Pillar was erected by a woman. And the language of the Georgians now utters praise. The forces of Armaz-Zadeni flee ... Come, the faithful ones and let us praise her in unison. For she is equal to the apostle. She was sent to the northern land. And delivered us through God's grace.'[48]

The pretences to the elect nationhood cultivated among the Georgian monks of Palestine are most dramatically reflected in an apocalyptic hymn, 'The Praise and the Glory of the Georgian Language', also written in Mar Saba. Here, Nino's illumination is compared to Christ's raising of Lazarus,

---

[45] *C'xovreba k'art'uelt'a mep'et'a*, ed. Kaukhchishvili, 18.24–19.2; https://titus.uni-frankfurt.de/texte/etcs/cauc/ageo/kcx1/kcx1lex.htm; Thomson, 26.

[46] *C'xovreba k'art'uelt'a mep'et'a*, ed. Kaukhchishvili, 15.23–16.6; tr. Thomson, 21.

[47] *C'xovreba k'art'uelt'a mep'et'a*, ed. Kaukhchishvili, 26.8–10; tr. Thomson, 26.

[48] Published in Kavtaria (ed.), *Cminda Nino*, 370. *Ianvrisa 14, cmidisa nino moc'ik'ulisay*: ɜ სასწაული საკჳრველთაჲ. რამეთუ სუეტი ივი ცხოვრებისა მომცემელი დედაკაცისა მიერ მჲის აღმართებულის, და დიდებისმეტყუელებს ქართველთა ენაჲ. დავლტიან არმაზ-ზადენითა ძალნი. და დიდებისმეტყუელებს ქართველთა ენაჲ. და ვლტიან არმაზ-ზადენითა ძალნი. მოვეცით, მორწმუნენო, და ერთობით ვაქოთ-ვსცემდეთ, რამეთუ ესე არს მსგავსი მოციქულთა. რომელი მოივლინა ჩრდილოჲსა ქუეყანად და მადლითა საღმრთოჲთა გამომიჴსნნა.

as similarly to Christ, Nino has unearthed Georgia from the soil of sin. As a result, Georgia now enjoys a crucial role in the universal salvation history, as spelt out in the following obscure lines:

> The Georgian language is buried until the day of [Christ's] second coming, to witness it. And so the language is asleep to this day, and in the Gospels this language is called Lazarus. And it was converted by the New Nino and Queen Helena so they are two sisters, like Mary and Martha. And friendship it spoke because every secret is buried in this language ... And this language, adorned and blessed in Lord's name, diminished and rejected, expects the day of the Lord's second coming and as a miracle it has ninety-four years more than other languages from Christ's coming until today.[49]

The trope of burying and unearthing is pervasive in the *Conversion* narrative. When Sarah Miap'or tells Nino to go and seek 'the North', she simultaneously conceptualises Christ's burial and the disappearance of his body in the Holy Land, with the burial of Christ's Tunic in the 'northern land' by the 'Jews of the north', which awaits discovery.[50] Language, history, memory, their forgetting and retrieval, all are encapsulated in the burning and unearthing of Kartli's foundational relics.

In the *Georgian Chronicles*, the formation of Iberian polity is, therefore, perceived as a herald of the reverse process in salvation history, a movement from multiplicity to unity. This antinomy of multiplicity and unity is epitomised in the Tower of Babel and Cross antinomy, and elaborated in the context of the theology of redemption, which can also be found in the *Teaching of Gregory the Illuminator* part of Agathangelos's history.[51]

> The Lord God, looking down on their lack of intelligence, mixed and gave them confusion of many tongues to drink. There he confused them one with another, whence the same place inherited the name Babel of confusion. They were scattered and separated from each other, and as a consequence, no man understood the language of its neighbour. And being thus disunited from each other, they were separated, and their work was abandoned, and what they had formerly put up, they themselves destroyed ... They were confused and scattered and separated from each other.[52]

---

[49] K'ebay da didebay, ed. Shanidze, 283.1–17; https://titus.uni-frankfurt.de/texte/etcs/cauc/ageo/kcx1/kcx1lex.htm; tr. Rayfield, *Literature of Georgia*, 18–20.
[50] Lerner, *Wellspring*, 160.
[51] Thomson, *Teaching of St Gregory*, 139–140, commentary on p. 23.
[52] Thomson, *Teaching of St Gregory*, 139–40.

After this scattering, Gregory speaks of Abraham who refused to partake in 'the plan to build what quickly crumbles' and has thereby preserved his tongue – Hebrew. From him are descended the inspired prophets who maintained the Law and raised 'the fallen of all the world'. Finally, Gregory contrasts with the Tower of Babel, the symbol of multiplicity and disunity, another construction, the Holy Cross, which encapsulates unity and truth: 'In place of the lofty and quickly ruined tower, the cross of truth has been set up, whose power is eternal and its glory God. As the prophet says: "To you the lord will be revealed, and his glory will hide you. Kings will come to your light, and the gentiles to the rising of your light (Isaiah 60: 2-4)"; "Instead of the wood which they worshipped, He set up his cross that he might send out the light of its rays to all creatures who were sitting in darkness and in the shadow of death (Psalms 106: 10; Luke 1:79)."'[53]

While in the early period, there are no relics associated with St Nino, the only and the principal foundation of the Old Kartli is the church of the Holy Cross, the Jvari, erected on the site of the first cross that Nino had erected on top of a hill overlooking Mtskheta. Jvari can thus be read as a symbol of the culmination of these unifying processes that in their totality constitute the conversion.[54]

Finally, the *Mok'c'evay* dramatically concludes the story of Kartli's conversion with the arrival in Kartli of another towering figure of Byzantine apocalyptic literature, Emperor Heraclius – 'another king of the Greeks', who completes what Alexander had begun.[55] Heraclius allegedly stopped in Kartli twice, first on his way to Jerusalem and then on his way back after retrieving the True Cross. Having besieged Tbilisi, Heraclius addressed the Persian commander of the fortress, who had mockingly called him a goat, with a quote from Daniel 8: 'The goat will come from the west and will crush the horns of the eastern ram', the prophecy that had been famously associated with Alexander. Having seized Jerusalem, he returned and made the citizens of Tbilisi, Mtskheta and Ujarma, Christians and fire-worshippers gather in churches, so all magi and fire-worshippers would be baptised or eliminated. They, however, did not wish to be baptised until he raised his sword against them. 'And in the churches, streams of blood were poured out. And King Heraclius cleansed the Christian faith and departed.'[56] Thus, Heraclius finalised the long history of conversion by decidedly 'cleansing faith' in Kartli.

---

[53] Thomson, *Teaching of St Gregory*, 141–2.
[54] In addition, Antony Eastmond also reads Jvari as a symbol of an encapsulation of religious unity and harmony in the Caucasus, on which see below.
[55] For the Alexander–Heraclius typology see Reinink, *Heraclius, the New Alexander*, 81–94.
[56] *Mok'c'evay k'art'lisay*, ed. Abuladze, 96.28–33; https://titus.uni-frankfurt.de/texte/etcs/cauc/ageo/gh/gh1/gh1.htm; tr. Lerner, 149–50.

## 2.6 From North to South

Another trope that the *Conversion* has generated, and has experienced particular vitality throughout subsequent centuries was the apocalyptic and political dichotomy of the 'North and South', and the transition from the former to the latter. In the *Life of Nino*, it is Sarah Miap'or Nino's original instructor in Jerusalem who first points to the North, where 'the northern Jews live', as the dwelling place of the Tunic. Then, just before experiencing a vision where she was instructed to proceed without fear, Nino gazed in terror at the Caucasus mountains: 'I looked upon the Northern Mountain and in the middle of the Summer days it was full of fog and bitter snow'.[57] Statements such as, 'Nino embellished this northern country of Mtskheta, the seat of great Kings',[58] or 'this land of North I have found in error', are pervasive in the *Conversion of Kartli*, and other narratives, hymns or homilies that ponder the history of Kartli. Nino invariably appears as the one who 'melts the ice of the north with the heat'.[59]

The 'North', as a biblical apocalyptic locus and a source of destruction (Jer 1:14–16; 4–6; 6:1–22; Ezekiel 38:1–3) was eagerly appropriated by medieval Georgian writing and internalised self-referentially. The Georgian word for North – *č'rdilo*, which also stands for shade, shadow or dusk, a common trope for sin – made a religious interpretation of this concept even more plausible. Evidently, originally self-identification with the 'northern regions' occurred in the communities in the Holy Land with reference to their distant homeland, and later adopted by writers in Georgia – hence the overdramatisation of the Caucasian peaks and Kartli's supposedly austere climate in the *Life of Nino*. This is how the Syriac *Life of Peter the Iberian*, for example, identifies Iberia, Peter's homeland: 'The country of the blessed Peter was the famous country of the Iberians, those northerners set toward the rising of the sun who are constantly fighting against the Romans and the Persians'.[60] Like the Georgians, the Armenian writers also identified

---

[57] *Mok'c'evay k'art'lisay*, ed. Abuladze, 116.
[58] Lerner, *Wellspring*, 153.
[59] The apocalyptic place of the North and of its inhabitants originates from the Bible. While apocalyptic events and the destruction of Jerusalem that originate in the North were already depicted by pre-exile prophets, Jesaia and Jeremiah, the main source for the Christian tradition is the prophecy of Ezekiel, especially Ezekiel 38:1–15. Among numerous studies, see van Donzel and Schmidt, *Gog and Magog*, 3–16
[60] John Rufus, *Lives of Peter the Iberian*, 5–7. For a brief overview of the concept of the 'North' in the Georgian and Armenian traditions, see Rapp, *Sasanian World*, 125–33. For a general overview of 'the North' in classical and medieval 'imagined geographies' with a focus on Western writing, see Rix, *Barbarian North, passim*.

themselves as 'northerners'. Due to Armenia's northern location in relation to Syria and the Holy Land, the Armenian authors also recognised in this geographic term religious implications. The Armenian tradition refers to St Gregory as the enlightener of the 'North' with all the attributes of this frosty region. Katholikos Xačik Aršaruni (c. 973–92) used the following imagery in his description of Armenia's Christianisation:

> We dwell within the boundaries of this northern country, which is swept by chilly gusts of frosty snowstorms and which had been frozen especially through the darkness of our spirits' former ignorance – a country where even after the dawn of the Evangelical light we had lingered for ages unreached by its rays. Yet, when the Sun of justice deigned to visit us from the heights through the valiant fortitude and the sufferings of the most blessed Gregory, the holy Enlightener and Christ's Confessor, it was with strokes of godly admonition and with miracles of divine wonderworking that he brought this people, and this kingdom of Armenia, from ignorance to the knowledge of the true God.[61]

Apart from the Bible, the Caucasian conceptualisation of the North echoes the apocalyptic topos of the 'northern regions' disseminated through the enormously popular Alexander legends in the wider region. Here, the images in which this 'North' was rendered were those of the land of constant darkness, unmelting ice and blinding snow.[62] Georgian authors internalised Alexander's legendary journey to the 'North' as his real invasion of old Kartli, by incorporating the Alexander legend into their salvation history, and by theologising on Georgia's former northerness and marginality, replaced by its eventual removal from the realm of the North, the 'Mountain of Darkness'. Alexander is described both as Christ's precursor in his universality, as he prepared the world for the dissemination of the Gospel by uniting it, and as a harbinger of Nino as a 'national' phenomenon. To incorporate Kartli in his oecumene, he 'cleansed' the land of Kartli from the Barbarians and

---

[61] Quoted from Dorfmann-Lazarev, *Christ in Armenian Tradition*, 217. See the chapter titled 'A Country Swept by Chilly Gusts of Frosty Snowstorms' for the discussion on the theological meanings of the North in Armenian writing. 'Gregory was also acknowledged as the Illuminator of the North because Syriac Mesopotamia remained an important cultural and religious reference for Armenia.' Dorfmann-Lazarev, *Christ in Armenian Tradition*, 222.

[62] Alexander's penetration into the darkness of the North became a religious metaphor also in the Islamic tradition, where Iskander's *Kosmokrator* image was completed through his exploits to the North, in search of the Fountain of Youth, behind the veil 'whose name is darkness'. Doufikar-Aerts, *Alexander Magnus Arabicus*, 171–80; Casari, *King Explorer*, 178–83.

pushed the boundaries of the North beyond the Greater Caucasus, thereby laying the foundation of Christianity and preparing the ground for the Tunic. Alexander also acted as a culture hero, since he introduced culture and infrastructure by 'planting a vineyard and constructing a conduit from the River Ksani'.[63] By removing Kartli from the 'angel of northern darkness', on a barely inhabited, wild and functionless land, Alexander founded a body politic, whose historical destiny would thereafter remain to guard the frontiers of the Oecumene and withhold the northerners until the final days.[64] Just before revealing the secret story of Mtskheta's relics, Sidonia also reveals the metaphysical and historical meaning of the 'North':

> It happened that God mercifully looked upon this forgotten northern land of Caucasus, the highlands and Somxit'i, and the entire kingdom whose mountains were covered with clouds and whose fields with the fog of terror and ignorance. And this northern land was [deprived] of the sun of the truth of the Advent and of God's acceptance, and it was rightfully called northern. It is not because it lacked the sunlight then or lacks it now. Every man living under heaven sees it and illuminates all. And although it deprives several lands of heat, it sheds its light on all places. It was not for this reason that the land was called northern; but it was because so many years have passed, and so many peoples, from Noah and Eber and Abraham. And among them was Job the Noble, examined by the Examiner, Joseph; Moses; Jesus; high priests and judges; and then in the order as we know it from the Holy Scriptures. To the Advent of Christ, five thousand and five hundred years had passed, and from Christ's birth to the crucifixion, thirty-three years, and from the crucifixion to the baptism of Constantine, the Greek-king, three hundred and eleven; and fourteen years later there came to our land the ambassador of the truth, Nino, our queen, as the dawn glows in the darkness and forms a rainbow, after which the great ruler of the day arises. This was our life, O Kartvelians [Georgians], for we turned back from the light

---

[63] For the episode from the *Conversion of Karti*, see Lerner, *Wellspring*, 139.
[64] Since the *Conversion*'s original conceptualisation, coupled with the internalised Alexander symbolism, in Late Antique and early medieval writing, the south–north trajectory was applied to any important missionary activity to Kartli, as a part of a recurring zeal to liberate Kartli from the 'realm of darkness'. Two centuries after Nino's evangelism, Ioane of Zedazeni and his twelve companions initiated a new journey from Syria 'to the North' to testify to Nino's evangelism, and were consequently honoured as Georgia's re-illuminators. The incorporation of the Syrian Fathers' cycle into the conversion narratives illustrates this political and geographic vision of the significance of Kartli's enlightenment. Martin-Hisard, 'Les 'Treize Saints Pères', 1, 141–68; 2 (1986), 75–111.

and lived in darkness, rested in joy and increased the grief for which there was no consoler.⁶⁵

In Sidonia's vision, Nino's evangelism pushed the realm of the North away from Kartli, incorporating it into the Christian commonwealth of the 'South'. The *Conversion of Kartli* takes off, culminates and ends with a focus on the 'North'. Georgia's landscape and the historical perception of the Caucasus mountains as a border zone contributed to the perpetuation of anxiety over the political and metaphysical belonging of its dwellers. Along with the biblical tradition, the Alexander legend and related apocalyptic writing, this perception was determined by Georgia's location in the foothills of the Caucasus and the historical experience of the costs and benefits of controlling the strategic north–south passes. The Iberian political experience of managing the few main Caucasian passes, especially the Gate of Alans (*Darial*) was over time linked with the teleological purpose of 'withholding' the barbarian tribes.⁶⁶ Thus, when 'this northern land' was illuminated by Nino, Kartli also acquired a strategic function as of the edge of the Christian oecumene. Since then, Nino has become permanently associated with this historic and geographic liminality.

Indeed, since the mid-seventh century, Georgia's geographic and metaphysical 'northern' isolation became a theme of woe for those who wrote under the Arabs. This angst over liminality and the anguish caused by the cold and gloom of political and spiritual desolation was often expressed in self-deprecatory terms, as if the author was not confident anymore whether the Georgians remained within the Christian oecumene, or indeed belonged to the realm of the North. Ioane Sabanisże's eighth-century *Martyrdom of Habo of Tbilisi* dramatically conveys this anxiety. It recounts the story of a young Arab man who had accepted Christianity, established himself in Kartli and was consequently martyred by the Muslims for his apostasy. Sabanisże laments the occupation of Kartli, 'the inlet of the world', by the Muslims, as the land's another and perhaps terminal removal from the stage of history, to which it had been brought with pain 'five hundred years earlier through the holy gift of baptism'.⁶⁷ For Sabanisże, the North, the 'land of Gog and Magog', was an *other*, and the Caucasian mountains were a passage into an alien realm: That is where the persecuted Nerse, duke of Kartli had to flee, to 'the land of the North, where there is the dwelling and the camp of the sons of Magog,

---

⁶⁵ *Mok'c'evay k'art'lisay*, ed. Abuladze, 124.23–125.24; https://titus.uni-frankfurt.de/texte/etcs/cauc/ageo/gh/gh1/gh1.htm; tr. Lerner, 168.
⁶⁶ Kavtaradze, 'Georgian Chronicles', 177–237; Preud'homme, 'Ancient Iberia and the Gatekeepers of the Caucasus', 155–72.
⁶⁷ Iovane Sabanisże, *camebay haboysi*, ed. Abuladze, 49–50.

who are the Xazars, wild men, fearsome of face, savage of character, drinkers of blood, without religion, except that they recognise God as their creators.'[68]

Among all early medieval compositions, it is the eighth-century *Life of Vakhtang Gorgasali 'the Wolf-Head'* that particularly keenly reflects on the concept of the North and political geography in general.[69] The *Life* is much unlike all the other narratives of the *K'art'lis C'xovreba* corpus of which it became part in the eleventh century. It is an epic story of a legendary fifth-century king, replete with grandiose campaigns, adventures and combats. In contrast to the *Life of Habo*, the *Life of Vakhtang* is devoid of any sense of inferiority. Here Kartli and its king appear in the virtual epicentre of the universal drama of history, and Kartli's northernness is re-evaluated as a definitive strategic advantage. It is not some other 'emperor' that embodies Alexander, but Vakhtang himself, who emulates the trajectories of Alexander's exploits. Just as 'Alexander came from the west, entered from the south and went up by the north', so did Vakhtang invade and fight the *bumberazis* (giants) of the North, of the East in India and the South in Ethiopia. Vakhtang's Kartli is no longer a barbarian North, instead the 'Wolf-Head' king was assigned to rule over the northern regions of the Oecumene. Emulating Alexander, Vakhtang repulsed the northerners, the Ovss (Ossetians) and the Khazars, and forbade them to leave the limits of the northern Caucasus without his or his House's consent. After an episode of dramatic battles with the Ossettians an undated insertion asserts, 'Vakhtang subdued the Ovs and the Kipchaks, and he created the gates of Ovseti (Darial), which we now call Darianisi [*sic.*]. And he erected high towers over them and established nearby mountaineers as their keepers. And since then the great Ovs and Kipchaks are not allowed to leave those gates without the permission of the Georgian kings.'[70] In the *Life of Nino*, the *Lives of the Kings* and the *Life of Vakhtang*, owing to Alexander and

---

[68] Iovane Sabanisże, *camebay haboysi*, ed. Abuladze, 58.7–11; https://titus.uni-frankfurt.de/texte/etcs/cauc/ageo/gh/gh1/gh1.htm.

[69] The dating of the *Life of Vakhtang* is complicated and is almost entirely based on circumstantial evidence of when and in which circumstances could such a text have been created. Most recently, Stephen Rapp has argued that the *Life of Vakhtang* is a pre-Bagratid creation, written before the rise of the Bagrationis in the ninth century. The main reason for such dating is the markedly non-Bagratid nature of the narrative and the absence of Bagratid ideology. It is not entirely clear in what circumstances the account was written, whether soon after the king's death or under the Arab occupation or even much later during the unification of the Georgian kingdoms. For further discussion, it is naturally essential to provide at least a working date of the narrative. However, I believe we are devoid of such means. We know for sure that the narrative was fully developed in the eleventh century, and whether or not it already existed two centuries earlier is a matter of speculation. For the questions of authorship, dating and historical contexts, see Rapp, *Studies*; Rapp, *Sasanian World*; Rapp, 'New Perspectives', 1–32; Martin-Hisard, 'Le roi géorgien Vakhtang Gorgasal', 207–42.

Figure 2.2  Nineteenth-century Russian photograph of a fortress in the Darial Gorge. Source: Library of Congress.

Nino, Kartli now acquired its own North identity-making *Other*, and has thus gained a political purpose – to withhold this apocalyptic *Other*. Later in the twelfth century, the metraphrastic editor of the *Life of Nino* reimagined Alexander's civilising journey into the Caucasus. For him, however, *Kedar*, the 'northern darkness' is no longer Kartli, but is located further north, beyond the Caucasian range, and beyond the Ossetes, 'where the mighty race of Kepcheks dwell'.[71] Over time, other kings and their writers have eagerly internalised Vakhtang's self-qualification as the guardian of the northern limits. Equally fascinated by this legend were the medieval western European writers about the region.[72]

The literary representation of Vakhtang as a gate-keeper has penetrated the lore of the mountainous border regions and has been internalised by the local population. The association of Vakhtang and St Nino has become particularly sturdy in Georgia's liminal spaces of the Caucasian highlands, such as Khevi and the Darial Gorge (see Fig. 2.2). In the nineteenth century, the founder of Georgian folklore studies, Petre Umikashvili, was reportedly told by the residents of Gergeti that the ancestors of the Gergetians had been ordered by Vakhtang Gorgasali to guard the gates in Darial.[73]

---

[70] Juanšer, *c'xovreba*, ed. Kaukhchishvili, 156. 19–21; https://titus.uni-frankfurt.de/texte/etcs/cauc/ageo/kcx1/kcx1.htm; tr. Thomson, 362–3, n. 7.

[71] Arseni Beri, *c'xovrebay*, ed. Abuladze, 46.27.

[72] 'Porro David, rex Georgianorum, qui cum suis predecessoribus Portas Caspias tenuit et custodivit, ubi sunt inclusi Gog et Magog . . . cuius terra et regnum contra Medos et Persas est nobis quasi antemurale'. Ansellus, *Epistola ad Ecclesiam Parisiensem*, ed. Migne, col. 729. Other medieval western European travelers (such as Marco Polo) and cartographers (for example the thirteenth-century Ebstorf Map) recount or illustrate a similar story.

[73] Kiknadze, *jvari da saqmo*, 33–4.

Vakhtang's association with crossing the Caucasian boundaries and subduing the Caucasus is preserved in a short oral verse:

> King Vakhtang was dear to God,
> he heard a toll from the heaven,
> He stepped his foot on Ialbuzi [Elbrus],
> the great mountains began to bend.

It is in the *Life of Vakhtang* that Nino makes a unique pre-thirteenth-century appearance and retakes her role of a political and historical mediator. In a chapter titled 'Here is the attack on Greece by Vakhtang Gorgasali', among his other valiant campaigns, Vakhtang, still an Iranian ally, launches a military expedition against the Romans to reclaim his ancestral lands that were taken from the Georgians in his youth. Vakhtang's army penetrates deep into central Anatolia where something dramatic and fundamentally new to the Georgian political discourse happens. Vakhtang was rebuked by his own bishops, Peter and Samuel, for marching against fellow Christians and looting Christian lands. Instead of alienating the Romans, they advised him to make friends with the Emperor. Vakhtang agreed, yet he wished to have a dream where he and the Emperor would meet and make friends. That same night he indeed saw the requested dream. St Nino appeared to him and took him to two thrones, one occupied by the Emperor and the other by Gregory the Theologian. Nino sat at their feet and brokered an alliance with the Roman emperor, by making Vakhtang swear that the enemies of the Romans will be his enemies and that he will always be guided by the Cross.[74] In the episode, Nino is introduced as a dynastic saint who reconfirms Vakhtang's allegiance to Christianity and to the Byzantine commonwealth. After Nino's appearance, Vakhtang, like his distant ancestor, Mirian, symbolically forgets his Iranian identity and adopts that of the Romans. Nino, therefore, sustains Vakhtang's double identity, of an Iranian yet Christian king, and reconfirms the political purpose of the House of Vakhtang – mediation between the Roman and Iranian realms, as articulated in the acclamation in the dream: '[Vakhtang], you will be the most faithful of all among the nation of the Persians!'[75] The king's transition from one identity to another is the central event of the narrative and the most mystical one, almost entirely unravelled in a royal dream. At the threshold of this rite of passage stands Nino, the principal symbol of Kartli's original transition from paganism to Christianity. The *Life of Vakhtang* has, therefore, appropriated Nino as a political

---

[74] Juanšer, *c'xovreba*, ed. Kaukhchishvili, 203; tr. Thomson, 184–6.
[75] Juanšer, *c'xovreba*, ed. Kaukhchishvili, 168; tr. Thomson, 185.

Figure 2.3 'Jvari' or the Holy Cross church, erected in the late sixth-century on the site of one of Nino's crosses, overlooking Mtskheta, with the Svetitskhoveli Cathedral in the background. Photo: Zurab Tsertsvadze.

cult that symbolised Georgia's detour from its Iranian past to the Christian future, an event prophesied by the apocalyptic vision of Mtskheta's women.

Antony Eastmond has recently argued that the church of the Holy Cross (Jvari), built in the late sixth century on the site where Nino's first cross was erected upon Kartli's conversion, epitomises similar liminality (see Fig. 2.3). In 591, the Roman Empire and Iran signed a new peace treaty, thereby dividing their spheres of influence. In the Caucasus, the dividing line was the River Mtkvari – Mtskheta to the west fell to the Romans, whereas Tbilisi to the east to the Persians. The church of Jvari was erected right on the border, overlooking both Mtskheta and the Mtkvari Valley. Eastmond interprets Jvari and its reliefs and inscriptions as a conscious project of 'accommodating' Roman and Persian powers: 'Jvari provided the ideal location to present a rival vision of Georgia as a state that reached into both spheres of influence, nullifying the idea of it being a border monument to Georgia's division.'[76] Eastmond's interpretation, and Nino's mediatory function, is supported by the Shatberdi redaction of the *Life of Nino*: Before embarking upon the trip, she inquires, 'Where is that Northern land, that is to say, where is the Tunic of Our Lord?' She was told that 'the northern land is the land of [between] *Somxit'i* [Armenia] and *Mt'iulet'i* [probably the Greater Caucasus], a pagan land, ruled by Greeks and Persians.'[77]

[76] Eastmond, 'Art on the Edge', 83.

Since the seventh-century *Mok'c'evay*, Nino also acts as a trailblazer who transcended the northern frontiers and took Christianity beyond the Caucasus mountains. Having converted the royal family, she proceeded further north, and with King Mirian's military involvement, forcibly converted the wild and unruly highlanders, Chartalians, Pkhovians, Tsilkanians and Tushetians. Most of these tribes, however, refused to accept Christianity.[78] These highland tribes were situated at the fringes of Georgia's political and religious realm, as while politically they were part of the Georgian kingdom, physically they lived on the northern side of the watershed. A part of medieval Georgian writing expresses worry over their liminal identity and their resistance to accepting the authority of the church and monarchy. Indeed, for the authors of the *Life of the Georgian Kings*, the land to the north of the Caucasus is a different and alien realm, since it 'was not the portion of T'argamos [the ethnarch of the Caucasian peoples]'.[79] There exists some documented evidence that Nino has been ingrained in popular memory as a guardian of Georgia's northern borders. By the late fourteenth century, the north-Caucasian border fortress of Gergeti where the Church of the Trinity stands was associated with Nino's only portable contact relics, the portable cross that Nino had made with twigs and had tied with her hair.[80] Not coincidentally, Nino's folk alter-ego, the boundary-crossing Minani, is specifically conceptualised as the one who travels between the two realms, the North and the South, and converts the northerners. In the *Description of the Georgian Kingdom*, Vakhushti Bagrationi (1696–1757) reports on Khevi, Georgia's small north Caucasian valley, west of Khevsureti, where the Minani story has crystallised, which through the Darial Gorge connects Georgia with the north Caucasian steppes. Bagrationi describes the Caucasian mountains with typical imagery of eternal ice and snow and takes the readers to the Gergeti monastery of the Holy Trinity, which can still be observed overseeing the Darial Gorge just under Mt Kazbegi (see Fig. 2.4). This was where the treasure of Mtskheta and St Nino's cross were traditionally

---

[77] *Mok'c'evay k'art'lisay*, ed. Abuladze, 331.29–31; https://titus.uni-frankfurt.de/texte/etcs/cauc/ageo/satberd/satbelex.htm; translation corrected from Lerner, *Wellspring*, 160.
[78] For the episode, see *Mok'c'evay k'art'lisay*, ed. Abuladze, 323–4, Lerner, *Wellspring*, 146. It is noteworthy that the two, the Šatberdi and Čeliši versions of the *Mok'c'evay*, differ in their presentation of the same events. While both editions attack the North, the Čeliši version, quoted above, is far more elaborate in its depiction of the opposition that Nino and the king experienced from the northerners against their incorporation into Georgia's political and religious body.
[79] *C'xovreba k'art'velt'a mep'et'a*, ed. Kaukhchishvili, 5; tr. Thomson, 6.
[80] The document, which lists the property of the church of Mtskheta and is dated to 1392, is published in Zhordania, *k'ronikebi* 2, 196.

Figure 2.4 The Trinity Church of Gergeti, fourteenth century, with Mt Kazbegi in the background. Khevi, Georgia. Photo: Badri Vadachkoria.

kept.[81] Recently, a previously unknown and rare fresco of St Nino was discovered in the church of the Gergeti Trinity. Considering the scarcity of medieval visual representations of Nino, and the very naïve depiction with the inscription 'St Nino, the mother of the Georgians', it can be argued that Nino's cult was particularly strongly preserved in Georgia's liminal zones such as the pass from the south to the north Caucasus.

The *Conversion*'s imagery and the dichotomies between centre vs periphery, isolation vs integrity, function vs aimlessness, being vs non-being, became powerful metaphors of political theology, both medieval and modern. Nino, who had been removed from the realm of the 'North', epitomised these tropes. Over time, the relevance of Nino's cult was directly tied with the persistence of these political tropes, or the emergence of new ones as it happened with the rise of the Bagratids.

---

[81] Vaxušti Batonišvili, *aġcera*, 320, ed. Kaukhchishvili.

# 3

# The Politics of Female Relics

## 3.1 The Proto-Martyr

The numerous reimaginations of the *Life of Nino* and the ways in which they problematised the feminine have made gender into a political as well as a religious issue in medieval and indeed modern discourses of sanctity. Although the Nino tradition had a long textual history, scholarship suggests that the surviving extended narrative is a later reconstruction and a reimagination of the fourth-century events. Chronologically, the earliest surviving securely dated piece of autochthonous Georgian writing is the martyrdom account of another female saint, Queen Shushanik, written in c. 480 by priest Iakob. Unlike the pseudo-epigraphic *Life of Nino*, there is little doubt that the claimed author had indeed witnessed the queen's martyrdom and recorded the story soon after her death.[1] The *Martyrdom of Shushanik* does not reveal any knowledge of Nino, let alone of her *Life*. Nevertheless, Shushanik's subsequent cult evolved in the same era and political contexts as that of Nino, and such, is a striking example of politicisation of a female saint and her relics. In fact, Nino and Shushanik were the only two early medieval cults whose significance transcended their hagiographic narratives

---

[1] For surveys, see Rayfield, *Literature of Georgia*, 40–9; Bíró, 'Shushanik's Georgian Vita', 187–200. Apart from the Georgian version, there exists an early Armenian *Martyrdom* also presumably dated to the fifth century. Nevertheless, the relationship between the two versions – the Armenian and the Georgian – is not entirely clear, and the two differ from each other substantially. While the Georgian version has a novelistic and expressionistic touch, claims to be a first-person narrative and reveals an intimate knowledge of the topography of the region, the Armenian version follows the typical pattern of a martyrdom account, presenting a much more abstracted perspective. Later, in or before the tenth century, a short Armenian redaction appeared, which was then translated into Georgian. Peter Cowe provides an overview of the Armenian version in Cowe, 'Armenian Hagiography', 299–322.

and whose memory and relics were integrated into political rhetoric. Apart from the Georgian, early medieval Armenian writing has also instrumentalised the two saints in their discourses of history, politics and identity. In both traditions, Shushanik and Nino had a mediatory function. While mediation, as well as transgression and transcendence, was inherent to the cult of Nino, Shushanik's cult was created and disseminated with concrete political implications, and was more directly involved in the religious controversies and ensuing memory wars of early medieval Caucasia.

The importance of the *Martyrdom of Shushanik* is determined by several factors. It initiated the most popular genre in Georgian literature – the lives and passions of saints. Shushanik was conceptualised as Georgia's first martyr, the proto-martyr and the exemplum for all subsequent martyrdoms. As such, she remains central also in contemporary Georgian ethno-religious imagery, since the *Martyrdom of Shushanik* is the first piece of literature taught in Georgia's high schools.

Secondly, Shushanik's martyrdom account contributed to the creation of an exceptionally sturdy image of a female martyr. Like Nino, Shushanik occupied a momentous place in the sequence of Georgian female saints, having authenticated the medieval claim of Georgia as the 'portion' or 'lot' of the Mother of God. Her image was echoed, reused and politicised several times in history, especially since the seventeenth century, after Queen Ketevan's martyrdom by the Safavid Persians had shaken the Georgians to their core cementing the narrative of Georgia's history as that of a story of martyred women.

Thirdly, already in the original martyrdom account, the interethnic and political nature of Shushanik's martyrdom was transparent to its readers, even though in the *Martyrdom* there is not even the slightest reference to the ethnicity or language of the protagonists. Nevertheless, Shushanik was an ethnic Armenian woman married to a Georgian duke, who then apostatised from Christianity, and tortured and murdered the queen. Whether or not this ethnic or cultural aspect transpires in the narrative, it was read, interpreted and problematised as such.

Finally, an aspect of Shushanik's cult is its relative absence and sporadic nature. Shushanik features far less prominently than Nino in medieval tradition and is almost entirely confined to hagiography and liturgical calendars. Known church dedications are non-existent from the medieval period, and her name does not transpire in hymnography either. Only in the eighteenth century, patriarch Antony I composed a short hymn in her honour, yet the hymn is tediously generic and unconcerned with any details of her life, death or cult. What ties together the cults of Nino and Shushanik is their appearance in specific political contexts, and their relative invisibility outside of these contexts. The place, time, circumstances and implications of Shushanik's martyrdom contributed to the politicisation of her cult almost immediately. Her literary representation and posthumous commemoration were involved in political negotiations and inter-religious and interethnic controversies in South Caucasia. The primary valence of Shushanik's cult was that of political mediation, a feature arguably determined by her ambiguous Armeno-Georgian identity, her literary representation as an Armenian bride given to the Georgians and, crucially, by the location of her martyrium in the political buffer zone between the Armenian and Georgian realms, and Tsurtavi, the town which has seemingly maintained such marchland identity for centuries. Therefore, Shushanik was from the beginning conceptualised as a border saint, symbolising the fuzziness of a frontier region. This feature makes Shushanik's cult a rare example of a relatively local tradition appropriated by larger political discourses, yet with varying success in Georgian and Armenian writing.

## 3.2 The Story

The *Martyrdom of Shushanik* was written as a point-of-view account by her court priest Iakob.[2] Shushanik was a daughter of the illustrious Armenian general Vardan Mamikonean (387–451), and as a daughter of such an important house, she was married to Varsk'en, the son of Aršuša II, the *vitax* (a frontier ruler of Iran) of Gogarane. According to Iakob, Shushanik's marriage to Varsk'en was initially a blissful one. The couple had prospered in the town of Tsurtavi, the capital of Gogarene, having happily raised three children. The drama started when, one day, Varsk'en returned from another sojourn in Iran. This time, unlike his earlier trips, it was revealed to the citizens of Tsurtavi that, to placate the Shah, their lord had apostatised from Christianity and converted to Zoroastrianism. Shushanik, a devout Christian, was appalled. She left home and refused to partake in family life, which spilled over into a family drama that takes the better part of the *Martyrdom*. She refused to share a meal with her family, to socialise with her relatives and effectively went on a hunger strike. Varsk'en was outraged by Shushanik's public display of dissent, and several times severely and publicly beat her. Shushanik left her home and withdrew into a cell, where she lived a life of severe asceticism. Yet there too her days turned into sheer torture and humiliation exacted by her ex-husband. Her fame spread across the entire region and people came to witness her miracles. After years of torture, Shushanik died in prison and was buried in the same town of Tsurtavi.

[2] An abridged English translation of the *Martyrdom* can be read in Lang, *Lives and Legends*, 44–56.

The tragedy that unfolded in Tsurtavi was essentially a family drama, similar in tone to the influential *Martyrdom of Vibia Perpetua and Felicitas*.[3] Yet, along with major typological similarities, there transpire some crucial differences between the stories of the two female martyr saints. Unlike Shushanik, Perpetua was a new convert to Christianity and suffered martyrdom on account of her rejection of her ancestral and imperial deities. Similarly to Perpetua, however, Shushanik's drama unfolded after she had rejected her family and privileged status within the community. In this, both Shushanik and Perpetua were 'transgressors'. Regarding Perpetua, Julia Weitbrech observes that female 'sanctification functions in the legends through the repudiation of normative "socially acceptable" roles. In this context, the virginal martyr enjoys extraordinary success, for she has already prevailed. A possible explanation is that the destruction and obliteration of the female body in martyrdom represents a form of disarming.'[4] The *Martyrdom of Shushanik* is effectively an illustration of Shushanik's liminality, of a rite of passage from being a woman of the highest social status into the 'bare life' of sainthood. Iakob constructs his 'male gaze' narrative upon Shushanik's gradual transgression of these 'socially acceptable' roles: withdrawal from social connections, a rejection of her husband, her in-laws, and finally and crucially, rejection of her children, which echoes Perpetua's culminating renunciation – of her newborn child.[5] Isolated in a cell and persistently ignoring her relatives' pleas to return to her palace, Shushanik gradually sheds her feminine self. She refuses to wear queenly garments, to groom, and does not wish to see anyone from her family. Shushanik consciously takes her body to the margins of everything that was considered normative to a woman of her class. Weithbrech's evaluation can be applied to Shushanik: 'The martyred mothers stand between integration and exclusion: until the end, they are both saints and mothers. Standing at the centre in an almost extreme manner, moreover, is the body of the mother, lactating and giving birth. This reproductive body appears as the antithesis of negation or extinction. In contrast to the virginal one, the maternal body can only be sanctified "afterward."'[6] Similarly to her fellow female martyrs in Rome, Iakob's Shushanik projects ambiguity by constantly fluctuating between her feminine self and the newly acquired 'masculine'

---

[3] For text, translation and studies, see Bremmer and Formisano (eds), *Perpetua's Passions*; Dunn, 'The Female Martyr', 202–25.
[4] Weitbrech, 'Maternity and Sainthood', 160.
[5] Cf. Agathonike's rejection of her child in the *Martyrdom of Karpos, Papylos and Agathonike*. CSLA.E00352 (E. Rizos).
[6] Ibid., 160.

steadfastness and perseverance.[7] In effect, her every utterance serves as meta-commentary to her martyrdom, and reflects on the transition between her old and new selves. Shushanik persistently refuses to partake in her family's daily life, as illustrated by a climactic episode that took place at the family dinner, where Shushanik was brought against her will. When her sister-in-law offered her wine, Shushanik said to her angrily, 'Whenever has it been the custom for men and women to dine together?' And stretching out her arm, she flung the glass in her face. Then Varsk'en began to utter foul-mouthed insults and kicked her with his foot. He picked up a poker, and crashed it on her head, splitting it open and injuring her eye. 'And he struck her face unmercifully with his fist and dragged her to and fro by the hair, bellowing like a wild beast and roaring like a madman.'[8]

Shushanik's enigmatic sentence whereby she protests the sharing of the meal between men and women has puzzled scholars for generations, as such rigid gender segregation was unknown to Late Antique Caucasia. However, arguably, rather than commenting on established gender roles, Shushanik thereby emphasises her liminality: she is not a member of the household anymore, not a wife to her husband, or a mother to her children – she is an alien. Shushanik is even more radical than Vibia Perpetua in her rejection of familial ties. While Perpetua's family is mostly embodied in her father, Shushanik's primary motivation is to explicitly sever ties of kinship with her entire family.[9] At one culminating moment, when Shushanik refuses to see her children and declares them apostates, the reader realises that the queen has entirely stripped herself from her self. In a soliloquy delivered in the cell in the author's presence, Shushanik mourns her old self, cursing her husband for what he had done to her:

> Varsk'en and I shall be judged where there is no count in the presence of the judge of the judges, of the lord of lords, where there is no distinction between man and woman, and where I and him will say equal words in the presence of our Lord Jesus Christ. The Lord will repay him, just as he unduly tore my fruits and extinguished my candle, and wilted by flower, he brought darkness upon the beauty of my goods, and destroyed by greatness. And may God be the arbiter between him and myself![10]

---

[7] On the masculinisation of Late Antique female martyrs, see e.g. Cobb, *Dying to Be Men*, especially 92–123 for literary examples.
[8] Iakob C'urtaveli, *camebay šušanikisi*, 6, ed. Abuladze, 16–17; tr. Lang, 49.
[9] Candida Moss notes that 'Perpetua's rejection of family is connected to the masculinisation of the female martyr, a literary and ideological topos clearly anticipated in the Maccabean mother.' Moss, 'Blood Ties', 194; Dunn, 'The Female Martyr', 202–25.
[10] Iakob C'urtaveli, *camebay šušanikisi*, ed. I. Abuladze, 26.28–27.1: https://titus.uni-frankfurt.de/texte/etcs/cauc/ageo/gh/gh1/gh1lex.htm.

The expressively laconic speech is a stunning display of anguish over her bygone life, rare in Late Antique female or male martyrdom accounts. In the same dialogue between her and her priest, where Iakob was appalled by the worms that were eating the queen's body, Shushanik says in a good Christian manner that earthly and mortal worms are better than the immortal ones. Yet, in a remark addressed to the reader, Iakob notes that only he knew that while on the outside Shushanik was dressed in an expensive Antiochean garment, inside she wore rugs, thereby once more stressing Shushanik's liminality.[11] Therefore, almost every episode of the *Martyrdom*, from Shushanik's early defiance to the descriptions of her final days in the cell, is dedicated to the explanation and dramatisation of her transitioning from one state to another.

## 3.3 Reciprocity

In this constant tension between her not-yet-abandoned and her not-yet-acquired selves, Shushanik's martyrdom is unique. Normally, martyrdom accounts of women try to neglect or downplay the protagonist's marriage or anything that could hint at her sex life. For instance, Perpetua's husband is absent in her *Passio*. In Shushanik's story, however, her marriage and its consummation are not ignored, quite on the contrary, they retain centrality throughout the narrative. During a dramatic exchange of insults, Varsk'en points to their marital bed, on which Shushanik, by her defiance, has 'sprinkled ashes'. This would be rare in Western female hagiographies, where even within marriage, female saints are presented as rather disinterested in sex and are virgins by disposition. Shushanik's answer is far from this:

> Is it not me who exalted your person? And it will be me who degrades it! Your father raised sepulchres for the martyrs and built churches, and you have ruined the deeds of your father and destroyed his good works. Your father invited saints into his house, but you invite devils. He confessed and believed in the God of heaven and earth, but you have renounced the True God and bowed down before the fire. Just as you have despised your Creator, so I pour contempt upon you. Even if you inflict many tortures on me, I will have no part in your doings.[12]

This is a crucial passage in the *Martyrdom*, whereby Shushanik's martyrdom transcends a mere family drama and takes the initiated readers to the

---

[11] This ambiguity of simultaneous feminisation and de-feminisation also transpires in Perpetua's story. See Moss, 'Blood Ties', 193–5.

[12] Iakob C'urtaveli, *camebay šušanikisi*, ed. Abuladze, 15.4–12; tr. Lang, 47–8.

realm of the political. With such an explicit emphasis on marriage, the marriage pact and its annulment, reciprocity permeates the entire narrative. The beholders of Iakob's story were the same people who had witnessed their queen's marriage, life in Tsurtavi and death. Most of the audience probably knew her personally or were at least familiar with the story, being also aware of the political nature of the marriage of their lords. The tragedy that unfolded before their eyes was a family as well as a political drama, and the queen's explosive reaction to her husband's apostasy had political connotations. Shushanik's marriage to Varsk'en was conditional. It was an exchange, and everyone was aware of this.

In the second half of the fifth century, the entirety of Caucasia was head-to-toe involved in an overt or covert anti-Iranian insurgency. At the battle of Avarayr in 451, in one of the most defining moments of Armenian cultural memory, Armenia suffered a catastrophic defeat at the hands of the Iranians. The rebellion was spearheaded by Shushanik's father, the great Armenian commander-in-chief and *naxarar*, Vardan Mamikonean, who was slain in the same battle. The anti-Iranian insurgency engulfed all of eastern Caucasia and continued until the end of the century. Later, the Georgian party of the wars was presided over by an equally legendary figure of lore and history, Vakhtang Gorgasali, the 'Wolf-Head' king. It was in the middle of this turmoil that Shushanik was born, raised and died. To strengthen the alliance with their northern neighbours, Shushanik was married to the Georgian ruler (*vitax/pitiaxš*) of Gugareti, known to late Roman authors as Gogarene, and Gugark' to Armenians.[13] This political marriage was initially supposed to strengthen the Christian anti-Iranian coalition in this strategic border zone. The seal of their contract was their shared faith in the politically volatile region, amidst the universal dominance of Zoroastrian Iran. During the verbal and physical standoff with her husband, this political significance of their marriage is Shushanik's principal line of defence: it was not her who broke the marriage contract, as the marriage, the original deal, was annulled the moment Varsk'en had apostatised. Consequently, since the opening paragraphs, the rest of Shushanik's martyrdom is a story of a systematic tearing of the marriage contract between the spouses, as exemplified in the following heartbreaking episode:

> [Varsk'en] said to me, 'Do you know, Priest, that I am leaving to fight against the Huns? I have no intention of leaving my jewellery with her, now that she is not my wife. Someone else will have to be found to wear

---

[13] A detailed history of the region from antiquity to the tenth century can be found in Toumanoff, *Studies*, 463–73; Allen, 'March-Lands', 150–6.

it. Go and bring whatever there is of it.' So I went and told this to St Shushanik. She was very glad and thanked God and handed everything over to me, and I delivered it all to the Pitiaxš. He received it from me, inspected it and found everything complete, and again said, 'At some later time, someone will be found to adorn herself with it.'[14]

The *Martyrdom of Shushanik* thus uncovers two valences of the holy queen's body: she is described as a liminal figure who took herself to the limits of everything, to a state of suspension between motherhood and virginity, the private and the political, the queenly and the abject. Second, Shushanik conceptualises herself as a gift, a grace bestowed upon her husband, which Varsk'en destroyed and jettisoned. In her final words Shushanik entrusts it to God to avenge the broken contract. Therefore, already in the original martyrdom account, perhaps the source of all other references to Shushanik, the holy queen is conceptualised as a gift or a loan given to her husband, which Varsk'en failed to reciprocate. Arguably, it was the idea of Shushanik as an 'unreciprocated gift' that determined the posthumous political life of her relics. For the fifth- and sixth-century Gugaretians, both ethnic Armenians and Georgians, the story was a reminder of their land's resistance to the Sasanians, and Shushanik's body buried in the town of Tsurtavi was a symbol of this Christian Armeno–Georgian coalition and religious unity. Yet, this image of Shushanik was soon to change, when religious unity was shattered in Gugareti and the entire Caucasia, and the frontier zone of unity changed into a space of alterity. In time, in the Armenian tradition, Varsk'en was identified with the Georgians, and Shushanik became Armenian par excellence, with their family story becoming a micromodel of the ensuing Caucasian conflicts.

As the Armeno–Georgian debates unfolded, Shushanik's liminality and her conceptualisation as a gift were even more internalised and integrated into interethnic polemic. In Armenian political discourse, Shushanik became not only an Armenian bride entrusted to the Georgian husband, but a symbol of the very Christianity that, according to Armenian tradition, the Armenians had gifted to the Georgians. By deviating from Orthodoxy, the Georgians violated the original contract and abused the 'gifts of civilisation' given to them by the Armenians. Due to strong associations of local politics with the memory and physical presence of Shushanik, her marriage and the broken contract, the conceptualisation of gift and debt became a central interpretive framework in medieval Armenian rhetoric of Caucasian politics.[15]

---

[14] Iakob C'urtaveli, *camebay šušanikisi*, ed. I. Abuladze, 19.1–9; https://titus.uni-frankfurt.de/texte/etcs/cauc/ageo/gh/gh1/gh1lex.htm; tr. Lang, 51.
[15] On the 'gift of Civilisation', see Grant, *Captive and the Gift*.

## 3.4 The Political Life of Shushanik's Body

Shushanik's physical death marked the beginning of her long political life, which in its practical influence outlived her illustrious contemporaries. Other than the literary tradition of her martyrdom, which relatively dwindled in the later medieval period, her living cult enjoyed success between the seventh and the tenth centuries, when Shushanik's material remains on the one hand, and her living memory on the other, acquired political expediency. Early medieval Armenian and Georgian historians envisaged Shushanik's death as a catalyst for the anti-Iranian policies of Caucasia's Christian rulers. The *Life of Vakhtang* recounts that, having heard of Shushanik's death by the hand of Vask'en (*sic.*), Kartli's King Bakur (probably Bakur II, 535–47) assembled his loyal lords, and ambushed the apostate duke. Varsk'en was cut into pieces and his body parts were hung on trees as a warning to all pro-Iranian traitors. Shushanik's relics were retrieved with a solemn procession and buried in Tsurtavi. Bakur immediately dispatched messengers to the Shah announcing to him what he had done, and asking him for forgiveness. Bakur's gamble proved to be a successful one. The Shah reasoned that punishing Bakur would have prompted the Georgians to shift their allegiance to the Romans. He ordered his men not to alienate the Georgians, and reluctantly forgave Bakur by conceding that avenging Shushanik's brutal murder was indeed justified.[16] This episode is one of many where Georgian rulers successfully blackmail Iranians and Romans in their continuous strife to maintain the balance of power in the region. It is, I believe, not coincidental that, while in the same *Life of Vakhtang*, the memory and cult of the Roman St Nino appear in the negotiations with Constantinople, and St Shushanik's body assumes a similarly mediatory role in the negotiations with the Iranians.

Yet the mediatory function of Shushanik's relics was most dramatically revealed in the context of Armenian–Georgian relations of which she became a symbol. This valence of Shushanik's relics emerged in the middle of Caucasian ethno-religious politics, caused by the spread of the Chalcedonian strife in the region and the ensuing memory wars over the history of Orthodoxy and the foundations of Christianity in the region. Shushanik's cult and relics were tied to the ethnic, linguistic and political idiosyncrasies of Gugareti, a region that became the epicentre of the Chalcedonian controversy in Caucasia, as well as later a military target of Georgian, Armenian and other powers. Arguably, Shushanik's original literary conceptualisation

---

[16] Juanšer, *c'xovreba*, 227–9. Armenian historian Łazar P'arpec'i claims that it was king Vakhtang Gorgasali who assassinated Varsk'en.

as a 'liminal figure' placed between the Armenian and Georgian realms, and the setting of her story in the virtual border-space between the two people, was the reason for her subsequent emergence as a border saint and a political mediator between the Armenian and the Georgian nations.

Shushanik was martyred in 475, soon after the 451 Council of Chalcedon, one of the most transitional events in the history of Eastern Christendom, and, with belated repercussions, also in the history of Caucasia. Having ripped apart entire regions, and arguably given rise to proto-national and ethno-religious identities, especially in the eastern fringes of the Eastern Roman commonwealth, the Council of Chalcedon saw the seeds of a religious discord that occupied the hearts and minds of writers of the Christian East, and especially of Caucasia, for centuries to come.[17] One hundred years after the Synod, the echoes of Chalcedon slowly, yet distortedly, reached Caucasia. There, among Albanians, Armenians and Georgians, where ethnic, linguistic and political disagreements had been sprouting throughout, the Chalcedonian controversy found fertile ground. As the entire Christian East, sixth-century Caucasia became engulfed in controversies over the nature of Christ's incarnation, the decisions of the Council of Chalcedon, and even over conflicting tendencies within non-Chalcedonian Christology. By the beginning of the seventh century, the debates over the nature(s) of Christ, amplified with political signifiers, exploded into a conflict between the Iberian and the Armenian churches, and, in time, decisively transformed the political and ethno-religious landscape in the region.[18] The Iberian Church chose a Chalcedonian confession of faith, and alliance with the Byzantines, whereas the early seventh-century leaders of the Armenian Church, although with ensuing internal opposition, adopted militant anti-Chalcedonianism.[19] Byzantium and Iran's struggle to secure control over the strategic lands of Caucasia further aggravated religious strife. The process and the immediate aftermath of the Ibero–Armenian schism are documented in the *Book of Letters*, an Armenian corpus of correspondence exchanged among the Armenians, Georgians, Albanians and other participants of the post-Chalcedonian polemic from the sixth to the eighth centuries.[20]

---

[17] For an exhaustive study of the reception of the Council of Chalcedon in Armenia and the Caucasus, see Garsoïan, *L'église Arménienne*, passim.
[18] I have discussed these debates in detail in Aleksidze, *Narrative*, passim. For other important studies, see, especially, Garsoïan, *L'église Arménienne*, passim; Mahé, 'Confession religieuse et identité nationale', 60–78; Mahé, 'La rupture arméno–géorgienne', 927–61; Zekiyan, 'La rupture', 155–74; Zekiyan, 'Le croisement des cultures', 81–96.
[19] On the Caucasian Schism, see Garsoïan, *L'église Arménienne*; Frivold, *Incarnation*; Zekiyan, 'La rupture', 155–74; Aleksidze, *Narrative*, 69–102.
[20] Schmidt, 'Das armenische "Buch der Briefe"', 511–33.

As we learn from the *Book of Letters*, the wellspring of the original Armeno-Georgian conflict was the region of Gogarene and its capital Tsurtavi, where Shushanik's martyrdom was located. Populated by both ethnic Armenians and Georgians, previously this area served as a buffer zone between the Armenian and Iberian kingdoms, and, after the annihilation of kingship, between Armenian and Georgian spheres of influence. By the fifth century, Gugareti was strategically a critical entity in Caucasia. Located in between the Armenian and Georgian realms, the Byzantine and Iranian spheres of influence, through Gugareti, winding roads proceeded towards the Caucasian mountains, and through the narrow Darial pass into the North Caucasian steppes; through mountain valleys, it offered the quickest passages from the Caspian to the Black Seas and further south-west into Anatolia. Since antiquity, the region migrated between the Armenian and Georgian realms, and larger imperial powers fought hard to secure control over this small rugged land. Indeed, the last military standoff over the region took place between the Armenian and Georgian republics in 1919. Due to Gugareti's strategic location and its liminality between the two major continental powers, its rulers were among the most powerful lords of Caucasia. While in its origin, neither Shushanik's story nor her cult had anything to do with inter-confessional debates, it was in the context of the Chalcedonian controversy and interethnic feud that the memory and cult of Queen Shushanik flourished.

According to the *Book of Letters*, throughout the sixth century and probably since the death of Shushanik, her martyrium in Tsurtavi ritualised the in-betweenness of Gogarene by uniting the Armenians and the Georgians. As insisted in the letters of the Armenian katholikos, at this holy site of memory, peace and brotherly love between the two people had been established and ritually performed. In the good old days, in Tsurtavi, at the martyrium of Shushanik, the Georgian and Armenian nobility used to meet, interact and even intermarry. In a letter addressed to his alienated Georgian colleague, the Armenian katholikos points out that 'the unity of faith and hospitality between our two lands was protected with a firm mediation by the Church of C'urtaw, where love, bodily kinship, and spiritual communion was performed with joy full of bliss. From here people would travel to the Cross of Mtskheta and from there – to the holy Cathedral.'[21] As a ritual re-enactment

---

[21] *Girk'Tłt'oc'*, ed. Aleksidze, 66–7: զիմիաւորութիւնհաւատոյևզասպնջականութիւն զերկուցունց աշխարհացս Յուրտաւայ եկեղեցին անշարժ միջնորդութեամբ պահէր, ուստի սէր և խնամութիւնք մարմնաւորականք և հաղորդութիւնք հոգևորականք կատարէին գնծալից ուրախութեամբ: Աստի, ի Մծխիթայի ի Խաչն գալով. և այտի՝ ի Սուրբ Կաթուղիկէ: . . .

of this tradition, the Bishop of Tsurtavi was elected alternately from among the ethnic Armenians and Georgians. The language of the liturgy too was both Armenian and Georgian, although the practical details of either of these arrangements are difficult to restore. The Georgian and Armenian polemicists of the *Book of Letters* univocally refer to the episcopal see of Tsurtavi as the mediator between the two realms, and to St Shushanik as the patron saint of this mediation. Shushanik's cult, therefore, maintained the region's function as a certain no man's land that shared both Georgian and Armenian ethnic, cultural and linguistic features.[22]

In Armenian rhetoric of the *Book of Letters*, voiced by katholikoi Movsēs and Abraham, the *phylax thronou* bishop Vrt'anēs K'erdoł, and Prince Smbat Bagratuni, the historical, political and religious harmony between the two nations and, moreover, the traditional moral dependency of the Georgians on the Armenians were symbolised by a host of saints. From the Armenian point of view, these were the Armenian illuminators of the Caucasian lands, St Gregory and the holy teacher Maštoc' (the famed translator of biblical books and creator of the Armenian alphabet): Gregory had converted, whereas Maštoc' further illuminated and created literacy for the Georgians. In addition, the Church of the Holy Cross of Mtskheta, by tradition associated with St Nino, was also evoked, though without any reference to the Nino tradition, either in its Georgian or Armenian guises. The most frequently evoked cult was that of St Shushanik, whose appropriate commemoration was adopted as a major rhetorical tool in the original Armeno–Georgian polemic and ensuing memory wars.

Our knowledge of Shushanik's cult stems, however, not from this period of unity that the polemicists reminisce about, but from that of disunion that the *Book of Letters* documents. The polemical exchange of letters between Armenians and Georgians is replete with mutual denunciations, most of which amount to accusations of forgetfulness of the former cohabitation between the two people, followed by allegations of heresy, schism and treason. The initial complaint that the Armenian patriarchs advanced against the Georgians was that the Georgians had allegedly forgotten the former days of solidarity between the two people and, by accepting the Chalcedonian faith, had rejected the symbols of this unity as ritualised by the appropriate commemoration of the founding saints of Caucasia. In the same letter, the Armenian katholikos complains, 'and now the Bishop of C'urtaw is persecuted, for [they say] why are you confessing the orthodox faith?! And I also heard that you have altered the

[22] Peeters, 'Ste Shushanik', 187–200.

Armenian service, established by Saint Shushanik. We considered this greater evil than death itself.'[23]

For the early seventh-century polemicists, as soon as the first struggle over remembrance broke out, in the absence of continuous institutionalised memory of the unity in faith, Shushanik's martyrium became a site of contested memory, and a symbol of divisive alterity, instead of that of former unity. The Georgians, from the Armenian perspective, were guilty of taking away from the region and Shushanik's relics the historically mediatory role. As well as expelling an Armenian bishop from the shared cultural zone, Kyrion, the Georgian katholikos, had also changed the language of the service ('Armenian service') allegedly established by St Shushanik herself. In his reply, Kyrion conceded that formerly 'Armenian noblemen, who had relatives in Georgia, used to arrive at the service of St Shushanik and at the Holy Cross [of Mtskheta]', but he also maintained that he had not changed anything – the tradition remained the same.[24] Therefore, the initial trigger of the heated polemic between the Georgian and the Armenian hierarchs, repeatedly voiced in the correspondence, was that the Georgians have, from the Armenian point of view, betrayed the religious and political union symbolised by St Shushanik.[25] Gugareti, from the Armenian perspective, was and must have remained a buffer zone, a guarantee of the balance of powers in Caucasia. The Georgian katholikos, through his actions, undermined this liminality by effectively nationalising the town and the region: he forcibly expelled the ethnic Armenian bishop of Tsurtavi and changed the language of the service into Georgian. Kyrion introduced rigid order, whereas, from the Armenian perspective, the traditional fuzziness of the region was its defining feature. In this, the rhetoric of the seventh-century Armenian Church hierarchs echoes Shushanik's own conceptualisation of her marriage contract and Varsk'en's betrayal of this arrangement.[26] For

---

[23] *Girk' Tłt'oc'*, ed. Aleksidze, 66–7: Այժմ գծուրտաւայ զեպիսկոպոսն հալածեալ է, թէ ընդէ՞ր խոստովանեմ հրամայես, զհաւատ ուղղափառութեան, և զպաշտաւնն հայերէն սրբոյ Շուշանկան կարգաւորեալ' լսեմ, թէ ի բաց փոխեցէք։ Մեզ մահուճափի իս չարագոյն թուեցաւ գործդ այդ.

[24] Ibid., 78.

[25] Martin-Hisard, 'Jalons', 53–78.

[26] Although the cult of saints as boundary markers has not been sufficiently explored in scholarship, comparable studies exist with regard to pre-Christian religious practices. Based on Campbell, Carin Green, for example, discusses boundary goddesses of ancient Rome, who 'marked the line dividing civilisation from wilderness; they fixed the distinction between the productive orderliness of the city and the unregulated chaos of everything else; they separated the place of law from the territory without law. They established the boundary of the land the Romans had to defend,

the early seventh-century Armenian elites, Shushanik's family drama now materialised into a political conflict, and as much as Shushanik was the symbol of the Armenian steadfastness in faith, so did Varsk'en become a symbol of Georgian apostasy and betrayal.

Shushanik's relics were an embodiment of the ambiguity and fuzziness of the region. Apart from physical boundary-marking, for both Georgian and Armenian participants of the controversy, Shushanik also marked the temporal boundary between the mythological past and the experienced present – in other words, the time of historical, yet forgotten regional unity and the current situation of schism. Even in subsequent centuries, the association of this land with Shushanik was so strong that the early eleventh-century Georgian katholikos Arseni Sap'areli believed that the entire diocese of Ttsurtavi had been established by her. Yet, even back in the seventh century, neither Georgians nor Armenians were able to explain what the essence of this unity was or what the 'service established by (for?) St Shushanik' truly meant: whether service in her honour or a specific service established by her. Indeed, most likely Shushanik originally had nothing to do with either of these, but, as a specifically Gugaretian martyr saint, was later conceived as the founder of the Church of Gugareti with its cultural peculiarities. The religious and political order, or rather the lack of it, in the region was maintained by an adherence to this fuzzy tradition. This made Shushanik's ambiguity both territorial as well as temporal. From the point of view of the seventh-century authors, the martyrium of Shushanik generated what Victor Turner called, *communitas*: at Tsurtavi, the rigidly structured categories of Georgianness and Armenianness, of the Georgian Church and the Armenian Church, became structureless. This 'structurelessness' was ritualised through the interaction between the allegedly spontaneous relationships between the Georgians and the Armenians, which turned Gogarene into what Turner would call, *normative communitas*, 'where, under the influence of time, the need to mobilise and organise resources and the necessity for social control among the members of the group in pursuance of these goals, the existential communitas is organised into a perduring social system.'[27]

Gogarane, with its saint, Shushanik, is presented as a liminal space, a zone of ambiguity and uncertainties. As theorised by Claude Levi-Strauss and Victor Turner, however, it is the nature of the liminal spaces to be extremely volatile. They inevitably create anxieties regarding the identity

---

and the boundary stood as evidence of their defense.' Green, 'Holding the Line', 283. Within the Christian context, so far the only parallel explored in scholarship is the cult of the Virgin Mary. Krueger, 'Mary at the Threshold', 31–8.

[27] Turner, *Ritual Process*, 132.

of the liminal, and require symbolic maintenance and ritualisation. The liminality of the area, which was sustained through a ritualised exchange, through a gift-and-debt dialectic, while seemingly sustaining stability, also generated a state of suspension, hence the emergence of largely invented traditions that even the authors of the *Book of Letters* find hard to explain. Such was the ritualised alteration of Armenian and Georgian bishops of Tsurtavi, the marriage alliances, the rather grotesquely accentuated bilingualism and lore generated in the same region.[28] The peace and love between the Armenians and Georgians, symbolised by the cult of Shushanik and ritualised in Gogarene, is from the point of view of the seventh-century authors, atemporal as it has 'always been such', and, therefore, truly temporary. Consequently, due to this state of suspension, as soon as this liminality was infringed, from symbols of a shared space, the liminal figures effectively transubstantiated into symbols of alterity and difference. Once, from the Armenian point of view, the Georgians had violated the tradition, the zone of ambiguity became that of 'nationalistic' certitude. What was seen as a symbolic annihilation of liminality, in the perspective of medieval Armenian writers, unleashed a series of catastrophes that befell the Caucasian region. From the seventh century, and especially in the tenth century, Gogarene was perceived as an Armenian land unlawfully taken over by the Georgians, and Shushanik too became a distinctively Armenian princess murdered by the Georgians par excellence.

## 3.5 Shushanik Revisited

The seventh-century Armeno-Georgian scandal, which was at least in part triggered by Eastern Roman and Iranian interests in the region, was merely the beginning of a conflict that, with varying intensity, spanned another millennium. Three centuries after the initial conflict, in the tenth century, with the decline of the Arab emirates, new kingdoms and principalities emerged in Caucasia. These Georgian and Armenian political entities occasionally allied with the Byzantines or the Arab Emirates in their zeal to gain control over the strategic regions of Caucasia. In this novel political context, the religious and political debates over the origins of the religious controversies were revitalised. With the renewal of territorial, religious and ethnic conflicts, both Georgian and Armenian historical writing became fixated on the border zones of Caucasia, such as Gugareti, Tao and other marchlands between Georgian and Byzantine, Armenian and Georgian,

---

[28] Aleksidze, 'Murder at Mt Kangar', 130–49.

and Byzantine and Iranian realms.[29] Especially Gogarene, during the Caucasian wars of the tenth and eleventh centuries, remained the central target of all the key players in the region. Exercising control over it could clear the way toward the last Arab stronghold in the region – the Tbilisi Emirate. This would also mean gaining control over all passages leading to the north, the west, and to Albania, as well as the roads leading through the southern valleys to Armenia. In other words, control over this central region would ensure control over the entire Caucasus. In this political context, the narrative of the old schism, or the story of the beginnings of the conflict, became an essential rhetorical tool in the ongoing memory war. Forged and developed in medieval Armenian writing, the memory of the original scandal became an interpretive framework through which the contemporary political status quo and its relation to the past were perceived. It is in these memory wars that a systematic conceptualisation of the political life of Shushanik's memory and relics was undertaken.

As a part of this effort, in the tenth century, Armenian historian Uxtanēs Bishop of Sebasteia produced an annotated edition of the *Book of Letters* and incorporated it into his *History of Armenia*. Uxtanēs dedicated an entire chapter to Shushanik with a brief account of her martyrdom. Nevertheless, Uxtanēs failed to refer to any of the versions of Shushanik's *Martyrdom*, either Armenian or Georgian. He admits that to research the story of the schism and Shushanik, he had travelled to Georgia and studied the history of the conflict. The Sebasteian bishop, seated far south from the original area of Shushanik's martyrdom, was indeed unaware of the standard martyrdom account. Instead, he was convinced that he was introducing Shushanik's story to his Armenian readers, while not expecting them to be knowledgeable of her life and deeds. Although Shushanik's Armenian martyrdom account had been written soon after her death, she was equally unknown to much earlier Armenian authors. One of the most famed children of the Mamikonean House and the dynasty's own martyr, Shushanik was ignored by the fifth-century dynastic historian of the Mamikoneans, Łazar P'arpec'i, whose primary purpose was to glorify the clan, particularly Shushanik's father. Łazar even relates the assassination of Shushanik's husband by King Vakhtang, but fails to say anything about the princess. Evidently, in the early middle ages, Shushanik was not yet celebrated as a major saint of the Caucasus, and the realm of her remembrance was confined to the region of Gugareti. Her Georgian and Armenian *Martyrdoms* too were written for this local audience. It was only after, and as a result of

---

[29] Cyril Toumanoff provides a comprehensive historic overview in 'Armeno-Georgian Marchlands', part of *Studies in Christian Caucasian History*, 437–99.

the Schism, that her fame left the boundaries of the region, turning her into a great Armenian and Georgian national saint.[30]

A regional saint whose relics marked the buffer zone between the two realms, and whose cult was far less vibrant, if altogether unknown, outside this particular geopolitical context, in Uxtanēs's writing was reimagined as a national saint. Due to the strong political expediency of Shushanik's cult, Uxtanēs believed that the revival of the memory of this fifth-century martyr was essential, 'especially because [C'urtaw] was a royal residence where the tomb of St Shushan and the site of her torture and martyrdom are also shown up to the present time. It is there that her holy and venerable relics are shrined where we also have gone on pilgrimage many times and have kissed that holy place.'[31] Uxtanēs wished to create a standard narrative of the Armenian relationship with the apostate Georgians, by breathing political life into and through Shushanik into the main political concern of his age – Tsurtavi. In these novel geopolitical circumstances, the peripheral region acquired centrality, and the city's as well as the region's patron saint was incorporated into the grand history of Christian Caucasia. Uxtanēs's *History* is structured in a way that the story of the

---

[30] Paul Peeters was convinced that the cult of Shushanik was in its entirety elaborated in the context of the Armeno–Georgian polemic and that both the Georgian and Armenian versions of her *Martyrdom* strove to 'nationalise' the saint in the post-Schism context. Peeters argued that the Armenian longer version of the *Martyrdom of Shushanik* was dependant on a Georgian prototype, because of several nonsensical passages that could only be explained by mistranslations from the Georgian. However, this source text, according to Peeters, was not the existing version of the *Martyrdom*, but an entirely different redaction created during the Armeno–Georgian debates of the early seventh century. Moreover, Peeters believed that the very cult of St Shushanik was a post-Schism phenomenon, and was created by the Armenian population of C'urtavi after the Schism in order to preserve the Armenian identity of the region. Shushanik was appropriated as a rhetorical device by both sides, which correspondingly resulted in a Georgian attempt to 'nationalise' the saint and the production of a Georgian version of her life. In response, the Armenians produced their own 'national' version of Shushanik's life. As for the extant Georgian *Martyrdom of Shushanik*, this version, according to Peeters, was created after the tenth century, as a response to Uxtanēs, who promoted the cult of Shushanik in his book without referring to any standard account of the princess's life. This Georgian creation was also supposedly a counterbalance to the shorter Armenian version, which was pro-Armenian in spirit and was translated into Georgian in the tenth century. Despite the elegance of this theory, Ilia Abuladze convincingly demonstrated in his critical edition of the *Martyrdom of Shushanik* that Iakob of C'urtavi's extant version is indeed an original fifth-century production and that the existing Armenian version was created soon thereafter. Peeters, 'Ste Shushanik', 245–307.

[31] Uxtanēs, *Patmowt'iwn*, ed. Aleksidze, 63; tr. Arzoumanian, 63.

Caucasian Church Schism is read as a historical re-enactment of Shushanik's death: an Armenian saint martyred by a Georgian interpreted as a holy marriage betrayed by her apostate husband, finally culminating in a holy union rejected by the apostate Georgians. Katholikos Kyrion of Iberia, the nemesis of Armenian cultural memory, who had allegedly orchestrated the Schism, was the new Varsk'en, a treacherous Georgian who once again killed Shushanik by betraying her memory and dishonouring her relics. An Armenian princess who found death in the hands of the Georgians mirrored the fate of Gogarene, an essentially Armenian land that found spiritual death in Georgia.[32] Shushanik, this seventh-century symbol of unity of the two Caucasian lands, was rediscovered in Uxtanēs's vision as a reminder of Georgia's original sin. In Uxtanēs's narrative, Shushanik was reimagined as an Armenian gift to the Georgians, and the symbol of the great debt that the Georgians owed the Armenians since their apostasy. For this purpose, Uxtanēs constructed an elaborate sequence of associations whereby, through a symbolic reference to Shushanik, the entire Armeno–Georgian relationship boiled down to the dialectic of the gift and the debt.

## 3.6 The Debt

The political significance of Shushanik's relics transcended the immediate geopolitical context in Uxtanēs's narrative, and acquired centrality in the grand narratives of Caucasian history. Since the Schism, over time, Armenians and Georgians have developed competing and sometimes mutually exclusive views of the origins of Christian cultures and Orthodoxies in Caucasia. While the Georgian narrative points to St Nino as their enlightener, the Armenian tradition, initiated by Agathangelos, declares St Gregory the Illuminator as the illuminator of all of Caucasia, including Iberia and its adjunct regions. Later, in or just before the eighth century, Movsēs Xorenac'i' made a compromise between the Armenian and Georgian narratives and introduced Nino into the Armenian historical discourse. Xorenac'i turned Nino's story into a sub-narrative of St Gregory the Illuminator's grand story, claiming that all Nino did was to act on Gregory's behalf and on his instructions, coordinating with the patriarch her missionary work, and reporting back to him. It was Gregory who commanded her to erect the cross on top of a hill near Mtskheta, one of the most sacred sites in Caucasia, so often referred to throughout Armenian

---

[32] This series of violence and treasons was further confirmed by another murder that, according to an oral tradition, took place in those same sombre days, when Georgians committed a similar offence in the same liminal zone. See Aleksidze, 'Murder at Mt Kangar', 130–49.

and Georgian writing.³³ In his revisionist history, Xorenacʻi attempted to repair the incongruence between the Georgian and the Armenian accounts of conversion. Xorenacʻi took the schema of the story of Iberia's conversion as known to late Roman historians and inserted it into his *History of Armenia*, by essentially repeating Socrates Scholasticus's account, which in turn is based on Rufinus's *Ecclesiastic History*.³⁴ However, he also altered the established story by shifting the centre of narrative gravity from Iberia and Constantinople to Iberia and Armenia. In Xorenacʻi's revision, the newly converted royal family dispatched an embassy with a request for a bishop, not to Constantinople, as told by Socrates, but to Armenia. Xorenacʻi and subsequent Armenian writers respect Nino greatly. She is honoured as a blessed miracle worker, a healer and a 'female apostle' (*arakʻeluhi*), yet her mandate is given to her by Gregory. Nevertheless, despite Xorenacʻi's rewriting, and his unmatched authority in medieval Armenian tradition, the Nino story was never incorporated into the original *Life of Gregory*. Ever since, these diverging accounts of the conversion of the Caucasus paradoxically existed side by side in the Armenian and Georgian literary traditions.

Uxtanēs adopted Xorenacʻi's rewriting and cleverly introduced it into his rhetoric. He essentially conceptualises the entire history of Armenian–Georgian relations as a gift–debt dialectical process, and places Shushanik within this sequence of debts that the Georgians owed to Armenians along with practically all markers of their Christian identity: 'Like Nunē [i.e. Nino] she [Shushanik] became a woman who filled the office of an Apostle, whose preaching spread all over the country of Georgia. And those who came to visit her were instructed by her in their piety, and many sick and afflicted who came to her were also healed.'³⁵ The comparison with Nino is not a mere acknowledgement of Shushanik's comparable missionary accomplishment in the region. Uxtanēs specifically pairs Shushanik and Nino as gift-givers of 'civilisation' and further commodifies the two saints as Armenian gifts granted to the Georgians, which the latter failed to reciprocate. According to this logic, therefore, Shushanik, like Nino, is effectively Georgia's enlightener. Like Nino's evangelism, Shushanik's mission too was accomplished from, or rather through, Armenia. By sending Nino, the Armenians gave Georgians the ultimate gift – Christianity. The figure of Shushanik was thus incorporated into a larger narrative of 'the gift of civilisation', making her a symbol of the eternal moral dependency of the Georgians on the Armenians. Just as earlier Movsēs Xorenacʻi

---

³³ Movsēs Xorenacʻi, *Patmowtʻiwn*, ed. Thomson, 235; tr. Thomson, 235.
³⁴ Rufinus, *History* 10.11, tr. Amidon, 396–400.
³⁵ Uxtanēs, *Patmowtʻiwn*, ed. Aleksidze, 200; tr. Arzoumanian, 129.

made Nino an envoy of Gregory by dismissing his sources, so did Uxtanēs's Shushanik become an ethnic Armenian woman whose purpose was to enlighten the Georgians on behalf of the Armenian nation. Consequently, in Uxtanēs's rhetorical framework, the 'apostasy' of the Georgians was a betrayal of Shushanik's memory and, by extension, a betrayal of the foundations of Christianity that the Georgians had previously received from the Armenians. In time, the political concept of the gift was extended to other aspects of culture, including the Georgian alphabet and writing, which, as the Armenian tradition maintains, was also created by the Armenian St Mesrop/Maštoc' along with the Armenian and the Albanian ones.

Uxtanēs's creation, the 'new' Shushanik, a mediator between Armenians and Georgians, was a gift as well as a gift-giver, and a reminder of Armenian moral superiority against the Georgians. After Uxtanēs, many Armenian authors deplored the forgetfulness of the Georgians and their alleged zeal to whitewash the true history of Caucasia. In the perception of the tenth-century Armenian theologian and monk Aharon of Vanand, for example, Christianity, as an Armenian gift to the Georgians, was embodied by these two female saints and embedded into the sacred objects associated with them. After Georgia's apostasy, Aharon's apocryphal story claims, Georgia's holiest relics, including Nino's cross, left Georgia and went (back) to Armenia. This happened through the labour of St Shushanik who had predicted Georgia's apostasy, that is their Chalcedonianism. For Aharon, the Cross of Nino was a symbol of religious and political stability in Georgia, whereas its removal and return to Armenia signalled Georgia's apostasy. Aharon creates an amalgam of existing historical narratives by reducing them to the story of Nino's cross. He tells how Nunē's (Nino in Armenian) holy cross and many other relics bequeathed by St Gregory were liberated from the 'bondage of foreign races' on Queen Shushanik's orders. Then a certain monk Andreas took the relics, then went to the hill where Nino's cross was kept (the Jvari above Mtskheta), cleansed and wrapped it in a white cloth and, with the help of local authorities, dispatched it 'to the west'. The cross was allegedly kept in the province of Sper, in the cave of Mt Parxar. He stayed there with the cross for seven years, until he heard about the death of Shushanik. Aharon then claims that his own monastery of the Holy Cross was founded on 'the Holy Cross of Mtskheta'. He also says that he had learned this story from Agathangelos, the *Martyrdom of Shushanik*, the *Life of Sahak* and other sources.[36]

---

[36] For the edition of Aharon's narrative, see Akinean, *Die Einführung des Christentums*, 105–13.

Although Aharon forwards the readers to Agathangelos, the *Martyrdom of Shushanik* and the *Life of Sahak* as his sources, none of the surviving versions of Agathangelos or any other text mentioned had anything to say about either St Nino or her cross. None of the details of the story is known to any of the several versions of the *Martyrdom of Shushanik* either. Instead, they point to an oral or at least apocryphal evolution of the Shushanik tradition specifically in the context of the Caucasian conflict. When the Georgians broke the spiritual marriage deal, the Armenians merely took away what they had brought as gifts – Christianity and its symbols – and this through the labour of this Armeno–Georgian border saint.

Thus, two of the greatest female saints of the wider Caucasian region were conceptualised in Armenian and partly Georgian rhetoric as objects of exchange. With Xorenac'i's rewriting, which became standard in Armenian writing, St Nino was essentially stripped of her agency, and reimagined as a mere mediator and further commodified as a gift. Their memory and material remains, such as Shushanik's relics, or Nino's cross, as well as the stories associated with them, were commodified as symbols of unreciprocated gift-giving. As such, they served as moral and political legitimisers to territorial pretences during the lengthy Caucasian conflicts, a trope that reverberated in many other aspects of Caucasian historical narratives. In other words, the value of the materiality and memory of both female saints resided in their convertibility to political capital.

# Conclusion to Part I
# Relics, Gender and Politics in Late Antique Caucasia

By the second half of the fifth century, when the first saintly narratives were written in Caucasia, the Eastern Roman emperors had an experience of utilising saints and their material remains to legitimise their rule. The relics were miraculously revealed, majestically transferred to the Imperial capital, and solemnly deposited in new foundations. Yet, what is absent in Eastern Roman narratives, is a deliberation on the deeper political or historical values of individual relics and relic assemblages, as well as how exactly they contribute to the political agenda of a monarch. The Caucasian foundational narratives on the one hand sourced their tropes from the foundational activity of Constantine and the conceptualisations designed by the first Christian emperors, yet also contributed to the political theology of saints and relics with a uniquely South Caucasian experience.

In Armenian writing, due to specific political circumstances, such as the newly abolished kingship, anti-Sasanian ideology and the necessity to sustain the Armenian nation's continuity, the ideological valence of saints' relics emerged as an integral component in the creation of a quintessentially Armenian vision of history. These ideas were both a result of the unique ethnic and religious experiences in Late Antique Caucasia and were indebted to Eastern Roman and Iranian concepts of legitimate kingship, political continuity and royal charisma. The narratives of the foundations of Christianity were deeply embedded in identity rhetoric, and some of the foundational texts discussed above became primary reference points for the South Caucasian writers of subsequent centuries.

In early Albanian, Armenian and Georgian historiography, the cult of saints and their relics projected a tripartite valence in the realm of the political: of historic time, territory and political authority. Relics were incorporated into the discourse of time, of the past (biblical, non-Christian, dynastic, Iranian) and the present, and were thus instrumentalised in identity rhetoric. They were used to circumscribe and mark the kingdom's limits and legitimise charismatic kingship. Crucially, the physical uncovering of hidden treasure, as a foundational activity, was accompanied by the discovery of narratives embedded in these relics. The miraculous manifestation of the relics was both physical as well as narratological, since along with material objects, the stories behind them (original Christianisation, stories of old kings, old martyrdom accounts) previously 'forgotten' were also revealed.

As objects of value, relics travel both between spaces and between different 'regimes of value'. As such, the treasure and the relics are their owner's 'inalienable possessions'. The material value of treasure and the religious value of relics conflate in their owners' political bodies, and are ultimately exchanged for political sovereignty, charismatic legitimacy or political stability. Thus, they are given away while simultaneously kept by their owners. These objects also act as stabilisers, as they slow down 'generation and change'.[1] P'arnavaz's Kartli and Vač'agan's Albania are stabilised by their foundational 'objects', whether treasure or relics, as opposed to their former precarity and ambiguity.

Arguably, these temporal, spatial and legal valences of sainthood, as illustrated by Armenian and Albanian narratives, were elaborated even further in early medieval Georgian tradition. Here, to this assemblage of values, yet another aspect was added – the gender of the saints and saintly remains. The Georgian *Mok'c'evay k'art'lisay* and the *Martyrdom of Queen Shushanik* raise additional questions: What happens to the temporal, spatial and legal valences of memory and materiality of saints when they are amplified with a feminine aspect? In other words, what happens when the political and the metaphysical are triangulated with the third 'hypostasis' – the feminine?

The early Nino tradition crystallised in the era when the Christian Empire faced an identity crisis and was engulfed in apocalyptic expectations following Heraclius's initial success and eventual catastrophe. The *Mok'c'evay*, in its broadest sense, is a 'nationalised' response to the dissemination of apocalyptic literature, in which the emancipation of Kartli and the Georgian language was celebrated in the face of the 'decline' of the Christian Empire. It was in this apocalyptic context that Nino's image and the grand story of the conversion that she embodied were conceptualised.

There are several conceptual innovations that the *Mok'c'evay* corpus has created. Here, relics retain their foundational 'value', yet generate further dynamism through their burial and discovery. Kartli's two principal relics, the Lord's Tunic and Elijah's sheepskin, their burial and discovery, are seen

---

[1] Serres, *Genesis*, 87. Cf. the study of holy objects and treasure as stabilisers of society and change in highland Svaneti: Batiashvili and Aleksidze, 'Symbolic Treasure, Care, and Materiality', *passim*.

as material manifestations of Kartli's history and the future. The structural symmetry of the *Conversion* narrative, which places Nino in the centre, and collapses upon the erection of the Living Pillar and the accompanying apocalyptic dream, forges a visual imprint of this history. Essentially, what the *Mok'c'evay* tries to achieve is a conceptual translation of the Holy Land from Jerusalem to Kartli through a dynamic interplay of Jewish and Christian identities, relics, their stories and the gender of its protagonist – St Nino.

The second innovation of the *Conversion* rhetoric is the conceptualisation of the 'exception'. Similarly to the charismatic preachers and founders of the Caucasian highlands, Nino as a woman was conceptually problematic. Imagining her as an exception, however, allowed for further saturation of her figure with historic, political and apocalyptic imagery. While Agathangelos inaugurated the usage of the cult and relics of saints in the deliberations over history and identity, Nino's gender, as an ambiguous phenomenon, contributed to an even further elaboration on historic time and political space. The reversion of gender roles signalled the grand detour in history. In the imagery coined by the *Conversion of Kartli* and the tradition based on this narrative, Nino is presented as a liminal figure who encapsulates the *raison d'être* of the Georgian body politic on the periphery of the Oecumene and at the foothills of the Caucasian borderland. Nino's evangelism was processed in political, geographic and apocalyptic terms, with her cult encapsulating Kartli's political body and its limits, especially its northern boundaries. Nino was established as a border-crosser, a traveller in the liminal and ambiguous time-space in between the two times of Georgia's salvation history and in between Georgia's belonging to the apocalyptic 'North' and the 'South'. These features of the cult of Nino, along with the discourse of ambiguity and exceptionality, were appropriated by the oral traditions ungarbled by theologisations and rationalisations of Nino's eulogists, and reimagined as exceptional figures such as Minani. The figures of lore, modelled after Nino, act as charismatic founders who, despite their gender, and due to emergency and the extraordinary times of history, transcend their feminine selves and acquire political and religious bodies. These ambiguous female figures travel between the two metaphysical realms, of men and gods, as well as the two geopolitical realms between the South and the North Caucasus.

Early medieval Georgian and Armenian tradition has celebrated yet another female saint whose feminine identity has arguably contributed to an exceptional space that she has occupied in literary traditions and cult practices. The cult of queen Shushanik the martyr developed independently, at least to a certain extent, from that of St Nino, yet converged in some important aspects. While Nino was conceptualised as a mediatrix between the two times of Georgia's history and two geographic realms, so the holy Queen Shushanik, due to the exceptional nature of her cult, symbolised the physical and conceptual no man's land in Caucasia, between the Armenian and Georgian realms, as well as the history of orthodoxies and heterodoxies in the broader South Caucasian region.

Claude Levi-Strauss's concept of the 'exchange of women', based on the earlier study of the exchange and commodification of women as gifts by Marcel Mauss, can help us understand the particularities of the political life of Shushanik's body.[2] Shushanik was perceived as a gift that required reciprocation well before her relics acquired any additional meaning. As explained by Mauss, the gift is not so much a gift but rather a loan that has to be repaid:

> In all these instances there is a series of rights and duties about consuming and repaying existing side by side with rights and duties about giving and receiving ... Food, women, children, possessions, charms, land, labour, services, religious offices, rank – everything is stuff to be given away and repaid. In perpetual interchange of what we may call spiritual matter, comprising men and things, these elements pass and repass between clans and individuals, ranks, sexes and generations.[3]

Giving while retaining was a feature that the relics of saints retained and which was particularly augmented in the middle ages, when the relics were used as diplomatic gifts, endowments, investments or loans. The question that Shushanik's and Nino's case raised, however, was whether the gender of the saint and her relics was a value added. Indeed, as we saw, the relics of a female saint have the potential of acquiring unique political implications by revealing exceptional relationships with body politic. In Nino's case, her femininity was conceptualised as an exception marked by the reversal of gender roles in her persona, whereas Shushanik was conceptualised as a gift that required recipcrocation. In both instances, the two female saints acted as mediators, as liminal beings of sorts travelling between two structures, existential, geographic, political or religious. The relevance of their cults was sustained precisely by this very function of mediation, and declined where mediation was not at stake.

Shushanik's political body has revealed two functions: she was a liminal figure who symbolised the buffer zone between the two realms, and

---

[2] Lévi-Strauss, *Elementary Structures*.
[3] Mauss, *Gift*, 11–12.

was conceptualised as a commodity of exchange between the Armenians and the Georgians. The relics of Shushanik were presented as symbols of the liminal space between the two political, cultural, ethnic and mnemonic realms. The initial and original function of Shushanik's martyr shrine was to ritualistically celebrate the border zone between the Armenian and the Georgian realms, Gogarene. In this discourse, Shushanik's political body projected two shades of liminality: first, the political and historic ambiguity of the buffer zone, and second, the ambiguities offered by blurred commemorative practices that separated the two times of Caucasian history – the legendary period of religious and political unity and the present state of schism. In between the two times was the fuzzy memory of transition from one to another where the memory of Shushanik was situated.

As a liminal figure, Shushanik marked the structureless situation between two structures, between *illo tempore* and the experienced past, Armenia and Georgia, Orthodoxy and heresy, and so on. Meanwhile, she also symbolised a process of movement of goods, by sealing a contract between the two realms. Along with Shushanik, Nino too, while absent in earlier narratives, was rediscovered as a gift. Both her and Shushanik were commodified as objects of value, as Armenian investments in Georgia, which, following the 'catastrophe' of the seventh century, Georgians failed to reciprocate. Since the Schism, Georgians have allegedly forgotten this great debt that they owed the Armenians by becoming Chalcedonian and apostatising from true faith. Therefore, all the symbols of this original gift had to be symbolically transported back to Armenia, since, one way or another, as Marcel Mauss had famously said, 'all gifts come back to the giver'.

The symbols of ambiguous unity, articulated in the *Book of Letters*, were transformed into symbols of distinct alterity in Uxtanēs's vision. Shushanik, a marginal saint, largely unknown to Armenian historians, acquired centrality in medieval national narratives when she became a symbol of mediation, of exchange, or rather of failed investment. Through the latter historian's political imagination, the drama of the Schism was assigned a specific realm of memory. The liminality of the Schism, as a transformative event in Caucasian history, was projected onto the geographic liminality of the region of Gugareti, and onto Shushanik, the ultimate liminal figure and mediator between the two realms. The place of Shushanik's martyrdom, Nino's cross of Mtskheta, and Gugark' became realms of memory that created 'another history' – the history of the separation of the Armenians and the Georgians.

By the turn of the millennium, while the Armenian tradition imagined the cult of Georgia's women as Armenia's gifts to the Georgians, as failed investments of sorts in their northern neighbours, the emerging Georgian historical and religious writing was reassessing its foundations. The emergence of a new Georgian kingdom with a new militant dynasty, the Bagratids, at its head created a new political and cultural horizon. Instead of Jerusalem, the Georgian writers began looking towards Constantinople and reassessing their religious identity with Constantinople in mind. Old saints were either neglected or being discovered in a new light, by serving the emerging idea of Georgia as the private 'allotment' of the Mother of God. Soon, by the end of the twelfth century, the kingdom of Georgia experienced something dramatically novel that defined Georgia's subsequent ideological history – a woman was crowned as a monarch. The coronation of Queen Tamar raised yet unseen religious and political problems, and many aspects of the cult of saints were re-evaluated with these political and religious conundrums in mind.

# Part II

# Introduction to Part II
# The Saintly World of the Bagratids

Out of several momentous events in medieval Georgian cultural memory, few were as traumatic as the invasion of Marwan II, nicknamed 'the Deaf', who later became the fourth Umayyad Caliph (744–50). By 736, 'the lands of Kartli, Armenia and Ran [Caucasian Albania] had been devastated and there were no buildings left, nor food for men, nor fodder for cattle'.[1] Tens of thousands of refugees left Kartli, and following upstream the River Mtkvari, they settled in the mountainous deserts of Tao and Klarjeti in north-eastern Anatolia. Yet, the members of the ruling Bagratid Dynasty were still nominally in power for a few more years in Kartli.

A new era in Georgian history began when the Bagratid Ašot (d. 826) was forced to flee the Arabs from his homeland and emigrate south-west, beyond the Javakheti Plateau in the region of Klarjeti, the upper banks of the Mtkvari/Kur River. As claimed by the eleventh-century chroniclers, Ašot was a son of the Klarjeti branch of the Bagratid House, and, as such, he must have considered himself a legitimate heir to his new homeland.[2] The previous rulers in the region had died out and warfare, epidemic and the devastating invasions had severely depopulated the territories that Ašot claimed. Yet, unlike central and eastern Kartli, there he felt safe, far from the Arabs and close to the then-friendly Byzantines and Armenian principalities. Ašot rebuilt as his residence Artanuji, a fortress on a high cliff that oversaw the strategic routes from the Black Sea to Kartli and

---

[1] Juanšer, *c'xovreba*, ed. Kaukhchishvili, 239.10–11: https://titus.uni-frankfurt.de/texte/etcs/cauc/ageo/kcx1/kcx1.htm.
[2] Sumbat Davit'isże, *c'xovreba da ucqeba*, ed. Kaukchishvili, 375–6. On Ašot's genealogy, see Aleksidze, 'bagrationt'a dinastiis šesaxeb', 120–8.

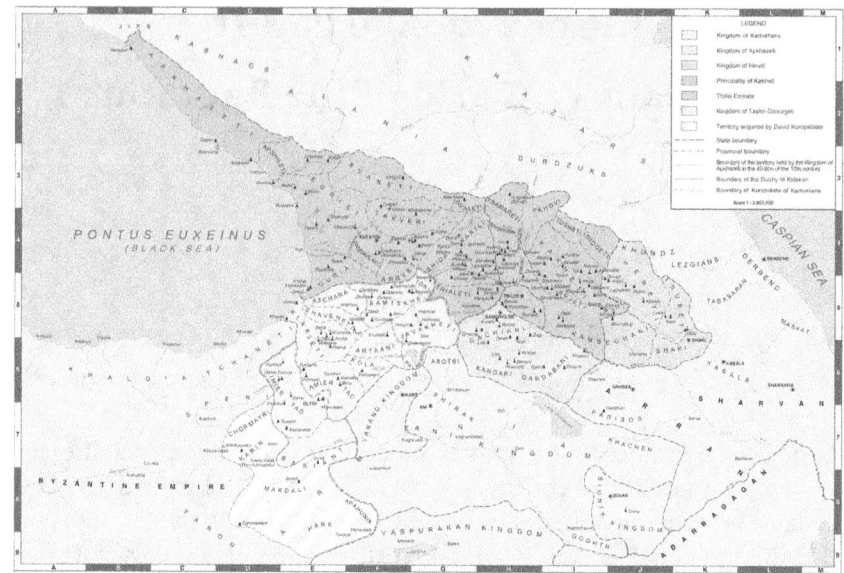

Map II.1  Georgian kingdoms and principalities in the second half of the tenth century. Source: D. Muskhelishvili, Historical Atlas of Georgia.

further to the eastern Georgian principalities.[3] He repopulated and restored the area with the help of previously migrated monastic communities and their greatest authority, archimandrite Grigol of Xanc't'a. By the tenth century, through the efforts of these two men, the area now commonly known as Tao-Klarjeti, ruled by the Bagratid House, became a cultural wellspring as well as a political magnet for all Georgian principalities and most of the Christian South Caucasus.[4] The Byzantines honoured Ašot with the title of *kouropalatēs*, the first of his house, while the Georgians hailed him as king (*mep'e*). Indeed, Ašot I, remembered as 'the Great', was the first Bagratid ruler to give an impetus to the emergence of the united Georgian monarchy. While for the next three centuries historic Kartli, Mtskheta,

---

[3] Constantine Porphyrogenitus characterises Artanuji as 'very strongly defended, and has moreover a considerable suburban area like a provincial city, and the commerce of Trapezus and of Iberia and of Abasgia and from the whole country of Armenia and Syria comes to it, and it has an enormous customs revenue from this commerce. The country of the city of Ardanoutzin, the "Arzyn", is both extensive and fertile, and it is a key of Iberia and Abasgia and of the Mischians'. Constantine Porphyrogenitus, *De Administrando Imperio*, 216–17. See, also, Evans, 'Case of Artanuji', 345–64.

[4] Martin-Hisard, 'Du T'ao-K'lardzheti à l'Athos', 34–46; 'Moines et monastères géorgiens', 5–64.

Tbilisi and their surroundings became part of the Tbilisi Emirate, Kartli as a concept had migrated to Tao and Klarjeti (see Map II.1).

As the first millennium was nearing its end, Georgian, Armenian and other principalities in Caucasia began to experience political, cultural and ideological transformations. Contemporary Georgian scholarship, although fed with primordialist sentiments, likes to see the ninth century as the dawn of the unification of the Kingdom of Georgia, a process which a century later culminated in the reign of King Bagrat III (960–1014), the first king of what was to become the united Georgia. In a sense, and should we abandon a historicist perspective, this is true, as starting from the ninth century, the principalities on the territory, and beyond what constitutes modern Georgia, engaged in a long struggle for supremacy in the Caucasus with a determination to unite the region under their sovereignty. By the early eleventh century, it was the Georgian branch of Bagratid House that was able to seize strategically the most critical regions, becoming first the most powerful, then the sole ruler of the united Georgian kingdom.

As Georgia's political centre of gravity shifted westward, Constantinople came into the religious and political focus of its royal and monastic elites. The relationship with the Byzantines was at times amicable but even more often hostile, a political dynamic that determined Georgian religious and political rhetoric for the centuries that followed, until the replacement of Byzantium by the Ottomans and the collapse of the united Georgian monarchy in the fifteenth century. Crucially for us, this relationship also created fundamentally new political and ideological representations of the cult of saints in Georgian writing and art.

The Byzantine–Georgian relations experienced a dramatic turn a century-and-a-half after Ašot's death, during the rule of his descendant, David *kouropalates* of Tao (983–1001). Apart from his foundational enterprises (such as the majestic churches of Khakhuli, Otkhta, Parkhali and others) and patronage of art and manuscript production, David's greatest political achievement which, in a sense, defined Georgia's further political and religious history was his military support to the Emperor Basil II (958–1025) against the rebellious Bardas Skleros. As related by the *Life of Ioane and Ep'tʻwime Mtʻacmindeli*, Basil's mother Theophano appealed to the Athonite monk and former commander Ioane-T'ornik to seek David's support against Bardas. T'ornik returned to Tao, and in 978 or 979, together with Bardas Phokas and David's twelve thousand cavalry, routed Skleros. In exchange, youthful Basil granted David the title of *kouropalates*, and rewarded him with a life-long ownership of the territories of upper Tao all the way to today's Erzurum. As for Ioane-T'ornik, he returned to Mt Athos and invested the amassed trophies in the foundation of a Georgian monastery now known as Iveron.[5]

The foundation of the Iveron Monastery was a momentous event in the history of the Georgian Church and its literary history. It was due to the extensive 'Byzantinising' effort of the Athonite monks that the Georgian Church abandoned the Jerusalemite liturgical practices and switched to the Constantinopolitan rite, a policy originally conceived by Grigol Xanc't'eli and his contemporaries. Old Hagiopolite liturgical books that stemmed from the Holy Land were abandoned, and Constantinopolitan ones were adopted. Iveron's *hegoumenoi*, Euthymios (955–1028), Giorgi (1009–65) and their successors initiated a massive translation project from Greek. Along with the appearance of new translations of virtually all existing genres of Byzantine literature, practically the entire Georgian corpus was retranslated and rewritten.[6] Somewhat later, Ephrem Mc'ire (the Lesser) (d. 1101) of the Black Mountain near Antioch and his companions and successors produced a corpus of what has now come to be known as Georgian *hellenophile* literature.[7] Rewriting was justified by the desire to emulate the Greek originals in their theological rigour, or to retranslate pieces that had been earlier translated through a third medium, mostly Armenian. Since the eleventh century, the spirit of rewriting has dominated Georgian monastic and royal scriptoria.[8]

The hellenophilism of the eleventh and twelfth centuries, and the Bagratid zeal to emulate the Byzantine emperors, however, was just one side of the complicated history of the Georgian–Byzantine relations. While the amicable relationship with the Byzantines reached its pinnacle during the reign of the Emperor Basil and David II *kouropalatēs*, it was soon thereafter that relations hit a new low, and have deteriorated since. Ten years after the victory over Skleros, David allied with Bardas Phokas (940–89), who quickly captured large chunks of Asia Minor. A partnership with the powerful general seemed reasonable. However, in 989 Phokas was defeated, and his allies faced Basil's wrath. As a punishment, Basil requested that David cede the territories that had been granted to him. While David bargained with Basil, and temporarily retained the lands, his

---

[5] Grdzelidze, *Georgian Monks on Mount Athos*, 56–9. See also John Skylitzes, *Synopsis of Byzantine History*, tr. Wortley, 300–13.
[6] Aleksidze, 'Georgian', 620–1; Gippert, 'Georgian Hagiorites', 75–83; Grdzelidze, *Georgian Monks on Mount Athos*, 68–70.
[7] Bezarashvili, 'Hellenophilism in Georgian Literature', 335–64.
[8] Aleksidze, 'Rewriting Histories', 101–19.

death in 1001 became a turning point. The lands known in Georgian as Imier Tao (beyond the mountains of Tao) were immediately upon David's death reannexed by Basil. As these lands constituted the core of both Byzantine and Georgian strategic interests, Basil's takeover provoked a series of wars between the two in the early years of the eleventh century. While Basil was busy fighting the Bulgarians, King Giorgi I (1014–27), son of Bagrat III (1008–14) David's adopted son, seized the opportunity, forged an anti-Byzantine coalition, and between 1014 and 1018 occupied the territory. In 1019, however, Basil crushed the Bulgarian resistance and turned his attention towards Giorgi, demanding that the Georgians vacate the territory. Giorgi refused and the 1021–3 Byzantine–Georgian Wars ensued. Despite Giorgi's attempt to secure an alliance with Nikephoros Phokas, the war ended in Georgian defeat, and Giorgi was forced to cede the territories back to Basil.[9] Giorgi lost far more than the original territories granted to David. Klarjeti, Kola and Javakheti were also ceded to the Byzantines. These lands together with several Armenian territories were integrated into the newly created Theme of Iberia.[10] The tensions with the Byzantines continued with the reign of Giorgi's son, Bagrat IV (1027–72). Finally, in 1030, Bagrat's mother Mariam Artsruni secured a treaty between her son and the Byzantines which ended in Bagrat IV accepting the title of *kouropalates* and marrying the daughter of Romanos III Argyros (968–1034).[11]

The relocation of the focus of Georgian political affairs from the Muslim emirates to the west, towards Constantinople, altered the geopolitical thinking and the conceptual apparatus employed in political rhetoric. Since David II, multiple inscriptions and documents attest to a new title in the style of the Georgian kings, where David II, Bagrat III, Giorgi I and Bagrat IV are honoured as the 'Kouropalates of all East'.[12] The 'of all East' addition to the Byzantine honorific titles granted to the Georgian kings by the Byzantines emperors was a specifically Georgian insertion unknown to the Byzantine sources. It conveyed the Bagratid claim to all the territories that had belonged to David *kouropalates*, and that were since his death an object of contention between the Byzantines and the Georgians.[13] The 'of all East' addition, with

---

[9] John Skylitzes, *Synopsis of Byzantine History*, tr. Wortley, 346–7.
[10] Rayfield, *Edge of Empires*, 76.
[11] Ibid., 76–8.
[12] Zhordania, *k'ronikebi* 1, 108. Nikolaishvili, *Byzantium and the Georgian World*, 69–70.
[13] Goiladze, 'Reflection', 423–8.

its ever-expanding connotations, clung to the Georgian kings until very late in the middle ages. The Bagratids now identified themselves in relation to Constantinople, and squeezed between the Romans and Seljuks and other eastern powers (Mongols and Persians), their imagined geographies were now saturated with East–West trajectories. Georgia's northernness, with its eschatological connotations, became an idea of history, confined to the historical discourses of sanctity and martyrdom.

At the height of the conflict with the Byzantines in the eleventh century, Georgian historians bitterly portrayed the Byzantine emperors and generals in an unambiguously negative light. Among the most opinionated anti-Byzantine campaigners were the anonymous *Chronicle of Kartli* (*Matiane K'art'lisa*) and Sumbat Davit'isże, the Bagratid chronicler. For Sumbat, Basil was a vile character and a nemesis of the Georgians. In his irritation with the Byzantines, Sumbat illustrates Basil's erratic nature: After another unsuccessful attack on the Georgian forces and the Byzantine retreat, 'King Basil was angered and brought the life-giving Cross [wrapped] in a holy cloth [*mandilit'a cmidit'a*]. And he threw it on the ground and said: "If you deliver me into the hands of the enemy I shall never worship you in eternity." And immediately, as he did and said this, Giorgi's armies, who were the first to arrive, were defeated and put to flight.'[14] In an even more hateful diatribe against Constantine VIII (1025–8), Sumbat describes the circumstances of his death: 'And as the entire East was thrown into disarray, the wrath swiftly reached the lawless king Constantine, similarly to the ungodly Julian, due to his mistreatment of our King Bagrat, and for plundering his fatherland [*mamuli*].'[15] Sumbat introduced a key anti-Byzantine rhetorical trope here, which appears repeatedly in monastic and court writing, criticising the Byzantines for the lack of steadfastness in Orthodoxy and reminding them of their dubious history of heterodoxy, particularly iconoclasm. Iconoclasm, which had blemished Byzantium and had supposedly left Georgia untouched, became an important tool for the development of the rhetoric of Georgian moral superiority against the Byzantines.

Since the eleventh century, until the formal termination of kingship in 1801, it was the religious and political ideology of the Bagratid House that dominated Georgia's political, literary and cultural landscapes. With other

---

[14] Sumbat Davit'isże, *c'xovreba da ucqeba*, ed. Kaukhchishvili, 384.18–21: https://titus.uni-frankfurt.de/texte/etcs/cauc/ageo/kcx1/kcx1lex.htm. For the same episode in a different chronicle, see *Matiane k'art'lisay*, ed. Kaukhchishvili, 287–8. tr. Thomson, 284. Corrected by Nikoloz Aleksidze.

[15] Sumbat Davit'isże, *c'xovreba da ucqeba*, ed. Kaukhchishvili, 386.18–20.

rhetorical devices, the cult of the saints acquired novel centrality in the emerging Bagratid ideologies, and underwent a drastic change, both as an evolution of the *Conversion* narrative, and as a departure from the pre-Bagratid foundational texts.

Four developments affected the transformation of the cult of saints in medieval Georgia. First, the geopolitical self-conception articulated by the *Conversion* tradition and the religious-political conceptualisation of Iberia as of a 'northern realm' became, in the current political state of affairs, rather obsolete. The political and religious attraction to Constantinople, and an almost simultaneous confrontation with the Byzantines over the north-eastern Anatolian regions, coupled with the growing antagonisms in the multi-ethnic monasteries in Byzantium, affected also the geopolitical focus and locus of the Bagratid authors. The imitation, emulation and confrontation with the Byzantines spearheaded by the Bagratids changed the political nature of the cult of saints for good. St Nino, although still celebrated in her *vitae*, lost her geopolitical significance. The cult of Shushanik also dwindled, as the polemic with the Armenians lost its political immediacy. New times brought new necessities and a search for new beginnings. Histories, and among them saintly narratives, were rewritten with an aim to create a novel idea of Orthodox continuity in emulation of the Byzantines. In their quest for a new rhetoric of legitimisation, the Bagratids, who boldly styled themselves as the kings 'of all east', also applied to the cult of saints, yet in radically different ways.

This effort of the Bagratids and of the Georgian monks in Byzantium resulted in the 'masculinisation' of the saintly pantheon, and a relative sidelining of old female saints. The traditional foundation narrative retained its centrality, yet alternative narratives were also elaborated, with attempts to override the feminine character of the original conversion account, and masculinise the foundation of Georgian Christianity, as well as its saintly landscape. Georgia's apostolic foundations were sought in which the Apostles' journeys to Georgia imitated and overrode the old Nino story. Nino's foundation activity was sidelined with a story of Andrew the First-Called, the allegedly original founder of Christianity in Georgia. Further, this 'masculinisation', prompted by the expansion of the royal court's militaristic culture, also manifested in the dramatic expansion of the cult of the male saint par excellence, St George, the biblical King David and to a lesser extent of other warrior saints.

Thirdly, the fusion of the Georgian monastic ideology in Byzantium with the Bagratid royal rhetoric resulted in an unmatched growth of the cult of the Mother of God. The result was a radical and long-standing conceptualisation of Georgia as the 'Lot of the Mother of God', a concept that significantly contributed to the formation of Georgian political theologies also much later, in the era of the Russian Imperial domination and in national discourses.

Finally, all these deliberations and rewritings were re-evaluated in a dramatic event – the coronation of Queen Tamar as Georgia's sole ruler. Tamar's reign, the necessity to legitimise her mandate as well as the legality of female rule and the formation of her posthumous cult redefined the place and the meaning of the feminine in medieval and modern Georgian political theologies. While the 'feminine' foundations of Georgia's Christianity were embraced, the ambiguity generated by this femininity has never entirely disappeared, and was retained in the problematic and ambiguous posthumous conceptualisation of the cult of Queen Tamar.

# 4

# Masculinising Saints: The Bagratids

## 4.1 In the Presence of Martyrs

The small single-naved Church of the Saviour (Mac'xvariši) was built by the end of the eleventh century in the village of Latali, in Svaneti, Georgia's north-western highland province. Svaneti is attested since Strabo as a semi-independent entity, which at various times was part of western Georgian kingdoms. In the eleventh century, it became part of the united Georgian monarchy. The interior of the church was decorated in 1140. The northwest niche of the church depicts the crowning of King Demetre I (1125–45), son of King David IV 'the Builder' (1089–1125). Demetre is blessed by Christ and crowned by archangel Gabriel. Two smaller figures of local dukes tie a sword around his waist. The north-east niche depicts the crowning of St Katherine of Alexandria with St Barbara standing next to her. The coronation of St Katherine with a royal and martyr's crown by an angel appears as almost a replica of Demetre's coronation. The apparent contrast between Katherine and Demetre, however, is their clothes: the former wears a kite-shaped imperial loros, whereas the latter appears in a Georgian robe.[1] The south-east niche has saints Marina and Irine, whereas the west wall and the south-east niche is occupied by the three great warrior saints: George, Theodore and Demetrios.[2] As with all medieval churches in Svaneti, the unimpressive architecture of Mac'xvariši contrasts dramatically with the artistic and symbolic richness of the interior (see Fig. 4.1).

In his book on *Royal Imagery in Medieval Georgia*, Antony Eastmond points out that 'The Crowning of Demetre' was not necessarily a centralised royal production and certainly not 'how Demetre would have liked to

---

[1] Eastmond, *Royal Imagery*, 84.
[2] Ibid., 73.

Figure 4.1  Coronation of King Demetre I (left) and Coronation of St Katherine next to St Barbara (right). Church of the Saviour (Mac'xvariši), twelfth century. Nakipari, Upper Svaneti. Photo: Zurab Tsertsvadze.

be seen'. Instead, it was an introduction and legitimation of the new king in this remote mountainous dukedom of Svaneti. It depicts the making of the new king, his investiture by local dukes and, most importantly, by Svaneti's local saints with the royal mandate in this area. 'Mac'xvariši would be a very concrete demonstration of the saintly sanction. It would certainly seem that the king's power was being mediated through the saints.'[3] As with other constituent parts of the united Georgian kingdom that came into being in the early eleventh century, the integration of Svaneti into the kingdom required an appropriate juggling of symbolism. Indeed, unlike the Byzantine emperors, who could evince their imperial authority from Constantinople and through mediation, throughout the entire history of Georgian monarchy, the Georgian kings had to negotiate there *in situ*, by being constantly present in Georgia's various provinces. Since unification, the Georgian kingdom was a constant work in progress, in need of physical, symbolic and narrative integration and reintegration. And while the Bagratid kings invested in their own mythologies and injected their cult of saints into the newly acquired domains, in some cases, such as Latali, the

[3] Ibid., 86.

process was reversed, and the king was virtually accepted and embraced by 'local' saints.

The iconographic ensemble of Mac'xvariši betrays yet another peculiarity of the cult of saints specifically in Svaneti – the predominance of female saints in the decoration of local churches. Even more unusual, and in fact, as Eastmond points out, unparalleled in Byzantine art, is the male monarch's association and legitimation through a woman saint. St Katherine and Barbara, and to a lesser extent Marina and Irene, were exceptionally widely present in dozens of eleventh- to fourteenth-century images in Upper Svaneti. The only other images that match and indeed surpass them in their prominence are of St George and St Theodore, who most commonly appear as paired riders – with St George slaying the Emperor Diocletian and St Theodore piercing a dragon.

The question of why female martyr saints were so prominent in medieval Svaneti will regrettably not be answered below, since this requires an altogether new study. Could this be caused by the Svans having internalised the tales spread in Eastern Roman geographies and histories where Svaneti was a land ruled by women? Or perhaps they were impressed by the eighth- or ninth-century *Acts of the Apostle Andrew* attributed to monk Epiphanius, which also claimed that Sosania (probably Svaneti) was ruled by women and was therefore easily converted by Andrew? This story was, after all, soon translated, internalised and expanded by the Georgian tradition. In any case, what clearly transpires from Svaneti's imagery, as well as, as we shall see below, in the evolution of the imagery of St Nino and of the cult of St George, is a tendency to pair (hyper-)masculine and female saints. This tendency, as it shall be argued below, transpires in art, as well as narrative and folk representations of saints, such as George and Nino.

## 4.2 The New Kartli

The migration of Georgian refugees and the translation of old Kartli made a deep impression on the writers of the age. The hagiographic production of the ninth–eleventh centuries, which consists primarily of monastic *vitae*, was infused with this sense of a beginning. The cult of martyr saints that flourished under the Sasanians and Arabs was replaced by that of the monastic founders.

Giorgi Merč'ule's *Life of Grigol of Xanc'ta*, written in 951, is particularly focused on this sense of novelty, and demonstrates an awareness of political and religious geography comparable to that of the *Conversion of Kartli*. The earlier narratives, the *Life of Nino*, the *Lives of the Syrian Fathers* and others, were focused on the saints' arrival and the enlightening of 'this northern land'. By contrast, Grigol and Ašot are the first founding figures to institute a new political realm in the mountainous deserts of Tao and Klarjeti, immediately adjacent and partly inside the Byzantine territories. Like his distant legendary predecessor P'arnavaz, and Albania's Vač'agan, Merč'ule's Ašot is conceptualised as a charismatic founder of a new political realm. Unlike the earlier accounts, however, Merč'ule ignores the Late Antique trope of the miraculous discoveries and distributions of historic relics by the king. Here the mystical continuity with the land is sustained by the discoveries and stories of the lost foundations on top of which the new fathers and kings built their own churches and monasteries.

In the *vita*, Grigol and Ašot effectively Christianise and sanctify the new Kartli, just like Nino and king Mirian had done six centuries earlier in the old Kartli. Instead of the Late Antique motifs of legitimation through materiality, treasures and relics, Merč'ule utilises the Old Testament models of the relationship between a king and a holy man. There are no hidden relics scattered across the deserts of Klarjeti awaiting a charismatic figure to be discovered, but St Grigol himself is the embodiment of historical continuity and the sanctity of the land. This intimate relationship with a living saint sanctions the king's sovereignty in the 'new' Georgia. Yet, both Archimandrite Grigol and King Ašot are aliens, escapees from the Old Kartli, strangers to these new lands. The core of the narrative, therefore, is Grigol's work to Georgianise the land and to legitimise Ašot's and his House mandate to rule in this land. In one of the most quoted paragraphs of the medieval Georgian corpus, Merč'ule redefines the conceptual boundaries of Kartli and offers a novel definition of its essence:

> Great Ephrem brought the greatest good to our country, for earlier the katholikoi of the East brought the myrrh from Jerusalem. But Ephrem, through Christ's order, instituted the preparation of the myrrh in Kartli, through the order and joyful resolution of the Patriarch of Jerusalem. But Kartli is called the entire land where liturgy is celebrated and all prayers are offered in the Georgian language, whereas Kyrie Eleison is said in Greek, which in Georgian stands for 'God have mercy'.[4]

The reason for the paragraph's popularity in contemporary national discourses is that it is often interpreted, albeit anachronistically, as a primordial confirmation of what allegedly constitutes the essence of Georgian unity.[5] Yet

---

[4] Giorgi Merč'ule, *šromay da moġuacebay grigolisi*, §44, ed. Abuladze, 290.33–40; https://titus.uni-frankfurt.de/texte/etcs/cauc/ageo/gh/gh1/gh1lex.htm.
[5] Aleksidze, *Narrative*, 183–8.

the fact that Merč'ule found it necessary to define the concept of Kartli voices the transformations that Georgia as a political concept underwent in these novel circumstances. Through Grigol's and Katholikos Ephrem's efforts, the Georgians were endowed with the right to independently produce myrrh, an event which, from the author's perspective, is a confirmation of the authority of the Georgian Church. Merč'ule dismisses Kartli's localisation, and defines it by the language of liturgy, which sets it apart from the co-religionist Byzantines. Considering the ethnic and linguistic diversity of the region, Kartli is now defined as a place where liturgy is celebrated in Georgian – a sign of the authority of the Georgian rulers.

Ašot, the new king, was technically an alien, as his original domains were located deeper in the Caucasus. As a new king, he required, what Marshall Sahlins calls 'naturalisation'. According to Sahlins, in investiture narratives the foreign king's right to rule over the new land is legitimised through his relationship with the autochthonous people, what Clifford Geertz calls 'a model of and for cultural order and historical action'.[6] Through a rite of initiation, the alien king is endowed with the right to rule in this new land: 'The ritual consists of a transfer of sovereignty in the course of which the stranger-prince is appropriated by the native owners of the land, and vice versa.'[7] After ritual rebirth, 'the headman then undertakes the new chief's maturation, as it were, by instructing him in the morality of the native society, while forcefully admonishing him to leave off the antisocial behaviour of his previous existence.'[8] A transitional event in Grigol's *vita* is a standoff between the king and Grigol over Ašot's deteriorating ethos, and the king's involvement with a concubine whom he had brought to his palace. Grigol's admonishment and rebuke of the newly arrived Ašot' over his transgressive morality is a point of transition in the relationship between the two men.[9] The conflict over the woman ended with the monastic community's victory, albeit achieved through deception, with the king being forced to relinquish the lover. Having listened to Grigol's closest associate mother P'ebronia's rebuke, the king repented: 'When the Kouropalates heard this, he was deeply ashamed by her pious rebuke and was immediately silenced, as if

---

[6] Graeber and Sahlins, *On Kings*, 175.
[7] Ibid.
[8] Ibid.,170–1. Here Sahlins quotes Geertz's ethnographic record: 'You are a mean, selfish fool, one who is bad-tempered ... But today you are born as a new chief ... If you were mean, and used to eat your cassava much alone, or your meat alone, today you are in the chieftainship. You must give up your selfish ways, you must welcome everyone, you are the chief! You must stop being adulterous and quarrelsome.'
[9] Giorgi Merč'ule, *šromay da moġuacebay grigolisi*, ed. Abuladze, 296.

defeated. For a powerful earthly monarch was overpowered by men strong in the spirit, armoured with the divine zeal. And perturbed Kouropalates said in distress: "Blessed are those who are not alive."[10] To formulate in Sahlins and Geertz's words, through this rite of passage, the new Georgian king converted to a new ethos, becoming a truly legitimate monarch.

The relationship between the saint and the monarch exhibits what was missing in Late Antique Georgian narratives – allusions to the Old Testament. The political rhetoric of legitimacy in Grigol's *Life* corresponds to the overall rediscovery of the Old Testament as a means of political legitimation by the Macedonian emperors.[11] 'No new event was wholly true nor any new emperor wholly authentic until they had been recognised and labelled by reference to an Old Testament model. In Byzantium, the Old Testament had a constitutional value; it had the same normative role in the political sphere as the New Testament in the moral sphere.'[12] Similarly to the rhetoric of the Emperor Basil' I's chroniclers, Grigol's *Life* too models Ašot after King David by dwelling on the typological similarities between the two kings. Unlike Basil, however, whose humble origins are often emphasised by the Macedonian historians and panegyrists, it is Ašot's strangeness to this land that contributes to this association. The real or fictional story of friction between Ašot and Grigol over the woman is an obvious mimicry of Prophet Nathan's rebuke of King David over his desire for Bathsheba.[13] After the 'conversion', Ašot praises Grigol and compares him to the Old Testament prophets. In response, Grigol blesses the king: 'O King, the son of the one anointed by Prophet David and the Lord! Christ God gave you his mandate and his virtues, and because of this I tell you: May the authority to rule remain with your children and their relatives on these lands until the end of times, and may they be as firm as rocks and everlasting mountains and glorified forever and ever.'[14] With these words, Merč'ule introduces the

---

[10] Giorgi Merč'ule, *šromay da moġuacebay grigolisi*, §55, ed. Abuladze, 297.36–41: https://titus.uni-frankfurt.de/texte/etcs/cauc/ageo/gh/gh1/gh1lex.htm.
[11] Dagron, *Emperor and Priest*, 199–200.
[12] Dagron, *Emperor and Priest*, 50.
[13] Claudia Rapp, albeit in the Byzantine imperial context, classifies this model as a 'more oblique way in which historians sometimes set an emperor in relation to Old Testament models. In these instances, authors did not make explicit statements, but rather crafted their descriptions in such a way as to hint that an emperor's conduct was evocative of an Old Testament figure.' Rapp, 'Old Testament Models', 181.
[14] Giorgi Merč'ule, *šromay da moġuacebay grigolisi*, §11, ed. Abuladze, 262.25–31: https://titus.uni-frankfurt.de/texte/etcs/cauc/ageo/gh/gh1/gh1lex.htm. On this episode, see also Rapp, *Studies*, 233–4. For parallel material in other regions, see Biliarsky, 'Old Testament Models'.

sturdiest concept of Georgian 'political theology' – the Bagratid Dynasty's descent from the biblical King David, an idea that the most successful members of the House have since endorsed ad infinitum.

We do not know whether it was indeed Grigol's *Life* that invented the Bagratid claim to Davidic descent, but it certainly is the earliest surviving evidence of the political cult of King David, and by association of the Mother of God.[15] Soon after Ašot's death, a visual confirmation of the claim appeared on the bas-relief on the church of Opiza. A century later, historian Sumbat Davit'idże constructed a genealogy of the Bagratids from King David until his own patrons, by referring to the Bagratid princes as the 'seed of David'.[16] Indeed, since Ašot's grandfather, David has been adopted as the most common name for Bagratid princes and the David-Solomon exemplum as a central trope for Bagratid historians with reference to the royal fathers and sons.[17]

The translation of the Old Kartli to the new 'Kingdom of the Kartvelians' is presumably reflected in the iconographic programme of the tenth- and eleventh-century foundations in Tao and Klarjeti. Zaza Skhirtladze and Ekaterine Gedevanishvili have argued that the churches of David II Kouropalatēs exhibit allusions to the Svetitskhoveli Cathedral in Mtskheta, revealed, among other ways, in the plans and sculptural decorations of the churches of Otkhta, Parkhali, Oshki and Khakhuli.[18] Gedevanishvili has further argued that the interior decoration of the church of the Khakhuli Monastery founded by David *kouropalatēs* conveys the transfer of the centrifuge of Georgian culture and history from old to new Kartli. This vision is reflected in the imagery of the ascension of Elijah, the favourite Old Testament saint of the Macedonian Dynasty. Arguably, along with the traditional eschatological meanings, it also conveyed historical references to old Kartli and its principal relic – Elijah's mantle. The association of Elijah with the story of Kartli's conversion is further cemented by the date of king Mirian's miraculous conversion. By tradition it falls on the feast of Elijah's ascension, on 20 July. It can be argued, albeit with caution, that the dating of Mirian's conversion to 20 July appeared in the ninth–tenth

---

[15] The Jewish origin of the Bagratids was originally elaborated by Movsēs Xorenac'i, but the Georgians were first to claim their descent from King David.
[16] Sumbat Davit'isże, *c'xovreba da ucqeba*, ed. Kaukhchishvili, 372–3; *Matiane k'art'lisay*, ed. Kaukhchishvili, 251; Rapp, 'Sumbat Davit'is-dze', 570–6; Eastmond, *Royal Imagery*, 223–5.
[17] See, e.g. the description of the coronation of Demetre I, son of David IV, in *C'xovreba mep'et'-mep'isa davit'isi*, ed. Kaukhchishvili, 363; tr. Thomson, 353.
[18] Gedevanishvili, 'Khakhuli Dome Decoration', 12–14. Skhirtladze, *Ot'xt'a eklesiis p'reskebi*, 107–78.

centuries after the four redactions of the *Life of Nino* had been finally formed, and was meant to coincide with the feast of Elijah's ascension. Another surviving example of the visual association of Elijah's ascension with the conversion of Georgia, that may corroborate this claim, is the diaconicon of the Gareja Monastery in Udabno, in eastern Georgia, where Elijah's ascension and episodes from Nino's life are represented side by side.[19]

The translation of 'old Kartli' and its foundation story happened at around the same time that the churches of Khakhuli and others were founded. The first edition of the *Conversion of Kartli* outside of the Holy Land was made or copied in the monastery of Shatberdi in Klarjeti originally built by Grigol of Xanc't'a. The codex was dedicated to Bagrat IV of Tao (d. 966). In the colophon, the editor Ioane Bera claims to have discovered the lost text of the *Mok'c'evay*.[20] It is indeed likely that the prototype of the Shatberdi redaction was taken from Kartli during the migration and has been lost over time. The rare pre-thirteenth-century visual depiction of St Nino also stems from the same period and the same context. The now lost bas-relief of St Nino was part of a decoration of the column in the south gallery of the church of Oshki, commissioned by Bagrat IV of Tao and completed in 963–76.[21] Yet, this depiction of Nino had nothing in common with Nino's later imagery, where she holds the Gospels and is equated to the Apostles. As if betraying the uncertainties towards her cult, this image of Nino *orans* is somewhat peripheral to the building, lost among other images of angels, birds and animals. She is represented as an *orans*, a holy mother, a deaconess, indeed a *k'adagi*, and not the great illuminator of the Mtskhetan and Palestinian traditions. Yet together, the Shatberdi codex and the Nino bas-relief testify to the translation and the attempts to establish this cult in New Kartli. However, whether or not this translation was successful is unclear, and if there existed more and more conspicuous depictions of Nino, they have not survived. One could argue that the Bagratids of Tao as well as the Apkhaz kings were busy crafting their own political cult of saints, and the ties with the old Kartlian story were weakening.

---

[19] Skhirtladze, 'cminda ninos c'xovrebis c'ikli', 369; Gedevanishvili, 'Khakhuli Dome Decoration', 12–13.
[20] *Šatberdis krebuli*, ed. Gigineishvili and Giunashvili, 20–1.
[21] Asmat Okropiridze identifies literary parallels between the Shatberdi redaction and the Nino image, specifically in her manner of praying, often referenced by her *vita*. Okropiridze, 'oškis cminda nino', 43–6.

We learn from the *Life of Grigol* and the foundations of Tao that the Bagratids strove to establish their unique mythologies and narratives of legitimacy. Yet, they faced the challenge of forging conceptual links among many disjointed traditions, saints and saintly narratives that were soaked in from Mtskheta, Byzantium, the Holy Land and other places where Georgian monks crafted, if not differing, then certainly nuanced visions of what constituted Georgia and its *raison d'être*.

## 4.3 The 'Grand Narrative'

It was the zeal of several energetic people as well as luck that led to the unification of the Georgian kingdoms. David of Tao did not have an heir so he adopted prince Bagrat, his nephew and son of Gurgen, the Bagratid prince of Kartli. In 978, King Theodosius III 'the Blind' of Apkhazeti was forced to abdicate and declare as his heir Prince Bagrat. Bagrat was crowned in the capital of Apkhazeti, Kutaisi. In 1010, he invaded and occupied the principality of Kakheti. By the end of Bagrat's reign, his title was 'King of the Apkhazs, Kartvelians, Rans and Kakhs, the *kouropalatēs*'.[22]

The unification of Georgia created political as well as ideological challenges. Along with an incessant struggle with old feudal houses who resented the new order, especially during Bagrat's tumultuous reign, there transpires a desire to craft a unified grand narrative of Georgia's history, by utilising and effectively rewriting earlier histories, chronicles, epic stories and hagiographies. The constituent parts of the Georgian kingdom, despite the common language, shared religion and some sense of unity, still required unification into a single story. Arguably, the outcome of this project was the *K'art'lis C'xovreba*, whose completion and edition is attributed to the enigmatic Bishop Leonti of Ruisi in the eleventh century. The project initially conceived by Leonti was a long one and practically all later chronicles have become incorporated into this massive, ever-expanding and continuously edited volume with an aim to create one, uninterrupted, and teleological narrative of Georgia's history.[23]

*K'art'lis C'xovreba* was a project of creating a unifying narrative of a newly emerging religious, linguistic and political concept – Georgia (*Sak'art'velo*), which literally stands for the land where those who identify themselves as Georgians (Kartvelians) live. As such, *K'art'lis C'xovreba*, as a work-in-progress, betrays anxieties regarding identity, history and

---

[22] Zhordania, *k'ronikebi* 1, 143.
[23] For an overview of the manuscripts, editions and structure of the *K'art'lis C'xovreba*, see Rapp, *Studies*, 17–43.

memory. Indeed, how eager was a western Georgian from Achara, Tao, Klarjeti, Apkhazeti or Meskheti, to accept Mtskheta's foundation story and its foundational saints? And what were the novel implications of the 'conversion of Kartli' for the new Georgia that encompassed territories and people far beyond the historic Kartli? Or what was the meaning of 'Georgian' in the new geopolitical realities? And what was the place of the Georgian language in these new realities? These were the questions that many authors struggled with in the first few centuries of the second millennium.

One of the ways in which Leonti addressed this challenge was incorporating a new edition of the *Life of Nino* into the *K'art'lis C'xovreba*. Leonti inserted it as a culmination to the *Lives of the Kings* by creating an impression that the entire narrative, the stories and deeds of pre-Christian kings, led to this culminating event.[24] Leonti relatively faithfully reproduced the Shatberdi edition of the *Life of Nino*, yet made it part of the royal chronicle. He achieved this by introducing the only Nino relic – her personal cross, which King Mirian incorporated into the royal crown and bequeathed it to his son and successor.[25] Leonti made Mirian imitate Helena and Constantine by merging the symbol of Georgian Christianity into the crown. Yet, it is unclear how successful Leonti's project was. If he wanted to reintroduce and establish the cult of Nino as a political cult of the Bagratids, he failed. By the eleventh century, outside specifically Nino narratives, she was still absent, and the Bagratids did not seem particularly keen on endorsing her cult either. The cross of Nino as a 'royal cross' began to feature only in the early modern era, and even then, the knowledge about this cross stemmed exclusively from the *K'art'lis C'xovreba*.

In the meantime, similar developments are attested in monastic writing. Among other fashionable literary trends of the era, Georgians have adopted the metaphrastic writing style, the largest Byzantine project of literary rewriting. Originally initiated by Symeon Metaphrastes in the tenth century, the purpose of the *metaphraseis* was to embellish existing hagiographic accounts by adding scriptural passages, expanding the details of a saint's life, and generally creating more ornate narratives. The Georgians too were drawn to the metaphrastic movement, and rewrote almost the entire earlier hagiographic corpus. The Georgian metaphraseis, however, had an additional purpose – to adapt earlier hagiographic accounts to contemporary ethno-religious discourse, to create tighter bonds between a historic

---

[24] Rapp, *Sasanian World*, 105–69.
[25] Leonti Mroveli, *mok'c'eva mirian mep'isa*, §7, ed. S. Kaukhchishvili, 130.10–16: https://titus.uni-frankfurt.de/texte/etcs/cauc/ageo/kcx1/kcx1.htm.

saint and their ethnic and communal identity, and to thus uphold the idea of uninterrupted orthodoxy vis-à-vis the ever-suspicious Byzantines.

In the twelfth century, monk Arseni was still unhappy with the dissemination of the story of Nino, and wrote a metaphrastic edition of her *Vita*. In a colophon, he made sure to register the already traditional complaint that such an important story had been nearly forgotten, with its bits and pieces scattered across various compendia. Yet even these narratives were 'dull and useless for the listener', so he wished to make them more accessible and ornate.[26] Arseni came up with a grandiose story of Nino supplemented with a lengthy introduction and presentist contextualisation to the narrative. It takes off with the mission of apostles Andrew, Simon the Zealot and Matthias to 'Georgia', invokes all the holy relics that have been translated to Georgia, and places Nino within this grand context. Yet, he does not name the places of Andrew's mission, trying to make a more abstracted image of what constituted Georgia in his time. His Nino, without specifying western or eastern Georgia, is the heir to the apostles' original mission.[27]

The cults and stories of Christ's apostles were introduced in Georgia for several purposes: to claim the apostolic foundations of the Georgian Church, to create a unified grand narrative of Georgia's Christianisation, and to masculinise the Nino story, making it more acceptable to the public. The national cult of Andrew the First-Called was an imported cult, and almost entirely sourced from the eighth- or ninth-century apocryphal *Acts of Andrew*. The ninth-century Andrew tradition as an apostle to Byzantium and the Pontus was originally forged to legitimise the authority of the Church of Constantinople and its apostolic foundations vis-à-vis the supposedly more prestigious See of Peter. The Bagratid writers swiftly hijacked the Byzantine invention and incorporated it into their own project. References to Andrew's mission in the towns of Pontus, Lazica and Abasgia started to sporadically appear in Georgian writing in tenth-century manuscripts (e.g. Klarjeti *Mravaltavi*). Yet all of these texts are translations of Greek authors and Andrew's sojourn is not recounted as 'our' story, and no first-person pronouns are used, which suggests that by then Andrew was still not conceptualised as the apostle to Georgia. The most fully evolved account of Andrew's legendary journeys was Epiphanius the Monk's *Life of Andrew*, which was well known to the Georgian monks of Mt Athos in the early eleventh century. Epiphanius claims that Andrew preached in Lazica, Trapezunt, Iberia, Phasis, Sousasnia, Pousta and Abasgia – the great Sebastopolis.[28]

---

[26] Arseni Beri, *c'xovrebay*, ed. Abuladze, 51.
[27] Ibid., 9–10.
[28] Epiphanius Monachus, ed. Vinogradov, 245.

They arrived in Iberia and Phasis, and a few days later they arrived in Sousania. The men of this tribe were ruled by women. The female nature is easy to persuade, so they easily hearkened (to the Apostles). Matthias stayed in those regions with his disciples. He preached and performed miracles. But Simon and Andrew went to Salania (*sic.*) (Alania) to the city of Phousta. They performed many miracles and taught multitudes and went to Abasgia. And when they arrived at the great Sebastopolis, they taught the Word of God.[29]

In 1011, a version of the *Acts*, due to its political expediency, was translated into Georgian by Ep't'wime Mt'acmindeli (Euthymios the Hagiorite).[30] The Andrew story was swiftly appropriated by Georgian writing. It was Ep't'wime's translation that was then incorporated into Arseni's metaphrastic *Life of Nino* as a prequel to the Nino story. In 1057, Giorgi Hagiorites used the *Life of Andrew* in his disputation against the Patriarch Theodosios of Antioch, by which he defended the independence of the Georgian Church: 'We are the allotment of the First-Called and his brother, his flock, converted and enlightened by him.'[31] A century later, Ephrem Mc'ire's handbook served the same purpose – to propagate the *Acts of Andrew* among Georgian monks so that they could defend themselves against Byzantine allegations.[32] The Andrew story also evolved as part of the *K'art'lis C'xovreba*. Here a reference to Andrew's and Simon's mission appears in passing, and both are credited with the conversion of Egrisi (Lazica), without providing any details comparable to Epiphanius' story. Yet, while the original account rather drily says in the third person how Andrew converted the Egrisians (Megrelians), a later insertion into the chronicle with an unknown date uses the all-inclusive *Sak'art'velo* as the destination of Andrew's mission, and offers an altogether new story of Andrew which shall be examined in the next chapter.[33]

While it is beyond our scope to provide a detailed study of these apocryphal stories, it will suffice to say that the literary production of the tenth to twelfth centuries betrays an anxiety regarding the geographic, political and historical meanings of *Sak'art'velo*. The rewriting was an archaeological project of discovering old saints and adapting them to contemporary

---

[29] Ibid., 257.8–15.
[30] *Mimosvla andria moc'ik'ulisa*, ed. Kobiashvili, 157–215.
[31] Grdzelidze, *Georgian Monks on Mt Athos*, 129.
[32] Ephrem Mc'ire, *ucqebay*, ed. Bregadze, 4. Ephrem Mc'ire surprisingly also refers to Bartholomew as the apostle to Kartli, a claim that must be a result of a confusion caused by the Armenian sources.
[33] *C'xovreba k'art'velt'a mep'et'a*, ed. Kaukhchishvili, 38–44.

needs.³⁴ The centralisation of the royal court and its ideology was effectively reflected in a tendency to seek, attune and incorporate old histories, whether hagiographic or historical, into a grand narrative such as the *Kʻartʻlis Cʻxovreba* project. The old saints became saints of a new political concept, and a new sense of unity. In this new narrative, each episode of Georgia's history reaffirmed the claim of uninterrupted Orthodoxy and association of a saint's Georgian ethnicity with his or her Orthodoxy.

## 4.4 An Old King for Modern Anxieties

Along with old saints, the *Kʻartʻlis Cʻxovreba* 'discovered' and a holy king of olden days, King Vakhtang the Wolf-Head. Those scholars who argue that Vakhtang's saga is essentially an old epic tale written down by the end of the eighth century are perhaps right. However, it was incorporated in the *Kʻartʻlis Cʻxovreba* project with a specific purpose – to create an image of a Georgian holy (and martyred) king as a certain counterbalance to the sacred aura of the Byzantine emperor, and to saturate his image and reign with very contemporary political tropes.³⁵

Within the *Kʻartʻlis Cʻxovreba*, Vakhtang was conceptualised as the last great king of Kartli, Georgia's own holy and martyred king, whose reign was restored by the Bagratids. The *Life of Vakhtang* is an epic saga, a mixture of history-writing and fiction of a fifth-century king, whose actual influence was most likely inferior to his grandiose image in the narrative. While the events of the *Life* unfold in a distant past, the political and religious messages that Vakhtang's stories convey are contemporary and reflect the geopolitical aspirations of the Bagratid kings in the eleventh century.

The story of Vakhtang is essentially that of a transformation, of a rite of passage from one identity to another. In this, Vakhtang's narrative is reminiscent of Vačʻagan's and Mirian's transformations. Both were members of an Iranian dynasty, yet through rites of passage, both 'forgot' their former identities and acquired new Christian political selves. This trope is certainly much older than the eleventh century, and was an integral part of the political conceptualisation of the conversion stories since Late Antiquity. Nevertheless, its adoption in the *Kʻartʻlis Cʻxovreba* was convenient. After a

---

[34] Yet another example of such 'rediscovery' is the Georgian version of the *Life of Peter the Iberian* and his depiction as a militant Chalcedonian, where Peter served as a 'proof' of Georgia's uninterrupted Orthodox history. *Cʻxorebay... petre kʻartʻvelisay*, 213–62. Aleksidze, 'Strangers in a Strange Land', 133–52.

[35] On the 800 date, see Rapp, *Studies*, 197–244; Martin-Hisard, 'Le roi géorgien Vakhtang', 226.

transitional moment, vision and prophecy, Vakhtang, an Iranian king by origin and an Iranian ally, befriends the Roman emperor and secures an eternal alliance with the Byzantines. It is a tale of Vakhtang's self-understanding and coming to terms with his Iranian background, yet Christian identity, which translates also into a political function. In the dream, the Emperor 'placed him by his throne and sat him beside him and gave him a ring from his hand in which was a very bright gem.' The Emperor asked Vakhtang to promise that he would always fight the enemies of the Cross. After this, Nino, bishops Peter and Samuel proclaim with one voice,

> 'We are guarantors, O invincible cross, that he will be the most successful of all' . . . And the bishop cried out three times: 'Vakhtang, Vakhtang, Vakhtang! You will be the most faithful of all among the nation of the Persians.' And the second time: 'Churches will be built by you, and bishops and an archbishop appointed.' And the third time: 'You will receive the crown of martyrdom!'[36]

The dream was essentially Vakhtang's canonisation by acclaim: he was to become a defender of Christendom, martyr and the founder of the independence of the Georgian Church. Vakhtang's house is conceptualised as originally Iranian yet essentially Christian, and this double-belonging of his house and his faith is symbolised by the greatest saint of his dynasty – St Nino, a Roman who converted an Iranian royal house to a new ethos and new political identity. After this episode, Vakhtang assumed the role of an arbiter between the Western and Eastern powers, Rome and Iran, brokering peace between the two superpowers. Vakhtang enforced the function that had been set by Alexander when he had distributed his universe among his four 'relatives' and 'gave to Bizintios Greece and Kartli and assigned to him the region of the north.'[37] As the *Life of Vakhtang* further boldly claims, it was Vakhtang who secured peace between the two eternal enemies, Romans and Iranian, through his control over the northern frontiers of the civilised world.[38] Vakhtang is presented as a great founding king who had laid the foundation to Georgia's current geopolitical status, its function and place in universal history.[39]

Like the writers of the tenth and eleventh centuries, the *Life* reveals a cognitive dissonance regarding the Byzantines. It opens with a reminiscence

---

[36] Juanšer, *c'xovreba*, ed. Kaukhchishvili, 168. 8–11: https://titus.uni-frankfurt.de/texte/etcs/cauc/ageo/kcx1/kcx1lex.htm; tr. Thomson, 185.
[37] Juanšer, *c'xovreba*, ed. Kaukhchishvili, 19, tr. Thomson, 27.
[38] Juanšer, *c'xovreba*, ed. Kaukhchishvili, 196–204.
[39] For an analysis of the *Life of Vakhtang*, see Rapp, *Sasanian World*, 271–330.

that the Greeks occupied the western Georgian territories when Vakhtang was still too young. It repeatedly fosters the idea of a historic injustice suffered by the Georgians from the Romans which Vakhtang restored, thereby betraying the anxieties during the formative period of the Georgian kingdoms and principalities on the verge of the millennium, and prefiguring the injustice that the Bagratid kings suffered under the Macedonian emperors. In an address to his army, Vakhtang explains the reasons for the forced relocation of the Georgians from the Pontus where their original domains were to the north: 'The Greeks took from us, the Georgians, the frontier to the east of the sea. Now the battlefield of our earlier kings was in Anżianżor, where is now the tomb of the great teacher Gregory, whence our kings fled. We have marched a journey of ten days and have turned to the north. We share in the religion of the Greeks, confessing Christ who is the true God of all.'[40] While the narrative opens with the vilification of the Greeks (i.e. Romans), it ends in Vakhtang's following testament: 'To all the nobles he said: "You, inhabitants of Kartli, remember my good deeds, because first from my house you received the eternal light, and I honoured you, my kin, with temporal glory. Do not despise our house, nor abandon the love of the Greeks."'[41]

While Vakhtang's *Life* is presented as an old tale, it was also reinterpreted as a new story, or rather a story of the new Kartli. He was a role model for Georgia's new kings – the Bagratids – with his career prefiguring their continuous manoeuvring between the Byzantines, Arabs and other greater powers. Indeed, in one episode, before a battle with the Byzantines, Vakhtang prays to God to give him the strength of David to defeat Goliath. It could indeed be the case that this aspect of Vakhtang's narrative was formed during the reign of Ašot or soon after his death. The conceptual ties with the era of the Bagratids of Tao are obvious – Vakhtang is claimed to be the original founder of the fortress of Artanuji, which was the residence of the Bagratids of Tao, of the Church of Oški, the founder of the independence of the Georgian Church, which was gained or regained in the ninth century by Grigol Xanc't'eli. The sense of novelty and foundations that permeates the Grigol narrative is ubiquitous in the Vakhtang story too. Both *vitae* reveal identical anxieties over the meanings of Georgia and Georgianness, Georgian language and territory, the place of Constantinople and Jerusalem in Georgia's Christianity, and the pervasive criticism of the Greeks. Like Giorgi Merčule, the author of Vakhtang's *Life* exhibits a

---

[40] Juanšer, *c'xovreba*, ed. Kaukhchishvili, 160.10–17; https://titus.uni-frankfurt.de/texte/etcs/cauc/ageo/kcx1/kcx1.htm; tr. Thomson, 175.
[41] Juanšer, *c'xovreba*, ed. Kaukhchishvili, 203.14–17; tr. Thomson, 222–3.

sense of territoriality and problematises Georgia as a historic and political notion.[42] Yet, in Vakhtang's *vita* there is still no St George or any other warrior saint of the Bagratids to fight by the king's side, and his guardian saint is Nino, the saint of old Georgia.

The political cult of Vakhtang was a successful one, one of the few that have made it into folklore. His cult was largely determined by his representation as the end of the old Georgia, but also a founder of the idea of the new Georgia. The Bagratids continuously sought an association with him, Georgia's own Constantine. The title of the metaphrastic *Martyrdom of David and Constantine* encapsulates this continuity: 'The martyrdom of the holy and glorious martyrs David and Constantine, who were martyred in the northern land, in the lands of Argueti, in the domain of the Georgians, after the death of the great king Vakhtang, who took the kingship of the land with him to the grave, under the ungodly king of Persia [*sic*.] Murvan Abul Kasim who was called the Deaf, who was the nephew of Mohammad, the false prophet.'[43] The fifth-century king, the seventh-century prophet, the eighth-century Umayyad Caliph and the ninth-tenth century amir of Azerbaijan are all crammed together in a single event of history – the termination of old Georgia. Old Georgia was buried together with Vakhtang but also with the relics of David and Constantine. At the end of the story, it is claimed that, centuries later, these relics were discovered by King Bagrat III, the first king of united Georgia, who built on the site the great church of the martyrs (*Mocamet'a*).[44] The *Martyrdom* is also particularly keen to introduce western Georgia to its readers, by casually referencing some of its main place names: towns, rivers and places, along with suggesting their etymologies. In the vision of its authors, Bagrat III who resided in in Apkhazeti's capital Kutaisi, is, through the story of the martyrdom of David and Constantine and by the virtue of their relics, a direct inheritor of King Vakhtang and his Kingdom of Kartli.

It is fair to say that the *Life of Vakhtang* was successful in that it established the only political cult before the emergence of the Bagratid holy kings. His memory became dear to the Bagratid kings who eagerly bore his name, and whose royal flag in the late twelfth century was referenced as *Davit'ian-Gorgasliani*.[45] In the same narratives the royal *Imitatio Constantini* is substituted with the imitation of Vakhtang. The image of Vakhtang

---

[42] Martin-Hisard, 'Le roi géorgien Vakhtang', 226.
[43] *Camebay davit' da konstantinesi*, ed. Abuladze, 248.8–16: https://titus.uni-frankfurt.de/texte/etcs/cauc/ageo/gh/gh3/gh3.htm.
[44] Ibid.
[45] *Istoriani da azmani*, ed. Kaukhchishvili, 68, 71, 104.

as a hero who challenged the Byzantine emperor, has inspired, or perhaps was inspired by, the emergence of the political cult of the greatest saint of the Georgian tradition – St George the Cappadocian.

## 4.5 St George

With the centralisation and consolidation of the Bagratid House, radical changes occurred in the political conceptualisation of old and new saints. By emulating a similar trend among the Macedonian emperors, the Bagratids invested in a political theological narrative for their House. Arguably, among other techniques, the Bagratid and monastic writers launched what can be called 'masculinisation' of the Georgian saintly pantheon. This tendency can in part explain the instability of the cult of St Nino, which was left beyond the rhetoric of the ruling elites. Instead, an emphasis was made on warrior saints. The greatest among them, whose name became strongly tied with Georgia, was without doubt, St George.

Nowadays, St George is hailed as Georgia's principal saint, a belief that stems from a phonetic, albeit erroneous association of Georgia and George. This analogy originates from medieval western European authors who were convinced that the Georgians derive their name from St George, by pointing out the particular veneration of St George by the Georgians and his featuring on Georgian banners.[46] This etymology was in late medieval writing also internalised by a part of the Georgian authors.[47] St George's unmatched popularity is confirmed by his two major feasts celebrated in Georgia: on 23 April (6 May) and 10 November (23 November), and multiple other local feasts, and hundreds of church dedications both medieval and recent.[48] In the eighteenth century, Vakhushti Bagrationi pointed out that 'there are no peaks or high hills upon which there have not been built churches of St George', whereas a popular Georgian toast still appeals to 'three hundred and sixty five St Georges' for intercession. Although Georgia, as a name, has nothing to do with St George, since the tenth century, there has been an outburst of St George's visual imagery.

The earliest association of St George with the ruling house appears in an eleventh-century manuscript from Mt Sinai, with Ioane Minč'xi's hymn

---

[46] An anthology of these sources with Georgian commentary can be found in Tvaradze, *sak'art'velo da kavkasia*, 125–77.
[47] Vaxušti Batonišvili, *ağcera*, 39–40.
[48] November in old Georgian was known as *Giorgobist've* (the month of St George). Kevin Tuite notes that 'Out of a sampling of over two thousand Orthodox churches from all regions of Georgia, over a third were dedicated to St George.' Tuite, 'St George in the Caucasus', 6.

dedicated to this megalomartyr. The colophon to the hymn reads, 'This hymn was written for the sake of King Giorgi by Minč'xi.' The nine short hymns make an acrostic: 'Saint George, have mercy on King Giorgi in the presence of the King of Kings and give him glory.'[49] Hymnographer Ioane lived in the tenth century and was originally from Inč'xi, a village in western Georgia, in the diocese of Martvili, then the Kingdom of Apkhazeti. As all his surviving manuscripts are housed in St Catherine's Monastery, it is possible that Minč'xi, like many of his prominent contemporaries, spent his adult life on Mt Sinai. The king to whom the hymn is dedicated is likely King Giorgi II of Apkhazeti (922–57) of the House of Ač'ba/Anč'abaże. Under Giorgi, the kingdom became particularly influential in the Caucasian region, and extended to most of Kartli and central Georgia. In the 920s, Giorgi marched further east and invaded Kakheti, and was even acknowledged as its sovereign. He became the most powerful of Georgian monarchs of his time, with his influence extending over all Georgian principalities including Tao and Klarjeti. Giorgi must have been particularly dear to Minč'xi's heart as the king was the builder of the Martvili Monastery and the founder of the Martvili diocese where Ioane had initially served.

The surviving evidence suggests that the cult St George originally expanded from tenth-century western Georgia. The earliest translation of the *Martyrdom of St George* has survived in two tenth-century manuscripts, one kept on Mt Athos (MS Ivir. Geo. 8) and the other in Sinai (MS Sin. Geo. 62). Should the translation be placed within the previous hundred-year period, the first translation of the *Martyrdom of St George* was either commissioned by or executed for Giorgi II of Apkhazeti. Yet another translation of the *Martyrdom* appeared soon thereafter, no later than the tenth century.[50] Other texts, such as the translations of Greek encomia, are also kept in an early tenth-century codex. Later that century, Ep't'wime Mt'acmindeli translated yet another encomium to St George.[51] In all likelihood, George/ Giorgi became the dynastic name of the Apkhaz kings in 861, when Giorgi I became king. Since then and until 1801, fifteen Giorgis ruled in Georgian kingdoms and principalities, not to mention hundreds of other members of the royal family. As a sign of special dynastic devotion, King Kostanti III (893–922), Giorgi's father, specifically went to pray in the Church of St George of Alaverdi in Kakheti, and decorated St George's icon with gold.[52]

---

[49] Ioane Minč'xi, *Poezia*, ed. Khachidze, 25: წმიდავო გეორგი შეეწიე გეორგის მეფესა წინაშე მეუფეთა მეუფისა და ადიდე.
[50] Gabidzashvili, *cminda giorgi*, 15–19.
[51] Ibid., 42–375.
[52] *Matiane k'art'lisay*, ed. Kaukhchishvili, 264. St George is commemorated in the same context in a 914 inscription on the Church of St George in Eredvi, a village in

The hypothesis that the cult of St George first emerged in Apkhazeti and was then adopted in the Kartvelian realm is further corroborated by the epigraphic commemorations of St George that are far more numerous in western Georgia than in the east.

Apart from Ioane Minč'xi's hymnography, the most detailed and earliest reference to the cult of St George in Georgia belongs to a thirteenth-century author Abuserisże Tbeli.[53] Tbeli's account is unique in that it is based on oral histories from Achara, Georgia's Black Sea region. Tbeli's collection also points to a rapid folklorisation of St George's cult and its incorporation in traditional religious practices. Arguably, in time, with Georgia's political unification, the cult of St George penetrated the eastern parts of Georgia and was inherited as a dynastic cult by the Bagratids, the direct descendants of Giorgi II.

Some of the surviving visual evidence may also help us understand the dynamics of the politicisation of St George's cult. Among the wealth of St George imagery, the early eleventh-century relief of the chancel of the church of Urt'xva, near Khashuri, in central Georgia, is altogether unique (see Fig. 4.2). A saintly warrior, identified by the inscription as George, is

Figure 4.2　Chancel of Urt'xva, early eleventh century, Shida Kartli, Georgia. Source: Ekaterine Gedevanishvili.

Kartli, which dates the foundation of the church to Kostanti's campaign in Kakheti and Hereti. *Kart'uli carcerebis korpusi*, ed. Shoshiashvili, 171–2.

[53] Abuseriże Tbeli, *sascaulni*, ed. Goguadze, Kavtaria and Chagunava, 58–70.

Figure 4.3    The Icon of St George in Nakipari, Upper Svaneti, eleventh century. Photo: Zurab Tsertsvadze.

seen with the head of his enemy mounted on a spear and marching away from his decapitated adversary. Vasily Putsko and Ekaterine Gedevanishvili have suggested, and I believe rightly, that this image of St George was inspired by the imagery of David slaying and beheading Goliath, a popular motif in the tenth- and eleventh-century Byzantine manuscript illuminations.[54] As such, the Urt'xva chancel appears as a certain iconographic hybrid of triumphant George and King David, and may be a visual reference to the Bagratid claim of Davidic descent. There may be an even more immediate reason for the commissioning of this hybrid image. The creation of the Urt'xva chancel coincides with the rule or the immediate aftermath of the death of King Bagrat III, the grandson of King Giorgi II of Apkhazeti and the adopted son and heir of David Kouropalates of Tao. This made Bagrat III an heir to the two thrones, and his official title became 'King of the Ap'xazs and the K'art'velians'. St George of Urt'xva may be a visual celebration of the unification of the two kingdoms, two dynastic names and two cults – the Apkhaz kings' cult of St George and the Bagratid cult of King David.

The appropriation by the Bagratid imagery of King David, Apostle Andrew and St George was both a means to emulate the Byzantines as well as an act of defiance. The Bagratid fascination with the cult of St George

[54] Gedevanishvili, 'Cult and Image', 152–4.

reflected the growing universal popularity of St George in medieval militant cultures, yet, arguably, it also served specifically the political rhetoric brewed under the Bagratids. This local variation of St George's cult is perhaps reflected in the most widespread imagery of the the triumphant St George, where the warrior saint slays a royal figure, commonly identified as Emperor Diocletian.[55] Most of these icons are concentrated in the mountainous regions of western Georgia, Svaneti and Rača, the transit areas between the north Caucasus and the Byzantine commonwealth. The emperor-slaying George motif also appears on the façade of the tenth-century Martvili Cathedral, which means that the motif was familiar also to Ioane Minč'xi.[56] Indeed, Minč'xi reflects this interchangeability of Dragon and Diocletian by calling Diocletian 'the dragon of hell, the pupil of the devil.'[57] As a visual confirmation of this simile, an eleventh-century repoussé icon of St George slaying Diocletian depicts the emperor in a scaly armour which resembles the scales of a reptile. In another unparalleled image, Diocletian is mounted on a horseback.[58] It has been argued, and I believe convincingly, that the surge in popularity of George slaying an emperor instead of the dragon reflects the strained relationship with Constantinople in the eleventh century. It may be a visual representation of the vilification of the Byzantine emperors as voiced by Sumbat Davit'isże, and especially by the authors of the *Life of Vakhtang*. One of the most remarkable examples of Diocletian imagery is the eleventh-century icon of St George kept in a small church in Nakip'ari village in Upper Svaneti (see Fig. 4.3). According to the inscription, the icon was commissioned by a certain Maruši. Paata Bukhrashvili argues that this unknown Maruš, who was most certainly a wealthy person, was a member of the powerful House of Marušiani. Bukhrashvili then suggests that since the Marušiani had originally been in charge of Georgia's southwestern provinces, after the regions had been occupied by the Byzantines, and the house had lost its domains, the king (Giorgi I or Bagrat IV) handed over to them the north-western areas, including Svaneti and the trans-Caucasian trade routes – a region comparable in its strategic importance to their previous domains. The icon then could have been commissioned

---

[55] Teodoro di Giorgio believes that the motif of Saints George and Theodore slaying the dragon originally appeared in the early middle ages as a celebration of Georgia's religious victory over the Sasanians. Di Giorgio, *San Teodoro*, 59.

[56] Iamanidze, *Saints cavaliers*, 82–4; Gedevanishvili, 'Cult and Image', 146–7. For a study of the dragon and Diocletian-slaying motif in medieval Georgian art, see also, Iamanidze, 'Dragon-Slayer', 97–110. For a broader regional study, see Pancaroğlu, 'Dragon-Slayer', 151–64.

[57] Ioane Minč'xi, *Poezia*, ed. Khachidze, 291.

[58] Gedevanishvili, 'Cult and Image', 149.

specifically as an anti-Byzantine piece of art by a house directly affected by the Byzantine takeover.[59] Though Diocletian is called an ungodly king, he embodies the current political climate by wearing a typical eleventh-century imperial chlamys. In two other twelfth- and thirteenth-century images, the slain Emperor also bears a halo, which Giorgi Chubinashvili considers as yet another indication that the George-Diocletian imagery implicitly attacks the sacred image of the Byzantine emperor.[60] Although the motif is specific to Georgia, Gedevanishvili points out possible typological similarities from other regions, such as the images of St Demetrius of Thessaloniki slaying the Bulgarian Tsar Kaloyan, or the image of St Mercurius killing the Emperor Julian Apostate. In a few rare images, St Theodore slays the dragon with a face of a man identified as a Persian ruler.[61]

It was especially, under David IV the Builder, that, as argued by Antony Eastmond, the 'royal imagery developed into a very sophisticated system that used complex and often indirect symbols to attain its goal of royal promotion'.[62] David's biographer claimed that St George had visibly helped the Georgian army at the 1121 battle of Didgori, and that everyone had witnessed this miracle.[63] An icon from Mt Sinai commissioned by David IV reflects both the centrality of the militaristic cult of St George and its political usage against the Byzantines. The icon executed by a master of St Catherine's Monastery depicts a royal figure with a Greek inscription identifying him as the 'pious *basileus* [emperor] of all east, Pankratonianos [Bagrationi].'[64] In the Georgian inscription he is called 'the king of the Ap'xazs, K'art'velians, Ranians and Kakhetians', a title that was assumed by David after he had added Kakheti to his kingdom. Antony Eastmond interprets this image as David's statement that he was wholly independent from Byzantium and sought for independent symbols of legitimacy. If earlier kings wished to emulate Byzantium, 'David wanted to replace Byzantium rather than to copy it.' By dropping the Byzantine title of *panhypersebastos* at the outset of his reign, 'David was able to break away from the shadow of Byzantium and convert its imagery to reflect only on himself, rather than on his relationship with the Emperor of Constantinople.'[65]

Gedevanishvili has suggested an even more immediate political connotation of the icon. The image of St George is the exact replica of the eleventh-century icon of St George of Bočorma, the most important fortification of

[59] Bukhrashvili, *cminda giorgi*, 42–53.
[60] Chubinashvili, *chekannoe isskustvo*, 325.
[61] Gedevanishvili, 'Cult and Image', 149–50 n. 35.
[62] Eastmond, *Royal Imagery*, 71.
[63] C'xovreba mep'et'-mep'isa davit'isi, ed. Kaukhchishvili, 341; tr. Gamqrelidze.
[64] Kldiashvili, 'sinis mt'is xati', 117–34.
[65] Eastmond, *Royal Imagery*, 70.

the Kingdom of Kakheti. In 1104, David annexed Kakheti without any particular effort when the dukes of Kakheti and Hereti seized and handed over to him Kakheti's unpopular King Aġsart'an II (1102–4).[66] The replication of St George of Bočorma on the icon of Sinai, which is dated to the same period, may have indeed served as a celebration of the annexation of Kakheti by David, and its integration into the Georgian body politic, an act that practically completed Georgia's unification.

By the twelfth century, St George was fully integrated into the Bagratid political ideology, visual imagery and written discourses. In visual and narrative imagery, St George appears both as an attacker who slays a Roman emperor, and as a rescuer, a motif that must have spread in the eleventh century, reflecting the insecurities deriving from the persistent menace from the Arabs and then Seljuks, by presenting George as the protector of the Christians.[67] This latter imagery appears in an unusual context where St George is paired with a female counterpart – the rescued princess of the city of Lassia. Indeed, as has been demonstrated, the earliest iconography of St George the rescuer is first attested in Georgia.

## 4.6 The Counterpart

The cult of St George was folklorised soon after its inception, and the military elites of Georgia and Armenia contributed to the spreading of the folk cult of St George across the entire Caucasus. The abundance of images of various St George legends across Georgia's peripheries contributed to the creation of spin-off narratives. One of the most popular cycles of St George in Georgia, and less popular elsewhere until the Crusades, was the 'saving of the princess'. In this imagery, the earliest of which is the late eleventh-century fresco of a small church in Hadishi, the defeated and tied dragon is led with a belt by the princess of Lasia into the city. More frescoes and icons from the eleventh to the fifteenth centuries depict this motif.[68] The Georgian pieces are the earliest representations of the said motif, and, while later Greek and Latin stories also recount a similar story, as Kevin Tuite observes, what is lacking in these narratives is any notion of partnership between a female and a male protagonist in the task of subduing the dragon.[69]

The mounted warrior, a dragon, and a fair princess leading the dragon next to a lofty castle inevitably triggered folk imaginations. Perhaps the

---

[66] *C'xovreba mep'et'-mep'isa davit'isi*, ed. Kaukhchishvili, 328–9.
[67] Tuite, 'St George in the Caucasus', 6.
[68] Gedevanishvili, 'Cult and Image', 159–63.
[69] Tuite, 'The Princess and the Dragon', 60–94.

exceptional popularity of female martyr saints in Svaneti was determined exactly by the necessity to pair them with the male warrior saints. The male–female partnership became central to the folk cult of St George. The woman that appeared next to George was reimagined as George's companion, antagonist, bride and at times all of these simultaneously. In folk traditions, the name of the woman who keeps appearing along with St George is Samżimari. The two are often conceptualised together as suggested by the formula 'George and Samżimari are one, one *xt'issvilni*'.[70] Tuite illustrates a tendency of pairing George with his mythological collaborators across the entire Caucasus, where George's balances the unruly and ambiguous females:

> Paired female and male divine beings, of which the female circulates between the hearth (the interior of domestic space, the 'interior of the interior') and the remote, uninhabited, unreachable outside ('exterior of the exterior'). Her male counterpart, usually named after St. George (Geo. *Givargi*, Svan *Zgeræg*), circulates between the public spaces of the community (the 'exterior of the interior') and those outside spaces exploited for the profit of the community (the 'interior of the exterior') ... The relationship between these two deities is the model for an institution Charachidzé called 'anti-marriage' (*cacloba*).[71]

Indeed, the most common quality of Samżimari is her gender ambiguity. Her folklorisation, like that of Nino-Minani, resulted in a problematisation of her gender. As a woman, she belonged to the realm of the *k'aji* (mythological evil creatures), yet she was saved (or kidnapped) by St George, tamed and masculinised. Since then, the Cross of Khakhmati, the principal anthropomorphised shrine of Khevsureti, was celebrated as a gender-ambiguous deity, a mixture of St George and Samżimari.[72] The foundation of Khakhmati in Khevsureti took pride in its female or rather binary identity. Unlike the foundation story of Karati, associated with a figure similar to Nino, the principal protagonist of Khakhmati is the extremely ambiguous Samżimari who often takes the form of mortal women and seduces men by particularly targeting the local *k'adagis*.

The only person in medieval chronicles with an almost identical name is Samżivari, the female ruler in Samtskhe, allegedly converted by the Apostle Andrew. Samżivari was a historic south Georgian feudal dynasty that went

---

[70] Kiknadze, *jvari da saqmo*, 85.
[71] Tuite, 'Lightning, Sacrifice', 489.
[72] Kiknadze, *jvari da saqmo 1*, 86.

extinct. However, their memory was preserved in sporadic references, especially in the apocryphal story of the mission of the Apostle Andrew. A widow, Samżivari is here the ruler of the kingdom and presented as the very first Georgian ruler to be converted to Christianity, a tale discussed in the next chapter.[73] But Was Samżimari a folk adaptation of this figure that appears in the *K'art'lis C'xovreba*? It is certainly tempting to identify the two, considering the propensity of the *K'art'lis C'xovreba* to generate folk spin-off narratives across the Caucasus. The problematisation of literary Samdzi(v/m)ari's gender and its ambiguity resonate well with similar gender ambiguities caused by the folklorised cults of St Nino, and as we shall see later in this section, of the Holy Queen Tamar.[74] Nevertheless, if the identity of the two names is a pure coincidence, which is unlikely, the phenomenon of Samżimari is clearly an extraction from literary and visual stories of St George and the princess.

A twelfth-century mural of the now destroyed Kldemaghala church in central Georgia accentuates this male–female antithesis of George's imagery. George slays and tramples a dragon who is then carried away on a girdle by the princess into the city. In this unique version, however, all figures depicted as the city residents are women: With her free hand the princess points to a group of pious women, and the entire scene is also overseen from the wall by two royal women. Gedevanisvhili suggests that the image was created in the early years of the reign of Queen Tamar, close in time to the composition of Nikoloz Gulaberisże's apology of the feminine foundations of Georgia's history. The city, arguably, symbolises the Georgian Kingdom, as ruled by a woman and dominated by female saints, yet additionally sanctified by St George.[75] What it certainly betrays is the uneasiness that medieval Georgians apparently experienced towards their Christian history and the role of the feminine in it, a Gordian knot that Katholikos Gulaberisże wished to cut with his homily and pro-Tamar policies.

St George, as a male counterpart, particularly transpires in the evolution of the cult of St Nino. Nowadays the two, George and Nino, are very closely associated and George effectively acts as Nino's masculine counterpart. While Nino is the most common female name in Georgia, Giorgi is an even more widely used male name. Many icons depict these two allegedly Cappadocian saints side by side, often stressing their common facial

---

[73] For a hypothetical association of the two female characters, see Charachidzé, *Le système religieux*, 559–65.
[74] For an alternative analysis of Samżivari's representations and parallels in Armenia, see Mahé, 'Mythe d'Ištar', 215–30.
[75] Gedevanishvili, 'Cult and Image', 162–3.

features and attire. George originally appears alongside St Nino in Arseni's twelfth-century redaction of the *Life of Nino*. In time, as the principal male saint of the Georgian calendar, both in literature and folklore, George featured as the counterpart of St Nino. In the ninth-century redactions, the martyrdom of George is merely referenced in the story of Zabylon, Nino's father, and is not elaborated in any detail. The episode is altered in Arseni's redaction: 'among other [martyrs], as the morning star, prominent among other shining stars, stood out the brilliant and invincible soldier of the great Lord, who stood bravely in front of God . . . the protector and helper of all believes, *and especially of our kin*, the great martyr George, who was martyred under Diocletian, who emerged to be praised by all residents of Cappadocia'.[76] Nino's father and his valiant deeds are recounted immediately after the summary of George's martyrdom. Here George also appears as a patron of the Georgians in general. Arseni claims in addition that the first church built by King Mirian on the spot of his conversion was dedicated to St George.[77] Further, in an abridged redaction of Arseni's version, written probably a century later, George and Zabylon are called 'fellow-believers and friends'.[78] The fourteenth-century Chelishi codex is particularly noteworthy. It consists of one of the four pre-metaphrastic redactions of the *Life of Nino* and a martyrdom of St George, along with a hymn to St George.[79] By the eighteenth century, Nino's father and St George are known as cousins, a belief that is commonly repeated in contemporary religious and ethno-national discourses.[80] St Nino's burial place was also allegedly dedicated to St George according to Nino's will. Arguably, the historical and hagiographic tendency to pair St George and St Nino for the legitimisation of the latter's mission and justification of her gender was ingrained in the conceptual and physical pairing of the two characters in oral traditions, and in the other oral reimaginations of medieval narrative sources.

By the eleventh century, St George acquired two functions: On the one hand his cult was adopted as the central cult of the Bagratid House, and on the other, it was used as a means of masculinisation of Georgia's religious history. An important valence of St George's cult in lore became to

---

[76] Arseni Beri, *c'xovreba . . . ninoysi*, §9 ed. Abuladze, 11.4–11: https://titus.uni-frankfurt.de/texte/etcs/cauc/ageo/gh/gh3/gh3.htm.
[77] Arseni Beri, *c'xovreba . . . ninoysi*, ed. Abuladze, 40.
[78] Ibid., 52.
[79] Kutateladze, *xelnacert'a agceriloba*, 52–4. The Chelishi codex follows the early tenth-century Sinaitic redaction of the *Mok'c'evay*, and diverges from the Shatberdi version. Aleksidze, 'Four Recensions', 99–106.
[80] Vaxušti Batonišvili, *ağcera*, ed. Kaukhchishvili, 39–40.

balance the dangerously ambiguous females. Arguably a similar tendency of pairing George with a female counterpart was revealed in his association with St Nino. While St Nino's cult was never entirely peripheral, her cult was constantly challenged and was subject to legitimation through masculinisation. As in Caucasian folklore, where George appears as a male counterpart to unruly or otherwise problematic female deities, most commonly to Samżimari, his cult was similarly utilised to balance the femininity of the Georgian pantheon. Throughout the *K'art'lis C'xovreba*, in the rare instances where St Nino was mentioned, she was conceptualised as the principal saint of pre-Bagratid history and kings, as symbolised by her cross that was inherited by the kings of Kartli. St George, however, was a Bagratid saint, who was in time paired with St Nino and her family, as part of a project of creating a charismatic continuity between the Bagratid Dynasty and that of Georgia's first Christian kings.

# 5

# The Lot(s) of the Mother of God

## 5.1 *Sak'art'velo*: A Project

The political cults of the biblical King David, St George and King Vakhtang of Iberia, crafted in the first century of the second millennium, remained central to the Bagratid rhetoric of power and identity. Until the end of the monarchy, Georgia's kings sought dynastic and even personal associations with these figures of biblical, Christian and Georgian histories, and promoted these ties through all available media. The royal crest of the Bagrationi family (the Mukhrani branch) still proudly bears the symbols accumulated over the previous millennium: One corner of the crest is occupied by King David's harp and sling; another by the scale of Solomon; it also features St George and the dragon, whereas a prominent place (sometimes in the very centre) is taken by the seamless Tunic of the Christ (see Fig. 5.1).

While these images have been fossilised in royal rhetoric and imagery, and are still perpetuated by Georgia's extravagant monarchist circles, the most enduring ideological concept that displayed vitality well after monarchy

Figure 5.1 Crest of the Bagrationi Family (one version). Source: Artanuji Publishers.

ended is the political cult of the Mother of God. The number of Marian dedications matches only the universality of St George's shrines across Georgia, with the two saints dominating the Georgian pantheon.[1] The story that, after Pentecost, Georgia had been allotted to the Theotokos for Christianisation was formulated by the end of the tenth and beginning of the eleventh century, blossomed in the twelfth and thirteenth centuries, and displayed longevity despite the general fall and dissolution of the united Georgian monarchy. The Marian discourse was revived in the early years of the Russian Imperial administration in Caucasia and reached unmatched popularity at the turn of the second millennium with the pontificate of Katholikos-Patriarch Ilia II. Yet, each new era provided a novel and unique context for the usage and interpretation of this old political and theological idea. To this day, the medieval belief that Georgia is the lot, allotment or portion (*cilxvedri, cilxvdomili*) of the Theotokos remains the most recurring, easily recognised, widely used and abused ethno-religious concept.

Arguably, the political cult of the Mother of God was shaped along with the formation of the very concept of Georgia in its modern sense. The unifying term *Sak'art'velo* began to appear in the eleventh century as a reference to all the lands that the Georgians considered as theirs politically, ecclesiastically and linguistically. While Kartli referred to a specific, albeit a fluid, historic land, *Sak'art'velo* gained currency as an imagined landscape where Georgians, or rather people who spoke and wrote in Georgian, who were loyal to the Chalcedonian Orthodoxy and to the Bagratid crown, lived. One of the earliest usages of *Sak'art'velo* appears in *Life of Vakhtang* as an antithesis to *Sa-berdzneti* (Greece), in a sentence that describes the boundary between the Roman and Kartlian spheres of influence. *Sak'art'velo* appears in the immediate vicinity of the Mother of God:

> When the Deaf one [*qru*] attacked Klisura, which at that time was the border of Greece [*Sa-berdzneti*] and Georgia [*Sak'art'velo*], he destroyed the city of C'xumi (Sokhumi) of Ap'šilet'i and besieged the fortress of Anakop'i, in which is the image of the all-holy Mother of God – not painted by a human hand but from on high. No one knows its origin; it was found finished on top of the mountain which is bounded on the south by the sea and on the north by marshland.[2]

---

[1] For the history of the visual representations of the Mother of God in medieval Georgian art, with an exhaustive bibliography, see Skhirtladze, 'Apocryphal Cycle', 103–17. The fascination with the Mother of God is also substantiated by the wide dissemination of Marian literature in Georgian. Van Esbroeck, 'Apocryphes géorgiennes', 55–75; 'Généalogie de la Vierge', 347–55.

[2] Juanšer, *c'xovreba*, ed. Kaukhchishvili, 235.4–9: https://titus.uni-frankfurt.de/texte/etcs/cauc/ageo/kcx1/kcx1lex.htm; tr. Thomson, 241–2. Slightly corrected by N. Aleksidze.

The fortress of Anakop'ia in Apkhazeti was frequently mentioned in *K'art'lis C'xovreba* as a stronghold disputed by the Romans and the Georgians, especially during the eleventh-century wars. However, outside of this specific context, the *acheiropoieton* icon of Anakop'ia is unknown to Georgian sources. This rudimentary legend of the Theotokos's icon must be a reflection the newly emerging and a much better-established legend of the travels of Andrew the First-Called to Georgia with the Theotokos's *acheiropoieton* icon. While in the Andrew legend, the icon is associated with the fortress and Cathedral of Acquri in Samtskhe, Georgia's southern littoral province, here a similar icon acts as a marker of the limit of what constitutes Georgia, a concept that evolved hand in hand with the evolution of the idea of the Lot of the Mother of God. If so, then, the *acheiropoieton* icon of the Theotokos must have been perceived as a guardian of Georgia's borders, especially against the Byzantines.

The evolution and spinoffs of the 'lot of the Mother of God' legend reflect the uneven process of Georgia's unification, with its uncertainties, as originally spelled out by Giorgi Merčule in *the Life of Grigol Xanc'teli*. It must not be coincidental that in the *Life of Vakhtang*, close to the above-quoted paragraph, *Sak'art'velo* reappears in a commentary of an unknown date, where the extent of the authority of the Georgian Church, and, by association of Georgia itself, is explained. It is claimed that the Sixth Ecumenical Council (680–1) granted to the Georgian katholikos the patriarchal title with all the associated rights:

> It is regulated by this council as regards the church of Georgia [*Sak'art'velo*], which is holy Mc'xet'a, that it should be equal in honour with the holy, apostolic, catholic churches, which are patriarchal; and the Katholikos of K'art'li should be equal to the patriarchs; and they should consecrate, appoint, and administer by (independent) right archbishops, metropolitans, and bishops, both over their own flock in K'art'li and beyond, in Kaxet'i, Šak'i, Širvan, and places nearby across the mountain, Suanet'i and the country of Ğ'erk'ezi, all Oseti and all Upper K'art'li, Samc'xe-Saat'abego. 'To him we entrust the churches of Georgia [*Sak'art'velo*]; let them be subject to him and under his authority; let them obey his laws and have him as pastor. We have given him authority to bind and to lose. What he binds will be bound in heaven, and what he loses on earth will be loosed in heaven. Previously he had been honoured by the council of Antioch, but by this council we have confirmed him as patriarch. So, let there not be metropolitan or bishop without the permission of the Katholikos. If anyone dares to oppose the Katholikos – archbishop, metropolitan, or bishop – either to seize

a title or church by force without the permission and agreement of the katholikos, or if a king is consecrated, or nobles, or archbishops, or metropolitan bishops, let him be deposed. Whenever he wishes to prepare or bless myron, let him bless it in his own church.[3]

All this, according to the author of the commentary, effectively constitutes *Sak'art'velo*. The first elaborate association of the Mother of God with this unified yet precarious concept appears in Arseni's twelfth-century *Life of Nino*, an account that surpasses all other versions of Nino's story in its ethno-religious ambitions. Unlike all the previous redactions of the *Life*, Arseni's version opens with a lengthy prequel to Nino's journey, listing and explaining all the grand events that preceded her arrival. We learn that after Christ's ascension and Pentecost, different nations were assigned individual apostles. Having hearkened the call, they preached the word of truth in every city and village. John the Evangelist was assigned Ephesus as his destination. Other apostles urged him to leave and proselytise, just as they had done, but John refused to abandon the Mother of God, whom he had served in her house in Sion. The Theotokos told him, however, that he should leave and preach alongside his peers and brothers. Initially, she planned to accompany him together with Mary Magdalene and her other companions. Three days later, Christ appeared to them and ordered John and others to leave and preach, but instructed his mother to stay at home in Sion, because 'the nation allotted to her was easy to convert'. The Mother of God thus died in Jerusalem, and was assumed by Christ into heaven. Many years later, it was revealed that it was Georgia and the Georgian people who were allotted to her. Then 'the glorious Queen looked at us from Heaven, and remembered in the Lord's and her Son's presence the land that had been her portion [*cilxudomili igi k'ueqana*] and our people, for we are her allotment [*nacil*], the Georgian people [*nat'esavi k'artvelt'ani*], and we are blessed and thrice blessed because we are called her allotment'.[4]

Since the eleventh century, the idea of the Lot of the Mother of God has begun to transcend the limits of the original Mtskhetan *Conversion* narrative. By the time Arseni was writing, along with the expansion of *Sak'art'velo*, the ethnonym *Kart'veli* had become a much broader term covering an area considerably larger than the fourth-century Kartli. Instead of specifically Kartli, 'the northern land' of the *Conversion* corpus, the Mother

---

[3] Juanšer, *c'xovreba*, ed. Kaukhchishvili, 232; tr. Thomson, 370–1. Slightly corrected by N. Aleksidze.
[4] Arseni Beri, *c'xovrebay ... ninoysi*, 26.13–18, ed. Abuladze, 16: https://titus.uni-frankfurt.de/texte/etcs/cauc/ageo/gh/gh3/gh3lex.htm.

of God was assigned to the Georgian people, in the broadest sense of this concept. While the legitimation of St Nino's female apostolic mission was certainly made possible through her association with the Mother of God, this association was not enough. Nino was the founder of the old Kartli. The extension of her mission to the new Georgia was impossible, and required the elaboration of a parallel and stronger narrative that would transcend the former geographic, ideological and indeed gender limits of Kartli's foundation narratives.

## 5.2 The Family

It can be argued that the 'Lot of the Mother God' was invented specifically to serve this idea of linguistic, ecclesiastic and territorial unity under the Bagratids. It was not necessarily invented at a certain point by some Bagratid ideologist and then disseminated. Instead, it seems that the Theotokos's political cult had at least two relatively independent origins that eventually converged into the concept of *Sak'art'velo*. The first source was the Bagratid mythology of their descent from King David, which was inevitably interpreted as a 'proof' of their kinship with the Mother of God. Constantine Porphyrogenitus (913–59) was aware of the Bagratid pretences of kinship with David (through adultery with Uriah's wife) 'and, consequently, to the Most Holy Mother of God' well before the consolidation of the Georgian kingdom. He seems to be bemused by this claim and suggests that it is for this reason that the members of the house of the 'couropalate' marry women from their own family to thus preserve the ancient ordinance. Constantine also adds an odd detail: 'they say that they originate from Jerusalem and were warned by an oracular dream to migrate thence and to settle over toward the region of Persia, that is to say, in the country where they live now.'[5] This report differs substantially from the claims of the Armenian Bagratids, who had allegedly immigrated in Caucasia during Nebuchadnezzar's reign. The only dream that vaguely resembles Constantine's report is the collective vision of the citizens of Mtskheta which heralded the symbolic translation of the Holy Land to Kartli.

The dynastic devotion of the Bagratids to the Mother of God also transpires in the visual imagery of the eleventh and twelfth centuries. The grandest confirmation of an extraordinary dedication to the Theotokos is the Gelati church and monastery, built on top of a hill near Kutaisi, the first

---

[5] Constantine Porphyrogenitus, *De Administrando Imperio*, 45.5–15, ed. Moravcsik, tr. Jenkins, 204, 205.

Figure 5.2    Apse of the Church of the Mother of God of Gelati. Source: Artanuji Publishers.

capital of united Georgia. The construction of the Church of Dormition was started in 1106 by David the Builder, and finished in 1130 by his son Demetre I. The interior of the church is dominated by the large mosaic of the Mother of God in the apse holding the baby Jesus and flanked by the archangels. The Theotokos is of the *kyriotissa* type, the iconography that was particularly dear to the Bagratid family (see Fig. 5.2).[6] Gelati was conceived as an epicentre of Bagratid ideology and Georgian unity, as an 'Athens of the East', a royal mausoleum of his house and a new centre of Georgian spirituality and scholarship. As such, Gelati was relatively disinterested in Mtskheta and its symbols, as the mythology that it encapsulated was far grander than that of Mtskheta. The images of the conversion story are absent both from the surviving twelfth-century frescoes and even from the ones restored in the sixteenth century. With his foundation and the rare usage of expensive mosaics, David imitated the magnificent churches of Constantinople.[7] The historian of David the Builder describes the foundation of Gelati in exhilarating words: 'This is now a foreshadowing of the second Jerusalem in the whole east, a school of all virtue, an academy of

---

[6] Eastmond, *Royal Imagery*, 61.
[7] Eastmond, *Royal Imagery*, 58–71.

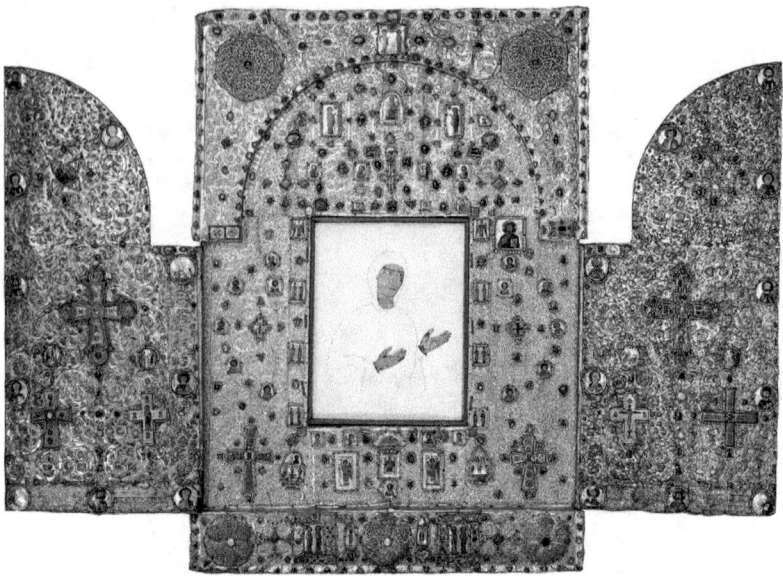

Figure 5.3  The Khakhuli Tryptich, twelfth century. Source: Artanuji Publishers.

instruction, another Athens but much superior to it in divine doctrines, a promoter of all ecclesiastical good order."[8]

In the early twelfth century, David the Builder had a triptych of the Mother of God brought from the church of Khakhuli in Tao for Gelati, where the icon was supposed to serve as an inalienable symbol of the Bagratid House. The Khakhuli Triptych, with over one hundred specimens of cloisonné enamel of various pre-twelfth-century dates, and with the icon of the Theotokos Hodegetria in its centre, is perhaps the most narrative material testament to the Bagratid claim of kinship with the Mother of God (see Fig. 5.3). In its richness, dedicatory inscriptions and imagery, the Khakhuli Triptych effectively acts as an encapsulation of the material, symbolic and genetic heritage of the Bagratid kings.[9] David's son, Demetre I, added a dedicatory inscription that announces the dynastic relationship between the donors, David and Demetre, and the Mother of God through the Davidic lineage of the Bagratids and the Theotokos:

> Just as you, o Queen, who have blossomed from your bosom through the grace of God, co-created from the beginning of times, you adorn and enrich yourself, the Temple of God, with various riches; just as

[8] *C'xovreba mep'et'-mep'isa davit'isi*, ed. Kaukhchishvili, 330–1; tr. Thomson, 322.
[9] Eastmond, 'Greeks Bearing Gifts', 88–105; Papamastorakis, 'Re-Deconstructing the Khakhuli Triptych', 225.

David, the descendent of David, dedicated himself to you, the Virgin, with all his soul, body and temple, similarly Demetre, the new Bezalel, Solomon by birth and authority, twice embellished your image with gold and silver, as the sun in the firmament, having put hopes in your intercession and co-ruling with you, Mother of God and with Christ.[10]

The second part of the inscription calls Demetre the new Bezaleel, the chief artisan of the Tabernacle, and compares him with Solomon, praising him for entrusting his kingdom to the Mother of God. The construction and completion of the Gelati Monastery and the embellishment of the Khakhuli Icon are compared to the construction of the Ark of the Covenant by Bezaleel and the founding of the Temple of Jerusalem by Solomon.

In time, the Gelati monastery became a virtual museum of Marian icons, relics and stories. Well after the collapse of the Georgian unity, local bishops and katholikoi proudly displayed these relics and recounted to foreign travellers (mostly Muscovite) all kinds of related stories that substantiated Georgia's allotment to the Theotokos. Seventeenth-century Russian diplomats noted in awe the sheer number of Marian icons and images, as well as reliquaries with extravagant relics: the Theotokos's tooth from when she was seven years old, parts of her hair that she tore when she saw the crucifixion of her son and drops of her milk.[11] Gelati was certainly the epitome of the Theotokos's political and dynastic cult, yet the material remnants of the Lot of the Mother of God, folklorised and blended with many local traditions, were scattered across Georgia's religious landscape and were entangled in subsequent power struggles, conveying both Georgia's unity and a reverse process of its disintegration.

## 5.3 Protector of Strangers

At first perhaps independently of Bagratid ideology, a dramatic impact on Georgian 'political theologies' was exercised by the growth and strengthening of the Georgian monastic communities in the Byzantine heartland. If we trust the numerous Georgian witnesses, these monks often lived in precarious circumstances where their Greek colleagues were extremely unhappy with their presence. Many of the monastic *vitae*, as well as other documents, of the tenth and eleventh centuries complain about the harassment and intimidation that the Georgian monks experienced in the monasteries in Byzantium. Some of these *vitae* then elaborate on alienation and strangeness as expressions of the Georgian minority's spiritual and moral superiority

---

[10] Quoted in Papamastorakis, 'Re-Deconstructing the Khakhuli Triptych', 226.
[11] Yevlev, *Stateinyi spisok*, ed. Tsintsadze, 52–3.

against the Greeks. It was in this abject context that the Georgian cult of the Mother of God flourished, and who then evolved into the exclusive patroness of the Georgians.

The earliest narrative where alienation is presented as an advantage and sign of Marian patronage is the anonymous tenth-century *Life of Ilarion the Georgian*. The *Life of Ilarion* reflects the history of tenth-century Georgia, and chronicles the origin of the Georgian Athonite colony, founded shortly before the *Life*'s composition, along with other Georgian monasteries across Byzantium and the Near East.[12] It introduces St Ilarion as a trailblazer who prefigured the religious and intellectual exodus from Georgia, having reached further west than any other Georgian has ever travelled, all the way to Rome. As such, Ilarion was one of the first saintly figures to receive an addition to his name *K'art'veli* 'Iberian' or 'Georgian', used primarily with reference to Georgian spiritual authorities who had lived outside Georgia.

The story of Ilarion's journey fictionalises the first encounter between the Georgian and Greek monks, the two co-religionist but in practice antagonistic people. By transforming the rhetoric of strangeness and powerlessness into that of superiority, it voices one of the earliest pieces of overtly anti-Byzantine rhetoric: Ilarion's and his companions' arrival at Olympus, where they eventually founded a monastery, immediately caused a scandal. When the Georgian brethren spent their first night there, suspicious of their incomprehensible language and alien looks, the Greek abbot grew wary of their presence and conspired to oust them. Before dawn, the abbot, however, saw a vision, where the Mother of God scolded him for plotting against her people:

> O the wretched one, why did you conspire to expel the strangers who have arrived here for the love of my Son and God and had abandoned their country, and you have not followed the law of the acceptance of foreigners and of the poor. Is it not known to you that there are many who have found their home here on this mountain who speak their own tongues and are saved by God? And whoever does not accept them are my enemies, for that nation was given to me [*rametʻu čemda moničebul ars*] by my Son for their steadfast Orthodoxy for they believed in the name of my Son and were baptised.[13]

This is the earliest attested claim that the Georgian nation 'had been given to the Theotokos'. Such explicit formulation, however, appears in the

---

[12] Martin-Hisard, 'Du T'ao-K'lardzheti à l'Athos', 34–46.
[13] *C'xovrebay ... ilarion k'art'velisay*, §18, ed. Abuladze, 20.10–20: https://titus.uni-frankfurt.de/texte/etcs/cauc/ageo/gh/gh2/gh2.htm.

Athonite version of the *Life of Ilarion*, and differs from with the somewhat later metaphrastic version. The metaphrastic *Life*, created independently from the Athonite recension a century later, although in tune with this passage in its rhetoric, lacks this specific formulation.[14] Although both recensions were created by Georgia's expatriate monks as pieces of anti-Byzantine rhetoric, a nuanced difference transpires between the two versions of the Theotokos's speech:

> Why, did you, the wretched one, dishonourably cast away the great labourer Ilarion and his companions? Why could you forget in your shamelessness the commandment of my Son and Lord, for he blesses the lovers of the foreigners and gives pain to the merciless and the evil ... and why did you give yourself to this foolish speech and believe that only the tongue of the Greeks is accepted? How come you do not know that all races who fear God and follow his commandments are agreeable to God? How come you alienated yourself from the prayer of my friend and from his blessing? For whoever does not accept them is my enemy!'[15]

While the two speeches are similar in scope and rhetoric, they also illustrate two evolving discourses. The Athonite version evokes the story of the Lot of the Mother of God and points to the Georgians as the Theotokos's exclusive allotment. Whereas in the metaphrastic version, the political and theological conceptualisation of Georgia as the 'lot of the Mother of God' is rudimentary. The metaphrastic version is more inclusive in its belief that the Theotokos is the protectress of all aliens, immigrants and linguistic minorities. It seems to be in line with the Palestinian Georgian rhetoric of the superiority of the Georgian language. In the Palestinian *Praise and the Glory of the Georgian Language*, the Georgian tongue is like Lazarus, buried until the end of time. It is 'adorned and blessed by the name of the Lord, yet wretched and unwelcome that awaits the day of the Lord's second coming', and, unsurprisingly, contains all the secrets of the universe.[16] The self-deprecatory qualifiers (alien, strange, forgotten, neglected) echo similar wordings of the Georgians in Byzantium, where their powerlessness of a minority is presented as an advantage. In the Palestinian hymn, however, the Theotokos is absent, and the exclusive nature of Mary's protection of the Georgians is yet unknown. While 'weakness as an asset' seems to have

---

[14] Both versions are edited and compared by Dolakidze, *żveli redakc'iebi*. See also, Martin-Hisard, 'La pérégrination', 101–38.
[15] *C'xovrebay... ilarion axlisay*, ed. Abuladze, 228.1–14: https://titus.uni-frankfurt.de/texte/etcs/cauc/ageo/gh/gh3/gh3.htm.
[16] *K'ebay da didebay*, ed. Shanidze, 283.

been an established trope in pre-Athonite Georgian rhetoric, as confirmed in the image of the archetypal weak alien, St Nino, the extrapolation of the 'Lot of the Mother of God' is a specifically Byzantine Georgian invention.

It was on Mt Athos and in its hagiographic and artistic production, and the resulting oral narratives, that the Lot of the Mother of God became associated with Georgianness par excellence. Unlike the Palestinian monks, the Athonite Fathers were also backed by a relatively powerful monarchy. George Hagiorites's *Life of John and Euthymios*, the first two *hegoumenoi* of Iveron, is an apology for the Georgian cause on the Holy Mountain. It is dedicated to defending the rights of the Georgians to own the Iveron Monastery, and to preserving the memory of the monastery's Georgian foundation. Throughout the narrative, the Mother of God repeatedly appears as the personal protectress of the Georgians: 'Thus the efforts of [the Greeks to take away first the Monastery and then the church from the Georgians] were to no avail as the Holy Mother of God granted her glorious church to us, the poor, assisting and protecting us, the unworthy and foreign flock of her glorifiers.'[17] Through the Theotokos's intercession, in spite of the Greek resistance, the Emperor Michael IV Paphlagonian (1034–41) officially confirmed the monastery together with its treasure as a Georgian possession.

The *Life* also records a unique miracle with the Mother of God at its core. Ioane reports that his son Euthymios's education was initially Georgian, and that he was raised as a nobleman. But once his father decided that Euthymios was to follow in his footsteps as a monk, the boy's education became entirely Greek, causing him to forget his native tongue. One day, youthful Euthymios fell ill. Once left alone in his cell, the Mother of God appeared and healed him, and, in addition, returned to him a perfect knowledge of the Georgian tongue. Mary told him in a vision: '"Nothing is wrong with you, get up, do not be afraid and [hence] speak the Georgian [language] fluently"', ... the blessed Ioane continued: "Until then, his Georgian had not been good and I worried for this reason but since then ceaselessly, like spring water, [the Georgian language] purer than of any Georgian flows from his mouth." Ioane told his newly healed son, 'My son, the land of Kartli is in a great need of books, for they lack many of them. I see what God has granted to you [so make sure that] with your efforts you multiply your gift from God.'[18] Later, in Giorgi Mc'ire's *Life of George Hagiorites*, who also became a *hegumen* of Iveron, the Mother of God is

---

[17] Giorgi Xuc'esmonazoni, *c'xovreba ... iovanesi da ep't'wmesi*, ed. Kaukhchishvili, 60–1; tr. Grdzelidze, 92–3.

[18] Giorgi Xuc'esmonazoni, *c'xovreba ... iovanesi da ep't'wmesi*, §§23–4: ed. Abuladze, 60–1: https://titus.uni-frankfurt.de/texte/etcs/cauc/ageo/gh/gh2/gh2lex.htm; tr. Grdzelidze, 67.

once again presented as the protectress of the Georgian language. To commemorate this miracle, the Georgian Athonites commissioned an icon of the Theotokos flanked by Euthymios and Giorgi, which was brought and placed on Giorgi's grave. 'Thus, the most Holy Mother of God glorified those who had glorified Her. She edified our nation by granting health and perfect knowledge of the Georgian language to one man and wisdom and intelligence to the other, and so both of them glorified the most glorious cause of our well-being according to their ability.'[19]

The miraculous anamnesis experienced by Euthymios is typologically identical to earlier conversion and foundation narratives, where the founders uncovered their true history and identity. The anonymous *Praise and Glory* specifically addresses the Georgian tongue as a buried and discovered treasure. The old trope of the founder's conversion to a new ethos, P'arnavaz, Mirian, Vakhtang or Ašot 'forgetting' their former identities and languages, is here reimagined as a new act of conversion to Georgianness with the Theotokos's involvement. Such a stress on language reflects the evolution of the idea of Georgianness together with the expansion of the Kartvelian sphere of influence across Caucasia and monastic colonies abroad. The Č'ordvaneli family to which Ioane belonged was originally precisely from such a multi-ethnic milieu in the surrounding of the Oshki Cathedral, where the anxieties over language and identity have been prevalent since Giorgi Merč'ule. It was, therefore, this expanding, fluid and indeed anxious concept of Georgianness, instead of specific geographic entities, that had been reimagined as Mary's lot.

Perhaps the most famous material attestation to this Georgian Hagiorite legend is the icon of the Mother of God of Iveron, the *Panagia Portaitissa*, or as known to Georgians and Russians, the Mother of God of Iveria. The icon was made in the late tenth or early eleventh centuries, soon after the foundation of the monastery by Ioane, Ep't'wime and Commander Ioane-T'ornik. By the thirteenth century, the fame of the icon spread across the entire Greece, and the Monastery of Iveron acquired an additional name, *Monastery of the Most Holy Theotokos Who Is Called Portaitissa*.[20] When in the mid-fourteenth century, the Greeks took the monastery away from the Georgians, the Church of the Portaitissa, where the icon was housed, remained in Iberian hands. The stories of the origins of the *Portaitissa* icon, spread on Mt Athos and beyond, reflected the Georgian pretences on

---

[19] Giorgi Mc'ire, *c'xovreba ... giorgi mt'acmidelisay*, §99, ed. Abuladze, 202.6–11; https://titus.uni-frankfurt.de/texte/etcs/cauc/ageo/gh/gh2/gh2lex.htm; tr. Grdzelidze, 158–9; Martin-Hisard, 'La Vie de Georges l'Hagiorite', 146.

[20] Chryssochoidis, 'Portaitissa Icon', 133–5. See also, Vocotopoulos, 'Note sur l'icône de la Vierge Portaïtissa', 27–30.

Mt Athos. According to the now famous legend, during Iconoclasm, a certain widow in Nicaea owned the icon. The iconoclast emperor's soldiers discovered the icon and threw it into the sea. The Panagia was lost for over a century and a half, until it made an appearance near the shores of Mt Athos as a column of light. No one, however, was able to retrieve the icon, as it would evade everyone who approached. The only person who was deemed worthy to remove the icon from the sea was a pious Georgian monk named Gabriel, who walked across the waves and retrieved the icon. The icon was then placed in the *parekklesion*, where it acted as the monastery's guardian and protector, hence her name *Portaitissa*.[21]

During the formation of the united Georgian kingdom, the Lot of the Mother of God became a concept that seemingly galvanised Georgia's political unity. It was a flexible cult that dialogised both with the old Mtskhetan mythology and opened new avenues for the shaping of new mythologies of the monarchy. On the one hand, the Theotokos was a relative and a personal patron of the Bagratids, the almost undisputable reigning dynasty, and on the other, via the Athonites, she became the protector of the Georgians par excellence. In the sacred image of the Theotokos, kingship, territoriality and language were united.

However, although united under a single crown, *Sak'art'velo* remained a project rather than a monolithic concept carved in stone. The persistence of confusing terms such as *K'art'li*, *K'art'veli* and *Sak'art'velo*, together with the medieval authors' recurring explanations of *Sak'art'velo*'s limits and repeated enumerations of its constituent parts, reflected the ambiguity of this unity. During the peak of its power in the late twelfth and early thirteenth centuries, this united Georgian kingdom was a centralised system, ruled by Bagratid symbolism and rhetoric. Yet, even then, the regional rulers struggled for autonomy, and some of the powerful regional houses across the kingdom, such as the Bagvaši, T'oreli, Mxargrżeli, Jaqeli, Kaxaberisże and others, vehemently opposed the centralising policies of the Bagratids. Other, formerly independent principalities retained memories, often institutionalised, of

---

[21] The Greek *Hypomnema* is edited in Bury, 'Iveron and Our Lady', 86–99. See also, Steppan, 'Überlegungen zur Ikone der Panhagia Portaitissa', 23–49. The legends became particularly popular in the post-Byzantine Russian tradition. In the mid-eighteenth century, diplomat and scholar Timot'e Gabashvili (1703–64) visited the Holy Mountain and collected local legends and sayings. By the time Gabashvili visited Athos, the legends that connected the Virgin with the Georgians had multiplied. Gabashvili proudly comments that the story of the discovery of *Panagia Portaitissa* and other miracles 'have been clearly displayed in favour and love of Georgia, by the Holy Virgin for the nation allotted to her'; tr. Wilkinson and Ebanoidze, *Pilgrimage*, 40, 82–5.

their former autonomy. The Katholikos of Apkhazeti, for example, although nominally subject to the Mtskhetan katholikos-patriarch, retained his prestige until the nineteenth century, and in the middle ages had the exclusive prerogative of anointing the kings of united Georgia.[22] Some of these great feudal houses, such as the Jaqeli, were offered highest hereditary administrative titles at the royal court to curb their separatist tendencies. When the Mongols invaded in the 1230s, the disintegration of the Georgian kingdom was already underway. It first split into two, then three kingdoms. Then even more principalities emerged. By the sixteenth century, Georgia's disintegration was a fait accompli. Along with the growing separatist tendencies, the question of what exactly constituted the Lot of the Mother of God lingered. Was it Kartli in its narrow sense, with Mtskhetan mythology at its core? Or did it imply Georgia in its broadest possible sense? If so, how broad? Arguably, the cult of the Mother of God embodied and projected this anxiety – since it was both a symbol of unity as well as a herald of Georgia's disintegration. From a barely realised project, *Sak'art'velo*, as a concept, was soon thereafter on its way to becoming a realm of sacred memory.

## 5.4 The Acquri Icon of the Mother of God

Although the concept of the Lot of the Mother of God was embedded into the conversion narratives, both eastern and western Georgian, and legitimised the female apostolic mission, the same motif was utilised as a groundwork for a parallel, and a rival narrative of the conversion, in part also intertwined with the problematisation of the feminine. This alternative conversion narrative that involved apostle Andrew, on the one hand, antedated the first appearance of Christianity on Georgian land to the era of the first apostles, and on the other, solved the Nino conundrum of the grand conversion narrative. In the literary tradition, Nino was continuously flanked by men (Syrian Fathers, King Vakhtang, St George, Apostle Andrew) who institutionalised, legalised and normalised her charismatic achievement. Near the end of the first millennium, yet another cycle was shaped in Georgian writing to complement the conversion narrative – the stories of Georgia's 'first' conversion by Christ's apostles, Andrew, Bartholomew, Simon the Zealot and occasionally others. As shown in the previous chapter, the Andrew story was eagerly internalised and disseminated by the Georgians, yet an element that found a specifically Georgian life was the episode of Andrew's conversion of a female ruler. Since Strabo,

---

[22] *Istoriani da azmani*, ed. Kaukhchishvili, 26.

the representation of the Caucasus and its tribes was fuzzy, which resulted in the series of geographic blunders. One of such legendary tribes that were localised in the Caucasus mountains were the Amazons.[23] By the ninth century, the association of the Amazons with the Caucasus had become so common that monk Epiphanius specifically pointed out Sousania, a mountainous region in the Caucasus, as a realm ruled by women.

Although since the translation of Epiphanius's *Life of Andrew* many authors have elaborated and commented on Andrew's mission to Georgia, the lengthy anonymous interpolation with an unknown date in the *K'art'lis C'xovreba*, which details Andrew's sojourn in Georgia, is altogether unique.[24] It narrates that following the Crucifixion, Georgia was allotted to the Theotokos. Yet, her journey to this country was interrupted by Christ, who instructed her to send Andrew the First-Called instead:

> Then the all-holy one said to the apostle Andrew: 'My son Andrew, it seems to my soul a serious matter that the name of my Son has not been preached in the land which is my lot. When I was setting out to preach my Son in that land which fell to my lot, suddenly my good Son and God appeared to me and ordered that you go and take my image and that of my good Son to the land which fell to my lot, so that I may direct their salvation, stretch out my hand and help them, and that none of their enemies may overcome them.'[25]

On her son's order, Mary fetched a board, washed her face, made an *acheiropoieton* icon of herself and handed it over to Andrew. Since then, Mary's image has guided Andrew on his journey to Georgia.[26] The deviation from the original *K'art'lis C'xovreba* notice is striking. While the original account refers to Megrelians, Apkhazeti and Egrisi in the third person, the insertion is a first-person narrative, an account of 'our own' conversion: Andrew first arrived in Trebizond, 'the city of the Megrelians', and then set off to Achara,

---

[23] For an exhaustive collection of ancient sources that localise the Amazons in or north of the Caucasus, see Gordeziani (ed.), *Encyclopedia Caucasus Antiquus*, vol. 1 (Tbilisi, 2010).

[24] The insertion is published together with the original text in Leonti Mroveli, *c'xovreba k'art'velt'a mep'et'a*, ed. Kaukhchishvili. However, the part is marked as a later interpolation. The dating of the interpolation is problematic, though it must have appeared after the thirteenth century, as it does not appear in the Armenian translation of the *Georgian Chronicles*.

[25] *K'art'lis C'xovreba*, ed. Kaukhchishvili, 38; tr. Thomson, 355.

[26] It is due to this association that in May 2019, the Georgian parliament passed a law that officially announced 12 May as the day of 'the lot of the Mother of God'. The same day had been earlier established as the feast of Andrew the First-Called.

'the land of Kartli.²⁷ The terminology used in this paragraph suggests a contemporary geographic vision, and a longer experience of a Georgian union. Crucially, the insertion also tears up the compositional structure of the *K'art'lis C'xovreba*, whereby a direct link was made between the Theotokos and her female apostle three centuries later, thereby disrupting the principal argument for female apostolicity, and placing Andrew as a mediator between Mary and St Nino. The inserted narrative is entirely disinterested in St Nino and is an altogether new foundational story, centred around the Church of Acquri in southern Georgia, in the region of Samtskhe.

Upon his arrival in Achara, the first properly Georgian region, Andrew converted the people and built a church of the Mother of God. The Theotokos instructed him to leave a miraculous copy of her icon for the local people, which he did. Throughout the narrative, Andrew is presented merely as a messenger, while the true agent is the icon of the Theotokos. Arguably, this trope is a reflection or was reflected in the traditional oral accounts of travelling *xatis* (icons) and their *dačerili* (captive or possessed) companions, the *k'adagis*. The rest of Andrew's travel is essentially a collection of the miracles performed by the Icon. Andrew then crossed a high mountain pass, Rkinis Jvari (Iron Cross) where he erected a cross, and reached the borders of Samtskhe, Georgia's southern province. He stopped near a mountain called Zaden Gora, and annihilated the local idols. In those days, Acquri, the centre of Samtskhe, was governed by a widow, Samżivari. The queen's son had recently died, and the city was engulfed in grief. One night, the locals saw a bright light emanating from the icon of the Theotokos. They discovered Andrew and reported to the ruler that a man had arrived who preached a strange, living god. When Samżivari heard that this god could resurrect people, she immediately summoned Andrew to her presence. Andrew told her whence he had come, and that he was the disciple of Jesus Christ, the son of God. The widow begged Andrew to bring back her son to life. Andrew only asked her to have faith in Jesus, and she thus accepted Jesus as her God. Andrew then placed the icon of the Virgin on the deceased boy and after a brief prayer, brought him back to life. The joyous woman immediately converted and was baptised. The good news spread across Samtskhe, and everyone gathered to witness the miracle. The priests of Artemis and Apollo, however, resisted and challenged Andrew. To challenge them, Andrew offered to leave the icon of the Virgin inside the temple of Artemis and Apollo, to see who would prevail. After a long night's prayer, they opened the door and discovered that the two idols had been smashed by the icon. Then the time arrived for Andrew to leave. The

---

²⁷ Thomson, *Rewriting Caucasian History*, 355–9.

widow begged him to stay but Andrew was destined to preach in other places too. So, he recounted to them the story of the *acheiropoieton* Icon of the Virgin, 'how the land of Samtskhe became the lot of the holy Mother of God. And that she had sent this icon here as a hope and protector of the land of her choice, and it is still here, resting here for ever and ever.' This is when the Meskhians (dwellers of Samtskhe) heard for the first time that their land had been allotted to the Mother of God. Andrew left the icon in a small church in Acquri, which later became a great cathedral. He then continued his journey in the 'lands of Kartli'. He went to Tao, to the banks of Chorokhi River. Then he turned north and arrived in Svaneti, which was ruled by a woman and he converted her too. He crossed the Caucasus, converted the Ossetes, turned back, went to Apkhazeti, arrived in C'xumi (Sokhumi) and preached there too. He left Simon there and went further to Jik'et'i in the North Caucasus. Those people were, however, wild and could not be converted. As a result, they remain pagan. So, Andrew went back, he fortified the faith of the Megrelians and the Apkhazs, and continued his way to Scythia, where the story ends.[28]

Andrew's journey to Samtskhe is essentially a replica of Nino's travels. It even hijacks some of the principal episodes of the original conversion narrative. Like Nino, Andrew erects crosses along the way and on top of the mountains adjacent to Acquri. He arrives at a hill called Zadeni, which was also the name of a hill near Mtskheta where the idol of Zadeni was destroyed by Nino's prayers. Like Nino, Andrew hid himself before emerging and presented himself to the ruler. The ensuing miracles are also identical to those performed by Nino. However, they surpass Nino's achievement in their magnitude – Nino merely heals the queen, whereas Andrew brings back to life the Queen's son.[29] Finally, it is Samtskhe, not 'the land of Kartli', that carries the prestige of the 'Lot of the Mother of God', since it had been converted far before Kartli.

Naturally, the question arises regarding the time and context of this legend's formation. In the late twelfth century, bishop Ioane of Anč'i, Tamar's contemporary, was aware of the story of Andrew's sojourn to Georgia. But to Ioane's knowledge, Andrew had brought the *acheiropoieton* icon of Christ, a ceramic copy of the Edessa *Keramidion*, the Anč'isxati.[30] Arguably, the Meskhetian insertion into the *K'art'lis C'xovreba* is a post-Tamar narrative, which was written after the downfall of the Georgian kingdom, and the rise of the House of Jaqeli in Samtskhe. Since Queen Rusudan,

---

[28] *C'xovreba k'art'velt'a mep'et'a*, ed. Kaukhchishvili, 39–43, tr. Thomson, 359.
[29] For the archaeological evidence, see Licheli, 'St Andrew in Samtskhe', 25–37.
[30] Ioane Anč'eli, *galobani*, ed. Sulava, 297–300.

Tamar's daughter and successor, until Georgia's official disintegration in the mid-fifteenth century, some of Georgia's regions, the most powerful being the Atabagate of Samtskhe, have claimed independence. The Meskhetian insertion can be interpreted as part of the south Georgian rulers, the Atabags project to sever ties from the centralised Georgian monarchy, its church and its foundation mythology by creating a rival foundation narrative for the Cathedral of Acquri.

Since the formation of the Georgian monarchy, Samtskhe, part of the larger historical region of Meskheti, has resisted the centralising policies of the Bagratids. In the eleventh century, it was controlled by the powerful Baġvaši House, the most dangerous rival of the Bagratids. In 1054, the Byzantines made Liparit IV Baġvaši the de facto ruler of the entire southern Georgia, before he was detained and exiled by Bagrat IV.[31] The region rose to strategic and cultural prominence during Tamar's reign as symbolised by another important foundation, which, similarly to Acquri, carried both strategic and religious significance. This was the cave city and church of Vardzia, another major foundation dedicated to the Theotokos. Vardzia reached the peak of its importance under Tamar, but was also destroyed by the same earthquake that razed Acquri. According to Tamar's contemporary historians, the Mother of God of Vardzia was the principal protectress of the Queen and her army.[32]

In 1266 Sargis I Jaqeli, the Duke of Samtskhe and the king's chancellor, requested the Mongols to grant him independence from the Georgian monarchy, an event that marked the beginning of the end of the united Georgian monarchy, only briefly restored by Giorgi V the 'Brilliant' (1299–1302, 1318–46). In 1285 Bek'a I Jaqeli ruled a large territory from central Kartli to Erzurum. In the early fourteenth century, an officially independent political entity, the Samtskhe Atabagate, was created, for centuries the largest and the most powerful principality in Georgia.[33] Since then, the Samtskhe Atabags have fought bitterly against the Georgian monarchy, even capturing king Giorgi VIII. A century later, Atabag Quarquare the Great (1451–98) initiated an ecclesiastic severance of the Seat of Acquri from the rest of Georgia, with a determination to establish an independent

---

[31] For these events, see Rayfield, *Edge of Empires*, 77–9.
[32] As a celebration of the victory against the Seljuks in the 1202 battle of Basiani, Ioane Šavt'eli composed an encomium to the Mother of God of Vardzia thanking her for the victory. Ioane Šavt'eli, *galobani*, ed. Sulava, 301–5.
[33] The *Atabeg* was a hereditary title of Turkic origin used as the highest military rank in the Kingdom of Georgia. The Atabags were first the Mxargrdzeli family and then the Jakeli House, who ruled in the South.

katholikosate of Samtskhe. Due to their increasing power and the vulnerable state of the eastern bishops, the Atabags secured the support of Constantinople. A Greek bishop was consecrated as the bishop of Acquri, and became a de facto katholikos, eventually receiving the right to ordain other bishops of Samtskhe. Therefore, it must have been under Quarquare or his immediate descendants that the insertion into the *K'art'lis C'xovreba* was made, as a codification of the Meskhetian version of the conversion into the grand Georgian narrative. Along with creating a new foundational mythology, the Jaqeli House strove to de-sacralise the Bagratid Dynasty by usurping their traditional saintly rhetoric, which is confirmed by the exceptional patronage that the Jaqelis demonstrated towards the *Panagia Portaitissa* on Mt Athos.[34]

Acquri was a cathedral seat since the ninth century, as attested in Giorgi Merč'ule's *Life of Grigol*.[35] In time the cathedral succumbed to frequent earthquakes, and archaeologists identify two main layers of the church, the tenth- to eleventh-century and thirteenth- to fourteenth-century layers. The church reached the peak of its influence by the eleventh century, and was then rehabilitated in the thirteenth under Queen Tamar. By the eleventh century, the Cathedral of Acquri must have been the largest church in the area, and was known as the 'great church of the Meskhians', rivalling the soon-to-be-completed Svetitskhoveli Cathedral. The Meskhetian interpolators of the *K'art'lis C'xovreba* ascribe to their cathedral church a grand history of foundation by circumventing the established tradition of the *Mokc'evay*. Another addition to the *K'art'lis C'xovreba*, specifically to the *Life of Vakhtang*, expands on the Emperor Heraclius's sojourn in the Caucasus, and ascribes to Heraclius the foundation of the Acquri Cathedral. Heraclius had allegedly heard of the wonder-working icon of the Mother of God, which was placed in a small chapel in Acquri, and went to worship it. 'Then Heraclius began to lay the foundations, and to build the large church at Acqueri. After that it was completed by pious men; and it was made into a bishopric.'[36]

---

[34] This is illustrated by Quarquare's dedicatory inscription on the icon. For text and discussion, see Skhirtladze, *iveriis xatis močediloba*, 3–27. The documents of Iveron also contain dedicatory letters of Quarquare's sons, K'aixosro and Mzečabuk with particular dedication to the *Portaitissa*. Skhirtladze, *iveriis gvt'ismšoblis xatis močediloba*, 9–10.

[35] Acquri was originally known as Acqueri. However, due to the rather inappropriate meaning of the Georgian word *queri* (testicle), the site gave birth to too many equally inappropriate foundation myths. Hence, in time, *queri* was changed to *quri* ('ear' in Georgian), and the place is currently known as Acquri.

[36] Juanšer, *c'xovreba*, ed. Kaukhchishvili, 224; tr. Thomson, 369–70. The author of these insertions may be the same person, someone closely acquainted with the geography of southern and south-western Georgia. In addition, the direction of the verbs that the author uses are always directed to the first person.

The history of the Acquri icon of the Mother of God took a similar path of 'nationalisation' as the cult of Queen Shushanik, who had been earlier venerated as a specifically regional saint of Gugareti, essentially the same territory that later constituted Meskheti, and was then nationalised by the Armenians and Georgians. This liminality of Acquri as a strategic fortress at the southern fringes of the Georgian kingdom and of its icon, and Meskheti's borderland identity between Christian Georgian lands and the Muslim powers, determined the subsequent claims of Acquri's historic centrality in the emerging ideology of the rulers of Samtskhe. Just as the Lot of the Mother of God was utilised in the Bagratid rhetoric as a mobilising force for the unification of the Georgian lands under their crown, the same concept was revitalised in the process of the disintegration of the Georgian kingdom, both political and ideological.

The Acquri Icon became strongly ingrained in Meskhetian identity, especially in their separatist claims. In the early eighteenth century, Vakhushti Bagrationi recounts the following story: When Uzun-Hasan the *šahanšah* of the White Sheep Turkomans (1453–78) pillaged Georgia, among other trophies he also removed the holy icon of Acquri from Meskheti. The Meskhians then left their land and migrated to Kartli. The captured icon performed numerous punishing miracles and was eventually returned to where it belonged. Immediately the gloom and darkness turned into light in Meskheti. When the Meskhians heard of this, they decided to return to Meskheti. The King of Kartli, however, prohibited them from leaving. Nevertheless, one night they left. Having discovered their flight, Kartli's king Konstantine chased them. A battle between the Meskhians and Kartlians ensued, and the Meskhians came out victorious having decimated the Kartlian army.[37] The Icon of Acquri is a symbol of local Meskhetian patriotism. Samtskhe's historic severance from Kartli was perceived through the biblical exemplum of Exodus.

In Caucasia, Samtskhe was not the only region to seek ideological severance from the kingdom, or to have created an alternative foundation narrative. West of Kartli, King Bagrat VI of Imereti (1463–1578) made the Patriarch of Antioch consecrate the Bishop of Tsaishi and Bedia as the Katholikos of Apkhazeti. In an encyclical letter that was supposed to confirm this fact, he made sure to say that, 'well before Kartli was converted by Nino, [west] of its borders, St Andrew had enlightened us with a shadeless light.'[38]

Further north-west, along the Black Sea coast, the Princely State of Odishi claimed a direct affiliation with the Mother of God. Like the south

---

[37] Vaxušti Batonišvili, *ağcera*, ed. Kaukhchishvili, 708–11.
[38] *mc'nebay sasjulo* (Teaching on Faith) is published in Zhordania, *k'ronikebi* 2, 294–7.

Georgian Jaqeli House, the Dadiani House ascended to power in the twelfth century. The region's secession from the central monarchy was a lengthy process, culminating in Levan I Dadiani's proclamation of independence from Imereti, a newly formed kingdom in western Georgia. The next few centuries, however, were marked by bloody and ugly wars between the princes of Odishi, Guria, the principality of Svaneti and the kings of Imereti and Kartli, accompanied by a formation of rival foundation myths. The Dadianis, who controlled the Black Sea coasts, created an independent chain of associations between the Mother of God and their principality, and had claimed that they possessed the robe of the Mother of God, and a fragment of her belt, still proudly exhibited in the Zugdidi museum. The owner of the robe was the Monastery of Khobi, which, as the local tradition claimed, had been founded by the Emperor Heraclius.[39]

There are no sources corroborating or confirming these stories before the seventeenth century, and we only know of them from later Russian and European accounts.[40] The legends of the Theotokos's robe and a fragment of her belt is believed to have first arisen in the sixteenth century with Dadiani's claim for independence. Their mission was identical to that of the Jaqeli: to claim that Samegrelo was the Mother of God's Lot, a claim more easily substantiated by the Dadiani's access to the Black Sea. Notably, the argument of the translation of the holy relics to Georgia stems not from the period after the fall of Constantinople, but rather from Iconoclasm. The pressing on this point, that Georgia was the only Christian region unaffected by Iconoclasm, was recommended by Ephrem Mc'ire in the eleventh century, to argue for an uninterrupted continuity of Orthodoxy in Georgia and Georgia as an abode of material veneration, as confirmed also by the story of the Panagia Portaitissa.

---

[39] For the history of the holy relics in Samegrelo, see Kalandia, *odišis saepiskoposoebi*.

[40] In 1652, Russian ambassador to the Kingdom of Imereti, Aleksey Yevlev, recounted the meeting with certain Athonite monks who had arrived in Imereti to collect taxes from their metochia and lands. The monastery and ethnicity of the monks is not specified but was most likely Iveron. From these monks, Yevlev heard about the Monastery of Khobi in the Dadiani Principality. The Church of the Dormition of the Khobi Monastery was allegedly founded by the Emperor Heraclius, and kept its most cherished icon, the robe of the Mother of God. The robe was allegedly brought to Samegrelo during iconoclasm by a certain librarian. Yevlev asked the Katholikos of Imereti whether he could confirm this story. The katholikos confirmed and said that he had venerated the robe numerous times. Aleksey Yevlev, *Stateinyĭ spisok*, ed. Tsintsadze, 63–4. Apart from Yevlev, other seventeenth-century Russian travellers also recount a similar story. See, e.g. Pavel Aleppsky, *Opisanie Gruzii*, ed. N. Asatiani, 71. The inscriptions on the reliquary where the robe is currently kept are also dated to the seventeenth century, more precisely to 1640.

## 5.5 Women at the Margins

It is noteworthy that the Georgians focused on the mysterious female ruler that Andrew had allegedly converted. But this ruler was in Svaneti, so the Meskhetian authors invented an additional female ruler, the widow Samżivari, who was converted even before the Svanetian queen. Interestingly, the appearance of this additional person, Samżivari, can be traced to Arseni's rewriting of Epiphanius's original account. While Epiphanius and Euthymios refer to a tribe of Sousania in the Caucasus who were ruled by a woman, Arseni removes this reference and places this female ruler abstractly within Georgia. This has allowed the Meskhetian creators of the Samżivari story to localise her in Samtskhe instead of the original Sosanigia. By the time this legend was crystallised, the feminisation of this narrative was already determined by several independent factors: first, this was caused by the original association of the Caucasus with the Amazons; second the existing Nino tradition contributed to this factor; and finally the memory and cult of Queen Tamar consolidated this association of women with transitional events in history.

The Meskhetian story poses an obvious question – is there any connection between the two most obscure names, the widow *Samżivari* and the mythological female *Samżimari*, or is this connection a mere coincidence? Jean-Pierre Mahé constructs an elaborate chain of argumentation, arguing that the two are in fact the same character with a slight phonetic variation. Samżivari is interpreted as the 'carrier of a pearl necklace'. Despite such a coincidence, it is hard to substantiate any relation between these two characters. Samżivari was an influential feudal house that is attested to have ruled in Samtskhe in the twelfth–fourteenth centuries. Their name is perfectly explainable from the Samżivari Valley. The house intermarried with other Meskhetian houses, the T'oreli and the Jaqeli. Yet, in a sixteenth-century list of Meskhetian feudal houses they are identified as extinct. Therefore, by the time of the crystallisation of Andrew's story, the Samżivari House was extinct or merged with the ruling House of Jaqeli. The narrative function of the female ruler was to mark the end of an era, a transitional moment in the history of Samtskhe, the end of the Samżivari House and the beginning of something new – perhaps of the Jaqeli. It could have also served as a reference to Queen Tamar, as a symbol of the Golden Age, yet also a marker of the end of the same age, and the beginning of the rise of Meskheti.

Since the reverse is impossible due to the historicity of the House of Samżivari, could it be the case that this account that made its way into the so-called *Axali* (New) *K'art'lis C'xovreba*, was folklorised, eventually ending up from Georgia's extreme south to the north-Caucasian lore? Due to the extraordinary similarity in names and the general propensity of Georgian writings towards folklorisation, this theory cannot be excluded. Perhaps the oddity of the name and its *mżivi* root made an impression on its listeners, causing the figure to spiral into the realm of lore and into a character of a pearl-wearing enchantress.

There is no way of substantiating this thought, therefore we can leave it as it is. Nevertheless, the fact remains that the feminine aspect of Georgia's conversion narratives was utilised in the power discourse of the rulers of Samtskhe. The Samżivari story was a post-Tamar phenomenon, when due to the lasting influence of the *Life of Nino* and the dramatic phenomenon of Queen Tamar, the feminine became strongly associated with extraordinary times, and liminal or transient political states of affairs. The rhetoric of the Nino story, coupled with the memory of Queen Tamar and her daughter Rusudan, where one marked the pinnacle of Georgia's strength and unity and the other symbolised its demise and disintegration, was embedded in the image of Samżivari, the first Christian ruler of Georgia, who was also, due to her widowhood, the last member of her House.

# 6
# The Queen's Three Bodies

## 6.1 The Two Queens

The title of the present chapter, with an intentional allusion to Kantorowicz's classic study, refers to the tripartite representation of a remarkably prominent person of Georgia's political history, cult, folklore and national myth – Queen Tamar. Indeed, no other figure in Georgia's history has received attention comparable to the centrality of Tamar in medieval and modern historiography, religious writing, encomia, prose, epic poetry and the echoing oral traditions. Today Tamar is firmly ingrained in Georgian national imagery, popular memory and ecclesiastic commemorations, with multiple historic locations, churches, bridges and ruins indiscriminately attributed to the Queen and her era (see Map 6.1). Essentially, across the

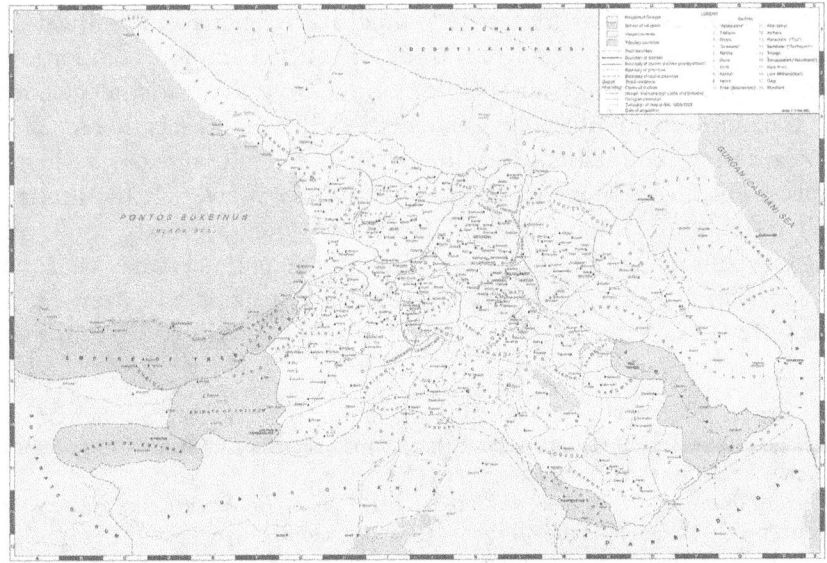

Map 6.1 The Georgan Kingdom during the reign of Queen Tamar. Source: D. Muskhelishvili, Historical Atlas of Georgia.

entirety of Georgia, any medieval monument without secure identification and dating is linked by local residents with Tamar.[1] The memory of Tamar and her 'Golden Age' constituted the core of romantic nationalism, especially since the 'reanimation' of her figure in nineteenth-century poetry.[2] Tamar's cult has transcended national historiography, and she has been venerated as a great saint, with multiple churches dedicated to her, in particular over the previous century. While her great grandfather, David the Builder, was the principal driving force behind Georgia's political achievements in the twelfth century, and was also canonised as a saint, neither his, nor indeed any other historic figure's, representation can match that of Tamar's centrality in commemorative practices. Rivalled only by St George and the Theotokos and their multiple feast-days, the church commemorates Tamar three times: 31 January, 14(10) May and the Sunday of the Myrrh Bearers.

With Tamar's political image as a factor, the political and national valences of other cults were merged into her charismatic persona. The cults of St Nino the Illuminatrix and the Mother of God were endowed with additional political values to sustain and promote the living and posthumous cult of the Holy Queen. The phenomenon of Tamar was so momentous that the entire political history of the cult of saints may be identified as the periods before and after Tamar. Five centuries after Tamar, the rapid dissemination of the cult of the martyred Queen Ketevan (1560–1624) was also determined by the previously established cults of the Mother of God, Nino and Tamar. As a result, nowadays, the four women of religious history constitute the axis of Georgia's Christian history and identity.

Tamar's imagery has transcended medieval religious and political discourses, and has penetrated oral traditions. It is common to traditional religious beliefs and practices to adopt saints from the Christian calendar and transform them into semi-pagan deities. This practice is shared across the Caucasian mountains where the Mother of God, and saints such as George, Elijah, Athenogenes, Barbara and others, have left the limits of ecclesiastic commemorations and have been integrated into traditional religious pantheons.[3] Yet, the only figure from Georgia's history to acquire similar centrality in folk cult practices, at least by name, is Queen Tamar. Currently, her cult occupies a prominent place across the entire Caucasian

---

[1] According to 1885 ethnographic records, the residents of Ushguli, the remotest village of the Svaneti region, believe that all major shrines in Svaneti were built by Tamar or during the prosperous years of her reign.

[2] See, for example, Akaki Tsereteli's (1845–1915) poem *The Beauty Has Risen*, which conceptualises Tamar as the symbol of Georgia's 'Golden Age'.

[3] George Charachidzé's studies are probably the most exhaustive in a western European language. See Charachidzé, *Le système religieux, passim*.

highlands and beyond, in many linguistic groups of the wider Caucasian region. While, in the same traditions, Georgia's 'historic' figure, St Nino, is modelled after her literary prototypes, and has never transcended the image of a *k'adagi*, Queen Tamar, along with other mythological figures, became a virtual deity of the Caucasian quasi-Christian pantheon.[4] A central aspect of Tamar's cult is the notable absence of her relics and a perennial quest for her grave. Tamar's grave and her body, and its mysterious revelations to the seeker and eventual disappearances, have become part of the legend of the Golden Age, and of a sizable corpus of folklore across the Caucasus.[5]

The only other royal figures, other than Tamar, who made it into folklore, were Vakhtang the Wolf-Head and King Erekle II (1744–98), Georgia's last great king (not a saint). Arguably, in both instances, the folklorisation of these figures was determined by their situatedness at the thresholds of history. Vakhtang's folklorisation was determined by a strong sense of the foundations that his image projected in *K'art'lis C'xovreba*, and by the efforts of the royal chroniclers to forge and institutionalise his cult. Since the composition of his *Life*, Vakhtang was perceived as the king of olden days, and the founder of the medieval Georgian political and religious body and of its *raison d'être*. Erekle II, on the other hand, was Georgia's de facto last king, the symbol of the old days begone, and Georgia's terminated independent monarchy. In the nineteenth century, his death was equated to the downfall of the Georgian kingdom and has produced a wealth of literature, hence his persistence in folklore. Tamar, however, was placed right in the middle of Georgia's history. Her figure personified its axis, the Golden Age, yet also heralded its downfall. The three folklorised monarchs mark the foundation and the end, the apex, and a transitional moment that embodies both the rise and the downfall, the beginning and the end. This historic liminality of Tamar merged with Tamar's problematic female gender contributed to the formation of her prominent, yet deeply ambiguous, cult. Due to this ambiguity, Tamar's lifetime and posthumous cult, her feminine, saintly and political 'bodies' exercised tremendous impact on the perception of the cult of other saints in Georgian written tradition, lore and national discourses.

---

[4] Although all samples of folklore associated with Queen Tamar were recorded in or after the nineteenth century when a scholarly study of folklore was initiated, it can be claimed with reasonable certainty that at least several motifs of Tamar narratives reveal archaic features and may remount to the aftermath of Tamar's death. For a collection of oral traditions, see Sikharulidze, *t'amar mep'e*.

[5] One folk tradition even claims that upon her death, Tamar was bodily assumed in heaven in a golden coffin.

## 6.2 The Theotokos's Kin

By the time of Tamar's ascension to the Bagratid throne, the 'lot of the Mother of God', a synthesis of the Georgian-Byzantine monastic and royal Bagratid ideological programmes had transcended the dynastic limits, and encompassed 'Georgia', as land, people and a political project. Yet, Tamar advanced this association further by introducing a personal aspect to the Theotokos's cult. This personal devotion to the Mother of God and the practice of *imitatio Mariae* was a source of sacral *basileia* since Pulcheria and the Theodosian empresses.[6] Tamar, however, doubled down on this rhetoric more than any other female monarch. While preserving and amplifying her dynastic kinship with Mary, Tamar strongly insisted on her intimate relationship with the Mother of God by framing her unprecedented mandate to reign in her own right as personally granted by the Theotokos. A similar exception, as Tamar's most loyal patriarch Nikoloz Gulaberisże preached, was allowed only once in history – when the mother of God chaperoned St Nino to Georgia. Evidently, the insistence on the disappearance of Tamar's physical body, and the alleged non-existence of her bodily relics too, was determined by her 'imitation' of the Theotokos.

The *History and Eulogy of the Monarchs*, written at the end of the twelfth century, is the most ambitious project of establishing intimacy between the Queen and the Mother of God. The *History* is partly a biography, yet mostly a bombastic eulogy of the queen. Among other encomiastic tirades, the author quotes iambic verses allegedly written by Tamar herself. They refer to the 1195 victory at the battle of Šamk'or (modern Shamkir in Azerbaijan) against Abu Bakr, the Atabeg of Azerbaijan, who was backed by the powerful Caliph of Baghdad. Tamar's husband, the Ossete prince, David-Soslan (d. 1205), commanded the Georgian army. To celebrate the victory, in emulation of her predecessors, Tamar gifted the Caliph's banner to the Khakhuli Icon of the Mother of God in Gelati Monastery, thereby attesting to the dynastic dedication to the Icon. The verses are addressed to the Virgin and thank her for the victory granted to the Georgian army. The final strophe reads,

> You the Virgin, for whose sake your kin David danced,
> Foretelling that the Son of God would also be Your Son,
> You have favoured me, Tamar; dust which will turn into dust [*mierive*]
>    [or: 'also the kin of David']

---

[6] Holum, *Theodosian Empresses*, 145; Cooper, 'Empress and Theotokos', 39–51; Limberis, *Divine Heiress*, 54; Homza, *Mulieres Suedantes*, 115–17.

You made me worthy of anointment and your kinship.
From Eden [East] to the Gates of Heracles [West], from South to
　North.[7]

Tamar's, or rather the author's, intention was twofold: to emulate her ancestors, by reconfirming her kinship between her House and the Mother of God through the biblical king David; secondly, and more importantly, to highlight the exclusive relationship that the two women had established, embodied in Tamar's unprecedented mandate to rule in the name of the Theotokos and in her own right. Another strophe, also attributed to Tamar, yet probably belonging to the thirteenth-century encomiast Ioane Šavt'eli, essentialises Tamar's personal association with the Theotokos:[8]

Bride, through the mystical mixture with your virginal blood,
Through the highest dispensation, you gave birth to the Son of
　God, for the life of all.
Me, Tamar, the descendant of the race of David, you adorned as your
　kin, glorified and elevated me.
And I too, adorned your Icon of the Mother and the Son. And me
　too and my son, protect us.[9]

By evidently trying to forge a political cult around her and David Soslan's son and successor, Giorgi, Tamar imitates the Virgin also as a mother. Upon his birth, Giorgi received an additional name, Laša, which means 'light' in Apkhaz. The promulgation of the political cult of her son must have been a successful endeavour, as Giorgi-Laša's memory was ingrained in the *Lašaris Jvari* (Cross of Lašari), a mythological deity of the eastern Georgian semi-pagan pantheon, yet entirely devoid of historical references to the

---

[7] *Istoriani da azmani*, ed. Kaukhchishvili, 75: შენგან, ქალწულო, რომელსა შენთვს დავით / როკვიდა, მისა ღმრთისა მეც შენდა ყოფად. / მე თამარ, მიწა შენი და მიერივე, / ცხებულობასა ღირს მყავ და თვსობასა. / ედემს, ლადიათად, სიმხნით, და ჩრდილოეთით. The English translation can be found in *History and Eulogy of the Monarchs*, tr. Gamqrelidze, 259–60. However, the interpretation is complicated, as several manuscripts offer variant readings. Here I am following Pavle Ingoroqva's reading. Sulava, *k'art'uli himnograp'ia*, 91–2.
[8] The poem is included in an eighteenth-century manuscript (H-2955), copied by Ose Gabašvili, who claims that the verses had been written by Tamar on the Khakhuli Icon. Other eighteenth- and nineteenth-century copyists attributed the verses to Rustaveli, while meanwhile retaining the claim that they were written on the Khakhuli Icon. Currently, however, no such verse has survived on the Khakhuli Icon.
[9] Ioane Šavt'eli, *galobani*, ed. Sulava, 295; for study, see, 100–6.

actual king. Giorgi's nickname ('light') is likely also an allusion to the verse from the *Akathist Hymn* – 'Mother of the star that never sets' (*Ikos* 5).[10] Other metaphors used with reference to Tamar are also borrowed from the encomia to the Virgin: 'Tamar conceived, and with her pure mind committed to the temple of God, the holiness of her body, her warm heart and enlightened spirit, she turned Tabakhmela [a hill near Tbilisi] into Bethlehem by giving birth to a son, equal to the son of God.'[11] Further explicit association of the Mother of God with Tamar and her son is found in Ioane Šavt'eli's *Abdulmesiani*, an abstruse encomium to the Queen and her husband:[12]

> From the seed of Jesse, a righteous child was born for [our] salvation,
> To be called King of the Lot of the Holy Virgin,
> As a pillar of Faith, and the wall of the soul,
> Who sets fire to the nation of Hagar.[13]

Šavt'eli's *Encomium to the Mother of God of Vardzia* retains this ambiguity by interchangeably and somewhat confusingly referring to the Theotokos and the queen.[14] Tamar's exclusive and inimitable mandate was the main line of defence of Tamar's historians, panegyrists and poets. Therefore, the encomiasts and historians stressed the total exceptionality of Tamar's persona by making these and other theologically scandalous allusions to the Theotokos. In this regard, one sentence from the *History and Eulogy* is perhaps the most perplexing metaphor: 'If earlier Nebuchadnezzar beheld one of the Trinity next to the three young men as the fourth; then here and now, together with the incomparable and honoured Tamar, the Trinity appears to consist of four.'[15] Other, theologically more acceptable, yet no less bombastic, panegyric, frames Tamar in Marian imagery, particularly as that of a great mediatrix between the realms:

---

[10] Cf. also the Georgian Iadgari: მზჱ სიმართლისაჲ სოფელს უშევ (And you gave birth in the world to the Sun of righteousness). Shoemaker, *First Christian Hymnal*, 324–5.
[11] *Istoriani da azmani*, ed. Kaukhchishvili, 56.14–57.2: https://titus.uni-frankfurt.de/texte/etca/cauc/mgeo/kcx2/kcx2lex.htm, tr. Gamqrelidze, 252.
[12] It is traditionally accepted that the poem was written in Tamar's and her husband's David Soslan's lifetime. However, the earliest manuscripts date to the eighteenth century. Lolashvili, *żveli k'art'veli mexotbeni* 2, 106–14.
[13] Šavt'eli, *Abdulmesiani*, §16 ed. Lolashvili, 122.1–4: https://titus.uni-frankfurt.de/texte/etcs/cauc/mgeo/abdulmes/abdullex.htm. For critical texts and study, see Lolashvili, *żveli k'art'veli mexotbeni* 2.
[14] Ioane Šavt'eli, *galobani*, ed. Sulava, 301–5.
[15] *Istoriani da azmani*, ed. Kaukhchishvili, 25.18–22: თუ მაშინ ნაბუქოდონოსორ სამთა ყრმათა თანა ოთხებად იხილა ერთი სამებისაგანი, აქა კულად სამებისა, თანა იხილვების ოთხებად თამარ, მისწორებული და აღმატებული, tr. Gamqrelidze, 239.

Those disobedient to her she belittled, but she raised up loyal subjects. She did not alienate her neighbours; she did not annex houses to her house, and lands to her land, but contented herself with her family estates, so that others did not think her to be unjust and greedy. And as the highest truth judges the righteous, she, too, exerted her influence upon her neighbours not through fear, but by personally protecting them from those who terrorised them, making them even frightening for their enemies. Ridding those around her of the insatiability peculiar to leeches, she never made fruits poisonous and deeds harmful. She sat as a judge between neighbouring kingdoms, making sure that nobody started a war or tried to coerce one another. And setting herself as an example for them, she was considered to be a second Solomon among kings. Whoever heard the name of the Queen began to long in his soul to see her; and if they were unable to do so, even great kings cursed their fates. She would have absorbed the whole sea, like a cloud that sprinkles its sweet rain equally upon everyone.[16]

The mediatory trope also seems to have been borrowed from the cult of the Mother of God, a feature that occasionally appears in the description of female rulers in Byzantium and western Europe. In those cases, however, the queen's pacifying power contrasts them with their militant husbands or sons. In this aspect too Tamar's imagery is ambiguous, as it simultaneously encapsulates both military ruthlessness and pacifying mediation. The last line of the paragraph is particularly cryptic with reference to Tamar's all-encompassing charisma and divine wisdom. Over time, with the dissemination of Tamar's cult, this mystical rhetoric transcended mere metaphors and was ingrained in Tamar's oral cult, which, influenced by the rhetorical ravings of Tamar's elite rhetoricians, envisioned Tamar as a demi-god of sorts. It appears then that the objective of Tamar's authors was to convey a sense of absolute exception in Tamar's figure, hence the exaggerated exaltations. The final strophe of the *History and Eulogy*, which allegedly quotes philosopher Arseni Iqalt'oeli, is entirely composed of religious metaphors. While Arseni's original intention is unknown, it is obvious that the author applies all these metaphors to Tamar:

The King, the Ruler, the Sion and the springs;
The youth, the virgin, the watchman and the watched;
The rein of foals, precious stones and Israel,

---

[16] Basili Ezosmoʒġuari, *c'xovreba*, ed. Kaukhchishvili, 148.15–28: https://titus.uni-frankfurt.de/texte/etca/cauc/mgeo/kcx2/kcx2lex.htm; tr. Gamqrelidze and Jones, 304–5.

The tower, the ferryman, the house and the father,
The Egyptian steed, Lazarus, hat.[17]

Both Tamar's gender and the legitimacy of her rule were problematic from the beginning of her reign. From the point of view of her loyal authors, the only solution to the conundrum was to resort to the imagery of two other exceptional figures, the Mother of God and St Nino. Ambiguity and exceptionality were, therefore, the central aspects of Tamar's political and cultic representation, as projected by her political, religious and gendered representations. This ambiguity and a coordinated venture of her writers to justify and legitimise her charismatic reign resulted in her sanctification, whereas in mountainous religious traditions, her subsequent deification.

## 6.3 The Two Crowns

In 1156, owing to the tremendous success of his grandfather David IV, Giorgi III (1156–84) inherited a relatively vast, multi-ethnic kingdom that covered almost the entire south Caucasus and parts of north-eastern Anatolia. His rule was that of perpetual campaigns both outside the borders of the kingdom and against the ever-rebellious nobility. In 1155 Giorgi married Guranduxt, the daughter of the king of the Ossetes, who gave birth to two daughters, Tamar and Rusudan.[18] In 1179, Giorgi made a surprising decision by declaring as his co-ruler his elder daughter Tamar. Just two years before Tamar's coronation, in 1177, Giorgi quelled the most dangerous rebellion against him led by the apparently popular Prince Demetre, nicknamed Demna. The controversy over succession began in 1150, when Demetre, son of David IV, had chosen his younger son Giorgi as his heir instead of the older David, the next in line. David conspired against his father, and in 1155 deposed him. His reign, however, was short-lived, and he died in the same year. The exiled Demetre returned from the monastery and crowned Giorgi as his co-ruler. Thus, the sacred formula of royal succession, somewhat later retrospectively reminded by Rustaveli that 'every king is to be succeeded by their (firstborn) son', was violated. In the eyes of the Georgians, Giorgi was likely a usurper, whereas the throne rightfully belonged to David's son, Demna. Prince Demna secured the support of

---

[17] *Istoriani da azmani*, ed. Kaukhchishvili, 113.9–14: https://titus.uni-frankfurt.de/texte/etca/cauc/mgeo/kcx2/kcx2lex.htm.

[18] Rusudan later married Manuel Komnenos, son of Andronikos Komnenos, and gave birth to Alexios I Komnenos (1182–1222), the founder of the Empire of Trebizond. Toumanoff, 'Founder of the Empire of Trebizond', 299–312.

some of the most influential aristocrats, and in 1177–8 staged a series of rebellions against his uncle. In 1177, Demna lost his cause, was captured, castrated and blinded. Soon after his demise, Demna died. He was declared a traitor and was universally condemned by the royal historians.

The challenge to Tamar's legitimacy was, therefore, twofold. On the one hand her dynastic legitimacy was dubious due to her father's actions and the injustice that Demna had suffered. The second problem, which augmented the first and made it even more flagrant, was Tamar's gender. From a medieval nobleman's perspective, Giorgi was highly provocative – himself a usurper, whose rule was not a model of clemency and peace, a person infamous for his ruthlessness against his foes, he now let his daughter rule the realm, crowning her as the monarch in her right. Part of the nobility seized the opportunity and immediately protested. The protest was followed by a series of armed standoffs organised by the royal treasurer who demanded the creation of a separate assembly, which would act independently from the monarch and her court, a bid that was duly neutralised.

As another act of resistance to Tamar's independent reign, almost immediately after her coronation, the nobility wished, to use Antony Eastmond's term, to 'manoeuvre' Tamar into marrying her to an agreeable political figure, the prince of Novgorod, Yury Bogolyubsky. Tamar's historians dismiss Tamar's first husband as an unworthy character. Due to his alleged wickedness, soon after marriage, Yury was expelled, and forced into exile to Constantinople. From there he tried to regain the throne, only to be defeated by Tamar's loyal commanders, the Mxargrżeli brothers. The disillusionment in Yury was perhaps an important step towards further legitimisation of Tamar, who vehemently defended her personal and inalienable right to the Bagratid throne. After this, Tamar was again pressed into marriage. Historian Basil Ezosmożguari stresses how much she opposed the marriage, and how nobles were worried by her childlessness, and the 'barrenness of her house' and how they 'vexed her soul, and crowded upon her', demanding a male commander of the army.[19]

The exact nature of these demarches is unknown, as we are presented with sole point-of-view narratives. It is, however, noteworthy that Tamar's rule and legitimacy remained subject to uncertainty until 1187/9, when the queen married the prince of Ossetia, David Soslan. From the first days of her enthronement, the nobility saw in Tamar merely a mother and a potential consort to the monarch, whose purpose, similarly to earlier Byzantine empresses, was to preserve the throne until the arrival of the true *basileus*. In opposition, Tamar and her loyal party forged an altogether

---

[19] Basili Ezosmożguari, *c'xovreba*, ed. Kaukhchishvili, 120.

different image of Tamar, of her virginity by disposition and of her inalienable and unique right to rule the kingdom in her own right. Indeed, while the resentment towards Tamar has very dimly survived in literature, its existence is confirmed through the vehement defence of her rule and apology of her gender.

Tamar embodied two seemingly irreconcilable attributes – of power and femininity – an indeed lethal mixture for contemporary Byzantine authors. Medieval Christian attitudes towards women in power range from cold silence to extreme misogyny.[20] The Byzantine history before Tamar had some experience of female rule, but even these women were regarded with distrust and hostility, and their power was always represented in relation to their husbands, sons or other male relatives. The association of women with power was viewed with suspicion, and zealous attempts were made to denigrate the will to power of the empresses, or to strip them from their political aura.[21] Instead, purity, humility, subservience and chastity were hailed as the guiding virtues of the royal women. Indeed, contemporary Byzantine and earlier traditions were almost entirely devoid of eulogies to powerful women, who were confined to mother figures, and the only context within which one encounters praise for women is their virginity or advanced age, or anything that divests women of sexuality.[22] This is especially true of saintly

---

[20] As an illustration, see Galatariotou's study of the famous twelfth-century misogynist, Neophytos the Recluse (d. 1214) in Galatariotou, 'Holy Women', 55–94. I particularly like Theresa Tinkle's explanation of the medieval male perception of the women in power as a carnivalesque inversion, in Tinkle, *Gender and Power*, 3: 'Women on top can represent an ideology of spiritual humility, and a rejection of ancient masculine gender roles. When a woman actively usurps a man's position, however, she becomes the bearer of entirely different and more mixed messages. In carnivalesque inversions, women on top typically symbolise the sensual desires that usurp the place of manly reason. By exposing men's inability to rule them, women on top contest the norm of male dominance, and invite other women to join in their rebellion. At the same time, the inversion teaches men to assert themselves more forcefully, to enact their role as superior reason. In this way, the trope subtly confirms the appropriateness of male dominance. Women on top thus have ambivalent implications in carnival contexts.'

[21] Quoting E. R. Leach, Galatariotou writes, 'The power of the witch is seen as a threat to the established order. The witch is illegitimate because her power is incompatible "with the interests of those who exercise authority in the social system". Since this system is patriarchal, it follows that any female who dares to hold – and exercise – power outside the influence of a male is, by definition, anti-social. If she further exercises this power against a male, then she would be deemed to have reached the ultimate in anti-social behaviour: witchcraft.' Galatariotou, 'Holy Women', 65.

[22] The hagiographer of the holy Empress Theodora, for example, presents her as a good wife and mother, pious and obedient to masculine authority, who finishes her life in a convent. Delierneux, 'Literary Portrait', 377.

women, who were denied not only their sexuality but their very sex to attain sanctity. As explained many times, their sanctity was revealed specifically in their ability to transcend their gender and to 'become male'.[23] Tamar was not an exception, nor was the Georgian tradition of the same period different from the Byzantine misogynistic rhetoric, nor was it particularly favourable towards women despite its 'feminine' religious foundations.

The only examples that could have served as models for Tamar were the purple-born sisters, the empresses Zoe (1028–50) and Theodora (980–1056).[24] Yet, the surviving rhetoric of power and gender regarding these empresses was unfavourable. The fact that they were women was repeatedly portrayed as their primary vice and an obstacle to holding political office, even if they were sometimes praised for their virtues. Michael Psellos was convinced that the sisters, and especially Theodora's claim to monarchy, were the principal reasons for the subsequent decline of the Roman Empire.[25] Psellos pointed out that he had no problem with the empresses' devotion and Christian ethos, that they were very pious indeed, yet what he would not accept was their political pretences. Psellos's cynical report that with Zoe and Theodora, the emperor's council turned into a *gynaekonitis*, is probably the most benign of his misogynistic tirades. The unlawful manner in which their house was rooted and planted in the ground further aggravated the problem of their gender.[26] Psellos claims to be objective by saying 'candidly' that 'neither were fit mentally to exercise single handed rule'[27] and that they confused 'the trifles of women's chamber with imperial matters'.[28] The empresses were vain, erratic, emotionally unstable. They spent the imperial treasury indiscriminately, indulged in gossip, mutual jealousy and all sorts of petty pleasures that Psellos considered as natural to women. It was mostly Theodora who baffled Psellos by deciding, contrary to all the previous exempla, to rule in her own right without a male emperor. Theodora was not given a talented ally like patriarch Nikoloz I Gulaberisże

---

[23] See, for example, Galatariotou, 'Holy Women', 85; Castelli, 'I Will Make Mary Male', 29–49.
[24] There exists a substantial corpus of scholarship on Byzantine empresses. For some of the important titles, see Herrin, *Women in Purple*. See Lynda Garland's introduction for an overview of the exceptional circumstances of the rise of empresses in Byzantium, in Garland, *Byzantine Empresses*, 2–7.
[25] Todt, 'Die Frau als Selbstherrscher', 149.
[26] Psellos, *Chronographia*, VI, 1.1–12, ed. Reinsch, 107.
[27] Psellos, *Chronographia*, VI, 5.3–4, ed. Reinsch, 109: οὐδεμιᾷ τὸ φρόνημα πρὸς ἀρχὴν αὔταρκες.
[28] Psellos, *Chronographia*, VI, 5.5–7, ed. Reinsch, 109: τὰ πλεῖστα δὲ τὰ τῆς γυναικωνίτιδος παίγνια τοῖς βασιλικοῖς κατεκίρνων σπουδάσμασι.

who would deliver a eulogy of the feminine in her defence; instead, she was challenged by a particularly hostile patriarch, Michael I Keroularios, who could not fathom the idea of a woman ruling over the Roman Empire.[29] Yet, contrary to all the challenges that she had encountered, Theodora was convinced that the empire was 'her inheritance and hers alone.'[30] Tamar was too, yet unlike Theodora, she succeeded in surrounding herself with the right people who would go to great lengths to substantiate her inalienable mandate to autocracy.

Practically speaking, Tamar's situation was even more precarious than that of Theodora. While Theodora could hide her gender behind the 'ever-present imperial mystique' of the court in Constantinople, due to the nature of the Georgian court and the non-existence of grandiose royal palaces, Tamar did not have the opportunity to create an aura of royal aloofness through ritual and seclusion.[31] Unlike her imperial peers, Tamar's court, as well as her visual representations were mobile, dispersed across Georgia's monasteries and churches.[32] Her persona and, therefore, gender were always present and manifest, and as such required perpetual defence. Another major difference that Antony Eastmond points out between the queens is the strategy of legitimation. Both Zoe and Theodora, although to various degrees, reached out to their dynastic belonging to legitimise their rule, a belonging that to a certain extent neutralised their unfortunate gender. All the support that the two empresses had, even if ambiguous and inconsistent, was due to their blood relation with Constantine VIII and Basil II.[33] Yet in Tamar's case, even after her marriage, the literary presentation of power 'was definitely around the cult and person of the queen', and not through her relation to other male royals.[34] It was the tension between the two aspects of her persona – the charismatic royal and the female – that court historians, poets, theologians and artists strove to overcome both in her lifetime and since her death, an opportunity that no Byzantine empress had ever had. As a result, and much unlike the purple-born empresses, while during Tamar's reign, the political discourse of royal chroniclers and artists was focused on the reconciliation of power and femininity, soon or immediately after Tamar's death, the two merged in her sanctity, which removed Tamar from the realm of history and transported her to the atemporal realm of myth.

---

[29] Psellos, *Chronographia*, VI, 220, ed. Reinsch, 568.
[30] Psellos, *Chronographia*, VI, 204.10, ed. Reinsch, 550.
[31] Eastmond, *Royal Imagery*, 131. See also, Eastmond, 'Royal Renewal', 288.
[32] For the mapping of Tamar's mobility, see, Baillie, *Prosopography*, 125–7.
[33] Hill, 'Imperial Women', 79; Todt, 'Die Frau als Selbstherrscher', 170–1.
[34] Eastmond, *Royal Imagery*, 131.

Tamar's ascension to the throne, the nature of the Georgian saintly cults, the immediate political circumstances of her enthronement, the necessity to legitimise her rule, the almost immediate decline and fall of the kingdom after her death, and the zeal to sustain her posthumous memory as a symbol of Georgia's Golden Age, all resulted in a unique biopolitics of Tamar that far transcended her biography. Due to the abundance of sources, we have an opportunity to observe the evolution of Tamar's cult of personality from her legitimation through her dynastic belonging to her personal charismatic mandate to kingship and eventually to sainthood.

The genesis of Tamar's cult can be found in the immediate circumstances of her coronation, and in the tactics by which the two biographers contrast her with the other female members of the House. Reportedly, Giorgi crowned and seated her to his right 'with the dispensation and support of the One high above who wills the destiny of the monarchs'.[35] Five years later, Giorgi died and was initially succeeded by the regency of his sister Rusudan. Rusudan, however, was never considered as the possible heir to the throne. Like Zoe, who was endowed with power during the fuzzy area of transition, Rusudan's mission was to safeguard the throne for the male heir, and her political identity resided solely in her liminality. Yet, unlike the Byzantine experience, here the throne was not safeguarded for a male heir, but for another woman. Yet, Tamar was not recognised as the monarch immediately following her father's death, and was summoned for another, independent coronation. Essentially the same ritual was performed twice, and, as the *History and Eulogy* recounts, the second coronation was even loftier than the first: The delegates of the entire kingdom asked Rusudan to let Tamar 'begin her reign, and be blessed as a crown-bearer, and [be] elevated to the throne of her parents by the Holy Cross and the blessing of Melchizedek, who had blessed Abraham, and to [let her] conquer the ends of the world and reign from sea to sea'.[36] So Tamar was coronated:

> ... the crown was brought and the singers, raising their voices, sang for her victorious reign and powerful autocracy; and they told her [the story of] the appearance of the cross to Constantine on the mountain of olives. And while praising and singing for her, they invited the worthy and blessed monk Anton Saġirisże, the archbishop of Kutaisi, to crown [her], for it was lawful prerogative of Lixt'-Imeret'i [western Georgia], to

---

[35] *Istoriani da azmani*, ed. Kaukhchishvili, 21: განგებითა და გაგონებითა ზენისა მის ხუედრისა შარავანდედთა მნებებელისათა.
[36] *Istoriani da azmani*, ed. Kaukhchishvili, 26.10–14: https://titus.uni-frankfurt.de/texte/etca/cauc/mgeo/kcx2/kcx2lex.htm.

crown the sovereign. On the other side stood Kaxaber, the *eristavi* [duke] of Rača and T'akveri. The eminent officials and noblemen – Vardanisże, Saġirisże and Amanelisże – placed the sword upon her. And the beating of drums, timbales, and cymbals, and the blowing of trumpets began; and there was exaltation, rejoicing and joy everywhere, and hope was restored among those who had long lost it. The armies of all the seven kingdoms bowed before her, blessed and praised her. And everyone took their proper place at the proper time. And Tamar, the like of the seven luminaries, was blessed by the One who in six days brought into being all that was to be brought, and rested on the seventh [day].[37]

Whereas, according to historian Basili, grief struck the Georgians upon receiving the news of Giorgi's death,

seeing Tamar before them, they ceased grieving and blew the trumpets, like it happened once for Solomon. And they placed the lofty throne of Vakhtang, the seat of David, which was prepared formerly for the moon by the King of Kings Sabaoth Elohim, to rule the world from sea to sea and from the rivers to the end of the world. The nobles lifted the sceptre, the wooden cross, and the banner of David which has never experienced opposing winds. And everyone and in unison handed to Tamar the parental sword together with the throne, handed over to her by her father.[38]

In contrast to her aunt, Tamar inherited all the royal insignia, charisma and mythology of the Bagratid Dynasty. In all the wealth of epithets and similes applied to her, she was never compared to any female figure from Christian or biblical history. Instead, through anointment, her genetic descent from David, King of Israel, her association with Constantine as a Christian ruler par excellence, and political descent from King Vakhtang Gorgasali were confirmed, as she bore her ancestors' sword by joining the ranks of the 'swords of Messiah'.[39] Through coronation, Tamar received the two crowns

---

[37] *Istoriani da azmani*, ed. Kaukhchishvili, 26.18–27.8: https://titus.uni-frankfurt.de/texte/etca/cauc/mgeo/kcx2/kcx2lex.htm; tr. Gamqrelidze, 239.

[38] Basili Ezosmożġuari, *c'xovreba mep'et'-mep'isa t'amarisi*, ed. Kaukhchishvili, 115.22–116.2: https://titus.uni-frankfurt.de/texte/etca/cauc/mgeo/kcx2/kcx2.htm; tr. Gamqrelidze, 287.

[39] Ibid. While her male predecessors and descendants' titles were the 'sword of Messiah', as attested in Arabic on their coins, officially, as a woman, Tamar was called the 'follower of Messiah'. For a catalogue of Tamar's coins, see *Online English–Georgian Catalogue of Georgian Numismatics*, http://geonumismatics.tsu.ge/en/catalogue/types/?type=68.

of medieval monarchy, 'the visible and material diadem as opposed to "invisible and immaterial Crown" – encompassing all the royal rights and privileges indispensable for the government of the body politic – which was perpetual and descended either from God directly or by the dynastic right of inheritance'.[40] While coronation is a legal unification of these two crowns, arguably, Tamar's double coronation, previously unattested in Georgian history, was the first sign of ambiguity of Tamar's person, which required double justification: the first coronation legitimised Tamar in her relation to her dynasty, whereas the second announced Tamar's personal mandate to rule in her own right. This tension and dialectic between her dynastic and personal mandates became a leitmotif of Tamar's reign, also expressed by visual means. The *History and Eulogy* was written after Tamar's death and beatification, and as such it neglected all the problems of legitimacy that Tamar had faced. Nevertheless, the necessity for a double coronation could indeed be a hint as to the residues of a scandal which blemished the early years of Tamar's reign.[41]

While Tamar's *potestas* was a fait accompli, her *auctoritas* required meticulous shaping both by recrafting her visual and narrative representations, and by re-evaluating the entirety of Georgia's religious history. Her *potestas* rested in the legal tradition of her heritage, yet her *auctoritas* was unique and could not be replicated.[42] No claim valid of Tamar could have been adapted to other queens, including her daughter and heir, Rusudan. Tamar was a total exception, a conceptualisation that transpires in thirteenth-century art, as well as in contemporaneous religious discourses, secular poetry, subsequent lore and posthumous representations up until modernity. Through a perpetual display of ambiguity, Tamar's charismatic persona suspended common law both on a metaphysical level and as a specific instance. It is for this reason that Tamar's historians refused to speak of Tamar or justify her reign by drawing analogies from either Georgian or Roman/Byzantine history or by comparing her to Byzantine empresses, even to the most powerful ones like Eirene or Theodora. While Tamar's predecessors for over two centuries modelled themselves according to Byzantine prototypes, Tamar's reign created an extraordinary situation, whereby applying the same models would have been useless and counterproductive.

---

[40] Kantorowicz, *King's Two Bodies*, 337.
[41] The news that Georgia was ruled by a woman soon reached the Holy Land. In a late twelfth-century French description of the Georgian Monastery of the Holy Cross in Jerusalem, the author claims that Georgia is also known as the 'land of the women' ('terre de Feminie'). See *La citez de Iherusalem*, ed. Tobler, 217.
[42] For the most recent elaboration of the concept, see Agamben, *State of Exception*, 50–88.

While Tamar was a rightful continuator of the Bagratid Dynasty, her biopolitical status of a female sovereign could not be replicated in history. Therefore, the solution to the 'problem' of Tamar's gender was to make it wholly irrelevant. The *imitatio Helenae*, or 'New Helena', a motif applied to female empresses and queens since the fifth century, is absent in Tamar's imagery.[43] Instead, Tamar is persistently presented as male, as the 'second Constantine', and her gender is subsumed in her political and religious splendour. Like Constantine, she 'sharpened a double-edged sword', and like Constantine she convened great and ecumenical councils.[44] Tamar's historians are keen to weave a third manifestation of the queen – the religious – and to further subsume her feminine and political identity in her sacred aura. Although Tamar was married twice and gave birth to successors, she was presented as a quasi-virgin who never wished to marry, and perceived marriage merely as a compromise for sake of her office. When Tamar was pressed into marriage, she reluctantly said, 'God is my witness that my heart never wished to have a husband, neither in the beginning [of the reign], nor now. I would have asked to release me of that necessity, had it not been the danger of futurelessness for my throne which has been entrusted to me first by God and then by my parents.'[45]

Tamar's visual imageries shed light on the contrast between Tamar's lifetime representations and her posthumous cult, as well as the evolution from the former to the latter. While in the literary evidence, Tamar's cult is fully formed, her visual representation points to an evolving process. Five medieval images of Tamar have survived across Georgia. Eastmond suggests that the images allow us to trace the evolution of Tamar's representation from her initial image as the co-ruler to the last years of her life and even posthumous representations. The contrast between Tamar's visual imagery and her textual representations is indeed striking. While Tamar's biographies written after her death stressed her resentment to marry, and underlined her inalienable mandate to rule, by discarding her gender, the images painted during Tamar's reign persistently represent her as flanked by men, and legitimise her rule in the context of family continuity. Before Tamar's marriage, this was her father Giorgi III, yet in time she appears with her husband Davit Soslan, and finally with her youthful and later mature son, Giorgi IV Laša.

---

[43] See McNamara, 'Imitatio Helenae', 51–80; Homza, *Mulieres Suedantes*, 33–79.
[44] Basili Ezosmożġuari, *c'xovreba*, ed. Kaukhchishvili, 485.
[45] *Istoriani da azmani*, ed. Kaukhchishvili, 47.2–6: https://titus.uni-frankfurt.de/texte/etca/cauc/mgeo/kcx2/kcx2lex.htm.

Figure 6.1  Queen Tamar and Giorgi III. Church of Dormition of Vardzia, thirteenth century. Source: Artanuji Publishers.

Arguably, the earliest representation of Queen Tamar in the Church of Vardzia reflects the political problems that Tamar faced in the early years of her reign (see Fig. 6.1). The fresco, which depicts Giorgi III and Tamar, legitimises not only Tamar's right to rule but the right of Giorgi's lineage, as opposed to Demna's. The inscription above Giorgi's head stresses his descent from Demetre I and the angel over his head symbolises the passing of power and divine approval from the Theotokos to the king. Tamar is placed only after her father, which underlines her legitimate legacy.[46] The stunning success of one family that had already ruled over Georgia for five centuries was the main legitimiser of Tamar's mandate. A century earlier, the same factor had contributed to the legitimacy of the rule of Empresses Zoe and Theodora.[47] While the incongruity of the visual and narrative representations of Tamar can be explained by the time of their composition, it can also be argued that the visual and textual imageries were created for different audiences: while Tamar's histories and eulogies were composed for the literate elites, her visual representations were designed also for the wider population, who was probably even less tolerant towards female rule and less exposed to the centralised propaganda.

Ambiguity became the principal attribute of Tamar's representation, both visual and literary. In Vardzia, Tamar is called *mep'et'a mep'e*, the king

---

[46] Eastmond, *Royal Imagery*, 108.
[47] Hill, 'Imperial Women', 82.

of kings, without any reference to her gender. On the same fresco, Tamar and her father are dressed almost identically, the only exception being Tamar's large earrings and other minor details of the garment. Tamar is not depicted as a male, and her female features and Persian ideals of beauty are sufficiently stressed, a mixture of feminine and masculine attributes also retained in *The Knight in the Panther Skin*. Since Vardzia, this ambiguity has become a paramount aspect of Tamar. As Eastmond observes, Tamar does not wear the kite-shaped loros that was often part of the dress of empresses in the eleventh century, and which is used in Vardzia to depict the imperial nature of the female saint depicted to Tamar's right. The patterning on Tamar's robes makes her the more striking figure in the ensemble. Tamar is shown as a ruler and not just as a ceremonial decoration to accompany any future husband.[48]

The latest of Tamar's images dates to the immediate aftermath of the queen's death, or perhaps the last few years of her life. The royal panel of Bert'ubani monastic church differs from earlier four images, where Tamar is always placed in between other men. By contrast, here Tamar holds a central position. This final image must have been commissioned by Giorgi-Laša who wished to be associated with his legendary mother, and legitimised his own rule through her. By then, 'Tamar had developed from a vulnerable queen, who was treated with much suspicion and faced open hostility, to a positive figurehead to whom later rulers could appeal.'[49] Provided that the fresco was executed after her death, Eastmond suggests that earlier images try to subsume her gender into the male figures surrounding her, and mediate her power through these men, whether her father or son. In Bert'ubani, however, her personality did not require to be circumscribed by men to make her acceptable: 'here she is no longer the ruling queen, whose power and position must be explained, but a dead figure, subject to myth and legend, whose reign can be glorified.'[50]

Even if the fresco were painted during her lifetime, and not after her death, the same interpretation still holds. Tamar is still the central figure of the composition. Whether dead or alive, Tamar has become a subject of myth and royal glory. She was no longer a young woman, whose femininity could have dangerously interfered with her political aura, and by the virtue of her age and charisma, she has fully transubstantiated into a political body devoid of any historical or biographic immediacy. It is precisely this stripping of Tamar from her biographic *Dasein* that was the next step towards her

---

[48] Eastmond, *Royal Imagery*, 109.
[49] Ibid., 175.
[50] Ibid.

appropriation from history by myth.⁵¹ To summarise in Eastmond's words, 'the legacy of imagery that Tamar inherited, with its rivalry between Georgian, Byzantine and Islamic manifestations of power, had to be adapted to fit this new situation: an image of strength had to be found that could depict the queen's authority but at the same time could confer on her all the necessary "female" virtues of the age.'⁵²

Tamar's tremendously successful cult resulted, perhaps even unintentionally, and as a side-effect, from this coordinated project to legalise her mandate. The literature produced during and soon after Tamar's reign, which includes her two historians, two lengthy encomia, Rustaveli's *The Knight in the Panther Skin*, at least one theological treatise and several religious verses, are in their own ways dedicated to the justification of Tamar's gender and her right to rule singlehandedly. All of these texts contributed to the formulation of the idea of exception in the image of Tamar that suspended all previously held rules and customs. It was this necessity to justify Tamar's reign that created a certain dialectic among Tamar's three 'hypostases': the feminine, the political and the sacred, which resulted in a unique theological and political conceptualisation of her holy body.

## 6.4 A State of Exception

By the time Tamar ascended the throne, the Bagratid mythology had sufficiently evolved from the original Kartlian foundation stories and cults. Yet, with Tamar and her challenges in picture, the religious authorities loyal to the young queen unearthed a crucial instrument in their rhetoric of legitimisation – the *Conversion of Kartli* and the saint of Old Kartli – Nino, another woman in Georgia's history whose authority suffered due to her gender. It was the prerogative of the rhetoric of Tamar's writers to rehabilitate Nino's cult and mould it into a power discourse. It was with the rise of Tamar in the late twelfth century that Nino's cult was rediscovered and refashioned to legitimise the queen's exclusive mandate. If only one image of St Nino has survived from before the twelfth century (the now lost Oshki relief

---

⁵¹ An unpublished manuscript dated to 1481 contains a curious collection of religious poetry, mostly akathists and hymns to the Virgin. In the middle of the manuscript four verses are inserted, dedicated to Mary of Egypt, George, St Theodore and Tamar. The verses immediately follow each other and their unifying theme is the motif of the sun and the halo light. The final verse is dedicated to Tamar: 'A golden sun of the halo shines under the sun, / Participates in the splendour of Christ's faith. / The light of the Universe is lit with the light of the One, / It covers the flowers with roses, / And the owner of cedars, Tamar is the daughter of David.'

⁵² Eastmond, *Royal Imagery*, 93.

from c. 960), with Nino's tradition being confined almost exclusively to her biographies, from the second half of the twelfth century, the depictions of Nino multiply across the Georgian kingdom: in Vardzia (1184–6), Kintsvisi (c. 1207), Bert'ubani (c. 1210s), Ani (mid-thirteenth century), Akhtala (late thirteenth century), Mghvimevi (1280s) and others.[53]

This Nino-Tamar project transpires in the most eloquent justification of Nino's gender in Katholikos-Patriarch Nikoloz Gulaberisże's (1149–78, 1184–?) homily *The Discourse on Svetic'xoveli, the Tunic of the Lord, and the Catholic Church*. Gulaberisże was summoned to Georgia and, having occupied the patriarchal throne under Tamar's patronage, remained her loyal supporter and fervent defender.[54] The homily was delivered on the feast of Svetitskhoveli, the Cathedral of the Living Pillar in Mtskheta, the patriarchal seat of the Georgian Kingdom. The homily starts off with a now formulaic complaint about how this foundational story had been forgotten for centuries. Yet, unlike his predecessors, Nikoloz's focus is now specifically on the Tunic of the Lord and the Cathedral of the Living Pillar. Then the patriarch recapitulates and explains the theological and political implications of the conversion of Kartli. In this, the homily is not particularly original. The novelty of the account, however, lies in the rhetorical purpose of its composition: to justify Nino's gender and explain its apparent incongruence with the Pauline prescription, 'But I suffer not a woman to teach, nor to use authority over the man: but to be in silence' (1 Timothy 2:12). Gulaberisże opens his discourse with a reference to the earthly 'reflection' of the Holy Trinity on the same spot where the homily was delivered – the cathedral church, the Tunic of the Lord and the Living Pillar – the yardsticks of Georgian Orthodoxy. Next he discusses the mission of the apostles and identifies Nino as the thirteenth apostle who was destined to enlighten this 'eastern land'. Then he immediately asks a rhetorical question, 'Why did God choose a woman to send to us?', and embarks upon a justification of female apostolicity. It is, however, obvious that the Patriarch's question is not merely theoretical, and that he challenges anti-Nino sentiments which, even if not dominant, were advocated in Georgia, obstructing the flourishing of Nino's cult.

---

[53] Skhirtladze, 'cminda ninos cxovrebis cikli', 364–5.
[54] Basili describes in detail Tamar's strained relationship with the ecclesiastic elites and her attempts to oust disloyal bishops. For the events, see Basili Ezosmożġuari, *c'xovreba*, ed. Kaukhchishvili, 117–19. Gulaberisże, Tamar's loyal patriarch, had been forcibly retired by Tamar's foe Katholikos-Patriarch Mik'el Mirianisże. Gulaberisże was then sent to the Georgian monastery on Mt Athos and then to Jerusalem to buy back from king Baldouin IV the landholdings of the Georgian Monastery of the Holy Cross, confiscated by the Crusaders. Rayfield, *Edge of Empires*, 108–9.

Gulaberisże breaks down his argument into three: first he addresses the analogy with the Theotokos. After Crucifixion, the Mother of God wished to spread the good news in the east, by thus justifying her name 'the truth of the Eastern light' (*aġmosaval mzisa simart'lisa*). However, her Son did not let her go, for she had another mission to fulfil. It was for this reason that the Mother of God had decided to send another woman in her stead in these 'final days': 'And since that woman was the most holy and most blessed of all women, men, and heavenly powers, for this reason, in these final times, God wished to bestow us with grace and salvation for our nation, He sent a woman [*dedakac'ive carmoavlina*], which, I believe, happened through the intercession of the Mother of God with her Son, for it was the Lot of the Mother of God. This should indeed be the one and indubitable reason.'[55]

As we saw earlier, this original association between the Theotokos and Nino had been sidelined and masculinised by the legend of Andrew and the Acquri Icon of the Mother of God. However, the pairing of the Theotokos and Nino was already implicit in the original *Lives* of Nino.[56] Before heading to the capital of Iberia, Nino hid in a wild blackberry bush, which is considered an allusion to the Burning Bush of Exodus, which, in subsequent patristic thought has been consistently interpreted as an allegorical reference to the Theotokos.[57] Gulaberisże brings back this argument by also subsuming it into the exempla from Byzantine rhetoric. The closest parallel to Gulaberisże's argument is perhaps Proclus's defence of the empress's femininity through the image of the Mother of God, where the Constantinopolitan patriarch attacked Nestorius, defending the Empress Pulcheria from Nestorius's 'misogyny':

> What we celebrate is the pride of women and the glory of the female, thanks to the one who was at once both mother and virgin. Lovely is the

---

[55] Nikoloz Gulaberisże, *sakit'xavi*, 2.9–4.27, ed. Qubaneishvili, 232–3: ხოლო ვინათგან იგი დედაკაცი იყო ყოვლადსანატრელი და კურთხეული, უზეშთაესი იგი დედათაცა და მამათაცა და ზეცისა ძალთაცა, ამისთვსცა უკუე უკუანასკნელთა ჟამთა, რაჟამს ღმერთმან ინება წყალობაი და ცხორებაი ნათესავისა ჩუენისაი, დედაკაცვე წარმოავლინა, ვითარ ვჰგონებ მე, გამოთხოით და ხუაიშნითა დედისა ღმრთისაითა მისი თჳსისა თანა, ვინაიგან ნაწილიცა იყო დედისაი ღმრთისი; ამისთჳს უფროისდა საგონებელ და საეჭუელ არს და ესე არს ერთი ჭეშმარიტი და უეჭუელი მიზეზი. A similar argument appears in the liturgical readings of St Nino.
[56] Bezarashvili, 'masalebi', 124–39.
[57] Bezarashvili and Coulie, 'On the Understanding of the Word *maqvlovani*', 56–70; Bezarashvili and Skhirtladze, 'The Symbol of the Thorn-Bush', 363–85. The hypothesis, although plausible, remains, to my mind, speculative.

gathering! See how both the earth and the sea serve as the Virgin's ten escorts: the one spreading forth her waves calmly beneath the ships, the other conducting the steps of travellers on their way unhindered. Let nature leap for joy, and let women be honoured! Let all humanity dance, and let virgins be glorified! For 'where sin increased, grace abounded yet more' (Romans 5:20). She who called us here today is the Holy Mary.[58]

Then Gulaberisże offers a second and a more pragmatic justification to Nino's 'unfortunate' gender: before conversion to Christianity, Georgians were a fearsome and barbaric nation, and as such, they could only have been pacified through the agency of a feeble, yet calm and rational woman. Gulaberisże launches a surprise attack on 'masculine wisdom' here: 'Nobody must dare and say idle tales and lies that philosophers' boldness and wisdom, or rhetorical prowess of some man has vanquished their evil ways'. Instead the bitterness was extinguished by the 'sweetness of clear stream's waters'. Gulaberisże quotes 2 Corinthians 12:9 ('for my strength is made perfect in weakness'), and presents Nino's female weakness as a divine dispensation analogous to God becoming man or Christ's disciples who were common men 'yet they "delivered arrows at the wise and the philosophers and wounded the hearts of the rhetoricians"'.[59] It is possible that apart from the scriptural references, the inversion of power dynamic and the presentation of weakness as an advantage was a trope that Gulaberisże had learned on Athos, where the Georgian monks had crafted a similar rhetoric against the Byzantines.[60]

Next, Gulaberisże politicises his discourses by referring to the events of the book of Judges and the role of women in the decisive victory of the Israelites – first this was Deborah who convinced the Israelites to attack the Canaanites. Then, in Judges 9, Abimelech the usurper, son of Gideon, was killed by a resolute woman. Throughout the book, energetic women are contrasted with indecisive and ever uncertain men, such as Gideon

[58] Quoted in Constas, *Proclus of Constantinople* (homily 1.1–13), 136; tr. 137–8. Proclus's homily on 26 December at the Virginity Festival addressed both Nestorius, who was present, and the empress. For commentary, see Limberis, *Divine Heiress*, 55–6.
[59] Nikoloz Gulaberisże, *sakit'xavi*, 6.36–41, ed. Sabinin, 233: https://titus.uni-frankfurt.de/texte/etcg/cauc/ageo/gh/ghqub/ghqub.htm.
[60] Theresa Tinkle in *Gender and Power*, 4–5 identifies this as a trope in early medieval exegetical literature: 'By praising and emulating the woman on top, exegetes reject traditional social hierarchies; they identify not with power but with weakness – with the omnipotent deity who allows himself to be crucified, with the children who shall inherit the kingdom, with the women who lack social and ecclesiastical status. By inverting traditional hierarchies, exegetes invent their authority as stemming from their difference within conventional social order.'

himself. Perhaps, apart from seeking for the examples of strong-willed women in the Bible, Gulaberisże also intentionally references the slaying by a woman of an usurper.

Gulaberisże then says that he had found yet another justification for 'the dignity and honour of women' (*ģirsebisat'vis dedat'a pativisa*) and refers to the Scriptural passage widely cited in Late Antique justifications of the sanctity of women, according to which women were the first to witness the resurrection of Christ. Gulaberisże adapts these familiar tropes of Byzantine rhetoric to the Nino tradition, and concludes this final argument with strict words of rebuke that betray the existing sceptical attitudes towards Nino's cult: 'For these reasons, close your mouths that denigrate wickedly and vainly the feminine nature of the preaching and of our conversion, instead we should rejoice even more and educate those who complain and thus speak to us out of their ignorance!'[61]

While the Patriarch speaks of distant times, biblical, New Testament and early Christian, and condemns misogyny towards Nino, his actual point of reference and immediate concern is a theological justification of Queen Tamar's debatable mandate to rule, veiled by the persona of Nino. On a psychological level, femininity, due to its mediatory character, is an asset both for Nino, as an apostle, and Tamar, as a monarch, since both had to manoeuvre among men. Both Nino's mission and Tamar's reign are mandated by their personal association with the Theotokos. Finally, all this is justified by the extraordinary nature of the event of the conversion, which allowed for the reversal of gender roles, for a new Deborah, centuries later reflected in the reign of Tamar, similarly to the mysterious dweller of Thebez who slew Abimelech and put men to shame, since extraordinary times require extraordinary measures.

The *Encomium to St Nino* by Katholikos-Patriarch Arseni IV Bulmaisimisże (early thirteenth century) compliments and contrasts with Gulaberisże's *Discourse*. Following the tradition that has been established during Tamar's reign, Arseni represents Nino as an instrument of the Theotokos in Georgia's enlightenment. Bulmaisimisże's pontificate fell immediately to post-Tamar era when the political cult of the great Queen was particularly strong, enhanced and advocated by her children and consecutive heirs, Giorgi IV Laša (1213–23) and Rusudan (1223–45). For Arseni, however, unlike Nikoloz, Nino is a genderless figure whose mission transcends boundaries of sex, class or history. The Theotokos is evoked several times and in all instances explicitly in the context of the

---

[61] Nikoloz Gulaberisże, *sakit'xavi*, 8.9–12, ed. Sabinin, 233: https://titus.uni-frankfurt.de/texte/etcg/cauc/ageo/gh/ghqub/ghqub.htm.

Georgian nation.⁶² Bulmaisimisże is far more rigorous and persistent in his references to the Mother of God than his predecessor, Gulaberisże. The final strophes of the *Encomium* refer to the patriarch's present, and praise the Queen of Georgia, whose rule is blessed and fortified through the intercession of Nino and the Mother of God.⁶³ Epithets used for Nino are no longer those of feminine powerlessness. Instead, Arseni's Nino is 'strong as a lion', 'wise in heart', with 'eagle's vision', and her apostolic mandate is validated by the Mother of God. This contrast is indeed understandable, as while Nikoloz's homily was dedicated to the justification of Tamar's femininity, for Arseni, the deceased queen's gender was no longer a problem, as her persona has already been sacralised and mythologised.

Yet, while Tamar's loyal writers produced elaborate rhetorical justifications of her right to rule, her persona was never utilised as a justification for the female rule in general, nor has it provided a licence to any subsequent women to rule singlehandedly. Even Gulaberisże's discourse, although seemingly a praise of the feminine nature, is a defence of the exceptionality of Nino, implicitly of Tamar's reign, and of the situation of emergency in which the two women operated. Meanwhile, Tamar's historians too consistently conceptualised her reign as a unique and exceptional state of affairs that had no exempla in history. Tamar was perceived both as a religious miracle and as a legal exception, which, according to Karl Schmitt, is an analogy to the miracle in religion.⁶⁴

St Nino's cult, at least its visual representations, faded away after Tamar's death. As Antony Eastmond points out, the cycle of Nino's life in Udabno Monastery is the last of such images, and does not reappear until the seventeenth century. This seventeenth-century image, however, was painted in the ciborium of the Svetitskhoveli Cathedral of Mtskheta, the place of Nino's cult's origin: 'Nino appears only in churches with strong court connections; as soon as one moves away from the court, the power of the cult wanes ... there was a disparity between the political requirements for St. Nino to represent the dynasty, which needed to encompass all the territories that the Bagrationis ruled, and the actual geographic limits of her cult, which never extended beyond the eastern provinces of Georgia that she evangelised.'⁶⁵ In elite representations, the problem of the Queen's gender had long lost its political immediacy, as she had transubstantiated into a religious figure. With Tamar's gender out of sight, Nino too retreated to the periphery.

---

⁶² Arsen Bulmaisimisże, *galobani ... ninoysi*, ed. Sulava, 326–8.
⁶³ Ibid., 328.
⁶⁴ Schmitt, *Political Theology*, 36.
⁶⁵ Eastmond, 'Local Saints', 723.

The sense of the emergency and the exceptionality of Tamar's reign is most narratively elaborated in the finest poetic justification of Tamar's mandate – Rustaveli's *The Knight in the Panther Skin*. Neither the exact date, nor the name of the author and the circumstances of its composition are agreed among scholars. While most accept that the poem was written in the zenith of Tamar's reign, some believe that it is a product of a post-Tamar era, written soon after the downfall of the Georgian kingdom and the beginning of the Mongol occupation. What remains evident, however, is that the poem was intended as a celebration either of Tamar's rule or her memory, and served as a poetic justification for Tamar's monarchy. At the outset of the poem, the first chapter discusses the advantages of female rule and implicitly recalls the events of 1177 by praising Arabia's King Rostevan for his wise decision to make Tinatin his co-ruler. Tinatin is praised for her maturity and wisdom, just like the Patriarch had justified Nino's mission by the advantages of female nature. In what is the most frequently quoted and controversial verse of medieval Georgian poetry, Rustaveli says,

> Although a woman, she is a sovereign, ordained by God's decree,
>   [more precisely: 'begotten through God']
> We are not flattering you, but even in your absence agree.
> Like her radiance, her deeds are as bright as the sunshine to see.
> Lion's whelps are equally lions, through female or male they be.[66]

While it is tempting to believe that the final line is an emancipatory manifesto of social equality of men and women, secularised from the Christian idea of their equality in the face of God, arguably it is not the gender of the lion's cubs that is of primary importance, but rather them being lions, that is, sovereigns. Indeed, as it transpires in the poem, Tamar's and her literary alter-ego's kingship are charismatic due to their womanhood. However, this charisma manifests only in political bodies, when political and feminine identities are merged. Tinatin, although a woman, through her impartial decisions, has entirely transcended her female self and has politicised her body, by thus temporarily normalising the exceptional. Rustaveli is keen to maintain this differentiation, and not to generalise the charisma of the feminine, by narratively demonstrating that the feminine, once left outside of the political body and the aura of *auctoritas*, becomes an irrational and destructive power. In contrast to Tinatin, who not for a single second abandons her political self, with her discourse always calm, rational and efficient, the poem's Indian protagonists, Princess Nestan-Darejan and General Tariel,

---

[66] Shota Rustaveli, *Knight in the Panther Skin*, tr. Coffin, 17.

bring destruction upon themselves and their realm with their unruly passion and recklessness.⁶⁷ The juxtaposition between the two impulses, the rational, embodied in Tinatin and Avtandil, and the irrationality of Nestan-Darejan and Tariel, propels the poem's plot. While the two male heroes are the active protagonists of the poem, Nestan and Tinatin set the story in motion. The former rolls the snowball of destruction due to her erratic nature that medieval readers considered as natural to women, and the latter orchestrates the eventual restoration of harmony by dispatching Avtandil to solve Tariel's problems.

Rustaveli's portrayal of princess Tinatin is in harmony with Basili Ezosmożguari's philosophising on the interaction of the feminine and the royal in the body of the Queen near the end of his account. Tamar is described as a philosopher king and a stoic sage, guided solely by reason, blending human and royal natures in a perfect mixture. She is presented as 'simple' (*martivi*) in a philosophical sense, and not allowing any admixture in her body, and remaining unaffected by passions.⁶⁸ Tamar's political aura subsumes and, as it were, girdles Tamar's gender. From a medieval perspective, the essentially transgressive nature of women is stabilised by their political hypostasis, something that, from the Georgian authors' point of view, happened only once, just as only once was a Virgin allowed to bear a child.

## 6.5 The Liminal Figure

That Tamar's popular cult has partly resulted from the active promotion of her living and posthumous cult by Georgia's ecclesiastic elites can be substantiated by the components of her myth, which can be broken down into several thematic strands: Tamar's foundations, motifs associated with Tamar's lost grave, deliberations on the ambiguities caused by her gender and monarchy, and Tamar, as a member of the eastern Georgian mountainous pantheon, and a founder of a political order. Yet, in all these variations, Tamar's memory and cult betray strong ambiguities. The three manifestations of Tamar – the feminine, the sacred and the political – as well as the tension among them, thoroughly whitewashed by Tamar's historians, are encapsulated in some of the oral stories below. Outside official narratives, Tamar is simultaneously represented as a mother and a virgin, a king and a queen, a saint and a political figure, the symbol of the

---

⁶⁷ Aleksidze, 'Let Us Not Obstruct the Possible', 167–84.
⁶⁸ Basili Ezosmożguari, *c'xovreba mep'et'-mep'isa t'amarisi*, ed. Kaukhchishvili, 148.

Golden Age and (implicitly) the reason for its downfall, a deity, a heroine and a villain, simultaneously projecting 'purity and danger'. The ambiguity of Tamar's representation resided in a simultaneous coexistence of the sacred and the profane in her body, which has been articulated in the wealth of mythological lore.[69]

Due to the exceptional prominence of Tamar in commemorative practices and national narrative, it may seem that once her political and religious cult had been established, her posthumous reputation has never been challenged. However, just as the legitimacy of her reign was fragile and in need of constant reaffirmation, equally ambiguous was her posthumous cult, split between reverence and misogyny. For a medieval person, women could cause destruction without even acting upon it, as proven by Tamar's daughter and heir, Rusudan. While through the pen of Rustaveli, Basili, Šavt'eli, Gulaberisże and scores of hymnographers, the stupendous success of Tamar's kingdom was paired with the glorification of her gender, the downfall of the Georgian kingdom under Rusudan was with a similar enthusiasm attributed to the new queen's feminine weaknesses as essential to her gender.[70] The dry report of the early fourteenth-century *Hundred-Year Chronicle*, also known as the *Mongol Chronicle*, of Rusudan's ascension to the throne after Giorgi-Laša's death, comes in sharp contrast to the joyful account of her mother's coronation. The ceremony of her coronation is related extremely laconically. Rusudan is described as beautiful, generous and politically wise, like her mother. Soon, however, everything deteriorated, and 'people of all ages began to display insatiability and idleness, and turned to evil. And because they had forgotten God, God subjected them to obscene curses and massacres at the hands of the heathens. Queen [*mep'e*] Rusudan adopted her brother's habits and indulged herself in idleness and amusement.'[71] And for this reason, great evil arose.

---

[69] Kevin Tuite summarises this sense of ambiguity as one of four characteristics of Georgian traditional religious practices: 'The contrast, or opposition, of male-linked/divine "purity" and female-linked/corporeal "impurity", the latter derived from an ancient representation of women as inherently powerful, but threatening to male/divine "purity". People, places and objects can be rendered more "pure" by the blood of sacrificed animals, which contrasted with the dangerous, "polluting" blood of women shed during menstruation and childbirth. Associated with this notion of opposed principles of "purity" and "impurity" is the seeming paradox that the survival of the community requires contact and cooperation between them.' Tuite, 'Lightning, Sacrifice', 489.

[70] Eastmond, 'Gender and Orientalism', 110–12.

[71] Żamt'aaġmcereli, *asclovani matiane*, ed. Kaukhchishvili, 168.7–15: https://titus.uni-frankfurt.de/texte/etca/cauc/mgeo/kcx2/kcx2.htm; *The Hundred Years' Chronicle*, tr. Gamqrelidze, 323.

For the anonymous author, Rusudan's gravest sin was that she, as a queen, was unable to transcend her feminine self, in this case her motherly instinct, which in Tamar's persona was suppressed by her Marian analogy. Rusudan, like her mother, was beautiful, but this beauty encapsulated all the 'feminine' vices. By repressing her brother's son David, Rusudan promoted her own son, also named David. This, according to the historian, was the principal cause of the catastrophe of the Mongol occupation and Georgia's political disintegration. The circumstances of Rusudan's marriage also contrasts with Tamar's reluctance to marry. Rusudan's passion towards her future husband and her overt sexuality are contrasted with her mother's desire for virginity: 'At this time Queen Rusudan had the son of Toġrili brought to her as a hostage. He was well-built and of mature age, his body was fair, and he was fearless and strong. When she met him, *Mep'e* Rusudan fancied him and decided to marry him, and so she did. She made Toġrili's son her husband and gave birth to a girl of sublime beauty, and she gave her the name of her blessed mother Tamar.'[72]

Unlike Tamar, Rusudan has never transcended her feminine self, having retained all the unruly traits that someone like Psellos would have considered as natural to women. As such, she never appeared in the liminal space of the feminine, the political and the religious. As a woman in power, Rusudan became the ultimate scapegoat for the catastrophe that befell Georgia, and the principal cause for the kingdom's eventual downfall and then breakup. Just as Tamar's eulogists praised, theologised and idealised their queen and her femininity, which brought about the Golden Age, so did subsequent historians blame her daughter's womanhood for its eventual demise. Much later, in the late eighteenth century, Rusudan's model was transposed on the last ruling queen of Georgia, Darejan (1762–98), the widow of King Erekle II. The end and eventual annexation of the Georgian kingdom by the Russian Empire were often, and entirely unfairly, blamed on the Queen and her alleged determination to endorse her favourite son as Erekle's successor. In these queens, the feminine, which constituted the essence of Tamar's sanctity and charisma, manifested in what a medieval author would consider natural for women – evil. Therefore, Tamar's paradigm has never resulted in a conceptual shift towards a reinterpretation of the feminine, not least its emancipation. On the contrary, Tamar remained an exception that proved the rule. It was this liminality of Tamar's representation between the divinely sanctioned

---

[72] Żamt'aaġmcereli, *asclovani matiane*, ed. Kaukhchishvili, 172.3–8: https://titus.uni-frankfurt.de/texte/etca/cauc/mgeo/kcx2/kcx2.htm; *The Hundred Years' Chronicle*, tr. Gamqrelidze, 324.

and charismatic exceptionality, on the one hand, and her essentially 'evil' female nature, on the other, which generated obsessions with her cult that transcended medieval historical narratives or panegyrics.

This ambiguous cult of Tamar conceived in the literary production of the thirteenth century demonstrated extraordinary vitality in folk traditions. While Tamar's court writers wished to resolve the tension caused by the problematic interaction of the royal, the feminine and the religious manifestations of the Queen, the popular tradition, free from the limitations of official narratives, has fully preserved and reproduced this tension. Tamar's artists veiled her gender in political and religious splendour, whereas popular poetry retained the ambiguity of Tamar's gender and her male and female attributes. A folk song spread across the Svaneti region of the Caucasus reveals a zeal to strip Tamar of all her feminine and social attributes, and to present her in bare, genderless life: 'Queen Tamar, you went to your father in law [repeated after each line], without a veil, without a skirt, without a dress, without shoes, without a horse, without a saddle, without reins.'[73] Another folk song, widely spread and performed in the Svaneti region, as well as, in other versions, in other highland regions, is similarly focused on and indeed baffled by Tamar's gender ambiguity:

> Queen Tamar arrived,
> She wore a helmet,
> She wore earrings on her ears,
> Her eyes were of hyacinth,
> Her teeth were gems,
> She wore a black necklace,
> Outside she wore an armour,
> Inside a silk dress.
> She wore shoulder plates,
> She wore chainmail on her thighs,
> And boots on her feet.[74]

Tamar's cult was initially most likely imposed and, perhaps forcibly, from above, and has met some resentment or at least misunderstanding among common people. Arguably, this resentment has been retained in a cognitive dissonance of sorts, reflected in several oral narratives, where Tamar is

---

[73] Ibid., 217.
[74] Sikharulidze, *saistorio sitqviereba*, 215. Svan is a South-Caucasian language, spoken exclusively in Georgia's north-western mountainous region of Svaneti. Georgian and Svan are not mutually comprehensible.

both praised as the maker of the Golden Age and implicitly blamed for its demise.[75] According to one such common story, Tamar had been seated on a throne on the Caucasus's highest peak, Mt Elbrus/Ialbuzi, where she had kept as a hostage the North Star, an arrangement that guaranteed everlasting Summer in her realm. One day, however, she left the box with the star to her maid who out of curiosity opened it and let the star escape. As a result, since then, the entire land has been covered in snow and Tamar too was no longer able to ascend Elbrus.[76] Understandably, winter symbolises the end of the Golden Age and the general downfall that followed Tamar's death. In this account, therefore, Tamar is both the reason of the Golden Age and its annihilation, an embodiment of the fragility of the Golden Age, reflected in the fragility of her feminine self.

There exists yet another oral story which essentially conveys an identical message. Here, Queen Tamar is presented as a virgin who wished to remain as such, a claim that resonates with Tamar's similar desire in the *History and Eulogy*. As a virgin, a living saint and queen, while attending the liturgy, Tamar never touched the church's ground with her feet. Instead she hovered slightly above the ground, with her clothes hanging on a sunbeam. One day, however, Tamar became pregnant, and the power of levitation left her. The perfect balance of her three hypostases was thus annihilated. The story of Tamar's pregnancy too generated several versions: one version points to the Georgian nobility who had secretly sent a man to her while she was asleep, and Tamar begot a child without her knowledge or consent. The second version is more pious and claims Tamar's immaculate conception. In both cases, a boy was born and was called Laša, the 'Light'. Tamar was deeply ashamed of her lost virginity and disposed of the boy. The boy, however, was raised by a deer as Georgia's future king.[77] Although this story underscores Tamar's sanctity and superhuman abilities, it also accentuates the inherent ambiguity of Tamar's persona. The reason that she hovers in the church could be both a sign of her sanctity, as the story claims, but also her, as of a woman's, impurity – as a woman she should have not stepped on the hallowed ground where women were banned from. Thus, as a saint, she was allowed inside a church, but as a woman, she avoided touching the church's ground with her feet. As soon as Tamar, due to her political

---

[75] In folklore, Tamar is also paired with her distant descendant and Georgia's last great and penultimate king, Erekle II. Some folk accounts call Erekle Tamar's son. Georgia's greatest and its last king embody the entire history of independent Georgia in a single mother–son relationship.
[76] Kiknadze, 'sami etiudi', 68–86.
[77] Sikharulidze, *saistorio sitqviereba*, 80–1.

responsibility, bore a child, her gift of levitation disappeared too, and neither could the rays of the sun hold her clothes.[78]

Other Tamar lore betrays overt misogyny and vilification of Tamar. In folk tales mostly spread in Georgia's lowlands, Tamar often appears alongside Shota Rustaveli, the author of *The Knight in the Panther Skin*, where she sometimes acts as Rustaveli's antagonist. A folk tale, known as *Shota Rustaveli's Grave*, tells a bizarre story: Shota Rustaveli presented his poem to Queen Tamar. Tamar was then betrothed to the son of Iury Bogolubsky, nevertheless she fell in love with Shota. Shota was, however, married, so Tamar decided to separate him from his wife. So she sent two 'black' men to seduce her, a mission that they accomplished. Shota witnessed one of such acts and beheaded the two men. When Tamar heard of this, she sought vengeance. Shota escaped to Greece and became a monk. Nevertheless, he was captured and beheaded. His body was left in Greece, whereas his head was brought back to Tamar. This is the reason why Shota Rustaveli's resting place is unknown. The existence of this unpleasant tale, even if peripheral, is a symptom of moral ambiguities generated by the ambiguities of her gender, a principal attribute of folk Tamar.[79] The common people among whom this legend circulated were entirely unaware of Tamar's literary representations, and just had a vague understanding of her as a powerful queen, a mixture that apparently begged for her vilification.

In the Caucasian highlands, however, Tamar had transubstantiated into a deity. Georgian scholars are keen to maintain that neither this nor any other folk Tamar had anything to do with the representations of the historic Queen. However, the fact remains that a Tamar has been absorbed from medieval narratives and visual representations into folklore, and has been transformed specifically due to the effort of her panegyrists to forge her cult. In one strand of lore Tamar is portrayed as a supreme deity served by the 'sons of god', simultaneously projecting male and female attributes of power, seated in between the realms and guarding the border between the two:

The Creator said:
When I placed the earth,

---

[78] Kiknadze, 'Sami etiudi', 80.
[79] Sikharulidze, *saisttorio sitqviereba*, 118–19; Fähnrich, *Georgische Sagen*, 19. For commentary, see Vashalomidze, *Die Stellung der Frau*, 242–4. In a Svan folk poem which I heard several years ago in Ushguli Village, Tamar was vilified and utterly condemned with utmost hatred. Unfortunately, I have not recorded the poem and despite years of my quest, I could not retrieve it. Therefore, I am unable to include the poem to further my argument. Curiously, when I inquired among folklorists, the very existence of such a poem was vehemently denied, as something 'impossible'.

With all its abundance,
Where mountains and plains met.
I encircled it with three seas.
The White, the Red and the Black.
I covered it with the sky,
The plate, the glass and the bronze (?),
I gave birth to the world,
A thousand kinds of faiths,
Sixty-three Saint Georges
Are located in all four corners,
For Christians to pray,
Have appeared as a cross.
For *xtissvilni*, begotten by God,
They serve as temples.
The sons of God [*xtissvilni*] have a saint
Queen Tamar,
She was ordered by the Lord,
To wear her father's sword.
She took her father's kingdom,
Though she herself is a woman.
She made the earth her own
She had sufficient power.
In the middle of the sea she placed the boundary,
The boundary is an iron rod.
To rule her realm,
She is seated on a dry hill,
In front of her on a hill stands
The cheerful *Lašaris Jvari*.[80]

In a more laconic variation, Tamar uses her veil to separate the two realms, the sea and the earth.[81] This motif with its numerous variations contains several important imageries. Tamar is presented as the creator of body politic par excellence, as God's representative on earth, who is endowed with the power to separate the two realms – the political and the natural.

---

[80] Chikovani, *xalxuri poezia*, 137–8; Sikharulidze, *saistorio sitqviereba*, 71–2.
[81] Chikovani, *xalxuri poezia*, 120: 'Seven-year-old Tamar arrived, / The Queen Tamar, / She took off her veil, / And dispersed the seas. / She placed a border in the middle of the sea, / Said – no dew shall cross this! / A youth arrived on a blue horse, / The joyful Cross of Lašari. / – Let us stand in front of each other, / And have servants! / She hung a bridge in-between / For crossing.'

> The lady king Tamar said: 'Mother, I saw a dream /
> I was handed over all the shores, but what if I cannot preserve them.'
> – When you were born, Tamar, it was already obvious,
> When you were three months old, you rose in your cradle,
> First you washed your hands and face, and then crossed yourself,
> You veiled yourself, and I could not tell where you went,
> You came back seven years later and said: 'I saw the middle of the sea...'[82]

Tamar guards the threshold of the two realms, that of the seas and the political. Finally, she embodies both female and male attributes, which makes it impossible to identify her gender. Arguably, Tamar's representation as of a guardian of a boundary, the crosser of the seas, the bridge-maker, which is present in almost all Tamar-related folk poems, and which is unique to her, as opposed to other male deities, draws on Late Antique Marian imagery, especially the Theotokos as the guardian of the threshold.

> Mary figures not as sacred space or womb but as the membrane separating the sacred and the profane, the pure and the polluted. Like her hymen, this boundary can be permeated without being violated, and thus the membrane both divides and joins the divine and the human, creator and create. The stories recounted by Moschos, Antony, and in the *Life of Mary of Egypt* place the Theotokos at the threshold, a penetrable barrier protecting sacred space. As such, she demarcates boundaries between heresy and orthodoxy, male and female, sin and redemption.[83]

The association of wisdom with waters goes back to the Vulgate version of the *Book of Sirah*: '8. I alone have compassed the circuit of heaven, and have penetrated into the bottom of the deep, and have walked in the waves of the sea, 9. And have stood in all the earth: and in every people, 10. And in every nation I have had the chief rule' (Sir. 24:8).[84]

This folklorised persona of Tamar has been ordered by God to wear her father's sword and to take up his kingdom, even though she was a woman. Then she is seated on the mountain of Lašari and faces the *Lašaris Jvari*, the

---

[82] Chikovani, *xalxuri poezia*, 118: ქალმა თქვა, თამარ ნეფემა: დედავ, სიზმარი გნახეო: / ჩამბარდა სახმელეთობი, ვაჰ, თუ ვერ შევინახეო. – მაშინვე ჩანდი, თამარო, როდესაც დაიბადეო. / მესამე თვე რომ გაგიხდა, აკვანშიითა ასდეო. / ჯერ ხელ-პირ ჩამაიბანე, მერე პირჯვარ დაისახეო. / ჩიქილა გადაგებურა, ვერ გავიგ, საد რა წახვეო. / მობვედი მეშვიდეფ წელსა, სთქვი: შუა ზღვაი გნახეო...
[83] Krueger, 'Mary at the Threshold', 38.
[84] Barker, 'Wisdom Imagery', 91–109.

principal deity of the Pshav and Khevsur pantheon, unambiguously based on the name of Tamar's son, Giorgi-Laša. Thus, like in Tamar's iconography, in folklore too, Tamar is paired with a male counterpart, *Lašaris Jvari*. In some versions, Tamar is paired with Iakhsar, an epic hero and demigod of the eastern highlands. Iakhsar is presented as Tamar's antagonist, although no further elaboration is provided as to what the reason of the battle between the two was. In this version, Tamar's formulaic story is narrated from Iakhsar's point of view as a part of Iakhsar's ritual dance song: 'Seven-year-old girl Tamar was declared king and queen. We met at the sea and made war.'[85] The representation of Tamar as an antagonist to one of the epic heroes and demi-gods can be yet another faint remnant of the ambiguity of Tamar's cult which in folk traditions required legitimisation through pairing with a male counterpart, similarly to Nino, in certain cases revealed in an armed standoff with the dominant male deity of the region.

---

[85] The poem is published in Sikharulidze, *saistorio sitqviereba*, 25: შვიდი წლის ქალი თამარი, მეფედ თქვეს, დედოფალიო. / ზღვის პირას შავიყარენით, შავგვექნა საომარიო. / ზღვასა გადაჰკრა ჩიქილა, გადააქანნა წყალნიო. / შუა ზღვას ჩადგა სამანი, არ გადმოსცილდეს ცვარიო. / კლდეზე გამართა ქალაქი, შააბა რკინის კარიო. / შიგ ააშენა სიონი, დაადგა ოქროს ჯვარიო. 'Seven-year-old Tamar was king and queen, / We met at the sea and made war. / She covered the sea with the veil, and dispersed the seas. / In the middle she placed a boundary: "may the waters not cross this"! / On the rock she built a city, and she hanged an iron door. / Inside she built the Sion, and she placed a golden cross.'

# Conclusion to Part II
# The Legacy and Myth of Queen Tamar

In earlier pre-Bagratid narratives, the gender of the saints implicitly contributed to the political and mediatory value of their cults and relics. By the turn of the millennium, with the rise of the Bagratids, gender became an issue in Georgian identity rhetoric. The old Mtskhetan foundation story posed two conceptual problems: first, it was too feminine, and second, its conversion narrative originally covered a territory far smaller than claimed by the Bagratids. Even if an overt challenge to the gendered aspect of the foundations of Georgian Christianity is not directly attested, Nikoloz Gulaberisże's ardent defence of Nino's femininity betrays the existing anxieties regarding this matter. Georgia in the eleventh century was not the same kingdom as the early medieval Kartli, and its kings were initially seated far from Mtskheta or Tbilisi, in western and south-western Caucasia. The population of these regions may have been even less impressed by the story of a solitary refugee girl being the founder of their Christian identity. Thus, the Bagratid mythology on the one hand projected a sense of novelty, yet on the other it dialogised with the olden stories, of old kings and their foundations.

The original *Mok'c'evay* narrative was essentially that of symbolic and material translation of the Holy Land to Kartli, embedded in the discovery of its foundational relics and stories, as well as the presence of the Jewish communities as memory-bearers of this continuity. This newly created entity, the Christian, 'northern' kingdom of Kartli was perceived by the authors of the *Mok'c'evay* as something radically novel, a last stage in world history and facing the eschaton. The endeavours of the first Bagratid kings were marked with a similar dialectic of foundation and translation. The old Kartli was politically and symbolically transferred to a new area, and while some symbolism of the old Kartli clung, most of them, including the political cult of St Nino, remained beyond the focus of the Bagratids, and struggled to gain foothold far from Mtskheta and the Living Pillar. The markedly feminine character of Kartli's foundational story was in all appearance shunned by the Bagratids, a tendency that transpires in Katholikos Nikoloz's eulogy. St Nino was sidelined by 'new' and masculine cults.

From the tenth century, warrior saints appear across Georgia's and Caucasia's churches and literature. From the Apkhaz dynastic cult, the Bagratids adopted St George as their patron saint by merging St George's imagery with the dynastic cult of King David. Apostle Andrew became Georgia's original missionary, King David was discovered as the ancestor and dynastic saint of the Bagratids, whereas the militaristic St George emerged as a quintessentially Bagratid and by extension Georgian martyr-saint. Due to the wide distribution of St George's visual images across Georgia's churches, he was conceptualised as a counterpart of the female characters of Georgia's religious history, of St Nino or her mythological alter egos. Thus, over time, Nino has become flanked by men: her mission was legitimised, and by the first apostles confirmed through her kinship with St George, institutionalised by the Syrian Fathers, and integrated into the making of the cult of the holy King Vakhtang. She remained a charismatic founder, a *k'adagi*, yet her charisma was subsumed in the aura of men. From a more theoretical point of view, there appears to be a more nuanced conceptualisation of gender. Arguably, the problematisation of the gender of the cult of saints was an important component in the Georgian project of creating an anti-Byzantine rhetoric and counterbalancing the rhetoric of the empire with that of the sovereignty of the Georgian kingdom. We shall see similar 'gendering' of the cult of saints much later, in the context of the Russian imperial discourse and Georgian nationalism in the nineteenth century. Indeed, the effect that the relationship with the 'co-religionist' yet aggressively expansive Byzantine Empire had on the formation of ideologies in Georgia is comparable to a similar relationship with the Russian colonialist policies in the nineteenth century. In both instances, these problematic relations were articulated in the idea of the 'lot of the Mother of God'.

Effectively, the cult of the Mother of God was the second context in which the saintly and political discourses were gendered. Originally, the 'Lot of the Mother of God' was designed to transform the tropes of weakness, alterity and alienation, into an advantage in the face of the dominant Byzantines. Yet this trope was internalised and transformed by the Bagratids into a symbol of exclusive prestige: just like they were related to the Theotokos, similarly was Georgia, a land united by the Bagratids, also conceptually united into a 'Lot of the mother of God'.

The third and crucial problematisation of the feminine occurred with the reign of Queen Tamar. With Tamar in the picture, the entanglement of the saintly, political and feminine once and most expressively became an issue. Tamar's rule was in urgent need of legitimisation, since her mandate to rule in her own right was unprecedented. The only exception that mandated a woman with a 'male' task was found in the *Mok'c'evay* story, hence the emergence of the cult of Nino since the late twelfth century. While the Mother of God remained the exclusive patroness of the Bagratid House and the Georgians, Tamar introduced a personal and intimate relationship with the Mother of God, which also affected the place and role of St Nino. Tamar was conceptualised as an exception, similarly to another exception allowed by divine dispensation when Nino was given an apostolic mandate. Both mandates were legitimised by the exceptionality of the Mother of God. Tamar's political and religious representation absorbed earlier cults and cult narratives and gave them new political meanings, especially to the original *Conversion* narrative. The cult of St Nino was re-evaluated and boosted with Tamar in the picture. Tamar, Nino and the Theotokos had one thing in common – they were absolute exceptions, hence intimately linked. Indeed, no image, trope or feminine category collected from the Byzantine or older Georgian writings was used to justify Tamar's gender and reign. Instead, exclusively Marian imagery and ambiguous religious tropes were used to characterise her.

Arguably, due to the tremendous effort of court writers to forge a cult of Tamar, her memory was adopted in oral narratives, where from a saint she transubstantiated into a quasi-pagan divinity.

The wealth of surviving evidence for the many manifestations of Tamar's cult suggests that the inherent ambiguity of her persona was the reason for the tremendous success of the queen's cult. The political cult of Tamar was initially forged by her elite entourage, and in time it became the greatest cult in Georgian piety and narrative. Although whitewashed in official writing, Tamar's popular representation inhibited a strong sense of ambiguity: she was a woman and monarch, king and also queen, a mother and a virgin, holy, yet, as a woman, unholy. She hovered in the church, yet her female impurity banned her from the holy site, she was the symbol of Georgia's Golden Age and a premonition of its downfall, she was a heroine and also a villain. Traditional misogyny and unabashed masculinity of the religious practices and cult sites came in sharp conflict with Tamar's gender, resulting in her unmatched aggrandisement. Her cult was augmented to an extreme, and the greatest saint of the Georgian Church also became the most prominent deity of semi-pagan religious practices across the Caucasus. In popular imagery and cult practices, Tamar became a liminal entity, the maker of the political realm, the 'maker of the bridges' and God's co-creator.

This 'gendered' trait of the cult of saints in Georgia, as largely determined by the representations of Tamar, became politically expedient in the eighteenth and nineteenth centuries, with Georgia's occupation and annexation by the Russian Empire. Georgia's 'feminine' history was duly noticed by the earliest Russian travellers and diplomats, a feature, which later, with Georgia's annexation, was used to forge the image of the Georgian colonial 'other'. Nino, Shushanik, Tamar, later the martyred Queen Ketevan and other female figures of Georgian lore saturated Russian imperial writing and rhetoric and contributed to the colonial vision of a subjugated, yet treacherous and unruly Georgia.

It was in the context of these ideological transformations and conundrums that *Sak'art'velo*, as a novel and a more abstracted unity, was born. *Sak'art'velo* projected a sense of unity but also harboured a potential for desintegration. *Sak'art'velo* and the 'The Lot of the Mother of God' were conceived practically simultaneously, as an effort to create a new mythology for this kingdom. 'The Lot of the Mother of God' was, however, an abstract concept, probably too abstract, in that it encapsulated the fragility of Georgian unity. Unlike the Lord's Tunic, it was not cemented in a specific space, except for the body of Queen Tamar. As such, it allowed interpretations. The question, which exactly was the Lot of the Mother of God, persisted, as we saw in the story of the Icon of Acquri, or the Robe of the Theotokos in Samegrelo. Over time, since the death of Tamar, the Jaqeli in the South or the Dadiani on the Black Sea coast claimed to be the real allotments to the Mother of God. Seemingly, the time from the formation of this concept to Georgia's political disintegration was too short to allow for its association exclusively to the Kingdom of Georgia.

'The Lot of the Mother of God', the entanglement of the feminine in saintly and political discourses, as well as the ambiguity of the cult of Queen Tamar all had an important role to play in the history of post-Byzantine Georgia. With Georgia's disintegration into smaller units in the fifteenth century, *Sak'art'velo* became a historical concept, as well as a project of unity. In this last section of our historical excursus into the cult of saints, we shall explore the rise of Russia to the north of the Caucasus and how it affected the perceptions of sanctity, gender and politics. What did not impress the Byzantines, impressed the Russians, who found in the Georgian claim to being the 'Lot of the Mother of God', as well as its coveted relics and stories associated with these relics, an opportunity for their imperial ambitions.

# Part III

# Introduction to Part III
# The Rhetoric of Gender and Sanctity from Imperialism to Nationalism

This final section of the book addresses the receptions of Late Antique and medieval concepts of sanctity and their political values. Although the section covers a vast period of time from the disintegration of the Georgian monarchy in the fifteenth century to modern days, it essentially addresses one conceptual problem – the manifestations of Russian imperialism and reactions against it in Georgia through the rereadings and reinterpretations of medieval concepts of sanctity. The Orthodox empire that arose to Georgia's north was particularly fascinated by the cult of saints and relics, masterfully integrating earlier concepts and tropes into its ever-evolving rhetoric of empire. The early modern and modern history of Georgia and Caucasia is essentially a story of conceptual, political and symbolic entanglements and disentanglements with the many instantiations of the 'Russian Empire' whether Muscovy, the Russian Empire, the Soviet Union or the Russian Federation with its neo-imperialistic ambitions.

In 1490, the nobility advised Georgia's King Constantine VII as follows: 'Because the Imeretian and the Kakhetians and the Atabags of Samtskhe stand firmly and loyally for their choices, we shall not fight them, and even if we do this later, we shall not be allowed to. Instead, let us wait, and perhaps one day God will return kingship to you.'[1] Thus, what had already been a political fact was also confirmed legally. Georgia's nominal unity was over, and what once was the united Georgian kingdom broke up into the kingdoms of Kartli, Kakheti, Imereti and the Principality of Samtskhe-Saatabago. Various branches of the Bagratid Dynasty ruled in Imereti, Kartli and Kakheti, whereas the powerful dukes, Dadiani of Odishi and Gurieli of Guria, controlled the Black Sea coast, and, until the Ottoman annexation, the Jaqeli ruled in the south. Kingship across the entirety of Georgia was never returned to a single house. What followed were four centuries of bitter and almost incessant warfare among the remaining political entities. Stories of treacheries, murders,

---

[1] Vaxušti Batonišvili, *ağcera*, ed. Kaukhchishvili, 303.

devastations, occasional alliances and guerrilla warfare against the Safavids and the Ottomans is the principal narrative arc of Georgian history between the fifteenth and the eighteenth centuries. Having turned into a battlefield of small and great powers, cultural life declined dramatically, only to be briefly reanimated in the eighteenth century. At various times and often simultaneously, all three branches of the Bagratid House believed that they were the legal heirs to the kingdom and until Russia annexed all of them in the early nineteenth century, expelling the Bagrationi claimants, they strove to unite the kingdom under a single crown. Georgian political unity was restored only four-and-a-half centuries later, in 1918, as the Democratic Republic. Yet, despite the absence of political unity, the concept of *Sak'art'velo*, which gained currency in the eleventh century, persisted as a designation of this imagined or projected unity. The idea of Georgia, while politically non-existent, remained ingrained as a memory, as an observable project and a religious phenomenon. Meanwhile, other neologisms also appeared, such as *Iveria*, with reference to the religious symbolism of the unity encapsulated in the ever-expanding *K'art'lis C'xovreba* corpus.

The diplomatic relations between the Georgian kingdoms and Muscovy began before the official disintegration of the Georgian kingdom. King Alexander I of Kakheti (1476–1511) addressed Ivan III, the Grand Prince of Muscovy (1462–1505), for help against the Muslim powers. Yet, Alexander's plea was rejected. The dynamics of Russian–Georgian relations for the next few centuries were determined by the zeal of the Georgian kingdoms to find Christian support against the Ottomans and Persians, and Russia's slow encroachment towards the Caucasus. The ties became deeper throughout the sixteenth and seventeenth centuries, when practically all other Georgian principalities were involved. Yet, the political orientations in Georgia varied. While some elites strongly supported Georgia's rapprochement with Russia, others were sceptical, whereas yet other groups were openly pro-Persian.

In 1783, King Erekle II of Kartli-Kakheti (1744–98) ratified a treaty with Russia, whereby this eastern Georgian kingdom became a protectorate of the Russian Empire. The thirteen articles of the *Treaty of Georgievsk* signed on 24 July of the same year acknowledged Kartli-Kakheti as a Russian dependency, and described the privileges and responsibilities that the two parties would henceforward have. The agreement was, however, never enacted, and not a single point was honoured by Russia. In 1795, at the battle of Krtsanisi near Tbilisi, Kartli-Kakhetians suffered a catastrophic defeat from Iran's Qajar Agha Muhammad-Khan (1789–97) and did not see the promised military aid.[2] This

---

[2] This event was obliquely acknowledged in articles 2 and 3 of the 1801 Tsar Alexander I on the abolition of kingship in Georgia. The manifest still claims, however, that the troops were dispatched but had to be unexpectedly withdrawn.

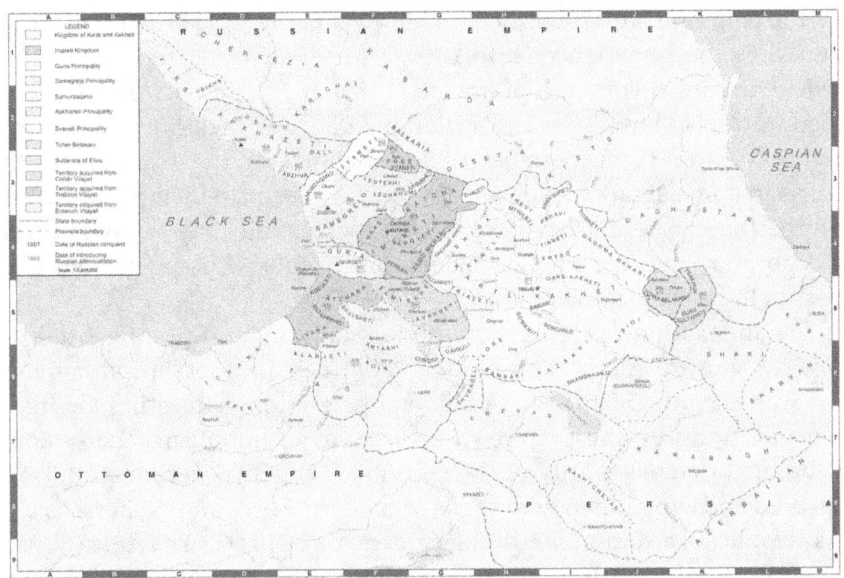

Map III.1  Georgian kingdoms and principalities as annexed by the Russian Empire in the early nineteenth century. Source: D. Muskhelishvili, Historical Atlas of Georgia.

was effectively the last major military standoff in the history of the Georgian kingdoms. Erekle II died in 1798 and was succeeded by his feeble and sickly son, Giorgi XIII (or, according to some other chronologies, Giorgi XII), who gave yet further concessions to Russia.

The decree of 22 December 1800 signed by the Russian Tsar Paul I (1796–1801) and issued on 18 January 1801 by his successor, Alexander I (1801–25), abolished the almost uninterrupted history of Bagratid kingship in Georgian lands, and annexed the kingdoms of Kartli and Kakheti (see Map III.1). This edict generated drastic social, political, ethnic and economic changes in virtually all aspects of the life of the people of Georgia. With these radical changes, the idea of the Georgian body politic too experienced dramatic transformations. After over 1,200 years of unchallenged rule, the senior members of the Bagrationi House were forcibly relocated to Russia, while the rest of them staged a series of unsuccessful anti-Russian rebellions. Having failed to gain local support, however, eventually, all of them were forced to leave Georgia. Eleven years later, the 1,500 years of the history of the Georgian Church too ended, and the local hierarchy was integrated into the Russian Patriarchate. Georgia's Katholikos-Patriarch Antony II was removed from his seat and transferred to Russia, where he reluctantly joined the synod of the Russian bishops, while his office was occupied by a Russian exarch. The language of the church service also became Russian, and the common law established by King Vakhtang VI (1716–24) was substituted by the Imperial code. In 1810, immediately after the death of the unyielding King Solomon II of Imereti (1789–1810), this western Georgian kingdom too followed the east's example and was incorporated into the Empire.[3] With a typically imperial gesture, however, the Tsar allowed the Georgian non-Bagrationi high and low nobility to retain their privileges and join the Russian feudal hierarchy, an act that significantly eased Georgia's incorporation into the Empire, indeed much unlike Russia's tedious conquest of the northern Caucasus.

The annexation of Georgia by the Russian Empire was an act of both political and religious significance. Political and territorial annexation was accompanied by symbolic appropriation, saturating Georgia's incorporation into the Empire with respective symbolism. The symbols of the historic sovereignty of the Georgian kingdom were methodically removed and supplanted with those of the Empire. Among others, as part of symbolic annexation, and replacement of Georgia's sovereignty with imperial rhetoric, Russian imperial discourse appropriated Georgia's religious imagery and the cult of the saints, incorporating them into the rhetorical arsenal of the Empire.

In the second half of the nineteenth century, however, the rising national movement sought to dismantle the imperial mystique, and salvage the tropes of sanctity by effectively desacralising the Russian Empire. Georgia's saints and historic relics appropriated by the Russian Empire as symbols of imperial authority were re-evaluated by nationalist discourses. Effectively, since then the modern dichotomies of Russia vs collective West, national vs Imperial, were born in their modern shape, and, as will be argued below, the cult of saints played a vital role in these conceptualisations.

One hundred and ninety years later, Russian rule finally came to an end in Georgia. On 9 April 1991, Georgia declared independence for the second time in that century. The independence brought about new hopes and new anxieties in practically all areas of the lives of the Georgian people. Nevertheless, Georgia continues to exist under the shadow of Russia's expansionist ideology. Consequently, in contemporary Georgian political discourses, internal as well as foreign, medieval and imperial tropes and the rhetoric of sanctity are deeply infused into the rhetoric of religious and political elites, contributing to or indeed undermined by the precarious process of nation-building.

---

[3] For an overview of the consolidation of the Russian rule in Georgia, see Gvosdev, *Imperial Policies*, 117–40.

# 7

# The Saints of the Empire

## 7.1 The Political Body of Queen Ketevan

Since its dismemberment into several kingdoms and principalities, Georgia, as well as the entire Caucasia, became a virtual battlefield among these emerging smaller powers and greater regional players – the Ottomans and the Safavids. With the 1555 treaty of Amaseia, what had constituted the Georgian kingdom was divided between the Ottoman and Iranian zones of influence. The west, beyond the Likhi range, was handed over to the Turks, and the east to the Safavids, an arrangement that, instead of peace, brought havoc to the Caucasus. In 1605, a young and charismatic Teimuraz I, one of the most tragic and controversial figures in Georgia's history, became King of Kakheti. He ruled until 1648 and during 1625–33 was also king of the united kingdom of Kartli-Kakheti. Teimuraz's education was entirely Persian, as was the case for most of the seventeenth-century Georgian elites. However, having written some of the finest verses of Georgian poetry, he became the most acclaimed Georgian poet after Rustaveli. For fifty years, Teimuraz led an anti-Iranian insurgency during which he orchestrated some stunning military victories and endured catastrophic defeats. Teimuraz saw the violent deaths of practically his entire family and the razing of his kingdom. He also fought alongside King Luarsab II of Kartli (1606–16), who was martyred by the Persians for refusing to abandon Christianity and was canonised as a result. The lengthy standoff between the outlaw king and Shah Abbas I, Teimuraz's victory at the Battle of Martqopi (25 March 1625) and defeat at Marabda (1 July 1625) became a theme of subsequent lore. For five decades he fought the Persians only to end his life in prison in Iran in 1661.

Early in Teimuraz's reign, the Shah was adamant to have Teimuraz fight on his side against the Ottomans. To guarantee Teimuraz's alliance, he demanded hostages. In 1614, Teimuraz reluctantly sent his mother, Queen Ketevan, and his two sons to Ispahan. The Shah also tried to lure Teimuraz, but the king did not show up and rebelled, allying with the Kartlian King Luarsab II and the Ottomans. The Shah retaliated and sacked Kakheti. In response, Teimuraz sought Russian, Ottoman, and Western European support. He struggled to free his mother, first through Muscovite diplomacy and then in 1618, as part of the Ottoman campaign against Iran, by attempting to forcibly set her free. Teimuraz was brutally punished for his efforts. The Shah castrated his sons. The older son lost his mind and the younger died soon thereafter. Meanwhile, the geopolitical state of affairs also changed against Teimuraz as the European powers now sought an alliance with Iran against the Ottomans, and would not antagonise the Shah. On 13 September 1624, as a punishment for Teimuraz's negotiations with the Russians and the Ottomans, and his continuous rebellions, Shah Abbas first demanded that Queen Ketevan abandon Christianity and accept Islam, and upon receiving a staunch refusal, had her brutally tortured and executed in Shiraz.

The brutal killing of his mother shook Teimuraz to his core and apparently affected his mental health. While scores of Georgians had been killed by the Iranians for centuries, such a public, inhumane and ritual execution was long unheard of. Ketevan's martyrdom resonated far beyond Iran and Georgia, and deeply impressed Catholic communities in Asia as well as western Europe. The circumstances, reason and method of her execution, the hiding of her body to discourage the Christians from venerating her, were reminiscent of the very foundations of Christianity and the stories of the first martyrs under the pagan Roman emperors and Sasanian kings.[1]

Teimuraz dedicated a bitter poem to his mother's death. The poem is a surreal mixture of Rustavelian tropes and descriptions of the brutal realities of Teimuraz's times. Ketevan is simultaneously compared to St Nino and Nestan-Darejan, the protagonist of *The Knight in the Panther's Skin*, who was imprisoned in the fortress of the *K'aji*, awaiting liberation. Yet, unlike Rustaveli, Teimuraz's poem has no happy ending. No Avtandil, Tariel or St George appear to rescue the queen. The poem is essentially a lamentation of Teimuraz's failure to emulate these figures of Georgia's history and literature and to liberate his mother and queen. Throughout the poem, Teimuraz crafted an image of Georgia personified by its most prominent woman. To describe her time in prison, he extracted tropes from Late Antique martyrologies, medieval romance and historical accounts. Teimuraz also applied to the traditionally ambiguous gender tropes, by simultaneously accentuating his mother's feminine beauty and underlining her fearsome and heroic

---

[1] Flannery, *Portuguese Agustinians*, 197–238.

character. Then Teimuraz carries on with a description of the gruesome details of her martyrdom, and, after several excruciating strophes, contrasts the marvellous deeds of her female nature with his male feebleness, now that he walks alone and aimlessly on the face of the earth.[2] Yet, seven months after Ketevan's martyrdom 'a miracle occurred', and Teimuraz's army defeated Abbas at the battle of Martkopi, temporarily liberating eastern Georgia from the Persians. After the battle, the Shah acknowledged Teimuraz's right to kingship in both Kartli and Kakheti. Georgian, Armenian and Portuguese historians perceived this victory as revenge for Ketevan's murder, while Ibrahim Peçevi pointed out that the Shah had not seen such a humiliating defeat in forty years.[3]

The news of the martyrdom of the Georgian queen spread swiftly among the Christians of Iran and beyond. Queen Ketevan was canonised immediately by the Georgian Church and became celebrated also in the Roman Catholic world. Her martyrdom was witnessed by Portuguese Augustinian missionaries who collected her relics, divided and dispatched them across the world. The Portuguese wished to canonise her as a Roman Catholic saint. However, the fact that she died Orthodox complicated the matter. In 1628, the Portuguese missionaries brought a portion of the Queen's skull and her right foot to Georgia. The queen's relics were deposited in the Alaverdi Cathedral in Kakheti.[4]

While lamenting her death as a personification of his kingdom's fate, Teimuraz fostered and instrumentalised the cult of his deceased mother. Indeed, no other Georgian martyr-saint has received international attention comparable to that of Ketevan. Unlike the martyrs of the olden days, she was probably known and respected by everyone in the small Kakhetian kingdom. For the Georgians of the time, Ketevan encapsulated everything that they had learned and knew about the history of their country, yet this history played out in the most gruesome way possible. For many non-Georgians, her story was practically the only thing they knew about the small kingdom of Kakheti. Apparently, in an attempt to recover from the tragedy, Teimuraz convinced himself that his success at Martqopi and eventual liberation from

---

[2] Teimuraz I, *cameba k'et'evan dedop'lisa*, ed. Baramidze, 126–38.
[3] Nachkebia, 'Ketevan', 569–70.
[4] Ketevan's martyrdom became a subject of western European literature. See, e.g. Gryphius, *Catharina von Georgian*. For a political theological study of the play, see Alt, 'Frauenkörper und Stellvertretung', 127–49. Ketevan's fame even reached the British Isles, where Scottish poet William Forsyth (1818–79) dedicated a poem to her martyrdom, *Martyrdom of Kelavane*. Some seventeenth-century titles include Gregorios Ieromonachos, *A Letter, Relating the Martyrdome of Ketaban* and Claude Malingre, *Histoires tragiques de nostre temps*, 469–532.

the Persians was accomplished with the aid of his mother's relics. Yet, guilt and certain masculine shame stayed with Teimuraz until his death as evidenced in many of his poems.

On 18 April 1656 Teimuraz, still overcome with guilt, sent a piece of Ketevan's relic to the Russian Tsar Alexis I with a note: 'I am hereby sending a piece of my mother's body from the thumb of her foot.'[5] The symbolism of the relic was staggering. Ketevan's death was at least in part caused by Teimuraz's effort to establish ties with Russia against the Safavids. Now, having turned Ketevan into a political commodity, Teimuraz encapsulated in this piece of his mother's body Iveria's history, and religious and political identities. As an act of desperation, he was now handing over this capsule to the Tsar, a gesture that was understood and eagerly received by the Russians. Teimuraz's act was the beginning of a new political life of saints, their relics and their stories. It signalled the rise of a new Orthodox power to Georgia's north with its novel imperial rhetoric and political mythologies. For the next four centuries, Georgia's, as well as the entire Caucasia's, political and religious life was determined by the continuous manoeuvring under the shade of Muscovy and its many incarnations.

## 7.2 Imperial Taking

Pieces of Ketevan's body arrived in Moscow amidst dramatic geopolitical changes in the wider region. Russia was slowly but steadily becoming a major regional player in Caucasia by balancing out the Ottomans and the Safavids. New imperial policies and rhetoric were initiated in Russia when in 1613, *Zemsky Sobor* elected Michael I of the House of Romanov as their Tsar (1613–45). Michael was the first representative of Russia's longest-ruling and last royal dynasty, whose sovereignty saw the greatest territorial expansion in Russian history. His son and successor, Alexis, was involved in the 1651–3 wars with Safavid Iran, the first major standoff between these two powers over the Caucasus. It was in 1615, during the reign of Michael I in Moscow, that Teimuraz in Kartli and Giorgi III in Imereti (1605–39) dispatched the first documented embassy to Moscow with a request for a military contribution to the struggle of the Georgian kingdoms against Iran, and they have maintained this relationship ever since. However, Muscovy was at that moment disinterested in the southern frontiers and was recovering from its internal troubles. In 1639, Teimuraz finally secured an alliance with Russia and took an oath of allegiance to the Tsar. In 1658,

---

[5] See Paichadze, 'masalebi', 456–7.

he even personally visited Tsar Alexis. Russia's support, however, remained entirely nominal and did not affect Georgia except for triggering Iran's occasional acts of revenge.[6]

The military and administrative achievements of Michael and Alexis were further aggrandised by their religious aura. For the two previous centuries, Muscovy's dukes had cultivated the ideology of Moscow as the Third Rome and invested in a material substantiation of this claim.[7] Part of the Russian tradition hails them as the first Tsars to bring to Moscow two of the greatest relics of Christendom – the Tunic of the Lord and the copy of the Panagia *Portaitissa* from Iveron Monastery – both items directly tied to Georgia. In the years that followed, Georgia and relics linked to or stemming from Georgia played a key role in the construction of Russian Imperial rhetoric. Perhaps for the first time in Georgia's history, the pretenses of the 'Lot of the Mother of God' were appreciated by a superior power with which the South Caucasian rulers negotiated for protection. The fact that the Byzantines had never taken the Georgian claims seriously whereas the Russians seemingly embraced them, was never forgotten and never forgiven by the Georgian Church, echoed even today in its relationship with the Patriarchate of Constantinople.

The Russian story of Christ's Tunic, and how it allegedly wound up from Georgia in Russia, reflects imperial pretences familiar to the imperial rhetoric since Constantine in the fourth century. The new centre of the Orthodox world required material substantiation of this centrality, and the Tsars initiated quests for Christianity's foundational objects. Russian diplomats, some of whom were also monks, rummaged across Georgian principalities, meticulously recording all the major and minor relics that various kings, dukes and monasteries possessed. Tsar Michael commissioned ambassadors Fedot Elchin and Pavel Zakharov to provide a detailed report on the principality of Samegrelo, its boundaries, politics and, crucially, the relics that it possessed. The Tsar specifically wanted to know 'whether there really was in the land of Dadiani a treasury of relics: the life-giving cross of the Lord . . . or his tunic, or the robe, or part of clothing, his or the Mother of God's, or her shroud or the belt'.[8] Georgian court and

---

[6] For some more recent titles about Russian–Georgian relations before 1801, see Gvosdev, *Imperial Policies*, 14–98; Suny, *Making of the Georgian Nation*, 42–96.

[7] The earliest proclamation of Moscow as an imperial city is found in the 1492 charter of Metropolitan Zosimus of Moscow where Tsar Ivan III is called New Constantine and Moscow 'New Constantinople', and Rus is placed in the centre of the universal history. Strémooukhoff, 'Moscow the Third Rome', 84–101; Poe, 'Moscow, the Third Rome', 412–29; Sinitsina, *Tretiĭ Rim, passim*.

[8] Gamakharia, *Materiali posol'stv*, 377–8.

ecclesiastic officials were glad to oblige. Moscow's claim to Roman heritage was familiar to Georgian officials, who addressed the Tsar as 'the great Christian autocrat, who earlier was in Rome, but not anymore'.[9] Georgian rulers shrewdly played the Holy Land card against Muscovy's pretences to Roman heritage. They boasted and eagerly recounted the stories from the *K'art'lis C'xovreba*, advertising the 'Lot of the Mother of God' in their dealings with their fellow Orthodox Russians. Russian diplomatic reports of the sixteenth and seventeenth centuries recount the eagerness with which the rulers of Georgian kingdoms and principalities exhibited their Marian relics – the Megrelian Principality of Odishi possessed her robe and a portion of her belt, the Imeretian katholikos boasted the ownership of bits of her hair and milk, whereas the Mtskhetans in the Kingdom of Kartli took pride in the foundational relic of Georgian Christianity – the Tunic of the Lord. They all exoticised and presented themselves as the most ancient and holy Christian land, indeed the Lot of the Mother of God, to emphasise the land's importance in Russian eyes and to hopefully secure their support against the Ottomans and Persians. When, for example, the Russian ambassadors asked the ruler of Odishi in Samegrelo whether he would be happy to send the Robe of the Mother of God to the Russian Tsar, Dadiani was not in principle against it, realising apparently the bargaining power of the coveted relic.[10] Indeed, arguably, it was specifically for Russian consumption that the idea of the Lot of the Mother of God was bolstered by Georgian rulers, both western and eastern, even more so than in their earlier dealings with the Byzantines, who were far less impressed by the Georgian claims. The idea of the 'Lot', as cultivated by the post-Byzantine Georgians, therefore, acted as a remembrance of the past unity, as a foreseeable political project, and as a means of diplomacy with the Russians. The project was successful, as the Russian pilgrims and travellers eagerly reproduced Georgian stories of the *K'art'lis C'xovreba* by nearly equating Georgia with the Holy Land.[11]

Among all of these relics, the Tunic of the Lord was certainly the most coveted. The Russian knowledge of the history of the Tunic and its travel from the Holy Land to Kartli derives entirely from the *K'art'lis C'xovreba* accounts that the Russian travellers recorded in Caucasia. Yet, in the Russian adaptation of the legend the Jewish component, central to the entire *Conversion* narrative, is silenced: it was allegedly a Georgian soldier who witnessed the event and, having collected the Lord's Tunic,

---

[9] For Shepeleva's commentary, see Likhachev, *puteshestvia russkix poslov*, 425.
[10] Aleksey Yevlev, *Stateinyi spisok*, ed. Tsintsadze, 63–4.
[11] Arseny Sukhanov, *Xozhdenie*, 112–14.

brought the Holy Relic to Georgia. Upon his return, his sister embraced the Tunic and being struck by the aura of the precious gift, died on the spot. Georgians buried the Tunic together with the woman, and a tree grew on top of the site where later the *Svetitskhoveli* cathedral was built, and where the Tunic was kept until the seventeenth century.

The most recent history of the Tunic, however, was intertwined with the political relationship among the three kingdoms: Russia, Persia and Kartli-Kakheti. Tsar Michael had offered Teimuraz protection against the Persian Shah Abbas I during the latter's pillaging campaigns in Eastern Georgia. According to some Russian sources, however, in 1622, after another punishing raid in Georgia, as a sign of peace, the Shah sent to the Tsar and the Patriarch Filaret Christ's Tunic that he had taken from the Svetitskhoveli in Mtskheta. In 1625 the Tunic, effectively Persian plunder, allegedly arrived in Moscow with great ceremony, where it was embellished with precious stones and where it is still kept today, although the original promise to the Georgian king was duly forgotten. The authenticity of the Christian relic gifted by a Muslim king was initially challenged. However, it was soon confirmed by the Patriarch after a series of miracles carefully enumerated in the respective documents.[12] The matter was settled without further investigation. The way the Russians dealt with the Tunic suggests that the authenticity of the Tunic was secondary to its political significance, which transcended the need to documentarily confirm its provenance.

The Tunic's removal from Mtskheta is rejected by the Georgian tradition. The story is challenged by other Russian reports that locate the Tunic in the Svetitskoveli Cathedral well after 1625. Twenty-five years after the purported events, the famed Russian pilgrim Arseny Sukhanov, the author of travelogues and descriptions of the Holy Land, sojourned to Georgia where he was shown Christ's Tunic. Arseny retold the well-known story without knowing anything about the Tunic's translation to Russia.[13] Travellers in Mtskheta are still shown the place where the Lord's Tunic is buried under the foundation of the Svetitskhoveli Cathedral. It is striking that the morality of this act – a Christian relic plundered by a Muslim king and gifted to a Christian monarch – has never been challenged, and the

---

[12] Belokurov, *Delo o prisyl'ke shakhom Abbasom*. The story is published on the official website of the Russian Patriarchate, and is titled *A Long Path to Moscow*. Archimandrite Avgustin, 'O Rize Gospodney', http://www.patriarchia.ru/db/text/330913.html (last accessed 11.08.2019). For an English translation, see http://www.pravmir.com/the-lords-robe-in-russia/ (last accessed 11.08.2019).

[13] For post-1625 Russian and Georgian references to the Tunic in Mtskheta, see Zhordania, *k'ronikebi* 1, 15–16; *k'ronikebi* 2, 57. Arseny Sukhanov, *Xozhdenie*, 112–14; Belokurov, *Snosheniĭa Rosii*, 433–88.

entire affair was interpreted as an acquisition by the Romanov Dynasty of the charismatic mandate to rule the Orthodox Empire, mimicking the Emperor Constantine's and his successors' zealous quest and appropriation of holy relics for their imperial foundations. Similarly to Constantine, Michael retrieved the relics from their old owners and translated them to his capital, thus marking the beginning of a new era, and the new Empire's mandate to collect, own and distribute the principal symbols of Christendom. Since the early Romanovs and until Putin's Russia, the Tunic has been a powerful instrument in the rhetoric of power of the Russian rulers.

Another relic associated with Georgia was the Icon of the Mother of God of Iveron, the *Panagia Portaitissa*, currently one of the most venerated Marian icons in Russia. In 1647 the Tsar commissioned a copy of the Icon, which arrived in Moscow a year later. The Slavonic stories related to *Panagia Portaitissa* are first attested in Old Russian in the fifteenth century and are very similar to Athonite and Georgian legends. They stem from the Greek *Hypomnemata* of the Icon, such as *On Iberians, and How They Came to Know God,* and are intertwined with other stories of Georgia's conversion to Christianity that the Russians had heard in Georgia and Mt Athos.[14] A short version of the account of the Icon, attributed to a Greek-Russian monk Maximus (d. 1556), locates an unidentified monastery in Georgia as the place of the Icon's origin.[15] By the seventeenth century, these Georgian and Greek stories, the Iveron Monastery on Mt Athos and Iveria (i.e. Georgia) were merged in Russian thinking. As a result, by the late sixteenth century, the idea of Georgia as 'the Lot of the Mother of God' further confirmed by the mythology of the *Iverskaya* Icon, was well known and utilised in official Russian correspondence. For example, Patriarch Iov of Moscow (1525–1606) addressed his Georgian colleague as the katholikos of 'the part and the lot of our All-Holy and Immaculate Queen and Mother of God and eternally Virgin, the land of Iveria'.[16] Later, bishop Dimitry of Rostov (1651–1709) almost verbatim reproduced the *Life of Nino* and the story of Georgia's allotment to the Mother of God, which he had partially collected from the Athonite tradition of the *hypomnemata*.[17] Russian accounts of 'Georgia's allotment' had two sources: One collected from Georgia proper and the other gathered from the Athonite tradition, according to which, although Georgia was the original allotment, Christ had ordered His mother to stay in Jerusalem. Later, she travelled to Cyprus to see Lazarus, but a

---

[14] Chryssochoidis, 'Portaitissa Icon', *passim*.
[15] Tolstaia, 'Iverskaia Ikona', 8–22.
[16] Belokurov, *Snosheniiā*, 91.
[17] Dimitry Rostovsky, *Zhitiiā*, 453–477.

storm forced her ship to land on the Athos Peninsula, where she destroyed Apollo's temple and sanctified the land.[18] These stories are attested in the Russian tradition as early as the first half of the sixteenth century and have crystallised by the second half of the seventeenth century.[19]

Even though Georgia had long ceased to exist as a kingdom, to the Russians the land of Iveria was a vague religious concept. It appears that *Iveria*, as a reference to Georgia, was coined specifically in the context of the *Iverskaia* Icon. The word in this form is not attested in Old Georgian, and the Georgians had in all appearance borrowed and internalised the word as a term for this historical and religious unity from the Russians. Since then, *Iveria* has referred to the entirety of the Georgian-speaking lands from east to west. This unified perception, despite independent diplomatic relations with these kingdoms and principalities, was represented by Marian relics. It was with the tremendous popularity of the *Iverskaya* Icon in Russia, coupled with the concept of the Lot of the Mother of God, that Georgia (Iveria) established itself in Russian ecclesiastical writing as a 'holy land'. Shah Abbas's gift too was perceived as the Shah's implicit concession of Georgia, the Holy Land by proxy, to Russia.

If the story of the Lord's Tunic, even if apocryphal, is a typical example of imperial appropriation, the story of another Christ-related relic, the Holy Nail, opens a new chapter in the political symbolism of Georgia's relics and is tied to the first Georgian emigration to Russia seventy-five years before Georgia's annexation. In 1724, unable to withstand Persian pressure, Kartli's king Vakhtang VI, along with his extended family and entire court, emigrated to Russia. Over 1,200 members of Georgia's intellectual elite left Georgia to seek refuge at the court of Russia's Peter I. Vakhtang, like previously Teimuraz I, was also a poet, having written, among many other pieces, verses that lament the fall of Iveria: *Woe, How Bitterly Was the Lot of Mary Burning!* The royal family took with them a large part of the royal treasury and library. Among others, it has been claimed that Prince Bakar (1700–50), son of Vakhtang, took with him the Holy Nail. In Russia, the Nail was allegedly kept in Prince Archil's family. However, Archil decided to send it back to Georgia. His intention was made known to Tsar Peter I who removed the Holy Nail from the Georgian family and ordered its translation to Moscow.[20] The association with Constantine's similar acquisition was obvious for eighteenth-century Russian writing, whereas for the Georgian readers, the removal of the Holy Nail as an act of imperial

---

[18] Shelonin, *Khronograf*, 498–501.
[19] Isachenko, 'Raĭ myslennyĭ', 200.
[20] Kluchevskaia and Makhanko, 'Kazanskaia I Tatarskaia Eparkhia', 183.

taking was reminiscent of the Emperor Heraclius's invasion, and removal of political sovereignty.

These oral and written narratives spread through different media, ages and contexts, contributed to the creation of a sacred aura of Georgia in Russian religious and political thinking, and were incorporated into the imperial rhetoric of appropriation. In the seventeenth and eighteenth centuries, together with the crystallisation of the ideology of Moscow as the New Rome, the perception of Georgia as the New Jerusalem was upheld and cultivated in the Russian–Georgian discourse. The political acquisition of this ancient Christian land together with the ownership of its symbolism, and religious and political mythology became integral components of the cultivation of the idea of the Orthodox Empire.[21]

The political and religious concept of the Lot of the Mother of God found sound resonance in Russian Imperial political theologies. A search on Russian websites for the 'Lot of the Mother of God' (*udel bogoroditsi*) will result in the following narrative, which ties together Russian piety and imperial ambition: Iveria (Georgia) is considered as the first lot, then comes Mt Athos, confirmed by various stories of the *Panagia Portaitissa*, followed by Kyivo-Pechorskaya Lavra in Kyiv, and finally, the fourth lot is the Saint Seraphim-Diveyevo Monastery near Nizhny Novgorod in Russia.[22] The last two sites were created by association: in the eleventh century, an Athonite monk from Rus founded the Pechera Monastery (Monastery of the Caves) and imported there the Athonite variety of the cult of the Virgin. Much later, in the mid-eighteenth century, a rich Russian woman arrived in Kyiv and became a nun. One night, the Mother of God appeared to her and told her the story of the monastery and ordered her to establish yet another 'lot' in the north of Russia. Today these narratives, mostly crystallised in the nineteenth century, are all associated with Russian Imperial pretences, and mark the lands that 'rightfully' belong to Russia, especially since Russia's 2008 war in Georgia and the 2022 invasion of Ukraine.

## 7.3 Imperial Giving

On 12 September 1801, the Emperor Alexander issued a manifesto abolishing kingship in the Kingdom of Kartli-Kakheti. The announcement, which the Emperor had allegedly made reluctantly, was a fusion of political, moral and religious justifications for Georgia's annexation, framed as an act of

[21] Tolstaia, 'Iverskaia Ikona', 8–22.
[22] See, for example, the Wikipedia article https://ru.wikipedia.org/wiki/Удел_Богородицы (03.06.23).

mercy: 'We are sympathising with your situation and have seen that the presence and mediation of the Russian army in Georgia is the only barrier against the bloodshed of our coreligionists and their eventual annihilation that has been prepared for you by your ravaging and infidel neighbouring people.' The Emperor then claims to have originally wished to maintain the political status quo and independence of the Kartli-Kakhetian kingdom, yet Georgia's extreme parochialism rendered his wish unrealistic. He was therefore forced to annex the kingdom. In other words, the Emperor saved Georgia from its self:

> The power of circumstances, your common sense and the plea of the Georgian people convinced us not to abandon and not to sacrifice the co-religionist language that had handed over its fate [*zhreby*] to the magnanimous Russian protection. Your reanimated hope will not be deceived this time. It was not for the sake of the increase in power, nor by avarice, nor for the sake of expanding the limits of our already vast Empire that we took upon ourselves the governance of the Georgian kingdom. It is solely honour, sorely dignity, and humanity that brings upon us this holy duty, the hearkening to the prayers of the oppressed, to stop their suffering, to establish in Georgia the rule which can strengthen the rule of law, personal and property's safety and to give to each the protection under one law.[23]

Thus, in the imperial language, annexation was wrapped as a gift. Arguably, the usage of *zhreby*, 'lot', a term that was so often referenced in Georgian religious and political imagery, was in this political edict a deliberate choice of words that channelled the traditional Georgian narrative into imperial ideology. The edict conveyed the idea that, just as Georgia was the lot of the Mother of God, similarly Russia had been allotted Georgia politically and religiously, thus fulfilling Georgia's metaphysical and political destiny. The 'gift' of annexation was sent together with another, material gift – the cross

---

[23] Beliaevsky, *Utverzhdenie*, 35: Сила обстоятельствъ сихъ, общее по сему чувство ваше и гласъ грузинского народа преклонили насъ не оставить и не предать на жертву бѣдствія языкъ единовѣрный, вручившій жребій свой великодушной защитѣ Россіи. Возбужденная надежда ваша сей разъ обманута не будетъ. Не для приращенія силъ, не для корысти, не для распространенія предѣловъ и такъ уже обширнѣйшей въ свѣтѣ имперіи пріемлемъ мы на себя бремя управленія царства грузинскаго; единое достоинство, единая честь и человѣчество налагаютъ на насъ священный долгъ, внявъ моленію страждущихъ, въ отвращеніе ихъ скорбей, учредитъ въ Грузіи правленіе, которое могло бы утвердить правосудіе, личную и имущественную безопасность, и дать каждому защиту закона.

of St Nino that had earlier, like many other relics and symbols of Georgian sovereignty, ended up at the Russian Imperial court.

This story of Nino's cross follows the same south-to-north trajectory as Georgia's other relics associated with the foundation of Christianity in the kingdom: Allegedly, due to incessant raids, the Cross was first transferred to Georgia's northern highlands, to Kazbegi and then to the Ananuri Fortress in the Aragvi Valley. From there, in 1749, Metropolitan Romanoz of Samtavro took the Cross to Moscow and presented it to his sister and wife of Prince Bakar, the heir to Kartli's throne, who, together with Kartli's royal family, lived as a refugee near Moscow. According to yet another version of the story, the Cross left Georgia even earlier, in 1688. The last station of the Cross appears to be the village of Liskovo where it was kept until 1801, the year when the Russian Emperor officially annexed eastern Georgia.[24] To mark the occasion, the pro-Russian branch of the Georgian royal family presented the Cross to Alexander I as a celebration of the Manifesto of 12 September. Up until this moment the relic had a history identical to other major relics housed in Georgia – Christ's Tunic or the Holy Nail – that were allegedly added to the imperial collection. However, a year-and-a-half later, the Emperor Alexander issued a decree ordering the Cross to be taken back to Georgia as a gesture of goodwill:

> Having been informed of . . . the pious reverence of the Georgian nation from antiquity toward the true and life-giving cross of St Nina, and that its preservation in its body was the sign of prosperity, whereas, the opposite, that its removal from the limits of Iveria was a sign of wars, quarrels and misfortunes, that has befallen this nation, we have been long contemplating to return to Georgia this Divine sign of grace and a mystical seal of its salvation. The Lord, who has blessed all our heroic deeds for the benefit of this nation, has earlier sent this priceless gift to our treasury. Having received it with due gratitude to His almighty dispensation, with great pleasure shall we forward it to the Georgian people, through the ruler of Georgia, Kovalensky. We hope that due to their experience our love for this co-religionist nation, they will receive this gift as yet another confirmation of our care. We, therefore, order you to announce publicly its translation to the Georgian land, in cooperation with the chief clerics, with due honour, and in accordance with faith and hope, to place it in the main church of Tbilisi, so that thus erected among the nation who righteously venerates it, it may become the reason for its happiness. And together with it, may peace and prosperity return to that country, and may the wondrous power of the cross heal many wounds

[24] Beliaevsky, *Utverzhdenie*, 36.

Figure 7.1 The Cross of St Nino, in a seventeenth-century metalwork. Source: Artanuji Publishers.

brought about by mutinies and internal strife and may the Lord's grace bring to a successful conclusion our aims and valiant deeds for the sake of the saving of the Georgian nation, for the sake of its glory and further success.[25]

In the same year of 1802 the Cross was carried in a solemn procession on the same, but reverse route from the northern Caucasus, via Vladikavkaz, through the Darial Gorge, Kazbegi and Ananuri to Mtskheta, where a service was celebrated in gratitude for the Emperor's benevolence (see Fig. 7.1).

[25] The letter, along with other documents related to Russian policy in the Caucasus, is published in Beliaevsky, *Utverzhdenie*, 36–7: Зная … сколь благоговѣйное уваженіе народъ грузинскій издревле сохранялъ къ честному и животворящему кресту св. Нины и что соблюденіе сей святыни среди его было знаменіемъ благосостоянія, такъ какъ, напротивъ, удаленіе ея отъ предѣловъ иверійскихъ было эпохою браней, раздоровъ и бѣдствій, страну сію постигшихъ, мы давно уже помышляли возвратить Грузіи сей залогъ Божія къ ней благоволеніия и таинственную печать ея блажества. Всевышній, благословящій всѣ подвиги наши въ пользу сего народа, ниспослалъ и сей безцѣнный даръ въ сокровищи наши. Воспріявъ его съ подобающимъ благодареніемъ къ всесильному Его промыслу, мы съ чувствомъ истиннаго удовольствія препровождаемъ его къ грузинскому народу чрезъ нашего д.с.с. и правителя Грузіи Коваленскаго. Мы удостовѣрены, что среди опытовъ нашея любви къ народу намъ единовѣрному, пріиметъ онъ сей даръ новымъ ознаменованіемъ нашего о немъ попеченія. Мы поручаемъ вамъ, возвѣстивъ всенародно о перенесеніи его въ страну грузинскую, учредить срѣтеніе его, по сношенію съ главнымъ духовенствомъ, съ подобающей честью, теплой вѣрѣ и твердому упованію сообразною, и поставить въ главномъ храмѣ тифлисскомъ, да водруженный среди народа, къ нему праведно благоговѣющаго, будетъ онъ залогомъ и утвержденіемъ его счастія, да вмѣстѣ с нимъ возвратятся въ страны сіи миръ и благоустройство, да чудесная сила креста сего исцѣлитъ безчисленныя раны, мятежомъ и внутренними раздорами нанесенныя и да благодать Вышняго увѣнчаетъ успѣхами намѣреніе и подвиги наши во впасаніе народа грузинскаго, въ славу его и въ преуспѣяніе предпріятые. The event is also described in Butkov, *Materialy*, 510.

On 9 April 1802, the Cross arrived in Tbilisi, and is to this day kept in the cathedral church of Sioni. The arrival of the Cross in Tbilisi on 9 April was immediately, on 12 April, followed by the most important political act in Georgia's history – the public announcement of the Manifesto of 12 September 1801, which abolished kingship, a declaration that came as news to most of the citizens. Thus, Alexander's two edicts – the abolishment of monarchy together with the establishment of a new colonial administration, and the return of the Cross of Nino – were published simultaneously, with the two acts framed as a single act of imperial gift-giving. The Russian emperor, therefore, symbolically gifted Georgia the gift of Orthodoxy while simultaneously taking its sovereignty and assuming its body politic. While keeping the relics of universal salvation history, he returned the national symbol of Georgia's participation in this history. Indeed, 'donating relics in the context of a diplomatic encounter served to underline the emperor's magnanimity and exclusive claim to ecumenicity on the one hand, and a recipient's indebtedness and loyalty to him on the other.'[26] Yet, in the Russian-Georgian context, the imperial gift also resolved the delicate problem that the Georgian Church was much older than the Russian. Thus, the 'gift of Empire', an expression coined by Bruce Grant, 'narrates the early Russian ideology of rule in the Caucasus. It speaks to a vision of sovereignty that opens with conquest and closes with victory, moving on to other affairs of state and other mythographies.'[27] Later in the book, Grant argues that 'while the gift of empire may ultimately be unilateral, it sets in motion a remarkably effective means of establishing sovereignty over others, hinging on a language of reciprocity that requires little or no actual reception among the conquered. It is the logic of sovereign rule where the act of taking – of lands, persons, and goods – is enabled by the language of giving.'[28] Imperial

---

[26] Mergiali-Sahas, 'Byzantine Emperors and Holy Relics', 48. Multiple examples exist of such gift-giving in the middle and late Byzantine periods. For example, in 819, similarly to Tbilisians in 1801, the Venetians celebrated the donation of a piece of the True Cross by the Emperor Leo V as the emperor's favour towards them. Ibid.; see also n. 37 for bibliographic reference.

[27] Grant, *Captive and the Gift*, xv.

[28] Ibid., 44–5. As an example, Grant discusses the famous Ditchley Portrait of England's Queen Elizabeth I (c. 1592) with an inscription: 'She gives, and does not expect. She can, but does not take revenge. In giving back, she increases': 'First and foremost, the queen gives. But what does she give? Perhaps like the sun, she gives light – she is the Enlightenment itself – and her gifts enable growth and prosperity. She does not expect return, but the inscriptions make clear that return is already in play. How, otherwise, and for what would she contemplate revenge? If she is giving back, what, then, has she taken? The point, of course, is that the quite substantial taking is lost amid the language of giving, an apparently selfless giving that requires no return.'

taking, in our case of political sovereignty, was thus framed in the language of giving the gift of Orthodoxy and a sense of newly found identity materialised as the Cross of St Nino.

Within a decade following the edict, Russia abolished the independence of the Georgian Church and thus (temporarily) ended its 1,500-year history. The Georgian katholikos-patriarch was violently removed from his seat and appointed as a mere metropolitan of a distant Russian province. The language of the service too was forcibly changed to Russian. Thus, the ritual return of Nino's Cross heralded the beginning of a new, 'purified' Orthodoxy gifted to Georgia by the patron of all Orthodox, the only Orthodox Emperor. In the Empire's rhetoric, this new Georgia did not require the unfortunate and wretched body politic which was invariably described by Russian writers as a history of misery and failure. The narrative forged and reproduced during the next century was that of constant internal strife and the external threat that Georgian kingdoms and principalities had experienced before Georgia's annexation, of trials and tribulations that effectively ended under the Russian Imperial crown. The absence of this Cross was perceived as a sign of war, whereas its presence in Georgia heralded everlasting peace. Paradoxically, this narrative was somewhat eagerly internalised by colonial Georgian elites. For those who were familiar with medieval Georgian chronicles, the Imperial act resonated with a similar act by the first pan-Orthodox emperor, Constantine, who gifted Iberia with the faith of the Cross, and all the accompanying insignia. Like Constantine, fifteen centuries later, the Emperor Alexander rebaptised Georgia by admitting it into the mystical body of the Orthodox Empire. While the Empire appropriated from Georgia the symbols of universal Christian history, it returned to Georgia the symbols of its participation in salvation history. There was no need to house the Cross of Nino in Moscow as Georgia itself had now become part of the Empire, and St Nino was incorporated in the discourse of *Pax Rossica*, of which Georgia was now finally an integral part. The events of 1802 and the ritual return of the Cross of St Nino to Georgia with its political ramifications gave new and modern life to the cult of this Late Antique figure. She was rediscovered in an imperial milieu, and, paradoxically, as a Russian imperial gift to the Georgian nation. To this day, Nino remains a highly venerated saint of the Russian Church, and thousands of Russian pilgrims travel annually to Bodbe, her alleged resting place.[29] Incidentally, as a sign of yet another

---

[29] In Russian popular lore, St Nino is also associated with the 1941–2 blockade of Leningrad. Allegedly, a Russian metropolitan saw St Nino in a vision who prayed to God to end the blockade. The blockade indeed ended on 27 January, on the feast of St Nino.

cynicism, the Russian general who was responsible for the atrocities during the quelling of the Kakhetian rebellion of 1812 was buried inside the church of Bodbe in Kakheti, next to the traditional grave of St Nino.[30]

The return of relics in exchange for sovereignty also happened as part of the annexation of another Georgian principality, Samegrelo. The Georgian tradition of an unknown date but attested since the sixteenth century claims that the Tunic and part of the Virgin's belt had arrived in Samegrelo from Blachernae after the fall of Constantinople. Grigol Dadiani, Samegrelo's dynastic ruler (1788–1804), entrusted the icon of Blachernae and the fragment of the Theotokos's belt to Giorgi XIII, the last king of Kartli-Kakheti. However, following the king's death, Giorgi's son David took the icon with him to Russia. Giorgi's daughter and Grigol Dadiani's widow Nino followed the icon and, having taken it away from David's family, presented it to the Russian Emperor. Nino's letter to the Emperor is an extraordinary witness to imperial taking and returning:

> I have been entrusted by a testament to present to Your Imperial Highness as a gift an icon – may the protection of your throne be established upon us forever, and on our sons and our descendants ... and may what has been lost by us, be returned to our House of Dadiani. ... I am presenting to you this gift, worthy of remembrance. For this is the image of the Mother of God of Blachernae, to which the belt of the All-Holy Mother of God Mary herself is attached that she had personally worn. This is the truth, our autocrat protector and monarch, and for this reason, it has been filled by the emperors with relics and adorned with precious stones and pearls. Currently, the Icon is kept in your capital in my above-mentioned brother's family, from whom my associate will collect the Icon and present it to Your Imperial Highness. Your most loyal servant Dadiani gifted you with the shores of the sea that had since antiquity belonged to Dadiani. And I, your most loyal servant, present the leader [*putevoditelnitsa/odigitria*] and the ruler of the seas through whose intercession may you acquire the throne of the first Emperors, now belonging to the Ottoman Porte.[31]

---

[30] Beliaevsky, *Utverzhdenie*, 100–1.
[31] Berzhe, *Akty II*, 504–5: Сдѣлано же мнѣ отъ него завѣщаніе принести въ даръ В.И. В. образъ, да покровительство престола Вашего утвердится во вѣки на насъ, на сыновъ нашихъ и на потомство наше, да призрѣны будемъ милосердо мы – вновь овдовѣвшіе и осиротѣвшіе и да похищенное врагами нашими у насъ возвращено будетъ дому Дадіани. Не оставивши открытъ сіе предъ престоломъ Вашимъ, я всеподданнѣйшая раба, съ сиротами моими приношу яко лепту, достойную памяти. Ибо образъ сей есть Влахерискія

The Emperor gladly received the icon. However, having adorned it with precious stones, he sent it back to Samegrelo in 1806, where he also ordered the building of a church dedicated to the Mother of God of Blachernae.[32] The church, which now serves as the episcopal see of Zugdidi, was built by Levan V Dadiani, son of Grigol, and completed in 1830. Nino's letter restates implicitly what has already been stated in other documents. Nino describes the Icon of the Mother of God as an embodiment of west Georgia par excellence. The strategic shores of the Black Sea have been now handed over to the Empire with all its religious symbolism. Yet, this imperial taking too was framed in the language of giving, and the relics were gifted back to where they belonged, together with the gift of membership in the imperial body politic. In rhetoric of the empire, the Black Sea shore of Samegrelo and Apkhazeti, the icon of Blachernae and the Marian relics have never been taken away, but instead gifted to the Georgian nation in its authentic, true identity. In other words, as a sovereign, the Emperor, to quote the inscription of Ditchley Portrait of Queen Elizabeth, 'gives and does not expect'. This was neither the first nor the last of such transactions, in which Georgia's relics, earlier appropriated by the Empire, were reinvested in Georgia as a sign of perpetual reaffirmation of Georgia's imperial belonging. The exchange of Georgia's historic relics for political sovereignty became almost ritualised, and was retained as a common practice well after the fall of the empires, both Tsarist and Soviet, as a component of Russia's soft power south of the Caucasian range.

## 7.4 The Sacred and the Erotic

As observed in recent scholarship, the feminisation of Georgia as an imperial and colonial 'other' was a powerful literary topos in nineteenth-century

---

Божіей Матери, къ которому прикованъ поясъ самой пресвятой Богородицы Маріи, коимъ была она опоясана. Вѣрьте истинѣ сей, самодержавнѣйшій покровитель и Государь нашъ, и потому наполненъ онъ отъ императоровъ мощами и украшенъ каменьями и жемчугами. Онъ былъ препорученъ отъ насъ отцу моему царю Георгію, рабу Вашему, по кончинѣ коего остался у брата моего царевича Давида. Не могли же мы его возвратить къ себѣ потому, что врагъ дома Дадіани не пропускалъ въ Грузію человѣка нашего. Нынѣ образъ тотъ находится въ царствующемъ градѣ Вашемъ у помянутаго брата моего, у коего по письму и просьбѣ моей взявъ, довѣренные отъ меня принесутъ въ жертву В.И.В. Всеподданнѣйшій рабъ Вашъ Дадіани принесъ Вамъ въ даръ берега морскіе, еще издревле принадлежащіе дадіанову владѣнію; я же, всеподданнѣйшая раба Ваша, приношу путеводительницу и правительницу морей, коея споспѣшествомъ да пріобрѣтете престолъ перво-бывшихъ императоровъ, а нынѣ Порты Оттоманской.

[32] Niko Dadiani, *k'art'velt' c'xovreba*, ed. Burdjanadze, 195.

Russian orientalist literary fiction. Feminisation and eroticisation of the colonial and imperial 'other' is certainly a familiar concept for a student of imperialism and orientalism and a shared trope across colonialist discourses.[33] In this sense, the Russian colonial experience in Caucasia is no different from European fantasies of erotic bliss in Asia, Africa or the Americas. In nineteenth-century Russian literature on the Caucasus, feminisation was one of the building blocks in the construction of an image of Georgia.[34] Russian cultural elites perceived the Caucasian frontier as a border zone between the Russia and Muslim superpowers, and as such a 'virgin' land. Georgia was feminised and sexualised as a frontier zone of ambiguity between the familiar Christian and strangely Oriental, at the same time alluring and dangerous, sacred and heretical, Orthodox yet also abject. In the Romantic literature of the Caucasus, Georgia was portrayed as a beautiful, seductive, yet treacherous Oriental woman in need of subjugation and taming. In her study of Russian imperial rhetoric and representations of the Caucasus, Susan Leyton examines the overwhelmingly feminine metaphors with which Russian poets and writers described Georgia.[35] Georgia was feminised and eroticised more than any other Caucasian region in Russian literature. It was conceived as a woman, a bride, a virgin, destined to be subdued, protected and owned by the hyper-masculine Russia. This rhetoric, as Layton points out, was determined by 'imperialist discourse's fundamental tendency to marginalise and to augment the alterity of the desired colony or the subject nation of an empire'.[36] By contrast, the colonial Georgia's literary landscape was almost entirely devoid of male characters, instead dominated by sensual femmes fatales. Similarly ignored were all the principal heroic male figures of history and lore, in contrast to the representations of the memorable tribesmen of the north Caucasus. Instead, these authors foreground native Georgian women, whose alterity is at once national and sexual.[37] Alexander Odoevsky's (1802–39) poem, *Marriage of Georgia and Russia*, is a typical example, in that it personifies Georgia as Russia's long-awaiting fiery dark maiden, a bride, and a virgin who longed for her northern husband's arrival and his everlasting protection. Russia,

---

[33] See, e.g., Spurr, *Rhetoric of Empire*, 170–83; McClintock, *Imperial Leather*, 21–131.
[34] Layton, *Literature and Empire, passim*. See, also, Tolz, *Russia's Own Orient*.
[35] According to Said, every nineteenth-century Western author who wrote about the Orient 'kept intact the separateness of the Orient, its eccentricity, its backwardness, its silent indifference, its feminine penetrability, its supine malleability'; Said, *Orientalism*, 206.
[36] Layton, *Literature and Empire*, 193.
[37] Ibid., 192–3.

her bridegroom, is a hyper-masculine giant, who, having defeated his rivals and her old suitors (Turkey and Persia), marches victoriously towards his chosen one.[38] Over time, the spread of the news of the martyrdom of Queen Ketevan also affected the Russian perception of Georgian Christianity and contributed even further to the Russian perception of Georgia as a land of female saints. As subsequent Russian writing on the Caucasus makes obvious, what had happened to Ketevan remained in the Russian memory as a confirmation of the Orientalist trope of Georgians not being able to take care of their women.

Besides traditional colonialist tropes, the Russian rhetoric of empire was nurtured by local traditions that had inherited the medieval Georgian literary entanglement of the feminine, the sacred and the political. In the wake of the annexation of the Kingdom of Kartli-Kakheti, along with the annihilation of the church, the Russian ecclesiastical tradition eagerly absorbed Georgian religious history and its saintly pantheon. Yet, the saints that were established in Russian commemorative practices were exclusively female: Nina, the queens Tamar(a) and Ketevan(a), and the fictional Dinara. These names were adopted in the Russian onomasticon, russified, and are still widely used with the feminine -*a* suffix. By contrast, no Georgian male name has achieved a remotely similar level of popularity in the Russian onomasticon. Georgia's men were utterly excluded from literature as well as religious imagery. Yet, even these female saintly figures, or rather their literary alter egos, were established in Russian literature as sensual, seductive and volatile women, far from their original saintly guises.[39] Nina and Ketevana appear as eroticised protagonists in Alexander Shishkov's rather unimaginative novel *Ketevana*, whereas Tamara was a famous antagonist in Mikhail Lermontov's *Tamara* and a victim of an evil force in the poem *Demon*. In the former, she is presented as a generalised Georgian woman, beautiful but also treacherous and dangerous.[40] These feminine names became associated both with Georgian femininity and with Georgia's treacherous nature.[41] Arguably, this wariness towards Georgian women originated from Princess Nino, the daughter of Georgia's last King Giorgi XIII, who participated in the 1832 anti-Russian conspiracy and was consequently exiled to Riazan. Another reason for the vilification of Georgian women was the wife of Giorgi XIII, Queen Mariam, who had mortally wounded the Russian general Ivan Lazarev when he was trying to forcibly exile the queen to Russia.

---

[38] Ibid., 190–1, 205.
[39] Ibid., 200–3.
[40] See Eastmond, 'Gender and Orientalism' 103–4.
[41] Ibid., 203–4.

Arguably, the Russian tendency to feminise Georgia rests in Georgia's religious history and cult practices as perceived and experienced by Muscovite travellers and diplomats centuries before the annexation of Caucasia. Early diplomatic relations with Muscovy were established in the fifteenth century but were intensified by the end of the sixteenth century with the Tsar's growing strategic interest in the Caucasus.[42] Since the seventeenth century, Russians have perceived Caucasia as a foothold and buffer zone for their diplomatic and military dealings with the Ottomans and the Safavids. While Muscovy was advancing towards the northern steppes of the Caucasus, their diplomats and travellers eagerly studied, collected and reported what they had heard and witnessed also south of the range. Due to the meticulous travelogues and records of Muscovite and then Russian diplomats, much of Georgia's religious history was vaguely known to Russian authors and travellers, and even fragments of the Georgian lore, albeit strongly distorted, have penetrated Russian storybooks. Pious Muscovites eagerly and uncritically reproduced legends and myths for centuries cultivated in Georgia regarding the sojourn and translation of various Christ- and Mary-related relics in Georgia. The saints of the Georgian Church, albeit in a rather distorted form, were known to enlightened Russians well before Georgia's integration into the Empire, so much so that there transpires a certain obsession in seventeenth-century Russian literature with Georgia's religious history, and fascination with Georgia's ancient Christian culture, which lay at the intersection of two Muslim powers.

A typical example of Russian adaptation of Georgia's religious lore is the story of Queen Dinar, now a saint of the Russian Church, yet an entirely fictitious character, unknown to Georgian history.[43] Queen Dinar was one of the earliest 'Georgian' characters to penetrate Russian religious mythology and the church calendar from the accounts gathered, revised and reimagined since the sixteenth century by Muscovite travellers in Georgia. A story with an epic title, *The Wondrous and Valiant Story of Bravery and Wisdom of the Chaste Virgin Queen Dinar(a), the Daughter of the Iberian King Alexander*, recounts that after the death of the pious King Alexander, his fifteen-year-old daughter inherited the throne and ruled

---

[42] For a study of these relations, see the first volume of Allen, *Russian Embassies*.
[43] Queen Dinar of Albania lived in the tenth century. Yet, practically nothing is known about her, and it is still a mystery how the name of this obscure medieval queen was entangled with Tamar's fame. In summer of 2019, however, an inscription of Queen Dinar was revealed in east Georgia, near the border with Azerbaijan, a discovery that confirmed the historicity of the person.

over Georgia wisely and piously.[44] Having learned that a girl reigned in Georgia, Persia's Shah ventured to capture the land and convert it to Islam. He sent envoys to Dinar requesting that she surrender her kingdom. Dinar responded that it was not in his name that she ruled the land, but on behalf of the Mother of God, and that her kingdom was the Lot of the Virgin. The enraged Shah insolently replied that he would allow her to be sovereign only if she reigned dressed in nothing but her underwear. Dinar responded that she accepted the challenge and that she would tromp him underfoot with the help of the Mother of God. The story is followed by a dialogue between the queen and her timid male noblemen on the nature of the feminine and the advantages of her womanhood. A conclusion is reached that the Georgians will prevail precisely due to the female nature of their monarch and the aid of the Mother of God. Dinara's army went to Tabriz to pray in the Church of the Theotokos, after which they attacked the Persians. The Georgians prevailed and Dinara personally slew and beheaded the Shah. She ruled for another thirty-eight years and even after her death no neighbour has ever dared to invade her land, as it remained under the protection of the Mother of God, 'and until our days the land of Iveria is unified. And they say of the Georgian rulers that they descend from David, the King of Israel, from the seed of Judas.'[45]

The story of Dinar is loosely based on the episodes from Queen Tamar's reign. It proudly references the campaign of Tamar's army into the depth of Iran. The Shah's rude letter is reminiscent of the misogynistic demands issued by the Sultan of Rum, Suleiman II. While the tale narrates details, although severely distorted, sourced from *K'art'lis C'xovreba*, it also problematises the simultaneous presence of power and holiness in a female body, and fictionalises the real or invented discussions on the advantages of female monarchy first articulated by Katholikos Nikoloz. The dialogue between the queen and the nobility reanimates the supposedly actual debates and uncertainties with regard to the feminine foundations of

---

[44] The popularity of the tale is affirmed by over 130 manuscripts, the earliest of which dates to the middle of the sixteenth century. Some of the earliest versions are added to the Russian Chronicle of 1512. According to the *Historian of Kazan*, during the siege of Kazan in 1552, Tsar Ivan the Terrible addressed his army with the story of Dinar to lift their spirits. See http://www.pravenc.ru/text/178261.html. For a critical study of the manuscripts, see Troitskaia, 'Rannie etapy'. The image of Queen Dinar riding a white horse can still be seen in one of the halls of Moscow's Kremlin.

[45] For the electronic edition of the original text with commentary, see http://lib.pushkinskijdom.ru/Default.aspx?tabid=5084. The edition is based on a sixteenth-century manuscript. Understandably, nearly all studies on the topic are in Russian and are kept only in the libraries of Russia, which are, for obvious reasons, inaccessible to me.

Christianity in Georgia and the equally feminine nature of its Golden Age; whereas the final paragraphs ponder the idea of Georgia's political unity as a sacred memory as well as a political project, by wrapping it in the idea of the Lot of the Mother of God. The Muscovite diplomats have familiarised themselves with these narratives during their visits to Georgian kingdoms or principalities, where the Georgian elites eagerly recounted to them stories as extracted from the ever-expanding corpora of the *Life of Kartli* and *The Knight in the Panther's Skin*, the two principal texts of late medieval Georgia. Over time, the story of Queen Dinar crystallised into typically Russian imperialist perceptions of a proverbial Georgian woman: seductive, fierce, pious, treacherous and rather dangerous.

The manuscript tradition of Queen Dinar is noteworthy. Half of the early manuscripts of the story of Dinar are an addition to the Russian Chronicle of 1512, and are written in the same hand as the story of the foundation of Mt Athos and Iveria's allotment to the Mother of God.[46] Indeed, it was the Georgian political and religious tradition of the Lot of the Mother of God, in Russian, *Udel* or *Zhreby Bogoroditsi*, that made a particularly deep impact on Russian writing, becoming an unusually attractive concept to the Russian religious and political elites in their dealings with Georgia. Unlike the Byzantines, the Russians were seemingly impressed by and have eagerly internalised the Georgian pretence to such prestige. Stories related to Georgia's allotment, as crystallised between the seventeenth and nineteenth centuries, still find resonance in Russia's ecclesiastical circles and are reproduced by the Russian Patriarchate. Over time, the story of the 'Lot of the Mother of God' became part of the rhetoric of the Empire and integrated into the gendered perception of the colonial other, and is still used in Russian neo-imperialistic discourses.[47]

Paradoxically, the Russian colonial imagery of the ambiguous feminine was self-referentially adopted and internalised in Georgian folklore within a few years after the establishment of Russia's rule in the South Caucasus. As a toxic hybrid of the political and the feminine, the image of Tamar became further entangled in the imperial and local representations of the feminine as well as the topography of the Caucasus. Some of these tales were tied to the liminal area between Russia and South Caucasus, the narrow Darial Pass in the middle of the Greater Caucasus Range. The Darial Gorge and the menacing Tergi/Terek were terrifying sights to see for Russian travellers. In time, once the Russian soldiers began to intensively

---

[46] Troitskaia, 'Rannie etapy', 30–1.
[47] A simple Google search of *udel bogorodicy* will reveal how popular this medieval Georgian idea is in Russian piety.

cross the pass, this liminal area gave birth to a legend that the pass was controlled by a certain woman Daria, an evil leader of brigands who forced travelling men to have sex with her, and that those she did not like, she threw into Tergi.[48] Mikhail Lermontov, however, who dedicated a poem to this character, calls her Tamara:

> Where waves of the Terek are waltzing
> In Dariel's wickedest pass,
> There rises from the bleakest of storm crags
> An ancient grey towering mass.
> In this tower by mad winds assaulted,
> Sat ever Tamara, the Queen –
> A heavenly angel of beauty,
> With a spirit of hell's own demesne.[49]

Evidently, this Russian literary image has made its way also into local Georgian lore causing a certain cognitive dissonance in popular imagination regarding the perception of the Holy Queen. In the late nineteenth century, ethnographer Alexander Khakhanashvili recorded an account from a local resident who related the story of twin sisters, both called Tamar. One of them was pious and chaste and lived in Ananuri Fortress, in the Aragvi Valley, on the Georgian Military Highway, between Mtskheta and Darial, whereas the other was a sorceress and had built a castle on the River Tergi in Darial pass. She too threw her sexual partners into Tergi. The witch was impervious to blades or bullets but was eventually killed by a Russian soldier who struck her with a button of his military uniform, which was, unsurprisingly, resistant to the witch's charms.[50] It appears, therefore, that while Tamar was rediscovered as a national saint by Georgia's Romantic authors, part of the Georgian lore has internalised the Russian ambiguous representations of the holy queen. Thus, by the time Tamar reappeared in the national context, in popular imagery, which was nurtured by Russian subjectivity and inherent misogyny, her image was split into two, between the holy and the unholy, revealing the anxieties of the age regarding its historical identity.

---

[48] The legend is recorded in several travelogues including the early nineteenth-century Caucasian travelogue of Jean-François Gamba. See, also, Canard, 'Les reines de Géorgie', 9–20. Canard compares this legend with an old Egyptian legend of an extremely promiscuous but powerful Georgian queen.
[49] Lermontov, *Tamara*, tr. Dickinson-Bianchi: https://allpoetry.com/poem/8527673-Tamara-by-Mikhail-Yuryevich-Lermontov (03.06.23).
[50] Khakhanov, 'Iz gruzinskis legend', 140.

In nineteenth-century imperial discourse, the annexation of Georgia was rendered in religious and gendered terms. With the annexation, Georgia became a certain embodiment of the coveted Iverskaya Icon in imperial theology. Georgia's body politic was essentially that of the Mother of God, encapsulated both in the famed icon as well as the mythology of the 'Lot of the Mother of God'. Nineteenth-century Russian ecclesiastic discourse developed an analogy that, while Georgia is the lot of the Mother of God, by association, Georgia is Russia's lot and this bond is mystical, and political as well as sexual, hence the abundance of marriage tropes in imperial literature. By appropriating the political cult of the Theotokos from Georgia, the periphery of the Empire, the Mother of God became the protector also of the Empire's boundaries. Georgia and Russia were united in mystical terms and in terms of a sacramental wedding in which Georgia was always a feminine 'other', as revealed in Alexander Odoevsky's poem on Georgia and Russia's marital union. One can still observe the cultivation of this early imperial belief among pious Russians and Vladimir Putin's expansionist rhetoric, as well as Georgia's contemporary Russophile and anti-Western intelligentsia.

In 1870, in the wake of the national movement, as yet another gift to the Georgian nation, a reliquary with the relics of Queen Ketevan and her small icon was sent from Saint Petersburg to Mtskheta, presumably those that were originally gifted by King Teimuraz I.[51] By then, Queen Ketevan had become not only a symbol of Georgia's feminine Christian identity but also of the essence of the historical relationship between Russia and Georgia. Ketevan was Georgia's greatest martyr-saint but also a reminder of how the Georgians, lacking a certain political stamina, were unable to take care of 'their women', a recurrent trope in Russian literature on the Caucasus. She served as a reminder of the circumstances of her martyrdom, of Georgia's failed historic body politic, how it turned towards Russia for help, and how it was saved and assumed under the imperial aegis.

Nineteenth-century Georgia's national elites realised the rhetorical power of the foundational texts and the symbolism generated and appropriated from these texts by the Russian empire. Since Georgia's annexation, every national movement, whether covertly or overtly anti-Russian, has applied this symbolism in its attempt to disentangle national imagery from the imperial rhetorical entanglement. The tropes of sanctity, imperial gift-giving and colonial feminisation that constituted the arsenal of the imperial rhetoric of the Caucasus were reclaimed by some of

---

[51] Nachkebia, 'Ketevan', 573.

the most influential leaders of the national movement. Similarly to the eleventh-century projects of the Bagratids to re-evaluate Georgia's historical pantheon of saints as part of their complicated relationship with the Byzantines, late nineteenth-century Georgian elites have shaped their own ethno-religious imageries in opposition to Russian imperialism. The young nationalist elites engaged with practically all medieval tropes of political sanctity as sourced from the *K'art'lis C'xovreba*, whether the political implications of masculine–feminine dichotomies, the new geopolitical implications of the Late Antique concept of the North, or the national valences of the cult of saints.

# 8
# The Saints of the Nation

## 8.1 'The Glory of Georgia'

In 1889, Mikheil Sabinin (1845–1900), a Russian-Georgian monk, historian and artist, painted and published an icon that he initially named *The Glory of the Georgian Church* (see Fig. 8.1). To this day, Sabinin's composition remains one of the most revered images of Georgian piety, displayed prominently in all major and minor churches across the country. The composition of the icon is dense: in the centre, the archangel raises the miraculous 'Living Pillar' of Georgia's first church, built by the newly converted royal family. In the upper section, just above the Pillar, the composition is presided over by Christ, the Mother of God, George, Andrew, Matthias, and the archangels. As a symbol of Georgia's allotment to the Mother of God,

Figure 8.1   Michael Sabinin, *The Glory of the Georgian Church*. Source: Artanuji Publishers.

the Theotokos extends her omophorion over the Georgian Church. Under the Pillar, clutching the Lord's Tunic brought by the first-century Jews to the capital of Kartli, lies Sidonia the Jewess. In the centre stands St Nino, extending her vine-woven cross as she supervises the raising of the Pillar. On both sides of the pillar, two kneeling monarchs can be observed: to the right, Georgia's first Christian king Mirian, who supposedly witnessed the miracle, kneels in awe. To the left stands Queen Tamar, who lived eight centuries after the events illustrated on the icon, yet is symbolically depicted in the immediate vicinity of the Holy Pillar, as a protagonist of Georgia's conversion narrative. Ascetics, priests and patriarchs have gathered behind her in awe while on the opposite side, behind Mirian, stand the saints of old Georgia: kings and soldiers, men and women, from the very beginning of Christianity up to the nineteenth century. In the distance, a burning church can be observed symbolising the carnage that the Georgian Church has experienced over centuries. Among this host of saints, the most prominent figures of the composition remain Nino, the architect of conversion, Queen Tamar and two other martyrs standing next to Nino – St Shushanik, tortured and murdered by her husband in the fifth century, and St Ketevan, even more brutally butchered and executed by the Safavid Persians in the seventeenth century. The latter saint stands closest to the Pillar. The only deceased person in the composition, the Jewish woman Sidonia, reposes under the pillar. The Mother of God acts as protectress of the entire realm, interceding with Christ on Georgia's behalf.

Sabinin painted the icon at the height of Russian imperial dominance in Georgia and on the eve of the national movement. By the last decades of the nineteenth century, Georgia, as well as the entire South Caucasus, was firmly integrated into the Russian Empire. Along with political sovereignty, Russia had abolished and then fully incorporated also the Georgian Church and its hierarchy. Therefore, formally, neither the kingdom nor the church existed at the time of the icon's creation. Meanwhile, however, the last three decades of the nineteenth century saw the rise of the national movement and the romantic struggle for emancipation together with a quest for Georgia's cultural and political belonging.[1] Young intellectuals and journalists sought to discover their fatherland's (*mamuli*) authentic self in colonial reality, and to deconstruct the nearly century-old idea of empire cultivated by Georgia's imperial administrators and colonial nobility.

Painted in such a transitional era, Sabinin's icon simultaneously voices two distinct and mutually exclusive narratives – the imperial and the

---

[1] For an overview of late nineteenth-century Georgian nationalism, see Suny, *Making of the Georgian Nation*, 63–143.

national. On the one hand, the aesthetics of the icon is closer to the Russian tradition than to the Georgian: the artist, trained in the Russian artistic milieu as most of his contemporaries, executed the painting in a markedly Russian style, having supplied the image with both Georgian and Russian captions. The icon projects a prominently feminine makeup of Georgia's religious history as well as the traditional Russian artistic, literary and political perception of Georgia through feminine imagery and tropes. The Georgian colonial and feminine imagery of the icon contrasted with the thoroughly masculine self-representation of Russian religious history.

Meanwhile, however, the icon also served as a political statement, articulating Georgian political and religious pretences of cultural superiority in the Orthodox world. While the original name of the icon was the *Glory of the Georgian Church*, soon after its creation it became known as the *Glory of Georgia*. This change is indeed noteworthy, as the Russian imperial administration, since its establishment, has consistently suppressed the usage of 'Georgia' as a political notion. Hence, the icon can be interpreted as an implicit reaction against this restriction. A few years later, Sabinin's icon became a symbol of the Autecaphalist movement that demanded and eventually regained the independence of the Georgian Church, an act that was soon followed by the declaration of independence of the Democratic Republic of Georgia. Therefore, as if split between imperial subjectivity and national identity, the icon sustains and projects certain ambiguity of Georgian identity and self-perception of the age – on the one hand, it depicts the ethno-religious narrative of Georgia's political body, and on the other, it internalises the Russian imperial vision of Georgia and Georgianness as an imperial and indeed feminine *other*.

The nineteenth-century Georgian national elites intensively theologised over the idea of the nation, and deliberated over the semantic, philosophical and religious meanings of 'Fatherland'. In this project of defining their national identity and revamping the nation's 'theology', Late Antique and medieval canonical narratives, united in the *K'art'lis C'xovreba* corpus, were rediscovered and re-evaluated. Some of the topics of the age scattered across journal articles, feuilletons, speeches and toasts were: How does sainthood interact with the body politic in the circumstances of annihilated Georgian sovereignty? How to reclaim and rehabilitate the cult of the saints appropriated by the discourse of the Empire and channel the same tropes, symbols and imagery into the nascent national framework? How to create a new theology of martyrdom when the principal adversary is the Orthodox Empire unlike old Zoroastrian and Muslim foes?

## 8.2 Gender Problematised (Again)

The nineteenth-century Georgian national movement was in many ways similar to the nationalistic projects across Europe. The generation of the 1860s closely followed and cheered for the Hungarians, Poles, Greeks, Italians, the Irish and others who, like them, struggled against imperialism and colonialism. On the other hand, Georgia's elites internalised imperial rhetoric with astonishing ease, and increasingly perceived themselves as colonial subjects. By the second half of the nineteenth century, Russian imperial ideology had successfully integrated the entirety of Georgia both politically and symbolically. A significant part of Georgia's nobility internalised the Empire's colonial tropes and proudly wore Russian regalia and titles. Even more successful was the Russian teleological narrative of Georgia's history, whereby the unity of Russia and Georgia was predestined since the Christianisation of Georgia. The Russian Emperor was seen not only as Georgia's de facto sovereign but as its legal and divinely ordained monarch. As a result, the Russian Emperor was rarely perceived as an aggressor or occupier. After the initial rebellions and conspiracies that effectively ended in 1832, until Marxist revolutionary ideas came into vogue, Georgia's nobility could not fathom rebelling against this sacred figure. The challenge that the new anti-colonial elites faced was to reclaim medieval Georgian political and theological tropes from imperial discourses and nationalise them. Disentangling Georgian identity from the imperial narrative was challenging, and required a thorough rereading of some of Georgia's 'foundational' narratives.

Thirty years after Georgia's annexation, the descendants of the royal family, the nobility and scarce intellectual elites conspired against Russian rule. The conspiracy consisted of an elaborate hierarchical organisation, of a web of networks and communications among various layers of Georgian society and the exiled claimants to the royal throne. The plan was rather brutal: the conspirators were to invite the entire Russian military command to a ball in Tbilisi and to arrest or kill them on site.[2] In 1832 the conspiracy was, however, betrayed, and all members were apprehended and punished according to the degree of their involvement. While many were exiled, the most severe blow that permanently ended any anti-Russian resistance until the revolutions of the following century was the most unexpected one – the imperial pardon. Some of the staunchest conspirators were pardoned and were in time awarded with the highest military and administrative

---

[2] For a history of the conspiracy, see Rayfield, *Edge of Empires*, 250–63.

ranks. The Emperor thus instilled in these people an emotion that resisted any hint of anti-imperial sentiment – gratitude, the Empire's another gift to the Georgian people.

Since the feminisation of Georgia by Russian imperial writing and the appropriation of the feminine pantheon of saints, the entanglement of the feminine and the political has seemingly become a leitmotif of Georgian–Russian relations. Such a tragic entanglement occurred in 1837, an event that encapsulated all the fears and anxieties of the Georgian elites. In 1837, for the first time, the Russian Emperor Nicholas I visited Georgia. In a typically colonial and Caucasian manner, the reception that the Georgians prepared for the Tsar was over the top, bombastic and expensive. On the fourth night of the Tsar's visit, the Georgian nobility organised a ball for the imperial guest. The Tsar had liked three women present. One of them was Maiko Orbeliani, a member of the Georgian high nobility, of one the oldest and most respected houses after the Bagrationis. Georgian nobles noticed the Tsar's interest and later that night brought the sixteen-year-old girl to him. Soon thereafter Maiko fell ill and died. The episode was largely silenced and repressed, yet indirectly reminded by the next generation as the ultimate symbol of Georgia's colonial subjectivity. For the generation that came after the event, this heinous act was similar to what happened to the daughter of Queen Rusudan and granddaughter of Tamar, nicknamed Gurji-Khatun, who was similarly, and as a teenager, married to a Muslim ruler. In the upcoming national movement, and its rediscoveries of old texts, the feminine, the sacred and the political were yet again entangled in the national rhetoric of liberation.

This story, although implicitly due to its delicacy, was reminded by the subsequent generation of nationalist authors as an attack against the 'generation of the fathers'. It was remembered as the extreme manifestation of colonial subservience practised by the Georgian elites of the first half of the nineteenth century. Nothing could have served as a better confirmation of the Russian imperial feminisation of the land. Gender, therefore, became a surprisingly central issue in the rhetoric of the nationalist authors. Arguably, Ilia Chavchavadze and his peers engaged in a 'masculinisation' of Georgia's religious history, an endeavour reminiscent of the eleventh-century Bagratid rewritings. Chavchavadze was behind the rediscovery of some of the major national male saints of medieval Georgia, such as the martyr-kings Demetre II (d. 1289) and Luarsab II (d. 1622). Chavchavadze's poem *King Dimitri Tavdadebuli* is a hyper-masculine account of Georgia's thirteenth-century martyr-king Dimitri. These figures were certainly known and commemorated by the church, yet they have not yet had currency in national discourse. Ilia's contemporary, Akaki Tsereteli, wrote a poem, *Tornike Eristavi*, dedicated to the general of the Georgian army and founder of the Iveron monastery on Mt Athos.

Chavchavadze was particularly focused on the reanimation of the memory of David IV the Builder, Tamar's great-grandfather. As a result of Chavchavadze's effort, today David the Builder and Tamar are often paired and conceptualised simultaneously as the two greatest holy monarchs. This Chavchavadze articulated in 1888, in a short, yet celebrated article, addressing the nation's collective remembrance. A century after the publication of this article no Georgian would have complained that David has been forgotten. On the contrary, today his persona constitutes the axis of Georgian national narrative, especially since the 2003 Rose Revolution when Mikheil Saakashvili swore the presidential oath on the king's grave. In 1888, David seemingly enjoyed much less popularity. Chavchavadze complains that while on 26 January the Georgian Church commemorates this great king, he is still not included in secular commemorative practices. Chavchavadze enumerates David's virtues and political achievements and concludes,

> This great king – what a great manly image [lit.: *manly man, kac'ur kac'i*, an expression particularly popularised by Ilia] he is for our eyes and what a great document for our pride. It is the commemoration of this kind of man that revitalises the nation and the oblivion of such a man must be considered as the nation's deadly sin, who gave birth to him and whose breasts nurtured him. Our protector, the Church, knew this well and it is for this reason that it established 26 January as the date of his commemoration so that at least once a year we may remember this great king, and wonderful man, and the source of our pride. A man must have two names – says our nation: – one to leave here and the other to carry with him. No other man has fulfilled this Georgian testament as has King David. Here he left the name of a Builder, of a king, of a man with a great soul – and there he took the name of a saint, and is adorned with the crown of glory.[3]

---

[3] *Iveria* No. 17, 1888: აი ეს დიდებული მეფე – რა დიდებულ კაცურ-კაცის სახესაც მოგვიგლენს თვალ-წინ და რა თავმოსაწონებელს საბუთს გვაძლევს ხელთა. აი ამისთანა კაცის ხსენებაა გამაცოცხლებელი ერისა და ამისთანა კაცის არ-ხსოვნა მომაკვდინებელი ცოდვად უნდა ჩაეთვალოს ერსა, რომელმაც იგი ჰშვა და თავის ძუძუთი გამოჰზარდა. ჩვენმა დამცველმა ეკლესიამ ეს კარგად იცოდა და ამიტომაც 26 იანვარი დააგვინიშნა, რომ წელიწადში ერთხელ მაინც გავიხსენოთ ეს ქართველთათვის თავმოსაწონებელი დიდებული მეფე, დიდებული კაცი. კაცს ორი სახელი უნდა ჰქონდესო – ამბობს ჩვენი ერი: – ერთი აქ დასარჩენი, მეორე თან წასაყოლიო. ეს ანდერძი ქართველისა ისე არავის შეუსრულებია, როგორც დავით მეფესა. აქ აღმაშენებლის სახელი დარჩა, როგორც მეფეს, და იქ, როგორც დიდ-ბუნებოვანმა კაცმა – წაიყოლა სახელი წმინდანისა, დიდების გვირგვინით შემკობილი. Reprints of this article are reproduced all over the Internet, for example http://www.orthodoxy.ge/tserilebi/ilia/agmashenebeli.htm.

By repeatedly stressing 'man' and 'manly' in his eulogy to David, Chavchavadze promoted a male military saint as opposed to the already successful cult of Queen Tamar and other female saints. The doubling of the word *kʻaci* (man) as *kʻacur kʻaci* (manly man) on the one hand amplified the person's virility and, on the other, removed the ambiguity from the word that stands both for man and a human being, just like its English analogue. Unlike his great-granddaughter, David the Builder had never made it into the ranks of the Russian imperial saints, and understandably so. David was strongly associated with the dramatic expansion of the Georgian kingdom and his saintly status was mostly determined by his political achievements rather than some inherently religious reasons. As such, as a male figure associated with Georgia's independent polity, Russian commemorative practices have never accepted the holy king. Chavchavadze aimed to replace the Georgian pantheon and saturate it with exclusively national saints associated with the Georgian body politic and dissociated with the established Russian imperial subjectivity.

Thus, gender became a central issue in the late nineteenth-century anticolonial nationalist discourse, which became further problematised by a discovery that happened close to Tbilisi. In an isolated valley about fifteen kilometres southwest of Tbilisi one can now visit a flourishing thirteenth-century monastery of Betania with a large church that houses impressive

Figure 8.2   The Royal Panel of Betania with Laša-Giorgi, Tamar and Giorgi III, thirteenth century. Author: Zurab Tsertsvadze.

frescoes. For centuries, the church was abandoned and was virtually rediscovered, and restored by a Russian painter and administrator in the Caucasus (and Mikhail Lermontov's close friend), Prince Grigory Gagarin (1810–93) in the 1850s. Among other heavily restored features of the church was the now famous fresco of Queen Tamar flanked by her father Giorgi III, and son, Giorgi IV Laša one of only five surviving images of the holy queen (see Fig. 8.2).

The discovery deeply affected the Georgian elites. Although four other frescoes of Tamar had existed and were known to antiquarians, Betania was close to Tbilisi and thus within an easy reach for Georgian intellectual and literary elites. Antony Eastmond suggests that with this discovery, Tamar's representation was dramatically affected. With the restoration, Tamar's features were subtly altered by the Russian artist: 'the Persian ideals of beauty that informed the thirteenth-century painting (visible in the queen's oval face, pale colouring and pearl-shaped eyes) have been subtly altered to show a more European, gentler face'.[4] Since then, this passive, gentle, asexual, softened and modest portrait became a canonical representation of Tamar, betraying the ambiguity of her representations in the colonial setting. Thus, her image fluctuated in Russian imagination and colonial Georgian representations from a ruthless, cunning, hypersexual mythological being of lore, to a valiant 'lioness' and military commander whose name evoked fear and adulation among Georgia's Muslim and Christian neighbours alike, and to a de-sexualised, modest yet beautiful, saint. Tamar's representation still suffers from a similar ambiguity, as we shall see in the final chapter.

It was perhaps indeed with this discovery that Tamar was incorporated into the national myth of the Romantic nationalists. It effectively became an iconic representation of the myth of Georgia's Golden Age. In 1887 the church was visited by poet Grigol Orbeliani (1804–83) who composed a poem while seated beneath the image of Tamar, titled the 'Image of Queen Tamar in the Church of Betania'. For Orbeliani, the portrait of the queen and her 'face full of beauty and radiant with sanctity' symbolises the long lost Golden Age of Georgia's history, which the poet continuously sees in his dreams and which he hopes to see restored through the intercession of the Holy Queen. He finishes the poem with a lament that of everything that he and all Georgians had remembered from the past and from Tamar's Golden Age, it is merely this abandoned and destroyed church in a murky forest with a faded fresco of Queen Tamar that is remaining.

---

[4] Eastmond, 'Gender and Orientalism', 106–7.

The fresco and Orbeliani's poem inspired tremendous obsession with Tamar in nationalist writing. Ethnographic expeditions were launched and Tamar-related lore was collected, which currently constitutes a sizeable part of Georgian folklore. The writers of the era attempted to retrieve a folk Tamar from the pit of national remembrance, an 'unadulterated', 'authentic' representation of the Holy Queen. Mythological and epic poetry related to Tamar was cherrypicked to chisel an image of the Golden Age. In 1892, Georgia's most celebrated poet, Akaki Tsereteli, published a poem titled merely 'Folk', with the opening lines – 'Beauty has risen' – where Tsereteli tried to fuse all the multiplicity of Tamar's representations – sanctity, gender and her political power: She is 'fairer than Eteri', a protagonist of the legend of *Abesalom and Eteri*, she is also the greatest saint, but she is also the autocrat in the 'Lot of the Mother God':

> The beauty has risen,
> Said: 'I've slept too much!'
> While a was awake,
> I feared no one.
> 'But recently treachery
> Has veiled itself;
> The enemy approached furtively,
> And secretly gave me poison.
> From now on I must be vigilant.
> Enough of so much sleep!
> [The country] is my responsibility [*samouravo*],
> The lot of the Mother of God.'[5]

Tsereteli thus utilises this unique mixture of sanctity, femininity and authority to create an image of a certain patron saint of Georgian nationalism. She is presented as 'risen' from oblivion, from centuries of gloom and destruction, colonial passivity and imperial subjectivity. With the rise of the national movement, she is now 'vigilant', retaking her role as the protectress of the 'Lot of the Mother of God'.

## 8.3 Roads Old and New

There was another trope extracted from medieval sources, which, due to the geography and topography of Russian–Georgian relations, was internalised,

---

[5] Quoted and discussed in Ghaghanidze, 'camodga mzet'unaxavi', 141–52.

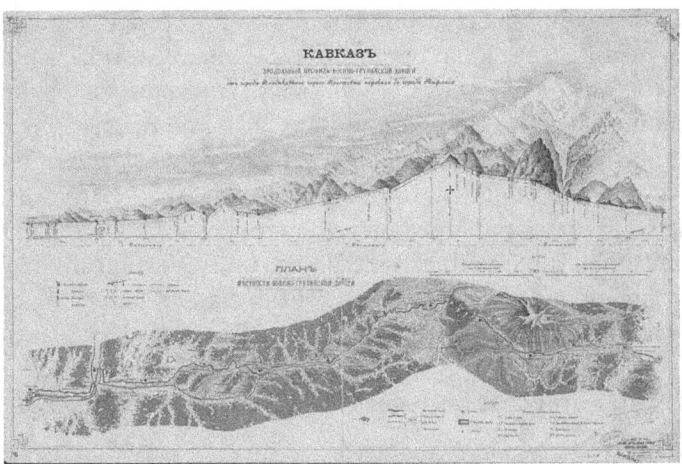

Figure 8.3  Russian topographic map of the Georgian Military Highway. Source: Library of Congress.

on the one hand, by imperial authors, and, on the other, by Georgian nationalists. This was the political and religious conceptualisation of the 'North', as originally embodied in the image of St Nino, in Georgia's grand conversion narratives. Contrary to the established tradition, Georgia's final Christianisation and acquisition of an authentic political body within the Orthodox Empire were reimagined as arriving from the North, which required a rewriting of the traditional tropes where the North was *Kedar*, the realm of darkness. In this, the reverse movement of St Nino's Cross to Georgia was symbolic – the key symbol of Georgian Christianity, now politicised and baptised in the imperial font, entered Georgia from the North, the new source of Georgia's enlightenment.

The northward road, the highway from Tbilisi, via Mtskheta, past Ananuri's strategic fortress, up to Kazbegi (St Stephen) and Gergeti Monastery, then through the narrow Darial Gorge and River Tergi (Terek Valley) to Russia's Vladikavkaz, is among Eurasia's most trotted literal and literary roads. Vladikavkaz, as its name suggests, was Russia's imperial foothold in the Caucasus, connecting the rest of Caucasia with the imperial core (see Fig. 8.3). The construction of the road, later known as the Georgian Military Highway, started in 1799 when the Russian army first marched in Tbilisi; it was then improved in 1801, and officially, yet nominally, opened in 1817. Although there were few other crosses from north to south, the Georgian Military Highway was effectively the only usable artery between Russia and the South Caucasus. A part of Georgia's colonial intellectuals internalised the imperial civilising discourse and viewed the highway as a tether connecting Georgia to the rest of the civilised world.[6]

Since the eighteenth century, following the exodus of Vakhtang VI's family, the 'Russophile' Georgian writers have internalised this civilising trope of the Caucasian pass, perceiving the road as a vessel of their 'true' Orthodox religious identity. In 1734, poet Mamuka Baratashvili, King Vakhtang's associate, and a prominent member of the Georgian diaspora in Russia, coined the infamous metaphor of Russia, still echoed over two centuries later. In his poem, the 'Praise of King Bakar', Baratashvili diverges from his main topic and praises the Russian Tsar Peter I:

> The enemy's army has been destroyed by our blessed and holy warriors,
> The hateful snake, the fatherland's foe vainly brags about their military power,
> The creature with the unsatisfied belly of Echidna was not satisfied by the blood of the righteous.
> The darkness has dissipated. *The sun has moved from the South to the North.*[7]

This last line inverts and invalidates the traditional medieval literary trope whereby the North was systematically conceived as an alien, menacing, uncivilised *other*, with its bitter frost contrasted to the cool shade of the south. As an elaboration of this new vision of the North, later, one of Georgia's most celebrated romantic poets, Alexander Chavchavadze (1786–1846), described the Caucasian range in a typically Romantic fashion of mountainous sublime. Yet, in his vision, the Caucasus is a barrier, and obstacle to northern enlightenment:[8]

---

[6] The road was described numerous times by Russian geographers, historians, poets and novelists both in the imperial era and the Soviet times. See Anisimov, *Voenno-Gruzinskaiā doroga*; Manning, *Strangers in a Strange Land*, 62–5. The Georgian intellectual elite of the 1860s was called the 'Drinkers from the River Tergi' (*T'ergdaleulebi*), a mock name derived from their European education, and their alleged disregard of traditional Georgian values. See, for example, Reisner, 'Travelling between Two Worlds', 36–50.

[7] Mamuka Baratashvili, *k'eba mep'isa bak'arisa*, 42 (emphasis added). See also, Shaduri, *Letopis' druzhby*, 59.

[8] Alexander Chavchavadze was one of the most typical members of the colonial elites. Until the end of his life he was a loyal military servant of the Russian Empire, and this has internalised his colonial status. His daughter, Nina, married the celebrated Russian poet Alexander Griboyedov (1795–1829).

> This [Caucasus] is the mountain, where the chained Prometheus,
> Had been cursed by the gods to have his heart torn open by a raven,
> A mountain raised with seemingly conscious design as a barrier,
> And recognized as impregnable since the creation of the universe;
> But then finally, he who was raised as a Russian warrior,
> The brave Tsitsishvili[9] approached it;
> And the [River] Terek, now checked, reverentially acknowledges its limits
> And the rock flung wide open its gates to the roads.
> Troops from the north penetrated through the granite,
> They feared neither the deep crevices nor the mountainous heights;
> The steel held in the hands cut through the stone,
> The artificial fire-breathing lighting
> Thundered, roared and rent asunder and the Caucasus, moaning,
> Was helped by its echo to understand its wounds [defeat]!
> The gates opened, and thereby the Iberians began once more to hope
> That enlightenment would enter their land by this road.[10]

This impregnation (for some authors, literal) of the Caucasus from the north was perceived as a beginning of a new era, a culmination of Georgia's everlasting zeal to participate in the civilised Christian world. The Caucasus barrier, the mighty River Tergi, was subdued by Russian enlightenment. The gate, built by Alexander or King Vakhtang, that served as a witholder of the apocalyptic enemy, opened, and instead, the troops of enlightenment marched in. Chavchavadze's poem, although relatively uninfluential, was nevertheless a watershed. Since then, one's attitude towards physical, political and metaphysical implications of the North essentially defined one's political and cultural belonging. Even today, a person's political stance is effectively determined by their political and metaphysical conceptualisation of this road, with the Russia vs West dichotomy remaining as the principal dividing line of political ideologies. A century-and-a-half after Baratashvili's poem, the message of the 'northern sun' resounded at the 25th Communist Party Congress in 1976. The First Secretary of the Georgian Communist Party and later president of independent Georgia, Eduard Shevardnadze, uttered the infamous,

---

[9] Pavel Tsisianov (1754–1806) was a general of the Russian Imperial army and the Commander-in-Chief of the Caucasus. He was infamous for his brutal methods of subduing the north Caucasians.

[10] For the quoted translation and discussion, see Ram and Shatirishvili, 'Romantic Topography', 8–9. Ram and Shatirishvili analysed the intertextuality of the poem and concluded that in its entirety the poem is an amalgam of various images and tropes gathered from Russian poetry.

yet historic, words that encapsulated and summarised the two radically different visions of Georgia's history: 'Comrades, they call Georgia a sunny land, however, our true sun has arisen not from the East, but from the North, from Russia, the sun of Lenin's ideas has risen. Georgia is a warm republic in the South, however, the true warmth has entered us from the North, from Darial Gorge. It – the warmth of Lenin's ideas – came to us via Georgia's historic road, the Military Highway, on the Russian–Georgian road.'[11]

While authors such as Alexander Chavchavadze have internalised the civilising role of the northern road, appropriating the imperial tropes into their patriotic rhetoric, the earliest, however dim, voices of opposition against the imperial rereading of medieval tropes were also heard in political and theological conceptualisations of the North. Part of the emerging anti-colonial movement was dedicated to reappropriating saintly imagery and topography to counter imperial political theologies. It was particularly the trope of the North's civilising gift-giving that needed to be challenged, and instead, Late Antique geopolitical narratives of the *Conversion of Kartli* reanimated as an objection to imperial claims.

Strikingly, as if emulating the female pseudo-narrators of the *Conversion of Kartli*, who had first established the concept of the North in medieval political discourse, the earliest authors to explicitly challenge the Russian civilising trope, by returning to the old St Nino imagery, were the women of the royal house. Princesses Mariam, Ketevan and Tekle, the daughters of King Erekle II, perhaps the most underappreciated poets of early nineteenth-century Georgian writing, were particularly sensitive to the political and religious implications of the North. While the principal subject of their poetry is the lamentation over the fall of the kingdom, their forced migration to Russia and the annihilation of their house, the imagery that they have adopted throughout is reminiscent of the wordings of the *Mok'c'evay K'art'lisay*, especially of Sidonia's prophetic speech. The presence of these metaphors in early nineteenth-century women's poetry, and their notable absence in the literature of the same period produced by men, can in part be explained by the general reading habits of men and women in Georgia. Until the nineteenth century, the women of the royal family and greater nobility were some of the most educated members of the elites. These women have particularly deeply internalised all three principal texts of the Georgian tradition – the Gospels, the *K'art'lis C'xovreba* and *The Knight in the Panther' Skin* – and arguably operated with the tropes gathered from these corpora on a deeper level than their contemporary male writers.

---

[11] Newspaper *The Communist*, 27 February 1976.

Mariam's poem *The Sweetness of the Times Has Become Bitter* is especially ambivalent in its tropes. Written in the first person, it laments the end of monarchy in Georgia and the annihilation of the authority of the Bagrationi House, through 'the evil messenger, the northern wind that blows mercilessly and implacably'. By the end of the poem, the speaker transforms into the Mother of God and deplores the devastation of her thriving garden 'famed in all four corners of the world'.[12] The princess thus creates a metaphorical association between her own body, as the last female member of the ruling dynasty, Georgia's political body and the Mother of God. In another poem, Mariam speaks of the 'northern sea that eternally shoots clouds and mist, and has separated us from the sun, and cast onto a lengthy road'. She also alludes to the trope originally coined by Mamuka Baratashvili, albeit in an opposite sense, which in Mariam's imagination was the premonition of apocalyptic doom: 'The sun sat in Asia, now it shines from the North.'[13] Mariam follows Sidonia's precedent in manipulating the word 'shadow', which also means 'north', by referring both to 'shade' and 'north', that is, Russia. The surviving poems of two other princesses, Ketevan and Tekle, are similar to Mariam's in their rhetoric. Ketevan's *How Shall I Say* was written just before her forced exile to Russia and, as such, her imagery is built upon her voyage to the North, the awaiting northern cold, clouds and winds, imitating St Nino's dread that she had experienced upon observing the eerie Caucasus lying ahead of her.[14]

During the upheaval of the early 1830s, there was one person, indeed a mastermind of the 1832 conspiracy, who was not pardoned due to his unfortunate social status. Monk P'iladelp'os Kiknadze was responsible for the preparation of the ideological groundwork of the insurgency. Among a handful of his surviving writings is a mystical poem *Vision of Jeremiah, Son of Aeneas, on the Situation in Iveria*. Here Kiknadze laments the observable degradation of Mtskheta, of Tbilisi and the entire Georgia in a few excruciatingly archaic verses. Rather unexpectedly for a person who masterminded the anti-Russian insurgency, the verses end in traditional praise for the Russian emperor, 'who burns our hearts with an inextinguishable stream of light and education'. Peace, enlightenment and other 'gifts of the Empire' presented to Georgia through imperial benevolence are all evoked here. The poem, however, consists of internal contradictions. While lamenting the fall of Mtskheta, Kiknadze extracted the old metaphors of the North from the original *Mok'c'evay*, of the menacing North from which, through

---

[12] Asatiani, *żveli sakart'velos poeti k'alebi*, 215–16.
[13] Ibid., 217–19.
[14] Ibid., 238–40.

the effort of Saint Nino, the land and the people had been rescued, but now again, 'the clear River of the north [River Aragvi] covers your lands with scorching sand', 'all has been kidnapped by the winds of the dark Pole'.[15]

Kiknadze's *Regarding the Love of the Fatherland* is the earliest surviving nationalist project in novel colonial circumstances written specifically for the insurgents.[16] Before Kiknadze's work, disunity, internal warfare and schisms that had permeated Georgia following its division in the second half of the fifteenth century made the abstract conceptualisation of the Georgian kingdom as a unified political body impossible. Instead, a historic and religious idea of Iveria, as the Lot of the Mother of God, lingered. Kiknadze faced a challenge that haunted the Georgian national discourse for the next century-and-a-half, while remaining a conceptual problem in certain ecclesiastic circles. While for centuries, the image of an enemy had been associated with a religious, mostly Muslim, *other*, Kiknadze had to mobilise his readers against the fellow Orthodox Russians – for many a holy Orthodox Empire – by creating a conceptual rift between Georgia's, as of a nation's, holy body and the holiness of the imperial body politic. Kiknadze had to overcome the unease that the conspirators may have experienced in imagining Russia and its Orthodox emperor as an antagonist, and to deconstruct the religious idea of the Holy Empire meticulously crafted throughout the previous decades. To this end, in an eloquent and archaic manner, he argues against the unity in faith as a sufficient reason for political alliance. Kiknadze creates a sacred image of the nation arguing that the death for one's nation is an act of martyrdom, which is identical to Christian martyrdom in its valour. In this discourse, the earthly universality of the Orthodox oecumene is neglected. Kiknadze wrote in a highly archaic, anachronistic and barely penetrable language, thus imitating the language of medieval theological texts. Until the mid-nineteenth century, Georgians were taught that there were two registers that one ought to use in writing: high Georgian for religious purposes and middle Georgian for all the rest. Kiknadze explicitly resorts to the former to stress that the subject of his discourse is religious rather than secular. The terminology that Kiknadze utilises in his description of *Mamuli* (the Fatherland) is also religious. His *Mamuli* is a certain Platonic projection of the universal Fatherland in heaven. Further, he applies to the medieval theological method of *communicatio idiomatum*, whereby everything said of Christ's divinity applies to his humanity and vice versa. The same, according to Kiknadze, is true of the two Fatherlands. Therefore, death for one's Fatherland, even if for

---

[15] Kiknadze, *siquaruli mamulisa*, ed. Kukava, 29–35.
[16] Ibid.

entirely secular reasons and even in opposition to the Orthodox Empire, is an act of Christian martyrdom. Thus, Kiknadze faced two objectives: on the one hand, formulating a theology of the nation, and on the other, declaring a certain theological state of emergency, whereby the sacredness of the Orthodox Empire is suspended in the face of national necessity.[17]

There is yet another aspect to Kiknadze's conceptualisation. It is devoid of references to Georgia's history or exempla from its past. There is not a single figure, king, saint or martyr mentioned as a role model for the upcoming rebellion. Arguably, the reason for such an overt refusal to reach out to history and ethno-religious symbolism is that by the time of its writing, the same symbolism has been firmly incorporated into imperial rhetoric. The symbols of Georgian historical Christianity too were incorporated into the Russian symbolic language, and the idea of continuity between the foundations of Christianity in Georgia, and Georgia's final incorporation into the Orthodox Empire, was propagandised. Indeed, from the point of view of political theology, kingship in Georgia was not entirely illegally abolished, as it was handed over as a testament to the Russian emperor by Kartli's last king. Since then, the title of the Russian emperor included three different words for Georgia: *Imperator Gruzinskiĭ . . . gosudar' Iverskia, Kartalinskia*, a title that encapsulated all the various shades, meanings and nuances of the Georgian body politic. Therefore, while Russia violated the secular agreement between the two kingdoms, from the religious point of view the emperor's mandate to rule over Georgia was legitimate. Kiknadze, therefore, endeavours to conceptualise something radically new, utterly cleaved from old concepts usurped by the Russian Empire, including the idea of sacred kingship and sanctity in general. Kiknadze and the generation after him had to overcome this tension and gradually deconstruct the sacred body of the empire by reclaiming authentic 'Georgian' symbolism. This project proved successful in 1917 when Georgians reclaimed autocephaly for their church without any strong official opposition from Petrograd.

Despite being unfamiliar with Kiknadze's work, Ilia Chavchavadze developed a novel and complex theology of nationalism, steeped in, among

[17] Kiknadze, *siquaruli mamulisa*, ed. T. Kukava, 50: თუმცალა მოვალეობა შემიკრავს ჩუენ ერთგულებისათვის მამულისა და მამეულთა სჯულისათვის, გარნა არა ითხოების ჩუენგან ამით, რათამცა დაუტევებდეთ ჩუენ უმთავრესსა მამულსა სჯულსა ზეციურსა მამისა, ეგრეთუე უმეტესადცა ვიყვნეთ ერთგულად თავ-დადებულ მამულთადმი ყოველთა ზეციურისა მამისათა მონიჭებულთა ჩუენდა და უკეთუ არა წინააღმდგომ იყოს ქუეყნიერისაცა მამულისა ერთგულებანი ზეციურისა მამეულისა თანა სჯულისა, მაშინ შევრაცხდეთ თავთა ჩუეენთა ერთგულებასა შინა მამულისასა და კმაყოფასა შინა ჩუენთასა.

other things, cults of saints. In his groundbreaking semi-fictional travelogue *Notes of a Traveller*, Chavchavadze addressed the traditional theological categories of the North and South to reorient Georgia's political and cultural aspirations from Russia towards Europe. The *Notes* chronicle young Chavchavadze's journey from Saint Petersburg through Vladikavkaz, on the Georgian Military highway back to Georgia, essentially parodying the most well-trodden road of the region.[18] The *Notes* appeared only a few years after the publication of Alexander Chavchavadze's *Kavkaz*, as part of the efforts to deconstruct the enlightening trope of this road espoused by the generation of Alexander Chavchavadze from imperial rhetoric:[19] On his way home, the author runs into a Russian officer with whom he engages in a comic Socratic dialogue in which the officer attempts to define 'civilisation' which the Georgians receive from Russia. In the end, the officer concludes that civilisation is defined by how many generals the country has, and by how frivolous the women are. As observed by Paul Manning, what Chavchavadze demonstrates is the emptiness and the inauthentic nature of the Russian civilising mission, compared to the authenticity of Georgian national imagery. Chavchavadze articulates his national manifesto in the words of a liminal figure of sorts, a highlander who lives between the Russian and Georgian realms in the Caucasian mountains and speaks in a strong local dialect.[20] The authenticity of the Khevian person's speech is contrasted with the empty form of the Russian officer's tirades.[21] Chavchavadze's original attack on the 'civilising North' was carried forward by his contemporaries, who, while not launching an all-out separatist movement, methodically demystified the North, instead bringing back its medieval implications. Akaki Tsereteli's *Begone the Northerner* is in this respect one of the most vocal statements:

---

[18] See Manning, *Strangers in a Strange Land*, 28–59, for an excellent analysis of the text.

[19] Manning, *Strangers in a Strange Land*, 29: 'The term *Terg-daleuli* itself undergoes a transformation and revalorization in the course of the text from the first sense to the second, as Chavchavadze becomes disenchanted with the promises of Russian civilisation and discovers authentic culture instead among the Georgian folk. This transition is mirrored in the natural order in the changes in the character of the Terek River itself from the placid, servile Terek in the Russian plains at Vladikavkaz to the torrential, free Terek in the Caucasus mountains.'

[20] Manning comments (*Strangers in a Strange Land*, 16–17), 'Aside from an early literary experiment by the writer Ilia Chavchavadze, it was not until the 1880s that Georgian novelists and ethnographers like Aleksandre Qazbegi, Vazha Pshavela, and Urbneli began to represent the lives of the mountaineers as being integral to Georgian identity. By 1892, as one commentator put it, Georgian mountain dwellers finally moved from being peripheral savages to becoming the highest representation of Georgian traditional culture, "our mountaineers".'

[21] Manning, *Strangers in a Strange Land*, 53.

Stay away from me, the northerner,
What do we have in common?
You, the wretched, and unpolished,
You can't possibly polish me.
Your poisoned and cold heart,
Can keep nothing but enmity,
From year to year and strangely,
Your brain is frozen in your head.

## 8.4 A New Nino

Chavchavadze's geopolitical programme drew its inspiration from Georgia's ecclesiastic history and conversion narrative. Less than fifty years after the failed conspiracy, with an implicit allusion to the *Conversion of Kartli* and the *Life of Nino*, Chavchavadze introduced St Nino in his political manifesto as the 'light from the south', as a reminder to the readers of the *raison d'être* of Georgia – a historical and a metaphysical ideal, and an observable political project. A short essay published in 1888 on the feast of St Nino redefines the role of the evangeliser in the circumstances where St Nino had become a favoured saint in the Russian Church, adopted in Russian political discourse as a symbol of Georgian colonial 'other'. Chavchavadze expresses the urgency to redefine the place of St Nino and her evangelism in Georgia's cultural memory. While previously, Nino was confined to the church tradition, and as such adopted in Russian ecclesiastical commemorative practices, and consequently imperial rhetoric, Chavchavadze prescribes the celebration of Nino's memory not only as that of a great saint but also, and most crucially, as the founder of the Georgian nation. Instead of the orientalist tropes internalised by the Georgian public, a re-evaluation of the place and meaning of the cult of St Nino in Georgia's national mythology is proposed:

> Georgians have added this new Faith, the new Covenant, to the old one – to the fatherland and nationhood ... Christianity, apart from Christ's teaching, meant among us the entire Georgian land. Even today in the entire South Caucasus, Georgian and Christian are synonymous. Instead of 'becoming Christian', one may often hear that someone 'became Georgian' ... The spread and establishment of Christianity is by itself a great achievement, but Christianity has also tied us together and has strengthened us as if by mortar ... This doubled, this magnificent labour has been handed over to us by our Illuminator Saint Nino. This is exactly why this day must be celebrated when our Church commemorates with glory this virgin and the equal to the apostles. ...

This apostle brought us the teaching that subsequently adopted our Fatherland, our nationhood, and has nurtured them down to our days.[22]

In Chavchavadze's vision, the cult of St Nino had transcended mere religious history and acted as a historical model and symbol of radical shifts, from the old to the new. He sees her as the founder of the Georgian nation par excellence, a few years earlier visually imagined by Sabinin. While not a single word of the article is factually original, or proposes a different interpretation of the meaning of Nino's evangelism, the rhetoric that Chavchavadze coined was new, and offered a new dialectic relationship between the Georgian nation and St Nino, and through St Nino the entire pantheon of Georgia's saints. Chavchavadze utilises bodily metaphors and presents Georgia as a political body that witnessed Christ's passion through the intercession of St Nino, and like Christ, Georgia was crucified for fifteen hundred years. While traditionally, Nino was praised for bringing salvation to Georgia, Ilia's rhetoric inverts the verbs, and paints Georgia as a martyr-nation that had saved Christianity: 'It was for this human-loving God that the Georgian nation was martyred, and to him, it offered everything that humans have for their happiness. It crowned itself with the crown of thorns, and carried it valiantly while covered in blood from head to toe, brought it to our times without blemish, and thus tortured and martyred, it passed [the crown] on to us, its sons, [saying] now it is your turn.'[23]

The emerging national movement has given Nino a new dimension in which her mission has been woven into the fabric of national identity. The universality of Nino's new religion was validated by the sacred particularity of the newly emerging nation. Such thinking was sensible in the circumstances of dominant Russian Imperial Orthodoxy, where Orthodoxy, as an imperialistic phenomenon could not have served as a bearer of national identity. In Chavchavadze's rhetoric, Christianity is the New Covenant, whereas the Georgian nation is an old and perennial one, historically reaffirmed and renewed through evangelisation.

The methodical cultural, political and theological reorientation of Georgia from the 'North' to the 'West' was a conscious undertaking that was evident in many of Chavchavadze's writings. For much of his writing career, Chavchavadze was dedicated to interpreting the current political,

---

[22] Chavchavadze, 'St Nino'; originally published in *Iveria* 9 (13 January 1888): http://www.orthodoxy.ge/tserilebi/ilia/ninooba.htm#sthash.nxyTr1SZ.dpuf (31.12.18). Aleksidze, 'Nation among Other Nations', 227–45.

[23] Chavchavadze, 'St Nino', originally published in *Iveria* 9 (13 January 1888). See http://www.orthodoxy.ge/tserilebi/ilia/ninooba.htm#sthash.nxyTr1SZ.dpuf (31.12.18).

cultural and social state of affairs through an analogical reading of Georgian foundational texts, the *Conversion of Kartli* and the *Life of Kartli*. He was a man of many talents, and his devilish intuition was one of them. One of his most successful projects that merged his pro-European, anti-imperial and nationalist rhetoric was his usage of an unexpected letter that he received in 1894. The letter, which he then published in his newspaper *Iveria*, was written by a young British woman, and later traveller and translator from Georgian, Marjory Wardrop. In near-perfect Georgian, Wardrop asked Chavchavadze for permission to translate and publish in Britain his poem *The Hermit*. The letter became a sensation. Georgians were deeply moved by this young British woman who had never been to Georgia, and had probably never heard spoken Georgian, yet took pains to learn this unapproachable language and boldly addressed their greatest authority. This, for many Georgians, came in sharp contrast with mostly Russian male colonial administrators, who spent their entire lives in Georgia without even attempting to learn the native tongue.[24]

Soon thereafter Marjory travelled to Georgia with her brother James Oliver, and translated important pieces of Georgian literature, such as *The Knight in the Panther Skin* and the *Life of Nino*.[25] While in time, Marjory and Oliver became celebrities and were carried around the country, it was Chavchavadze who foresaw and conceptualised the place that Marjory subsequently occupied in the imagery of the Georgian people. The Wardrop Collection at the Bodleian Libraries at Oxford has preserved letters, poems and even toasts offered in praise of Marjory, from Georgia's capital to its remotest villages. In a passionate toast delivered to Wardrop in January 1895 at a party thrown in her honour, Kote Bakradze echoes what Chavchavadze had in mind for her. Bakradze starts his toast with a reminiscence that Georgia is the 'Lot of the Mother of God': 'Our people believe that this small country had become a lot of the Mother of God, when the apostles divided the world as they knew it among themselves to spread Christ's faith. She received our fatherland under her protection and for a long time, she has not averted her protective eye from us. The particular love and attention of the Mother of God toward our country is visible in our entire past, our history.' Then Bakradze points out that there are very few countries in the world where women were as influential as in Georgia:

---

[24] The letter and Marjory's persona were incorporated in the nascent Georgian feminist movement. In the discourse of the nineteenth-century intellectuals, Marjory Wardrop was conceptualised as a showcase to demonstrate the possibility of the intellectual emancipation of Georgian women.

[25] On Marjory, see, among others, Aleksidze, *Georgia*.

'the equal to the apostles, Nino brought into Georgia Christ's faith ... she was followed by other numerous famous women who gave their lives for faith, among whom were, in particular, Shushanik, Ketevan and finally, the great Tamar'. Yet, continues Bakradze, today (meaning in the circumstances of Russian imperial dominance) women ceased to be as influential as they used to. And then Bakradze directly addresses Marjory Wardrop:

> But the Georgians have not despaired and they are still expecting consolation from their protectress (the Mother of God). Maybe the Blessed One has chosen you to show her care; maybe it is you, a feeble person, to whom She has entrusted this monumental mission? ... From whence have you arrived that you encountered us and studied us and introduced us to Europe? You have raised their sympathy for us, with hopes that this forgotten land may leave the darkness. God willing, our expectation will be met, God willing, you fulfil this great mission. God willing, our women will be emboldened through your good example and will regain the importance that they have temporarily lost in the life of their people.[26]

In a way, Bakradze's rhetoric is typical of the nascent national discourse – the idealised past contrasted with the unfortunate present, and the future that must be sought and discovered in that same past. The peculiarity of Bakradze's toast resides, however, in his perception of Georgian history as entirely constructed on the lives of Georgia's holy women. This nineteenth-century intellectual, who, from the Russian Imperial perspective, lived in a distant province of the Russian Empire, saw the future emancipation of Georgia in a messianic revival of the historic role of holy women. A Georgian listener would have immediately realised that the tropes and similes utilised by Bakradze with reference to Marjory are entirely borrowed from the *Conversion* narrative and the *K'art'lis C'xovreba*. In Bakradze's perspective, which became typical, Marjory's trajectory to Georgia replicated that of St Nino: St Nino was a young Roman woman who had travelled to this distant, 'northern' and hostile land, and having learned the complicated language she introduced enlightenment in Georgia, a story that was emulated by Marjory. Marjory too was an alien woman who had arrived in Georgia to bring Western enlightenment to Georgia, and to return Georgia to Europe, by delivering it from the realm of the North. In this discourse, the civilising role of the North is entirely ignored and replaced by its original, Late Antique perception. Just as fifteen hundred

---

[26] Bodleian Library Collections, MS. Wardr.d.20 (21).

years earlier, Nino had changed Georgia's historic trajectory, so did Marjory stand at the threshold of Georgia's history. It was a similar sense of a beginning that Chavchavadze wished to instil in his readers by reminding them of the importance of Nino's mission for the modern Georgian nation.

The deliberations over the feminine, the religious and the political have not ended with Chavchavadze's rhetoric. This triangulation of sorts retained its centrality in many subsequent identity discourses. Without going into details, as a conclusion, it is worth having a look at one such instance of the usage of the cult of St Nino in a similar nationalist context. In 1917, the Georgian Church regained independence taken away a century earlier by Russia. One year later, the Democratic Republic of Georgia declared independence, yet less than three years later, the Georgians were defeated by the Bolsheviks, and the country was captured by Soviet Russia. In 1926, on the feast of St Nino, Georgia's Katholikos-Patriarch Kalistrate I read a homily on St Nino, where he addressed the issue of gender, originally posed by his distant predecessor, Nikoloz I Gulaberisże. Effectively, Patriarch Kalistrate's sermon served an identical purpose as Patriarch Nikoloz's discourse: he wanted to offer his answer to the question 'Why a woman?', along with a eulogy to Nino and her female nature.[27]

Patriarch Kalistrate started with reasons identical to those described by Gulaberisże: the inhabitants of Iberia had been wild and bloodthirsty, and the divine providence had therefore appointed a woman to pacify this unruly nation with her sweet words. It is for the same reason that all of Nino's disciples, instrumental in Georgia's evangelisation, were women – Shroshana, Sidonia, Nana, Salome, Anastasia and others – some of these names added later to the list of Nino's companions. It is this feminine foundation of Georgian Christianity that makes Georgian religious aesthetics, polyphony and architecture so refined and even sensual, says the Patriarch. (Incidentally, he does not forget to smugly contrast the alleged graciousness of Georgian church architecture to 'brutish' Armenian architecture, whose founder was a man!) Immediately after this, the discourse takes an unexpected turn and the Patriarch dives into politics. What he essentially argues is that it was due to Nino's gender that Georgia succeeded in avoiding what he describes as Roman and Byzantine 'caesaropapism', and that from its inception Georgian Christianity was secular, with a rigid differentiation between religious and secular realms. As such, concludes the Patriarch, Georgian Orthodoxy is perfectly compatible with Soviet religious policies, which nominally guarantee the freedom of religion and the

---

[27] Tsintsadze, *sitqva*, 16–23.

separation of church and state: 'Religion is a private matter of every citizen; every citizen can confess the religion which he prefers, or if he so wishes – none. The Church is separated from the state ... Every citizen is granted the right to preach religion or anti-religion.' This rather cynical clause of the Soviet Constitution, considering the ensuing destruction of churches, was perceived by the Patriarch as essential to Georgian Christianity, a trait that remounted to its 'feminine' foundation. In the Patriarch's vision, inherited from Patriarch Nikoloz I Gulaberisże's original thesis, the 'feminine passivity' was re-evaluated as an active and positive identity.

# 9
# The Sacred, the Feminine and the National

## 9.1 Guardians of the Borders: Saints and the Nation State

In this concluding chapter, with the help of a few contemporary vignettes, I would like to briefly illustrate the persistence of medieval tropes of sanctity and their lasting entanglement with contemporary political and gender discourses. In recent decades, an increasing tendency can be observed of theologising on the nation state and injecting liturgical tropes into modern Armenian and Georgian ethno-religious and political discourses. In this rhetoric, the cult of saints often appears at the forefront, mediating between the physical and mystical bodies of the nation state in the rhetoric of ecclesiastical and political elites. While as illustrated in the introductory vignettes of the present book, in Armenian political rhetoric, the cult of saints was discovered with new vigour in the context of the Genocide, in Georgian discourses, the medieval tropes of sanctity have been introduced in recent political and geopolitical rhetoric, particularly in the context of Euro-Atlanticism and Eurasianism.

A striking feature of this politicised sainthood is the tendency to suspend the canonical practices of canonisation for the ever-changing requirements of the nation. This is a common feature of Orthodox Christian nations elsewhere, where together with the rise of national movements and romantic nationalism, 'national' saints have appeared saturating liturgical calendars. The sanctity of these figures was determined not necessarily by their martyrdom for faith or their illustrious Christian lives, but rather by their service to the 'Fatherland'. This suspension of the canonical and the instrumentalisation of sainthood is often justified by urgent national requirements, such as the necessity to merge the Late Antique concept of martyrdom with the modern legal definition of Genocide in the Armenian case. In contemporary Georgia, two political problems can be considered as a source of national anxiety comparable to that of the Genocide in Armenia: the country's territorial integrity and the ever-widening rift between the Euro-Atlantic and Eurasian aspirations of the Georgian public.[1] Both of these sources of contemporary political anxieties and public policies have spilled over into the old entanglement of sanctity, gender and political rhetoric.

In the late twentieth century, the two South Caucasian nation states with a predominantly Christian population experienced a dramatic revival of Christian spirituality. In Georgia and Armenia, the deepening scholarly and ideological interest in the Middle Ages, coupled with nationalist sentiments, irredentism and the general rise of medievalism, resulted in a recurring interpretation of the present in (pseudo-)medieval categories. Analogously, medieval history is still often read and interpreted through the lens of the modern nation state and largely anachronistic interpretive schemata. The middle ages are prospering in these countries, with Late Antique and medieval literature and histories constituting the axis of national narratives and identity rhetoric. At a young age, children are introduced to the foundational narratives of medieval corpora, mostly the lives of saints. In addition to symbolism, visual and textual imagery, literary tropes and rhetorical metaphors have been extracted from these corpora, revitalised and embedded in modern conceptual networks.

Arguably, there has never been a time when Georgia's cult of saints has enjoyed such political and social relevance as under Katholikos-Patriarch Ilia II. His pontificate, which began in 1977, stretches across two seemingly contrasting eras – the last decade of the Soviet regime and the period of national independence. Since Georgia regained independence from the Soviet Union, Ilia II orchestrated the rise of Christian piety, the establishment of dozens of new monasteries, the building of hundreds of new churches, accompanied by an exponential growth in the number of the clergy, splitting of episcopal dioceses, and a staggering expansion of the church's power. The dramas of the verge of the millennium – economic collapse, civil war in the centre of Tbilisi, the coup, and the fall of Georgia's first government, two proxy and one direct war with Russia, followed by years of corruption, stagnation and nihilism – all these factors gave rise to apocalyptic fears and ethnic nationalism. Amidst the general chaos and decline that Georgia experienced in the last decade of the twentieth century, the Orthodox Church emerged as the sole stable, powerful, relatively wealthy and reliable institution, with hundreds of thousands of men and women of all ages flocking to the churches. By the time of the writing of this book, Ilia II still enjoys unmatched authority among the Georgian populace, both old and young.

---

[1] Batiashvili, 'Europeanisation and the Russian-Georgian Brotherhood', 157–73.

As Georgia's most powerful religious and indeed political authority, Ilia II became the principal author of modern ethno-religious ideology and political theology. The Patriarch's vision of his ethno-national Orthodoxy was probably first vocally articulated in the middle of the *Perestroika*, on Easter 1989, when, possessed by nationalist sentiments, the Patriarch added an illicit insertion to the universal formula: 'Christ is risen! Christ is risen! Georgia is risen!'[2] The words were uttered just seven days before the 9 April anti-Soviet demonstrations and ensuing massacres in Tbilisi. Since then, in the Patriarch's rhetoric, liturgical and national terminology have been used interchangeably.

Owing to the Patriarch's charisma and political capital, the end of the millennium saw a revival and a growing interest in medieval religious imagery, especially in saints. Indeed, in no other period of Georgia's history have so many individuals been canonised as during the pontificate of Ilia II. Figures of national importance, even if their Orthodox careers were rather dubious, such as Ilia Chavchavadze, Ekvtime Takaishvili and others, were canonised as saints of the church. Other figures remain constantly on the verge of canonisation and are subject to a controversy between the church and the nationalists.[3] It is Patriarch Ilia's favourite theological and political concept – 'Heavenly Georgia', a nationalised version of Heavenly Jerusalem or Heavenly Kingdom – which he does not fail to mention in his sermons on important feast days as a justification for such aggressive canonisations. 'Heavenly Georgia' is in the Patriarch's rhetoric a certain metaphysical prototype of Georgia's political body. Georgians who achieve the rank of sainthood perform the same duties in Heaven as in earthly Georgia, according to the Patriarch. While here they served Georgia's physical body, in heaven, they became servants of Georgia's mystical body. In 1987, the canonisation of Ilia Chavchavadze was announced in the following words: 'Now dwelling in heavenly Georgia, the companion of earthly Georgia, Ilia's bright and immortal soul still shines upon us!'[4] In the following thirty years, the concept has been repeated countless times. Using liturgical terminology, the Patriarch likes to describe some major national and religious feast days

---

[2] Cf. György Geréby's analysis of modern the insertion of the Hungarian national anthem in liturgy in 'Angels of the Nation', 823–4.

[3] See my discussion on secular saints in modern Georgia, in Aleksidze, *Narrative*, 175–94. These canonisations must not be confused with the concept of 'cultural saints', i.e. figures who play almost identical roles as medieval saints in national narratives and collective remembering, yet are not saints in the strict sense of this word. For an in-depth study of the phenomenon of cultural saints in Europe, see Dović and Helgason, *National Poets, Cultural Saints*.

[4] http://www.orthodoxy.ge/patriarqi/qadagebebi/skhva/iliaoba.htm (30.05.18).

as a 'mystical union of the earthly and heavenly Georgia'. In theological terms, 'Heavenly Georgia' is absurd. Similarly to the apologetic literature produced in defence of the canonisation of the Armenian Genocide victims, where the formula *necessitas legem non habet* was adopted as a guiding principle, a similar methodology was adopted, although implicitly, in the patriarchal policy of beatification. This novel, national discourse of sainthood too was entangled in Russian Imperial and Soviet legacies, as well as contemporary political anxieties and the rereadings of classical saintly narratives.[5]

Another person who wielded the idea of 'Heavenly Georgia' in the wake of Georgia's independence, was Zviad Gamsakhurdia, a Soviet dissident, leader of the national movement, and finally Georgia's first president. Until his ousting and alleged suicide that followed the coup, Gamsakhurdia was the Patriarch's political rival cherishing a typical mistrust towards Soviet clerics. While both men had a similar understanding of sainthood in their rhetoric, Gamsakhurdia was Ilia's rival also in the struggle over the authorship of the theology of the nation. Gamsakhurdia wished to create a parallel, and from the church's point of view, an illicit host of saints, to which he added Merab Kostava, his co-dissident, who had died earlier in mysterious circumstances, and whom he declared as 'blessed'. Gamsakhurdia's speech on 26 May 1990, which commemorated the declaration of independence of 26 May 1921, was explicitly religious resembling the ravings of a medieval church father, and blurring the lines between sacred and secular:

> My friends, may there be no enmity and treachery among us on this day, on this holy ground, where the spirits of our ancestors are still among us, where the blessed Merab [Kostava] watches us from celestial Georgia, from where Saint Ilia the Righteous too watches over us, the same Ilia the Righteous whom we have martyred . . . The nation of Georgia! Two roads are ahead of you. Your national-liberating

---

[5] Katherine Verdery has studied similar usage of the bones of the monarchs in contemporary Yugoslavia. Verdery, *Political Lives*, 98: 'Post-Yugoslav corpses have also aided in reshaping time. The six-hundred-year-old bones of Prince Lazar, borne from monastery to monastery throughout all the areas containing Serbs, not only established the territorial claims of a new Serbian state. They also compressed time, as if his death in 1389 had occurred just a few days ago. In this way the new Serbia was re-joined with its days of glory as the first medieval state formed in south-eastern Europe, prior to the Ottoman conquest. Reburying Vlatko Maček in Zagreb reconnected the new Croatia with pre-Communist (1930s) politics, as if the communist period had not existed. The same exercise takes place by reburying the dead of World War II precisely as new dead are being produced in their name.'

movement has reached a crossroad. Behold the road of Ilia the Righteous, behold the road of sanctity, of virtue, behold the road of democracy, behold the road of truth and innocence, and behold the road of robbery and treachery, behold the road of terrorism! Choose, nation of Georgia! Choose Christ's road and the road of the good, choose the road of Ilia the Righteous, for this road shall take you to the Purgatory! And he who takes the road of perdition, the road of Barabbas, shall be cursed for eternity![6]

In these exhilarated words, the leader of the national movement usurped the patriarchal rhetoric, striving to overshadow his rival Patriarch and act as the sole 'theologian' of the nation. A striking quality of the theology of saints, as preached by President Gamsakhurdia and Patriarch Ilia, was a very literal understanding of Georgia's mystical alias and the territoriality of the saints. Their 'Heavenly Georgia', as a metaphysical category, was not the universal 'Homeland', the 'Heavenly Jerusalem' of all Christians, but a replica of Georgia's physical body. In this, Ilia's theology of the nation transcends that of P'iladelp'os Kiknadze. From Kiknadze's abstract 'Heavenly Fatherland', under Patriarch Ilia, 'Heavenly Georgia' has evolved into a very tangible imagined geographic category, with the nation state receiving its direct metaphysical analogue.

Patriarch Ilia and President Gamsakhurdia shared a profound understanding of medieval metaphorical language. As a medievalist by training, and an established philologist of Old Georgian, Gamsakhurdia was perfectly articulate when it came to recycling medieval conceptual frameworks for modern purposes, and so was Ilia, owing to his education in the classics of Georgian religious writing. Gamsakhurdia's death, however, left Ilia II as the only hermeneut of the medieval corpus, and, as such, the only sovereign in matters of the theology of the nation. To paraphrase Karl Schmitt, it was now only the Patriarch who could 'decide on the exception'. As the only theologian of the nation, Ilia II felt free to interpret Christian requirements and inject liturgical and theological themes into political discourses, which Georgia's political elites, ever zealous to placate the church, readily adopted. The suspension of canonicity and the Patriarch's power to 'decide on the exception' are in practice manifested in Ilia's very political perception of sainthood. Effectively, the church's policy of canonisation became a direct reflection of the immediate political requirements and national anxieties present since the nineteenth century – Georgia's historic and current unity, ethnic separatism and linguistic diversity. In effect, saints

---

[6] http://qartuliazri.reportiori.ge/news_print.php?id=22974&lang=1 (30.05.20).

were put in service of the country's political cohesion. A certain political geography of sainthood was charted, where saints were assigned to Georgia's regions, thereby incorporating the frontier areas into the nation state's mystical body and ideally also into its physical body. Now, Georgia's marginal regions with a history of liminality have been provided with a local saint whose task was to secure the place of the region in the mystical and physical body of the nation.

For example, in 2002, a thirteenth-century writer, Abuserisże Tbeli, was canonised. This person authored an obscure astrological treatise, two hagiographic narratives and a short chronicle. In normal circumstances, he would not qualify as a saint. The only reason for his canonisation, however, was his association with Georgia's marginal region Achara, with all the accompanying religious and historical problems. For over three centuries, Achara was a province of the Ottoman Empire and its population had become predominantly Muslim, while during the Soviet period, it served as a frontier zone between the Soviet Union and NATO, and was thereby largely inaccessible. Since Georgia gained independence, Patriarch Ilia has been actively proselytising Achara, by organising mass baptisms, building and rebuilding churches, and even establishing an Orthodox University in the region's remote mountainous and predominantly Muslim settlement. In addition, several decades earlier, as a certain invented tradition, the festival of Tbeli (Tbeloba) was instituted, as a ritual reaffirmation of Achara's belonging to the mystical and physical body of Georgia.

Further north, along the Black Sea coast, another medieval saint was discovered. Tsotne Dadiani, a thirteenth-century nobleman, who, apart from several passing historical references, is known for one indeed impressive act of bravery. All the rest concerning this figure, including his religious belonging, is sheer speculation. Nevertheless, due to the House of Dadiani's historic association with the Samegrelo region, he now serves the same purpose as Tbeli. Samegrelo's distinct regional identity and language, related yet different from Georgian, was a source of anxiety for national sentiments since the birth of the national movement in the nineteenth century. Dadiani's canonisation was, therefore, a testimony to Samegrelo's belonging to Georgia's physical body, or rather of Patriarch Ilia's 'Heavenly Georgia'. In the logic of the new theology of the nation, Tsotne was a Megrelian hero, therefore – a national hero and, correspondingly, a saint of the Orthodox Church. Similarly, the feast of Tsotneoba, yet another neologism, is now celebrated annually in Samegrelo's region of Khobi.

Further, also in 2002, a certain late medieval bishop Zosime of Kumurdo was canonised. Virtually nothing is known about this person except that he restored and dedicated the Church of Kumurdo in the ethnically heterogeneous Javakheti region. For many centuries, Javakheti has been a source of discord between Georgians and Armenians. It was in this broader region that many centuries earlier, St Shushanik's cult served the purpose of first sustaining regional unity and then marking ethnic antagonism. The church of Kumurdo, an indeed impressive monument of medieval architecture, is considered a monument of Georgian national heritage, and is also claimed by local Armenians as a monument of Armenian heritage. Therefore, canonising and reanimating the memory of this Georgian Zosime serves the purpose of effectively Georgianising the church. A short biographical sketch of this figure, available on the patriarchal website, includes the following line, full of rhetorical appeals, but without any historical reference: 'The episcopal see of Kumurdo has always been a defender of the unity of the Georgian Church and a pillar of the religious and national idea in the country.'[7] The canonisation of this otherwise obscure figure is effectively justified by this statement which ascribes to this figure concepts that were non-existent in his time.

Finally, recently many martyrs have appeared whose very existence is a conjecture. However, their inclusion in the imagined community of Georgian saints was essential for the national narrative. The church canonised a group of martyrs they called 'Three Hundred Laz Martyrs'. The canonisation of this host is based on a sole assumption: We know of the existence of religious persecutions in the Ottoman Empire, the Lazs used to be Christian, this land is still inhabited by the Laz, therefore there must have been Laz martyrs, so why not canonise them?! The anonymity of these martyrs is staggering. The Lazs, whom the Georgian national narrative considers as quasi-Georgians, as 'familiar strangers' of sorts, living on the other side of the Turkish border, were thus included in the imagined community of Georgianness. They were perceived as lost Georgians who must be embraced into the mystical union of the Georgian nation, as stated in the introductory sentence on the same website: 'Lazeti is the bosom of the Colchian culture. It was the main artery of the definition of Georgian statehood and the oldest site of our culture.'[8] In all these instances, the peripheries of the modern nation state, in its actual or irredentist visions, are conceptualised as historic centres of Georgia's identity, substantiated by the memory and canonisation of their holy figures.

Saints act as realms of memory, as the pillars on which the imagined geography of the nation is grounded. They have become symbolic manifestations of national anxiety over the past, ethnic identity, political and historic borders and the limits of the nation state. The canonisation of these figures would have been problematic in western Christianity or indeed in

---

[7] http://www.orthodoxy.ge/tveni/maisi/01-zosime.htm (30.05.22).
[8] http://www.orthodoxy.ge/tveni/aprili/29-lazebi.htm (30.05.22).

most Christian traditions. Patriarch Ilia's theology of the exception, however, allowed for such digression. The presence of a copy of Sabinin's icon the *Glory of Georgia* in practically every Georgian church and the recent creation of the Armenian Icon of the Martyrs of the Genocide, reflect the merging of the sacred and the national in ecclesiastic as well as public spheres. Due to pressing historical circumstances, an additional layer of representation is added to the icons, as they can now be observed and venerated as singular images of the nation. The state of exception is a guiding principle of the canonisation of non-saintly historical figures, where the immediate requirements of national cohesion suspend the canonical theology of the saints.

In addition to the ongoing incorporation of saints into national discourse, the contemporary rhetoric of sainthood also reflects and interprets some essential aspects of medieval and early modern narratives, such as the problematic overlapping of the feminine, the religious and the political.[9] The 'feminine' aspect of Georgia's cult of saints, promoted by Russian Imperial rhetoric, was reanimated with particular vigour in Ilia II's theology of the nation. Here the imagery of Ilia II projects certain 'cognitive dissonance' typical of colonial Georgian thinking. It is a mixture of two seemingly incompatible beliefs that stemmed from his biography: a patriotic Georgian born in the centre of the Caucasian highlands in the middle of Stalin's regime who received his entire religious education in Russia. While Ilia II is well-read in medieval Georgian religious corpus, the Patriarch's self-perception, as often transpires in his speeches, was essentially Imperial Russian and viewed through a Russian Orthodox prism. For the Patriarch, Georgia's emancipation from the Russian Empire resided in its moral or historic high ground – of Georgia being the 'Lot of the Mother of God', a concept that the Russian Imperial Church had eagerly internalised.

Independently from the Patriarch's rhetoric, however, the 'feminine' component of Georgia's religious history has also been embodied in Georgia's public discourse. The staggering longevity and influence of medieval narratives, disseminated primarily through school curricula, resulted in a repeated interpretation of Georgia's recent history in gendered terms. The perception of 'woman at the threshold', conceived by the *Conversion of Kartli*, and universalised by the cult of Queen Tamar, became a common trope in the late twentieth and early twenty-first centuries for the processing of Georgia's most recent past. Even the supposedly archaic and medieval concept of the Lot of the Mother of God found a surprisingly new life in contemporary Georgia. Consequently, contemporary Georgian

---

[9] Aleksidze, *Narrative*, 175–94.

public discourse, entangled in these medieval concepts, is split between conservative and liberal rhetoric, as illustrated in the following vignettes.

## 9.2 Blasphemy

In 2015, Georgia was shaken by unusually frequent occurrences of domestic violence. As soon as the outrage over one murder subsided, another news headline broke of a jealous husband killing or seriously injuring his current or former spouse. Statistically, 2015 was not particularly outstanding in this respect, as women were murdered before that year and after. However, it was due to a new development that these killings became particularly prominent and affected all layers of Georgia's society. Perhaps for the first time, femicide became a matter entangled between religion and politics, cultural memory and identity discourse, and this was due to the deplorable involvement of the Georgian Patriarchate.

On 15 October of the same year, Georgia's leading Ilia State University hosted a temporary exhibition of contemporary Georgian artists. Among other exhibits was also a painting by Lia Ukleba, whose boldly deviant art had already gained moderate fame among liberal circles. Ukleba's exhibited piece depicted a pregnant woman who bore an unambiguous resemblance to the Mother of God. With her left hand, Mary supported her pregnant belly, and in the right hand she held a pistol aimed at her whisker (see Fig. 9.1). The painting may have gone unnoticed, if not for an existing Georgian icon of the pregnant Mother of God, to which Ukleba's painting bore an uncanny resemblance. Ukleba's image was, therefore, exhibited as an open parody, or polemic with the existing, albeit until then largely unknown, icon of the pregnant Mother of God. The artist explained that her painting, or rather performance, protested the killings of women and the intolerant, violent, misogynistic and homophobic atmosphere prevalent in the country. Through her attempted suicide, Mary refused to bring the child into this world and take

Figure 9.1   Lia Ukleba, 'Mary with a Toy Gun'. Source: Lia Ukleba.

Georgia under her protection. In other words, she would rather die than accept Georgia as her lot. As such, Ukleba's performance was arguably the first explicit protest against this pivotal trope of the Georgian national narrative.

The public display of the painting triggered a violent reaction and, as usual, divided the Georgian public. Social media was flooded with posts condemning and defending the painting, with elaborate argumentation appearing across the spectrum. In the same year, the Charlie Hebdo massacre happened in Paris, an event that found resonance in Georgian social networks as well as debates over the limits of freedom of speech and religious offence. In a heated polemic, the opposing sides debated whether it was appropriate for a university to display blasphemy publicly and whether it violated the rights of members of the faculty and students. That same Sunday, the Patriarch furiously reacted to the display of the painting: 'There is an exhibition at the University of St Ilia the Righteous, where the All-Holy Mother of God is depicted holding a pistol and killing herself. This is an offence against our faith and Georgia. I am stunned that the rector and the professors allowed such blasphemy. Never has Georgia seen such indignity. Georgia is the lot of the All-Holy Mother of God, and I hope they will come to their senses.'[10]

Patriarch Ilia was certainly right to have his patriotic (along with religious) feelings hurt, as the painting was perhaps the first unambiguous and public criticism of the dominant trope of Georgian religious imagery. The Patriarch's assessment would not have been unusual if not for two circumstances. First, his comment was rather unambiguously a call for censorship in a secular institution, and second, it was uttered when the nation was traumatised by frequent news of femicide. Liberals were outraged by the Patriarch's comment and pointed out that not even once had the Patriarch condemned domestic violence, or called for equal opportunities for women. Yet, he was quick to condemn 'blasphemy' against the 'main woman' of the Georgian Church tradition, as he liked to call the Theotokos.[11] In the patriarch's many sermons read over his long reign, Georgia's historic women served as models of subservience rather than political empowerment. St Nino, Queen Tamar, martyr Queen Ketevan and others feature prominently in patriarchal discourses. Paradoxically, despite his obsession with the feminine components in Georgia's history, never has the cult of the

---

[10] https://ipress.ge/new/ilia-ii-ilias-universitetsh/ (03.06.23).
[11] The highlight of that Sunday was perhaps our colleague's humorous Facebook post, which was widely shared and reposted, which very sharply ironised the Patriarchate's statement: 'Don't worry, my fellow citizens, the Patriarch has finally condemned the death of a woman. This is by all means a step forward.'

Mother of God, so deeply ingrained in the fabric of the Georgian Church and religious imagery, been used to endorse women's emancipation. Instead, the medieval idea that the Mother of God, Tamar and Nino were ambiguous exceptions that prove the rule was faithfully retained.

A tense intersection of the political, the feminine and the sacred had occurred also earlier, in 2001, when a young and still relatively little-known author and son of a much better-known artist, Laša Bughadze, had published a short story titled *The First Russian*. The story fictionalised the marriage between Queen Tamar and her infamous first husband, the Rus's prince Yury Bogolyubsky. The story focuses on the first conjugal night of the Queen and the prince of Novgorod as a metaphor and a premonition of the ill-fated Russian–Georgian relations – hence the title of the story. This night, according to Bughadze, fictionalised the first and ominous meeting of the two nations that determined the dynamics of their subsequent relations.

The story found perhaps the single most scandalous reception in Georgia's recent literary history. The church condemned it as blasphemous. The author faced death threats and verbal abuse from pious Georgians. Bughadze was even summoned to the Patriarchate and threatened to either publicly apologise or face excommunication. Nine years later, well after the dust of the controversy settled down, Bughadze, now a bestselling author, published an essay *The Story of the First Russian* and later an award-winning novel, *A Small Country*, where he recounted the previously untold details of the aftermath of the publication and his meetings with the clergy. *The First Russian* was far from graphic, but even a hint about Tamar's sex was deemed offensive and blasphemous. The church had conceptualised the mother of two as a dedicated virgin.

Thus, in these two unrelated instances, the bodies of the two main women of Georgia's history and imagery became entrapped in religious, political and identity debates. Although medieval historians painted the Russian Yury as an epitome of sexual perversion, nevertheless the Patriarch, while offended by the sexualisation of Tamar's body, was seemingly equally concerned with the vilification of Yury as a personification of Russia. After all, he was one of the only two men who had sex with the Holy Queen. According to Bughadze, the audience with the Patriarch, which Bughadze describes with a touch of sarcastic piety, opened with a most unexpected dialogue:

> The Patriarch sat me next to him and told me that Tamar is the most beloved saint of the Georgian nation and one ought not to offend her. I replied that I had not written anything bad about Tamar, and that the

story was about the Russians. – But aren't you worried that Russians will start a war with us for this reason? – asked the Patriarch. The question was so unexpected (back then at least) that I was at a loss, not sure how to respond.[12]

The Patriarch's concern for the feelings of the Russians which betrayed the deeply Russian subjectivity that Ilia II had espoused throughout his life, came as a particular surprise to the young author. The story of *The First Russian* reflects a deeply ingrained anxiety in Georgian cultural memory over the three manifestations of the Holy Queen: the sacred, the political and the feminine, reanimated in the post-Soviet Georgian public discourse specifically due to the dominance of Patriarch Ilia's spirituality. While Tamar's feminine body remains taboo, her political manifestation is also downplayed, and as such, she is removed from the grey zone of the liminal and transposed to the clear-cut realm of the sacred. By ignoring the norms of the medieval Georgian language, contemporary Georgians are generally eager to explain the reason why Tamar is called king (*mep'e*) and not queen (*dedop'ali*), which almost invariably boils down to the argument that she, as a ruler, was as brave and wise as any man, and, implicitly, has shed her femininity. Perhaps the most illuminating example of downplaying Tamar's feminine and political bodies is the Patriarch's sermon on the feast of Tamar:

> Today we celebrate and commemorate Holy Queen Tamar. She was indeed exceptional, elevated from among our nation. Queen [*mep'e*] Tamar stands out with her particular spirituality and her great dedication. One day, Tamar saw in a dream two thrones – one was magnificent and the other was smaller. Tamar wanted to be seated on the more prominent throne, yet she was told – this is not your throne! Whose is it then? – she asked. They replied – your servant's. What has the servant done? – Tamar asked in surprise. They said – She sewed garments for twelve priests and in twelve churches the service is now held with these garments. Then Tamar brought wool by herself, set it up by herself, weaved by herself, and knitted by herself, and thus she completed this assignment, the vision.[13]

---

[12] The original article has disappeared from the web together with the online journal where it was published. Luckily, however, it was reproduced elsewhere. For the Georgian text, follow the link to the secondary website. https://forum.ge/?f=29&showtopic=34070414 (03.06.23).

[13] http://guardian.ge/25312-ilia-meore-thamar-mefe-gardaicvala-sul-akhalgazrda-magram-thamaris-ckhovrebis-periodi-aris-chveni-istoriis-oqros-khana.html (03.06.23).

Crucially, in the parable, while Tamar does indeed occupy the throne, it is not hers, and does not belong to her, a claim that goes against the rhetoric of Tamar and her contemporaries who pressed Tamar's inalienable and personal right to rule in her name. There is yet another noteworthy aspect in Tamar mythology as perpetuated by the Patriarch: Tamar serves the clerics and the church, and therefore submits her political aura to that of the church, in contrast to her biographers' univocal claims that Tamar heavy-handedly controlled the church, convoked church councils and appointed patriarchs. While Patriarch Ilia read the same medieval sources and stories as anyone else, he has adopted a certain filtered image of Tamar, similar to the misogynistic lenses through which the folk narratives had perceived the queen.

Practically all sermons delivered by the patriarch on Tamar's feast days are littered with similarly ambiguous references to the Queen's power and gender. Another pious anecdote, also often recounted by the Patriarch, tells how one day Tamar was in the middle of adorning herself with precious stones and royal garments when she was told that a beggar had come to the palace asking for alms. Her response was to ask the beggar to wait a moment, and that she would arrive as soon as she had completed her preparations. When she finally finished, the beggar was gone. Tamar was deeply saddened that she had missed her chance to do good because of her vanity, so she immediately removed all the jewels and donated them to the icon of the Mother of God.[14]

The source of these stories remains unknown, at least to me, yet have become canonical in Tamar-related sermons published by the Patriarchate. In both sermons, the patriarch downplays two of the three manifestations of Queen Tamar. Both her female and political bodies are suppressed, with only her religious hypostasis remaining. In this rhetoric, Tamar denies not only her sexuality and her sex to become a saint, but also rejects her charismatic body as a monarch. Implicitly, despite the medieval sources' insistence on the opposite, in oral narratives reproduced by the Patriarch, she is still suspected of being unable to fully transcend these two other bodies. Both of these legends, although not attested in any of the medieval accounts, nowadays, since their popularisation by the Patriarch, widely circulate on the web, reflecting the ambiguous representation of saintly women in religious discourses. The greatest historic monarch, under whose reign Georgia achieved unmatched political success and cultural

---

[14] http://www.orthodoxy.ge/patriarqi/qadagebebi/2009/14-05-2009.htm. Originally published in the *Bulletin of the Patriarchate* 16 (2009).

splendour, a person who was famed for her diplomatic prowess and strategic vision even in her lifetime, and whose reputation transcended history-writing, in the Patriarch's rhetoric is utilised as merely another metaphor of female subservience, and specifically subservience to the church.

## 9.3 *Cilxvedri*

The scandal that erupted following the exhibition of the suicidal Theotokos marked the beginning of a very modern and yet unknown political life of the 'Lot of the Mother of God' – its criticism. Since independence, the Patriarch has been doubling down on this metaphor and secular authorities too happily reproduced the patriarchal rhetoric. Meanwhile, over the last two decades, the liberal public has developed a strong criticism of ecclesiastic rhetoric and all of its aspects, from human rights to the church's views on Georgia's foreign policy. In this latter aspect the church was always suspect of anti-Western inclinations and Soviet or pro-Russian nostalgia. The Russian Imperial idea of 'co-religionism' that had justified Georgia's annexation two centuries ago, and reanimated in Vladimir Putin's neo-Imperial ambitions, was eagerly internalised by Georgia's conservative public and ecclesiastics.

While the 'Lot of the Mother of God' was increasingly frequently heard in the patriarchal discourses, over the past couple of decades, the same concept was appropriated in liberal discourse, albeit with a diametrically opposite meaning. Georgia's liberal elites, particularly critical of the ethno-religious nationalism advocated by the church and its candidly pro-Russian sentiments, came up with a mock word to describe Georgia's current state of affairs – *cilxvedri*, literally meaning 'the Lot' from *ġvt'ismšoblis cilxvedri* (Lot of the Mother of God). Statements such as 'I am returning to the *cilxvedri*' or Facebook posts with pictures of filthy streets and ironic hashtags #cilxvedri, referring to the government's yet another anti-Western and implicitly pro-Russian behaviour, became a common marker of alterity, of differentiation between *us*, the liberal, pro-Europeans and them – nominally conservative, ecclesiastic and arguably, at least in part, pro-Russian groups.[15] In liberal language, *cilxvedri* essentially became synonymous with everything that went wrong in the country.

The liberal reaction towards this concept became particularly furious after the August 2008 war with Russia. Secularly minded Georgians, the civil rights, feminist and other activists, consolidated in their condemnation

---

[15] A simple Google search of *cilxvedri* will make this obvious.

of the idea of the Mother of God as Georgia's protectress, as well as the very concept of chosenness. Since the nineteenth century, the political implications of the 'Lot of the Mother of God' have become woven into Russian Imperial ideology, and the concept of 'the Lot' was duly associated with Russian imperialism. Indeed, this medieval Georgian idea originally coined as a marker of superiority against the Byzantines, remains popular among Russian religious and political writers, common believers, pilgrims and, incidentally, travel agencies. As a result, the political implication of the Lot of the Mother of God acquired dangerous ambivalence. On the one hand, before Georgia's annexation by Russia in the early nineteenth century, it constituted the core of Georgian messianic political theology. On the other, the same concept became strongly associated with Russian Imperial subjectivity. Contrary to the patriarch's vision, the contemporary Georgian liberal public views the very notion of the 'Lot of the Mother of God' as a manifestation of a certain imperial subaltern and colonial passivity. The passive and arbitrary connotations of 'being allotted to someone' contributed to this perception. For the liberal elites, the necessity to free Georgian identity from the subjectivity of *cilxvedri* has been tied together with the zeal to free Georgia from Russian subjectivity. The criticism of the ecclesiastical discourse, however, originated mostly from non-governmental liberal elites, and never from political groups who desperately required ecclesiastic support to accumulate political capital. The icebreaker came in May 2014, when the speaker of the parliament of Georgia, David Usupashvili, uttered what arguably was a historic speech. Usupashvili opened a church-organised conference dedicated to the cult of the Mother of God across the Orthodox Church. He started with a lengthy quote of the Georgian author Jemal Karchkhadze, written soon after the collapse of the Soviet Union but since neglected:

> Two thousand years have passed since we started believing that we are the lot of the Mother of God (I believe, in this symbol also lies the key to the national mission), and in these two thousand years we have not approached by a single step this high goal. On the contrary, we zealously try to go back, to such extent that from time to time we make attempts of spiritual suicide. Let us, for a brief second, imagine a small religious miracle: The Mother of God wished to see her land. What will she see? She will see idolaters overcome with the sickness of slavery, who believe that freedom is merely a change in lords. She will see rich Pharisees who do philanthropy merely for the eyes, while real people really die with real deaths. She will see deceivers who perform piety and have turned faith into a matter of bargain. The Holy Mother of God, I

ensure you, would have rejected such a country. The legend will end and the symbol will be erased. Apparently, the metastasis of Communism has been rooted deep into our national body. If we look closely, and consider the fact that the Mother of God has never seen her country, we must think that Georgia is merely potentially the Lot of the Mother of God, whether or not it becomes such in reality, depends on us and only us.[16]

After quoting Karchkhadze, Usupashvili criticised the detrimental effects of the hundred years of Russian colonial rule and seventy years of Soviet rule on Georgian national character and ardently defended Georgia's liberal democracy. He particularly attacked the idea cultivated by the Georgian Church that the West is an essential opponent of Orthodoxy, whereas the Russian Empire in its many guises was its protector. Usupashvili concluded his speech with a rhetorical question, whether the church will be able to follow the principles of secularism: 'It must do so, and if it succeeds, then we will not be ashamed of the [eventual] visit by the Mother of God.'

A few months later, Usupashvili stepped down and for good reason – he was too liberal both for the church and the current political regime. The speech that he had given in the presence of Georgia's high clerics was an attempt to restructure the national paradigm. The bishops and the patriarch seated next to him were used to delivering theology into politics. However, it was for the first time in their post-Soviet experience that a secular authority challenged the ecclesiastic narrative in their presence and subverted the religious paradigm that they had embodied. Usupashvili implicitly criticised the Patriarch himself and his favourite trope of the Lot of the Mother of God. The Patriarch's personal devotion to the Theotokos and their exceptional relationship, was the framework within which all of Patriarch's sermons were delivered. It was in this idea that the Patriarch promised Georgia's salvation, its unification and reanimation. In Usupashvili's paradigm, already embedded in the liberal discourse, the Lot of the Mother of God was reimagined as a trope of passivity, of imperial and colonial subjectivity, which needed to be changed into that of activity. Essentially, the traditional political cleavage that has emerged since the middle of the nineteenth century between the conservative Russophiles (the so-called *Rusetumes*) and the liberal elites, and originally articulated by the *Tergdaleuli* national elites of the 1860s, widened even further during Georgia's independent life, articulated in, among other things, the cult of

[16] https://www.youtube.com/watch?v=VQpwyvhtBUs (03.06.23). For the original quote by Jemal Karchkadze, see *C'iskari*, March 2016, p. 3; http://dspace.nplg.gov.ge/bitstream/1234/155058/1/Ciskari_2016_N3.pdf (03.06.23).

the Mother of God. A new and deep cleavage was about to tear Georgian society apart, and the 'Lot of the Mother of God' was about to mark this polarisation.

The political conceptualisation of the feminine and its symbolic role in the interpretation of Georgia's past and present were rejuvenated following the 2003 Rose Revolution, when Patriarch Ilia encountered the biggest ideological adversary in his career – Georgia's president-elect, Mikheil Saakashvili. Saakashvili was by no means anti-clerical, and he paid all his due to the church. Just like the ageing Patriarch, however, Georgia's young president had an acute sense of the importance of historic tropes for the mobilisation of his voters. In May 2004, Aslan Abashidze, the self-installed ruler of Georgia's Achara region, with severe separatist and pro-Russian aspirations, was ousted from Georgia, and constitutional order was reinstated in the region. The central government initiated a series of drastic reforms to quickly incorporate the region into Georgia's political body, and turn Achara from a peripheral region with the sole purpose of hosting Russian troops into a centre of Georgia's political, cultural and touristic policies. Saakashvili was convinced that people's attitudes could be changed by the appropriate usage of symbolism. He decided to commemorate Achara's return to Georgia's political body with an erection of a lasting symbol. Paradoxically, of all the symbols, he commissioned the erection of a tall and imposing statue of Medea, the mythological daughter of King Aeëtes of Colchis, in Batumi's central square. The square was simultaneously with the instalment of the monument renamed into Europe Square.[17] In a symbolic gesture, Medea's statue now looks westward, extending the Golden Fleece, as if gifting the western newcomers, the Argonauts, this precious gift – the gift of civilisation.[18] Commenting on the erection of Medea's monument, Saakashvili said,

> There have been a lot of rumours about the erection of the statue of Medea in Batumi. However, the first myth through which Georgia became a part of European consciousness is the story of the Argonauts. Medea is associated with this myth and with medicine. This monument is a symbol of Georgia's Black Sea coast and is its attribute thereof.

---

[17] The previous occupier of the square, Memed Abashidze, was relocated to a corner of a minor street. Memed Abashidze (1873–1937) was a leader of pro-Georgian Muslims in Achara and one of the architects of the region's integration into Georgia.

[18] The village of Sarpi cut into two by the Turkish border annually celebrates the arrival of the Argonauts and Medea in a feast called *Kolkhoba*. For the festivity, see Pelkmans, *Defending the* Border, 61–7.

Georgia's Black Sea coastline begins in Achara and ends at the River Psou [in Apkhazeti]. That is why Medea has to be raised exactly in Batumi.[19]

Medea's representation was ambiguous since the earliest stories of the Argonauts, where she was presented as a traitor to her homeland, a murderer of her brother, and in later versions and Euripides' tragedy, as a slayer of her children. From heroine she became a tragic figure, and from a tragic figure, she was transformed into a villain. As a literary character, Medea was introduced in Georgian discourse through the Russian medium in the nineteenth century, and was not previously identified with Georgia. Eventually, in modern Georgian discourse, Medea acquired a new role: first and foremost, she was Georgian, a daughter of the king of Colchis, of an ancient Georgian kingdom. The history of the kingdom of Colchis is now taught as a part of the history of Georgia, as an argument for a three thousand-year history of uninterrupted statehood. Soon thereafter, however, Medea was incorporated in national narratives, as a symbol of national pride. Medea became a 'Georgian woman'.[20] Anthropologist Tamta Khalvashi comments on the contemporary significance of Medea imagery:

> The tectonic political shift in Georgia that happened as a result of the Rose Revolution of 2003 was thus a counter-reaction to the chaos and uncertainty brought by the postsocialist state formation. The revolution suggested a popular denial of this past and a remarkable reversal of a country whose post-socialist transition had gone awry. In this context, the Medea mythology and its monument in Batumi emerged as tropes of the complex negotiation of past and future in Georgia's latest revolutionary regime change. In fact, 'Europe started here' became a slogan of the Rose Revolution government to promote Georgia as a founder of European civilisation. In a way, the revival of hopes and optimism for capitalism and Western modernity as a result of political change re-emerged concomitantly with a re-enchantment of economic, social, and political circumstances and landscapes. The Medea mythology

---

[19] Quoted from Khalvashi, 'Horizons of Medea', 8.
[20] Akaki Tsereteli, a venerated poet and one of two leading figures of the Georgian national movement, even created a revisionist version of the drama, where Medea is a daughter of the glorious Kingdom of Colchis, who desperately falls in love with an alien man. Nothing of her primary crime is mentioned. A century later, in the 1970s sculptor Merab Berdzenishvili erected a statue of Medea in the town of Bichvinta. Medea is covering her children with her veil in an attempt to protect them, maybe from the sea, or even from her own self, or perhaps from posterity. For discussion on Medea in modern Georgian culture, see Nadareishvili, 'Medea', 1–16. Cf. Akaki Tsereteli's romantic rediscovery of Prometheus's Georgian alter ego, Amiran.

contained such a capacity of re-enchantment to sustain the dreams of the Rose Revolution.[21]

Despite never explicitly being contrasted with the Mother of God, the political message of Medea and justifications for the erection of her statue engage in the gendering of Georgia's political discourse. The liberal criticism of the Christian concept of 'the Lot of the Mother of God' with entailing ethno-religious meanings, and especially those of feminine passivity, is with the Medea imagery substituted with a pagan woman that stands literally at Georgia's westernmost gate. The image of 'new Medea' was saturated with identical tropes that were generated by the rediscovered imageries of Nino and the Mother of God. Like Nino, Medea mediates between the two realms: she turns her back to the past and looks towards the feature, equally does she turn her back to both the North (Russia) and the East (Asia) and looks westward. Having turned her back to Russia, Medea actively chooses the West, an image that contrasts with the passive allotment to the Mother of God, and by analogy to the Russian Empire. She is an active protagonist, a chooser symbolising Georgia's perpetual choice to become part of the European commonwealth. As Georgia's first woman, she imitates her historic successor and symbolic predecessor, St Nino, who, according to Ilia Chavchavadze and since Chavchavadze, the liberal Georgian narrative, made the first pro-European choice, defining the country's further political trajectories.

For the ageing Patriarch, something unthinkable was happening: Liberal Georgians were becoming increasingly critical of the 'Lot', with *cilxvedri* fading away from their ethno-religious imagery and self-perception. Like Medea, young Georgians were looking to the West. The contrast between how the Georgian elites were abandoning his favourite idea and the eagerness with which the Russians maintained and reproduced it by consistently

---

[21] Khalvashi, 'Horizons of Medea', 8: 'the paradox of the Georgian government commemorating a mythical hero who is publicly seen as facilitating the theft of the Colchian treasure, indexes the ambivalent imaginaries of the modernising reforms undertaken by the Rose-revolutionary government. Moreover, it captures the contested nature of the myth of Medea, which effectively reflects and channels ideas of statehood, modernity and culture not only in the eyes of political elites but of the general public as well.' Khalvashi has recorded a multiplicity of reactions, most common of which is encapsulated in the following statement: 'Medea is a woman who betrayed our country and killed her children. Yet our government put up a monument to her. It is because our government is like Medea. It sends the message out that we sell out our country like Medea did; that we want every piece of Georgian land to be bought by foreign investors! It's a shame to have monuments like these!' Khalvashi, 'Horizons of Medea', 9–10.

hailing Georgia as *Udel Bogoroditsy* was striking. No European institution or Georgian liberal would have said anything reminiscent of Russian Priest Rafael Karelin's following dithyrambic words towards Georgia:

> The guardian angel of Georgia is the Queen of the Heavens herself... The historical road of the Georgian Church is that of martyrdom, a millennial battle for Orthodoxy, against paganism and the Muslim world. The history of Georgia is a book written in the blood of the martyrs and tears of the blessed, illuminated by the pyre of fires and blinding thunders of battles. There were times when Georgia was an island in the trepid sea of heterodoxy which broke upon it with thunder and calamity, when it seemed that Georgia would be finally devoured by the merciless abyss. But the grace of the Queen of Heavens was with Georgia, her shiny omophorion was spread over the Georgian Church. Great empires of the Huns, Khazars and Mongols were erased from the face of the earth. Of many nations we know merely from an erased inscription on a stone or a coin found by chance; other nations and tribes disappeared without even leaving a trace in the annals of history. Georgia, however, having repelled the storms of centuries, retained in its heart – the name of Christ, and as soul – Orthodoxy... If Christians do not exchange in their souls these three virtues, on other, apparent goods, then her shiny omophorion, as the wings of the angels, will keep protecting the Church of Georgia in the times of trouble.[22]

The Russian priest's eulogy effectively summarises the Georgian church's vision of its past and future, a vision allegedly shared by the Russians and denied by the EU, or even by the Church of Constantinople. The Patriarch resented what he saw as Georgian denialism of their identity, a resentment on which Russia's soft power has since capitalised. Putin's determination to cultivate the idea of *Russkii Mir* in *blizhnee zarubezhie* (Former Soviet and Eastern Bloc countries), and a vision of Russia as a protector of traditional values against Western liberal encroachments, found an ally in the Georgian Church and the Georgian Dream government. In 2012, with the defeat of Saakashvili's United National Movement in parliamentary elections, the Patriarch found his revenge. Georgia's Euro-Atlantic aspirations were nominally retained but in practice restricted, and the entire Georgian government made sure to cosy up with the church. Seven years later, in April 2019, Georgia's prime minister, whose cabinet was often accused of

---

[22] Karelin, *Khristianstvo i Modernizm*, 79. http://www.pravoslavie.ru/orthodoxchurches/39716.htm (12.12.21)

betraying Georgia's pro-Western trajectory and flirting with Russia, commissioned the parliament to quickly adopt new legislation whereby 12 May, the feast of Apostle Andrew's arrival in Georgia, would be declared as the day of *cilxvedroba*, that is the day when Georgia became the Lot of the Mother of God. The law, which was swiftly and pompously adopted, and inscribed into the Constitution, utilised bizarre religious language, and quoted the *K'art'lis C'xovreba*, an authoritative source for such a decision. The clause proclaims that the traditional belief of Georgia's election by the Mother of God was the guarantee of Georgia's political longevity and sovereignty. The act which was aimed at placating the church for the upcoming elections and at hunting for the votes of pious Georgians became the most ridiculed decision in recent history among those whose who had some basic knowledge of the source material: The markedly late and political insertion in the *K'art'lis C'xovreba*, which has never claimed to be an authentic part of the original corpus, and which most likely appeared there as an articulation of Meskheti's separatist claims, was now carved in the Constitution. The Lot of the Mother of God became a legal entity.

## 9.4 The Witches of Independent Georgia

I would like to conclude the present book with one final vignette from Georgia's recent history, to show just how deeply ingrained in contemporary political imagery is the medieval entanglement of the sacred, the feminine and the political.

April 1989 was perhaps the most dramatic month in Georgia's late Soviet history since Georgia's occupation by the Red Army in 1921. On the eve of 9 April 1989, the Patriarch of All Georgia stood on Rustaveli Avenue in front of tens of thousands of Georgians who had gathered there to protest the Soviet regime and its policy in Georgia's region of Apkhazeti. Ilia II was confident that his mesmerising style of speaking and his command of all the tropes that rang the bells of the Georgians would once again do its trick, when he addressed the protesters with a 'blessing' to end the demonstration and gather in the nearby church for prayers: 'You know that Georgia is the lot of the Mother of God. For many centuries, She and God protected Georgia from danger. And now, once again, I can see that the danger is close, the danger is imminent. It comes fast and may be here in a matter of minutes. Therefore, I give you my blessing to end the meeting and to assemble in Kashveti church for prayers.'[23] The footage of the fateful night

---

[23] The footage of the events and the Patriarch's address are widely available online.

has recorded the staggering silence that followed the patriarch's speech and vague echoes of 'no!' reverberating across the crowd. Minutes later, tanks rolled and armed Russian soldiers marched on the avenue, violently cracking down on the protesters and killing twenty-one people. Seventeen of the victims were women. The oldest was seventy, the youngest – sixteen.

The 9th of April marked the beginning of the story of independent Georgia, but not of the church. The most important day in Georgia's history happened without the church's involvement and in defiance of the Patriarch. The Patriarch was close to remaining outside the single most transformative event of Georgia's history. Philosopher Giorgi Maisuradze argues that 9 April 'was the act of the creation of that commonwealth of people which is now called the Georgian nation. A proper evaluation of this event is possible not so much through political and legal theories, but rather through mythological and mythopoetic configurations and paradigms.' Maisuradze sees the 9th of April as a ritual re-enactment of the Georgian national narrative, essentially a replication of foundational martyrologies. Over time, argues Maisuradze, 'Georgia found itself in this huge fictional and imaginative world, written during mass protests, which brought it to a complete alienation from reality and adequate rational activity.'[24]

Indeed, in subsequent narratives, 9 April was seen as an act of the foundation of the Georgian nation, saturated with an ambiguous mixture of secular and religious tropes, marked by the absence of the patriarchate, yet a strong presence of medieval imagery. Yet, there seems to be an even more specific narrative embedded both in the 9th of April and its subsequent re-enactments and commemorations. The protagonist of the event was not the Patriarch's favourite Mother of God, who 'failed' to protect her people, but rather the activist women. As the footage of the massacres shows, women were at the forefront of the clashes, and consequently, most of the victims were also women. The overwhelming predominance of women on that day, also previous days and the days that followed, has been universally noticed and acknowledged (see Fig. 9.2).[25] Among tens of thousands, three blind women stood out who every day assiduously went to the square and sang, including that fateful night. Their high-pitched voices can be heard from all angles of the surviving footage of the events of 9 April. The four blind women (Lela Vepkhvadze, Zaira Gelashvili, Donara Tskhodiashvili and Tina Birkadze) of 9 April were immediately mythologised in urban

---

[24] Maisuradze, *mart'lmadidebluri et'ika*.
[25] Tamuna Gegidze, *k'veqnis mcvelebi – k'alebi 9 aprilidan* (protectors of the country – women from 9 April), News.On.Ge, https://go.on.ge/11sc (02.10.23).

Figure 9.2 An iconic photo of a woman (Nana Makharadze) carrying a black flag the day after the 9 April massacres. Iury Mechitov's photograph has since become the symbol of 9 April and of the eve of Georgia's independence. Notably, for decades, most people were convinced that the woman held the Georgian flag due to the bright white background. Author and source: Iury Mechitov.

lore. Three of them died soon after the tragedy. Only Lela Vepkhvadze survived, only to spend her life in utter misery. For years, during their daily commute in Tbilisi underground, citizens of Tbilisi saw her singing with her young daughter by her side and witnessed her gradually fade away from the view and memory. Back on 9 April 1989, however, during the serene few hours before the massacre, the Georgian public eye noticed and adopted in its imagery these four women. As blind *k'adagis* of lore, they kept standing and singing in the face of the imminent danger, heartening the terrified protesters. As Lela Vepkhvadze recalled, she was aware that she was about to witness the birth of a new Georgia. The blind female singers symbolised this rite of passage, as midwives attending to the birth of a nation. The imagery of these women echoed the original mystical visions of St Nino's female entourage of the *Mok'c'evay K'art'lisay*, their prophecy of a dramatic birth of new Georgia, the devastating invasions of the Zoroastrians and the rise of the new martyrs. Similarly, the singers of Rustaveli Avenue were conceptualised as the new *k'adagis* who in their ecstatic performance foretold the miserable yet thrilling future of the nation as born on Rustaveli Avenue.

Maisuradze is right to interpret 9 April as a new foundation myth, which can only be comprehended in the language of mythology. But it is also the medieval Georgian literary corpus that comes to our aid. The events of 9 April and its feminine imagery caused yet another cognitive dissonance with regard to that event. Many, including Maisuradze, believe that while a new paradigm was born on this day, what one may indeed call the Georgian nation, it was also a birth of utter irrationality that embodied the ensuing catastrophe. For many Georgians, the irrationality of 9 April was the only way to comprehend the real irrationality that unfolded in the few years to follow that tore Georgia apart. In this vision, a direct continuity is seen from the reckless nationalism of 9 April and the ensuing civil wars in Tbilisi, Apkhazeti and Tskhinvali, fuelled by ethno-nationalism and chauvinism that simultaneously caused and were generated by those events. Although never written, in conversations, the holders of this position never fail to point to the same blind women as the symbols of this irrationalism of Georgia's subsequent downfall, with the sound of their singing still making them shudder. Thus, echoing the deeply rooted cognitive dissonance regarding the feminine in Georgian identity discourse, and split between the two contrasting visions of nationhood, the four women of 9 April are simultaneously hailed as heroes and condemned as 'witches' with whom rests the blame for Georgia's subsequent downfall.

As a commemoration of the victims of 9 April, Jemal Sepiashvili, an *estrada* composer beloved by the Soviet establishment, recorded a song titled 'Let Us Give Each Other Tulips'. The sentimental song, which immediately became a hit, was simultaneously performed by all famous singers of late Soviet Georgia, swiftly becoming an anthem of Georgian unity in the aftermath of 9 April. Thirty years later, Sepiashvili recorded a remake of the old hit and announced its premier on 9 April, 2019. While Sepiashvili's music has long lost its appeal, on 9 April social media was flooded with the video. It was the same song, sung by several singers, yet this time, every performer was male. No woman was given a single line. Effectively Sepiashvili whitewashed the 9 April imagery by removing all the female imagery that had been a hallmark of the event. Facing the backlash, he even acknowledged that he intentionally chose an all-male ensemble, because he believed that 'men were the protectors of the nation'.[26] Once again, the female imagery of Georgia's foundation narrative encountered a staunch resentment.

The 9th of April gave rise to Georgia's first president, Zviad Gamsakhurdia, a controversial figure in Georgia's recent history. Gamsakhurdia simultaneously generated outright hatred and adulation. His supporters saw him as Georgia's saviour, while his opponents condemned him as Georgia's destroyer. In their attempts to attach an aura of irrationality to Gamsakhurdia and his policies, his enemies devised a political trope – 'Zviadist women'. In the early 1990s, the preponderance of female imagery in Georgia's mass

---

[26] Tamuna Gegidze, *k'veqnis mc'velebi – k'alebi 9 aprilidan* (protectors of the country – women from 9 April).

protests and women's active involvement led to a widespread myth that most of Gamsakhurdia's followers were women. They were painted as his obsessed cheerleaders, as irrational maenads unleashing destructive forces who had no purpose but to sing paeans to their charismatic leader. The civil war that ensued in 1992 between Gamsakhurdia and the opposition razed Tbilisi and further triggered two more wars in Georgia's regions. The war ended in Gamsakhurdia's ousting and then death in mysterious circumstances. For the next few years, a military council presided by a triumvirate of warlords took over. The leader of the temporary triumvirate was Jaba Ioseliani, a former gangster, professor, novelist and general of a paramilitary unit *Mkhedrioni* (Georgian for 'knights'), a heavily armed regiment of mostly unprofessional militiamen. Following Gamsakhurdia's ousting, in one of the interviews on Russian television, the triumphant Ioseliani delivered a hateful tirade against the president in hiding and expressed wonder regarding the 'femininity' of the president's entourage and supporters. Ioseliani even suggested that psychologists or anthropologists should study the Gamsakhurdia phenomenon and explain the predominance of women among his supporters. He repeatedly and derogatively used the words 'feminine' and 'irrational' against Gamsakhurdia and his supporters, by describing these women as 'ugly and unattractive'.[27] In this and other speeches, Ioseliani framed the civil war as a certain primordial battle between Georgia's male (Mkhedrioni) and female *archē* (Gamsakhurdia). Surprisingly, one can even find a Wikipedia article dedicated to an invented mock term, *Mdedrioni* (*mdedri* is Georgian for female), which describes the feminine alternative to the masculine *Mkhedrioni* during the civil war:

> The core of the protesters were the so-called 'women of the tents'. Next to the stairs of the parliament, they have set tents, where a certain group of protesting women permanently lived. They were mostly past middle age, as people said, often, due to excessive political activism, they experienced problems in their families. These women were particularly aggressive. Their activism and aggression were so noticeable, that they were known among people with nicknames ... This aggressiveness, the entirely unknown mentality for the Tbilisians of that era, caused antipathy among the citizens of Tbilisi ... Due to all these reasons, the citizens of Tbilisi responded with humour. They paraphrased [*sic*] the mighty organisation *Mkhedrioni* and thus created *Mdedrioni*.[28]

---

[27] The short Russian documentary can still be found online: https://www.youtube.com/watch?v=4SkSuqBqe2c (03.06.23).

[28] https://ka.wikipedia.org/wiki/მდედრიონი (03.06.23).

The article is understandably written by a strong opponent, if not a hater, of Gamsakurdia, and illustrates the deeply ingrained misogynist incompatibility between the political and the feminine, the masculine coolness of the capital's citizens and the erratically female attributes of the 'villagers' who had 'flocked' into Tbilisi in Gamsakhurdia's support and had 'blemished' Tbilisi's urban landscape. Just as Ioseliani and Sepiashvili could not fathom simultaneously the feminine and the political, so did the anonymous author of the Wikipedia entry attempt to strip the women of their political agency, and paint them as certain faceless priestesses of their god.

The entanglements of the feminine, the political and the sacred continue to haunt Georgian public discourse in many forms and guises. A big fraction of Gamsakhurdia's supporters split from another Gamsakhurdia group after his alleged suicide. Their principal problem was the persona of Manana Archvadze, the president's widow, whom they blamed for constantly supplying the president with irrational advice that had eventually caused his downfall. Yet, every day, and for many years since her husband's passing, 'the Widow', as she has been commonly called, stood together with a small group of supporters in front of the parliament building in Tbilisi. They never acknowledged the legitimacy of any subsequent government and restlessly demanded the restoration of constitutional order. Due to her ritualised performance, her perseverance and unyielding stubbornness, she consolidated a sizeable number of supporters, who saw in her a manifestation of an old order, of a parallel time and embodiment of the legitimacy of her husband's government as opposed to the illegitimacy of the present state of affairs. Archvadze wore the same black outfit year after year with the same extravagant hat and heavy white makeup, never altering her tragic and fossilised expression in public. She intended to remain in the public eye as a fresco-like image frozen in time, as a symbolic bearer of the legitimate government, as a liminal entity perpetually awaiting the restoration of the legal order.

# Conclusion to Part III
# The Modern Lives of Old Saints

In contemporary Armenian and Georgian religious and political discourses, the nation state is often conceptualised in a certain 'state of emergency', where the immediate national requirements allow for improvisations on such an old Christian concept as the cult of saints. Throughout various eras, the cult of saints was tweaked and adapted to emergent political needs – to legitimise the reign of a female monarch, to create a rival rhetoric against the Byzantines, to claim an uninterrupted continuity of monarchy, or as, in modern times, to forge a religious image of the nation state with all its current challenges and anxieties. In the Armenian discourse, the cult of martyrs has been adapted to the legal concept of Genocide. While in the rhetoric of Georgia's ecclesiastic elites, the cult of the saints often serves the nation state's territorial cohesion, in both instances, the nation's urgent requirements justify otherwise problematic canonisations. There are however, more nuanced ways in which the cult of saints and relics were politicised and problematised in Georgia during the last two centuries.

At the beginning of the second millennium, the Bagratids initiated a rereading of foundational texts and a reinterpretation of old saintly narratives for their rhetoric of power. This effort was largely determined by a zeal to simultaneously imitate, emulate and ward off the Byzantines, both in the Caucasian region and in the Georgian monastic foundations across the empire. New political cults, such as that of the quintessential warrior, St George, and the idea of the 'Lot of the Mother of God', were elaborated in these transitional circumstances. The cult of St George and the 'Lot of the Mother of God' served the consolidation of the Georgian kingdom, the legitimisation of its ruling dynasty, as well as the fermentation of a sense of moral superiority against the Byzantines. The Bagratid project was successful, since in time, both St George, as Georgia's patron saint, and the 'Lot of the Mother of God' became inextricably associated with the Georgian body politic, whether real or imagined. The fall of Constantinople, earlier the refusal of the Georgian bishops to sign the acts of the council of Ferrara and Florence, or the historic memory of the absence of iconoclasm in Georgia, contributed to the deepening conviction that Georgia, due to its steadfastness in Orthodoxy, was indeed the Lot of the Mother of God. This conviction further proliferated holy relics in different Georgian kingdoms and principalities, especially Marian.

By the end of the same millennium, it was another Orthodox empire that prompted similar rereadings of older narratives and reappraisal of the cult of saints and foundational relics. Since Russia's appearance in South Caucasia, Moscow has remained the principal source of political anxiety for all South Caucasian political entities, but especially Georgia. For centuries, Russia was seen as a potential ally and a safe haven against the Muslim Ottomans and Persians. With Georgia's annexation, however, these perceptions changed or at least became deeply ambivalent. For the Georgians, Russia's conception as an imperial foe, yet also a co-religionist, became a conceptual trap in which the country and its citizens still remain entangled, perhaps stronger than ever. Therefore, in some surprising ways, the strategies of politicisation of sanctity were similar to the efforts of the Bagratids, yet also dramatically novel. While the Byzantines were not particularly impressed by the Georgian pretences to being the Lot of the Moher of God, the Russians were, or at least swiftly identified the political expediency of this claim for their imperial ambitions. In the absence of a united monarchy, the 'Lot' maintained a certain sense of historic unity, often expressed in the concept of Iveria, while materially in Christ's and Marian relics scattered across Georgian kingdoms. Russians perceived 'Iveria' as a single religious entity, as a coveted holy land of sorts, and the Georgians of these lands gladly fed these imperialistic sentiments by self-aggrandising as a holy land by proxy, and thereby flattering Muscovy's ambitions as the 'new Rome'. Thus, the 'Lot' became permanently entrenched in the gendered discourses of empire, colonial subjectivity and national sovereignty.

The concept of the Lot has maintained ambivalence and relevance in contemporary religious and political discourses, both internal and foreign. Together with the expansion of literacy, standardisation of school curricula, Stalin's nationalism or the ensuing national liberation movements, interest in Georgia's medieval past was rejuvenated with new vigour. Merged with nineteenth-century imperial rhetoric, old and foundational texts were read, reinterpreted and integrated into the national narrative. The constant anxiety provoked by Russia's threat and Georgia's shaky Euro-Atlantic integration were expressed in, among other things, the conceptualisations of medieval cults. Thus, as never before, in the late twentieth and early twenty-first centuries, the cult of saints found a new life. There are three contexts in which the cult of saints has been integrated into political rhetoric since the emergence of the Russian Empire on the Caucasian frontiers until today: that of gender, imperial gift-giving and political topography.

The Russian Imperial discourse perceived Georgia and its saintly pantheon in strongly feminine terms, subsuming its imagined femininity into the discourse of imperial power. While in the Russian perceptions of Georgia, St George faded away, Georgia's female saints came back to the fore. After all, in Russian, Georgia is *Gruzia* and does not offer any intuitive connections with the Cappadocian warrior saint. In response, in the wake of the national movement, gender became passionately politicised and theologised by liberal elites. The feminine, which symbolised passivity in the face of Russian imperialism, and which required 'enlightenment' and 'guidance' on the part of the hyper-masculine Russian *Ispolin*, was problematised in Georgian national discourse as a quest for Georgia's authentic self. Thus, from a symbol of colonial subjectivity, St Nino turned Ilia Chavchavadze's rhetoric into a symbol of Georgia's European identity that Georgia had acquired together with Christianity. The late nineteenth-century liberal discourse engaged in a virtual quest for historic reaffirmations of the feminine as a premonition of Georgia's emancipation, as exemplified in Bakradze's toast to Marjory Wardrop. The prominence of St Nino and her relics in imperial piety was in accord with the Russian perceptions of Georgian piety, and of Georgia as an Oriental 'other'. Whether by masculinising Georgia's historic figures, or challenging the concept of the 'Lot' as a symptom of passivity, or creating alternative female (active) imagery, Georgia's liberal elites often expressed their anti-colonial and anti-imperial sentiments in gendered terms. The leaders of the National Movement, however, reimagined the role of the feminine in Georgia's history, and reappropriated its early medieval symbolism by associating femininity with transition, with a passage from non-being to being, from ethnicity to consolidated nationhood. From a passive instrument of proselytism, Nino was reimagined as an active converter and as the founder of the Georgian nation, an imagery that found resonance also in the image of Medea in Batumi.

From medieval narratives, Georgian collective memory and national narrative have inherited a strongly ambiguous perception of the place and role of women in Georgia's religious and political history. Contemporary political, and geopolitical aspirations too, owing to the tremendous influence of the medieval corpus, became strongly gendered, whether during the civil war or the ensuing uncertainties in the 1990s. Georgia's recent history has been saturated with female imagery, with political antagonism also often expressed in gendered terms. The readiness with which the ecclesiastic and public discourses have adopted women as liminal figures as markers of transition has been, apart from the general tendency of placing women in the realm of the ambiguous, also determined by the strong living presence of the medieval literary corpus. Georgian religious and political imagery of the twentieth century has accumulated a long experience of presenting its holy women as liminal figures. Yet, like earlier, during and immediately after Tamar's reign, the Queen's feminine nature was presented as the reason for her unmatched glory, though it was the femininity of her daughter and successor Rusudan that was presented as the reason for all the calamities that befell Georgia under the Mongols. Similarly, the very notion of the feminine, coupled with sanctity and politics, became a matter of contention in modern Georgia, simultaneously perceived as a quintessentially Georgian phenomenon and a reason for Georgia's 'irrationality'.

Another powerful trope conceived in the Russian imperial discourse of Georgia and the Caucasus is gift-giving as an instrument of imperial rhetoric of power. In the early nineteenth-century imperial discourse, it was not merely the enlightenment or the 'gift of civilisation' that was generously 'gifted' to Georgia and the rest of Caucasia. A sense of religious rebirth in a new political body was vigorously bolstered, expressed, most vividly, in the re-evaluation of Georgia's pantheon of saints and its historic collection of relics. While the Imperial Church eagerly adopted Georgia's saintly pantheon, it also conceptualised some of Georgia's historic saints and their relics as gifts given (back) to Georgia and redistributed among its newly acquired subjects of the emperor. The act of Georgia's political annexation was framed by imperial rhetoric as Georgia's baptism in the font of Imperial Orthodoxy. Russians perceived Georgia as one of the oldest centres of Orthodox Christianity, directly linked to Jerusalem, and so the political annexation of Georgia into the empire was interpreted and presented to the Georgians as a realisation of their religious predestination. The idea of the 'gift', originally articulated in Emperor Alexander's manifesto, remains firmly entrenched in the Russian perception of Georgia and the Caucasus. And since the collapse of the Soviet Union, and Georgia's determination to join the European Union and NATO, Russians have often expressed frustration over Georgian 'treachery' and the unreciprocated gift. Arguably, the internalisation of this trope by some of the most powerful Georgian ecclesiastic elites perhaps explains their pro-Russian sentiments and anti-European rhetoric even in the aftermath of Russia's war in Georgian in 2008.

The final aspect of the cult of saints in the rhetoric of the empire is religious and political topography. The first text in which the 'North' was problematised as an apocalyptic other and a nemesis of Georgia's newly acquired identity was *Mok'c'evay k'art'lisay*. During the Bagratids, the North has briefly lost its relevance, due to the relocation of Georgia's political nexus towards Constantinople. With Russia's appearance from the North, however, everything changed. The multiple rereadings of the narratives that have expanded on the foundational *Mok'c'evay*, as well as Georgia's exceptional location that controlled the Caucasus's strategic passes, instilled an acute sense of political and religious geography in nineteenth-century writers. With the translation of political and religious focus to the North, in Russia, the concept of *Kedar*, 'the northern realm of darkness', that had been so firmly engrained in medieval Georgian religious and political rhetoric, found surprisingly new vitality in Georgian thought. Inevitably, the Late Antique concepts of 'North' and 'South', together with their religious implications, were adopted and instrumentalised in pro- and anti-imperial discourses, symbolised by, among others, the figure of St Nino. The North and the West still remain two of the most charged political, religious and, in a sense, gendered concepts in Georgian discourse. Thus, the medieval entanglement of the sacred, the political and the feminine found a new life in the fears and trembling of the modern Georgian people.

# Final Remarks

The incorporation of the cult of saints and saintly relics in political and identity rhetoric was a common theme in early Caucasian religious narratives, inaugurated probably by the fifth-century Armenian writers. As reported by Agathangelos and other authors, the cult of saints was introduced together with the establishment of Christianity, and the declared purpose of these new cults was to define Armenian, Georgian or Albanian identities in the context of the universal salvation history. The *Lives* of Armenian Gregory the Illuminator, Albanian King Vač'agan and Georgia's Nino ponder the meanings of time, history, geography, belonging and identity through the prism of the cult of relics, whether of biblical saints or recent martyrs. The early medieval Georgian tradition has internalised all these valences and values of the relics and memories of saints, having also enriched the problem of sanctity and authority with that of gender. Since the creation of the *Conversion of Kartli* corpus, the entanglement of sanctity, gender and politics has become a defining character of much of Georgian religious and political thinking.

The entanglement of sanctity, the political and the feminine was a familiar conundrum to many cultures across the premodern world. The ambiguity over the role of the feminine, as engrained in the foundations of Christianity, produced further conceptual problems with the rise of the cult of saints, of the Theotokos and further with the appearance of several powerful female monarchs. The Georgian literary tradition was particularly receptive to the problem, as two of the defining moments of its history were associated with female saints – the foundation, that is Christianisation and the 'Golden Age'. With this in mind, the aim of the present book was first to identify some of the central rhetorical tropes of sanctity in Late Antique political and identity discourses, and then to follow the many recurrences of these tropes in subsequent literary traditions. I hope I managed to demonstrate that Late Antique Georgian writing has posited a fairly unique problematisation of the feminine, the sacred and the political in its foundational narratives, the *Conversion of Kartli* and the many *Lives of Nino*.

The question posed in the Introduction was whether the femininity of a saint, as a factor, added to the political valence to the said saint's cult? As I hope I managed to demonstrate, it did. Anthropological studies have demonstrated that premodern societies are prone to commodifying women as a means of exchange, to classifying them as inherently transgressive, dangerous and ambiguous entities. As such, the major female saints of the Georgian and Caucasian traditions have also acquired mediatory functions. Placed in the fuzzy geographic, temporal or metaphysical zone, the material relics and remembrances of these holy women symbolised transcendence, spatiality and temporality. St Nino's original conceptualisation was that of a mediator between times and spaces, both metaphysical and physical. She symbolised the end of the old and the beginning of something radically new. She also heralded Georgia's metaphysical transposition from the realm of the North to that of the South. All these spatial, temporal and metaphysical concepts were embodied in the long history of the imagery and cult of St Nino.

While the cult of Queen Shushanik developed independently from that of St Nino, from its inception, it also served a mediatory function. Her martyrdom account conceptualised her as a transgressive human, who had abandoned all the socially accepted norms, and even her feminine self, to sacralise her body. In her *Martyrdom*, Shushanik is presented as a mediator between the Armenian and Georgian realms, whose mediation was violated by her husband, which in turn legitimised her violation of the marital pact. These conceptualisations and tropes of marriage and gift-giving were internalised in Shushanik's posthumous cult, when the holy queen became a symbol of mediation and then of alterity in the grey zone between the Armenian and Georgian realms.

The transformations that the Georgian principalities and kingdoms experienced on the verge of the millennium required a re-evaluation of old cults and a new deliberations on the nature of the feminine in political and religious experience. The formation of the royal court and court culture seemingly contributed to the masculinisation of the religious tradition and saintly imagery, especially through the aggrandisement of the cult of St George. Nevertheless the almost simultaneous emergence of the political cult of the Mother of God created a new level of ambiguity and anxiety over the feminine component of the ethno-religious symbolism. The idea of Georgia as the Lot of the Mother of God was established as the sturdiest political concept of Georgia's history. Essentially, since the eleventh century, the integration of the Georgian kingdoms and the disintegration of the united monarchy since the thirteenth century were rhetorically embedded in the re-evaluations of this political cult of the Mother of God.

The cult of Queen Tamar encapsulated in itself all the anxieties generated by the incongruence among the feminine, the political and the religious, which resulted in the creation of Tamar's image as that of an absolute state of exception. Appropriated by folk cult practices, Tamar became a deity of mediation par excellence: she was perceived as the bridge between nature and culture, the wilderness and polity, and this due to her ambiguity. As perhaps demonstrated in the pages above, the ambiguity of the feminine manifests itself both in the realm of the religious and the political. Due to the markedly 'feminine' character of Georgia's religious history, subsequent Georgian historical, political and religious authors were often prone to problematising the nature of the feminine in religious and political discourse. The ambiguities inaugurated by the conversion narrative and later encapsulated in the cult of Queen Tamar projected the same ambiguity on other aspects of historical and identity experience. The mediatory nature of the ambiguous figures was in time ascribed to all major female figures of Georgia's history. While Queen Tamar was hailed as the reason for Georgia's Golden Age, the creator of, as it were, ideal Georgia, it was her gender that was placed at the centre of this creative force, and thus sacralised. It was, however, the same feminine gender that was implicitly and often explicitly condemned as the reason for Georgia's subsequent downfall under Tamar's daughter, Rusudan. While unable to criticise Tamar due to her sacralisation even in her lifetime, the misogyny of medieval authors was unleashed on her immediate successor who allegedly failed to transcend her female body, and assume body politic, a unique achievement of her mother. Other female figures of Georgia's history followed suit – for example, in contemporary historical discourse, especially the kind taught in schools, Queen Darejan, the widow of King Erekle, became the symbol of Georgia's final downfall due to her inability to transcend her motherly instincts, an act of 'bad faith' that caused the annihilation of Georgia's body politic.

Arguably medieval Georgian political and religious rhetoric was particularly dedicated to the disentanglement of the conundrums created by the foundational text of the medieval Georgian culture the *Conversion of Kartli* and the corpus of which it has later become part – *K'art'lis C'xovreba*. Until the late nineteenth century, the education of the Georgian elites was based predominantly on three canonical texts: *K'art'lis C'xovreba*, Rustaveli's *Man in the Panther's Skin* and the Bible. It was through these three corpora and their numerous sequels, prequels and spinoffs that the Georgians were exposed to political, religious and ideological imagery. The *Man in the Panther's Skin* was seen as a poetic imagination of Georgia's history and specifically of its Golden Age under Queen Tamar. Stories, characters and tropes from these texts have permeated folk traditions, identity narratives and national imaginaries. The problem of sanctity, gender and politics was one of such conundrums extracted from these principal corpora of Georgian literary tradition. Princess Tinatin became firmly associated with Tamar, whereas Tamar symbolised the feminine foundations of Georgian culture, and embodied all the ambiguities related to the pairing of power and femininity, and femininity and sanctity.

The deliberations over the feminine in Georgia's identity narrative kept appearing in modern ethno-religious discourses, in the nineteenth-century imperial setting and since. The events of the night of 9 April and the predominance of female victims among the massacred were interpreted as a reconfirmation of Georgia's original foundation story in the fourth century. The political and religious vision of Nino and her female companions was mimicked by a similar act of the birth of a new Georgian nation. Just as the original foundation narratives experienced constant ambiguity due to their femininity, so was the feminine component of the events of 9 April politicised and even mocked in subsequent years.

Meanwhile, Georgia's current patriarch also forged the narrative of the feminine in his religious discourse. While the nationalist discourse entirely ignored the nineteenth-century conceptualisations, the Russian-educated Patriarch's vision of Georgia's metaphysical body was saturated by tropes formed in imperial discourses. It was for this reason that his favoured concept of Georgia as the Lot of the Mother of God became the cornerstone of controversy between the ecclesiastic and liberal elites. While the former saw in this image Georgia's exceptionality, the latter increasingly perceived the idea as that of passivity and subservience.

Georgian literary tradition opens many avenues for the study of the many usages and shades of sanctity. The histories of the cults of individual saints that have been either sporadically addressed or largely ignored in the present study may indeed become fascinating objects of inquiry. Although much has been written on the paganisation of the saintly pantheon, a proper study of the adoption of Christian saints in the mountainous religious practices is yet to be written. Such a study will certainly transcend the limits of Kartvelian studies and will include many Caucasian languages and cultures. Individual Caucasian regions also provide their unique perceptions and idiosyncrasies of sanctity, such as the warrior saints in Svaneti or a curious tendency to depict only women in their churches.

Even in contemporary Georgia and Caucasia, sanctity and sacralisation are re-emerging in political discourses. Caught between Euro-Atlanticism and Eurasianism, Georgia's national elites reach to medieval texts and saintly narratives to interpret the present. Depending on the reader, the same saintly account can be read as a premonition of Georgia's Euro-Atlantic zeal or a stamp on its Eurasian fate. Therefore, in contemporary national discourses, the cult of the saints is alive and well. The 'new theology' of the nation, as articulated by the church, is presented essentially as a state of emergency, a necessary secular swerve from the rule, justified by pressing political and national requirements in the face of the eschaton. In this rhetoric, saints serve the purpose of sustaining the historical continuity and territorial integrity of the physical and mystical bodies of the nation. As such, the cult of saints persists in contemporary national, ethnic and religious anxieties. New controversies keep emerging over the place of an individual figure in ecclesiastic and national imageries, and almost without exception, each act of canonisation is saturated with political meanings. This, however, is no news for students of Late Antiquity, and Peter Brown's qualification of the rise of the cult of saints is still applicable to twenty-first-century Georgia:

> ... the lurching forward of an increasing proportion of society toward radically new forms of reverence, shown to new objects in new places, orchestrated by new leaders, and deriving its momentum from the need to play out the common preoccupation of all, the few and the 'vulgar' alike, with new forms of the exercise of power, new bonds of human dependence, new, intimate, hopes for protection and justice in a changing world.[1]

I hope that the present inquiry succeeded at least in problematising the crossroads of the religious, the feminine and the political by looking at a relatively small part of the Christian world. It is my belief that should we attempt a wider study of the phenomenon, we shall be able to discover universal and particular traits of the crossroads whether in narrative texts or oral traditions, which will significantly expand our understanding of the phenomenon of holy bodies and body politic.

---

[1] Brown, *Cult of Saints*, 21–2.

# Bibliography

## Medieval Narrative Sources in Georgian

Abuseriże Tbeli, *axalni sascaulni cmidisa giorgisni* [New miracles of Saint George], in N. Goguadze, M. Kavtaria, R. Chagunava (eds), Abuserisisdze Tbeli, *t'xzulebani* (Tbilisi, 1998), 58–70.

Antiochus Strategus, 'The Capture of Jerusalem by the Persians in 614 AD', tr. F. C. Conybeare, *English Historical Review* 25 (1910), 502–17.

Arsen Bulmaisimisże, *galobani cmidisa moc'ik'ulisa ninoysni* [Hymns of the holy apostle Nino], in N. Sulava, *XII–XIII saukuneebis k'art'uli himnograp'ia* [Georgian hymnography of the 12th and 13th centuries] (Tbilisi, 2003), 326–8.

Arseni Beri, *c'xovrebay da mok'alak'obay da ġuacli cmidisa da ġirsisa dedisa č'uenisa ninoysi* [The life and work of the worthy and holy Nino], in I. Abuladze (ed.), *żveli k'art'uli agiograp'iuli literaturis żeglebi* 3 (Tbilisi, 1971), 7–51.

Basili Ezosmożġuari, *c'xovreba mep'et'-mep'isa t'amarisi* [The life of Tamar, Queen of Queens], in S. Kaukhchishvili (ed.), *K'art'lis C'xovreba* 2 (Tbilisi, 1959), 115–51.

Basili Ezosmodzghvari, *The Life of Tamar, the Great Queen of Queens*, tr. D. Gamqrelidze, in S. Jones (ed.), *Kartlis Tskhovreba* (Tbilisi, 2014), 287–314.

*Camebay davit' da konstantinesi* [Martyrdom of David and Constantine], ed. I Abuladze, in I. Abuladze, *żveli k'art'uli agiograp'iuli literaturis żeglebi* 3 (Tbilisi, 1971), 248–63.

Č'axruxaże, *k'eba mep'isa t'amarisi*, ed. I Lolashvili, in I. Lolashvili, *żveli k'art'veli mexotbeni* 1: *c'axruxadze, k'eba mep'isa t'amarisi* [Old Georgian Panegyrists 1: C'axruxadze, Praise of King Tamar] (Tbilisi, 1957), 181–216.

*C'xovreba mep'et'-mep'isa davit'isi* [Life of David, King of Kings], in S. Kaukhchishvili (ed.), *K'art'lis C'xovreba* I (Tbilisi, 1959), 318–65; tr., R. W. Thomson, *Rewriting Caucasian History: The Medieval Armenian Adaptations of the Georgian Chronicles* (Oxford, 1996), 309–53.

*C'xorebay cmidisa mamisa č'uenisa iovane zedaznelisay*, in I. Abuladze (ed.), *żveli k'art'uli agiograp'iuli literaturis żeglebi* 1 (Tbilisi, 1963), 191–217.

*C'xovrebay da mok'alak'obay cmidisa mamisa č'uenisa ilarion axlisay* [The life and work of our holy father, Ilarion the new one], in I. Abuladze (ed.), *żveli k'art'uli agiograp'iuli literaturis żeglebi* 3 (Tbilisi, 1971), 227–8.

*C'xovrebay da mok'alak'obay cmidisa da netarisa mamisa č'uenisa ilarion k'art'velisay* [The life and work of our holy and blessed father Ilarion the Georgian], in I. Abuladze (ed.), *żveli k'art'uli agiograp'iuli literaturis żeglebi* 2 (Tbilisi, 1967), 9–37.

*C'xorebay da mok'alak'eobay cmidisa da netarisa mamisa č'uenisa petre k'art'velisay, romeli iqo že k'art'velt'a mep'isay* [The life and deeds of our holy and blessed father Peter the Georgian, who was the son of a Georgian king], in Abuladze (ed.), *żveli k'art'uli agiograp'iuli literaturis żeglebi* 2 (Tbilisi, 1967), 213–62.
*C'xovrebay da mok'alak'obay ġirsisa da mocik'ulta scorisa netarisa ninoysi* B [The life and work of the worthy and the equal to the apostles, blessed Nino (B)], in I. Abuladze (ed.), *żveli k'art'uli agiograp'iuli literaturis żeglebi* 3 (Tbilisi, 1971), 53–83.
Ephrem Mc'ire, *ucqebay mizezt'a k'art'velt'a mok'c'evisasa tu romelt'a cignt'a šina moixsenebis* [The history of reasons for the conversion of the Georgians and in which books they are narrated], ed. T. Bregadze (Tbilisi, 1959).
Giorgi Mc'ire, *cxorebay mamisa čuenisa giorgi mt'acmidelisay* [Life of our father Giorgi Hagirotes] in I. Abuladze (ed.), *żveli k'art'uli agiograp'iuli literaturis żeglebi* 2 (Tbilisi, 1967), 101–207; tr. T. Grdzelidze, *Georgian Monks on Mt Athos: Two Eleventh-Century Lives of Hegoumenoi of Iviron* (London, 2009), 97–164.
Giorgi Merč'ule, *šromay da moġuacebay grigolis ark'imandritisay* [Life and work of Archmandrite Grigol], I. Abuladze (ed.), *żveli k'art'uli agiograp'iuli literaturis żeglebi* 1 (Tbilisi, 1963), 248–319.
Giorgi Xuc'esmonazoni, *c'xorebay mamisa č'uenisa iovanesa da ep't'wmesi* [Life of our fathers John and Euthymios], in I. Abuladze (ed.), *żveli kart'uli agiograp'iuli literaturis żeglebi* 2 (Tbilisi, 1967), 38–101; tr. T. Grdzelidze, *Georgian Monks on Mt Athos: Two Eleventh-Century Lives of Hegoumenoi of Iviron* (London, 2009), 53–98.
Iakob C'urtaveli, *camebay cmidisa šušanikisi dedop'lisay* [The martyrdom of the holy queen Shushanik], in I. Abuladze (ed.), *żveli k'art'uli agiograp'iuli literaturis żeglebi* 1 (Tbilisi, 1963); tr. D. W. Lang, *Lives and Legends of the Georgian Saints* (New York, 1956), 44–56.
Ioane Anč'eli, *galobani anč'isxatisani*, ed. N. Sulava, in N. Sulava, *XII–XIII saukuneebis k'art'uli himnograp'ia* [Georgian hymnography of the 12th and 13th centuries] (Tbilisi, 2003), 297–301.
Ioane Minč'xi, *Poezia* [Poetry], ed. by L. Khachidze (Tbilisi, 1987).
Ioane Šavt'eli, *abdulmesiani*, ed. I. Lolashvili, in I. Lolashvili, *żveli k'art'veli mexotbeni 2: ioane šavt'eli* [Old Georgian Panegyrists: Ioane Šavt'eli, Abdulmesiani 2] (Tbilisi, 1964), 117–52.
Iovane Sabanisże, *camebay cmidisa da netarisa mocamisa k'ristesisa haboysi* [The martyrdom of the holy and blessed martyr of Christ Abo] in I. Abuladze (ed.), *żveli kart'uli agiograp'iuli literaturis żeglebi* 1 (V–X ss.) (Tbilisi, 1963), 46–81.
Ioane Šavt'eli, *galobani varżiisa ġmrt'ismšoblsani* [Hymns for the Mother of God of Vardzia] in N. Sulava, *XII–XIII saukuneebis k'art'uli himnograp'ia* (Tbilisi, 2003), 301–5.
*Istoriani da azmani šaravandedt'ani* [History and eulogy of monarchs], in S. Kaukhchishvili (ed.), *K'art'lis C'xovreba* II (Tbilisi, 1959), 1–114; tr. D. Gamqrelidze, *The History and Eulogy of Monarchs*, in S. Jones (ed.), *Kartlis Tskhovreba: A History of Georgia* (Tbilisi, 2014), 227–86.
Juanšer, *c'xovreba vakhtang gorgaslisa* [Life of Vakhtang Gorgasali] in S. Kaukhchishvili (ed.), *K'artlis C'xovreba* 1 (Tbilisi, 1955), 139–244; tr. R. W. Thomson, *Rewriting Caucasian History: The Medieval Armenian Adaptations of the Georgian Chronicles* (Oxford, 1996), 153–251.
*K'ebay da didebay k'art'ulisa enisay* [The Praise and the Glory of the Georgian Language], ed. A. Shanidze, in A. Shanidze, *sinuri mravalt'avi 864 clisa* [The Sinai Mravaltavi of 864] (Tbilisi, 1959), 283.

Leonti Mroveli, *mok'c'eva mirian mep'isa da mis t'ana qovlisa k'art'lisa ninos mier* [The conversion of King Mirian and with him of all of Kartli by Nino], in *K'art'lis C'xovreba* 1, ed. S. Kaukhchishvili (Tbilisi, 1955), 72–140; tr. R. W. Thomson, *Rewriting Caucasian History: The Medieval Armenian Adaptations of the Georgian Chronicles* (Oxford, 1996), 84–153.

Leonti Mroveli, *C'xovreba k'art'velt'a mep'et'a* [Life of the Georgian kings], in S. Kaukhchishvili (ed.), *K'art'lis C'xovreba* 1 (Tbilisi, 1955), 3–72; tr. R. W. Thomson, *Rewriting Caucasian History: The Medieval Armenian Adaptations of the Georgian Chronicles* (Oxford, 1996), 2–83.

*Matiane k'art'lisay* [The Chronicle of K'art'li], in *K'art'lis C'xovreba* 1, ed. S. Kaukhchishvili (Tbilisi, 1955), 249–317; tr. R. W. Thomson, *Rewriting Caucasian History: The Medieval Armenian Adaptations of the Georgian Chronicles* (Oxford, 1996), 255–308.

*Mimosvla andria moc'ik'ulisa*, ed. M. Kobiashvili (Tbilisi, 2008), 157–215.

*Mok'c'evay k'art'lisay* [Conversion of K'artli], in I. Abuladze (ed.), *żveli k'art'uli agiograp'iuli literaturis żeglebi* (Tbilisi, 1963), 83–165; tr. Lerner, C., *The Wellspring of Georgian Historiography: The Early Medieval Historical Chronicle the Conversion of K'artli and the Life of St. Nino* (London, 2004).

Nikoloz Gulaberisże, *sakit'xavi svetis-c'xovlisani, kuart'isa saup'loysa da kat'olike eklesiisay* [Discourse on Sveticxoveli, the Lord's Tunic and the Catholic Church], in M. Sabinin, *Sak'art'velos Samot'xe* (St Petersburg, 1882), 69–118, reprinted in M. Ghlonti, *cmiday nino, embazi k'art'lisay* [St Nino, Kartli's baptismal pit] (Mtskheta, 2015), 286–344.

*Šatberdis krebuli meat'e saukunisa* [Shatberdi collection of the tenth century], ed. B. Gigineishvili, E. Giunashvili (Tbilisi, 1979).

Shota Rustaveli, *The Knight in the Panther Skin*, tr. L. Coffin (Tbilisi, 2015).

Sumbat Davit'isże, *c'xovreba da ucqeba bagratoniant'a* [Life and history of the Bagratonians], in S. Kaukhchishvili (ed.), *K'art'lis C'xovreba* 1 (Tbilisi, 1955), 372–85.

*Synaxaria*, in I. Abuladze and E. Gabidzashvili (eds), *żveli kart'uli agiograp'iuli literaturis żeglebi* 4 (XI–XVIII ss.) (Tbilisi, 1968).

Żamt'aaġmcereli, *asclovani matiane* [The hundred-years chronicle], in S. Kaukhchishvili (ed.), *K'art'lis C'xovreba* 2 (Tbilisi, 1959), 151–325; *The Hundred Years' Chronicle*, tr. D. Gamqrelidze, in S. Jones (ed.), *Kartlis Tskhovreba: A History of Georgia* (Tbilisi, 2014), 287–314.

## Early Modern Georgian Literature

Mamuka Baratashvili, *k'eba mep'isa bak'arisa* [Praise of King Bakar], in *Complete Works*, ed. G. Mikadze (Tbilisi, 1969), 58–60.

Niko Dadiani, *k'art'velt' c'xovreba* [Life of the Georgians], ed. Sh. Burjanadze (Tbilisi, 1962).

Teimuraz I, *cameba k'et'evan dedop'lisa* [Martyrdom of Queen Ketevan], in *Complete Works*, ed. A. Baramidze (Tbilisi, 1934), 126–38.

Timot'e Gabashvili, *moxilua cmidat'a da sxuat'a agmosavlet'isa adgilt'a* [Pilgrimage to the holy and other place of the east] (Tpilisi, 1852); tr. J. Wilkinson, M. Ebanoidze, *Pilgrimage: Timothy Gabashvili's Travels to Mount Athos, Constantinople and Jerusalem, 1755–1759* (London, 2016).

Vaxušti Batonišvili, *aġcera samep'osa sak'art'velosa* [Description of the Kingdom of Georgia], in S. Kaukhchishvili (ed.), *K'art'lis C'xovreba* 4 (Tbilisi, 1973).

## Medieval Narrative Sources in Armenian

Agathangelos, *Patmowt'iwn Hayots'* (History of the Armenians), R. W. Thomson (ed.), a facsimile reproduction of the 1909 Tiflis Edition (Delmar, NY, 1980); tr. R. W. Thomson, *Agathangelos, The Lives of Saint Gregory: The Armenian, Greek, Arabic, and Syriac Versions of the History Attributed to Agathangelos* (Ann Arbor, 2010); R. W. Thomson, *Agathangelos, History of the Armenians* (Albany, 1976).
*The Epic Histories Attributed to P'awstos Buzand (Buzandaran Patmut'iwnk')*, tr. N. Garsoïan (Cambridge, 1989).
Lazar P'arpec'i, *The History of Łazar P'arpec'i*, tr. R. W. Thomson (Atlanta, 1991).
Movsēs Kałankatwac'i, *Patmowt'iwn Ałowanic' Ašxarhi* [History of the Land of Ałuank'], ed. M. Ēmin (Tiflis, 1912); tr. C. J. F. Dowsett, *The History of Caucasian Albanians by Movsēs Dasxuranc'i* (London, 1961).
Movsēs Xorenac'i, *Patmowt'iwn Hayoc'* [History of the Armenians], ed. M. Abełean, S. Yarowt'iwnean (Tiflis, 1913), reprinted in R. W. Thomson (ed.), a facsimile reproduction of the 1913 Tiflis edition (New York, 1981); tr. R. W. Thomson, *Moses Khorenats'i, History of the Armenians* (Ann Arbor, 2006).
Step'annos Orbelean, *History of the State of Sisakan*, tr. R. Bedrosian (Long Branch, 2012–15).
Uxtanēs, *Patmowt'iwn bažanman Vrac' i Hayoc'* [History of separation of the Georgians from the Armenians], Armenian text with a Georgian translation, ed. Z. Aleksidze (Tbilisi, 1975); tr. Z. Arzoumanian, *Ukhtanes of Sebastia, History of Armenia Part II, History of the Severance of the Georgians from the Armenians* (Fort Lauderdale, 1985).

## Late Antique, Byzantine and Medieval Sources

Ambrose of Milan, *Political Letters and Speeches*, tr. with an introduction and notes, J. H. W. G. Liebeschuetz and C. Hill (Liverpool, 2010).
Ansellus, *Epistola ad Ecclesiam Parisiensem*, ed. J. P. Migne, *Patrologia Latina* 162 (Paris, 1899), cols. 729–32c.
*The Book of Ceremonies*, tr. A. Moffatt and M. Tall (Leiden, 2017).
*Chronicon Paschale*, ed. L. A. Dindorf (Bonn, 1832); tr. *Chronicon Paschale, 284–628 AD*, translated and notes with introduction by Michael Whitby and Mary Whitby (Liverpool, 1989).
*La Citez de Iherusalem*, in T. Tobler (ed.), *Descriptiones Terrae Sanctae* (Leipzig, Buchhandlung, 1874), 197–224.
Constantine Porphyrogenitus, *De Administrando Imperio*, ed. G. Moravcsik, tr. R. J. H. Jenkins (Washington, DC, 1967).
Epiphanius Monachus, ed. A. Vinogradov, in A. Vinogradov, *Grecheskie predania o sv. Apostole Andree* [Greek stories of Apostle Andrew] (St Petersburg, 2005), 236–65.
*Historia ecclesiastica*, ed. J. Bidez and G. C. Hansen (Berlin, 1995).
*The History of Alexander the Great: Being the Syriac Version of the Pseudo-Callisthenes*, tr. E. A. Wallis Badge (Cambridge, 2013).

John of Damascus, *Oratio in Nativitatem Sancti Dei Genetricis Mariae*, in B. Kotter, *Die Schriften des Johannes von Damaskos* V (Berlin, New York, 1988), 162–83; tr. M. B. Cunningham, *Wider than Heaven: Eighth-Century Byzantine Homilies on the Mother of God* (Crestwood, NY, 2008), 53–70.

John Rufus, *The Lives of Peter the Iberian, Theodosius of Jerusalem and the Monk Romanus*, ed. and trans. C. B. Horn and R. R. Phenix Jr (Atlanta, 2008).

John Skylitzes, *A Synopsis of Byzantine History, 811–1057*, tr. J. Wortley (Cambridge, 2010).

Michael Psellos, *Leben der Byzantinischen Kaiser (976–1075), Chronographia*, ed. and tr. G. R. Reinsch (Berlin, 2015).

Paulinus of Nola, *Carmina*, ed. F. Dolveck (Turnhout, 2015).

Rufinus of Aquilea, *Church History*, tr. P. R. Amidon (Oxford, 1997).

Procopius, *De Aedificiis*, in J. Haury (ed.), *Procopii Caesariensis opera omnia*, vol. 4 (Leipzig, 1962–4).

Socrates, *Ecclesiastical History*, tr. Zenos, in P. Schaff, *Nicene and Post-Nicene Fathers*, series II, vol. 2 (Buffalo, NY, 1890).

Theodoret, *Ecclesiastical History*, tr. B. Jackson, in *Nicene and Post-Nicene Fathers*, series II, vol. 2, ed. P. Schaff (Buffalo, NY, 1890).

## Early Modern Russian and Western Sources

Aleppsky, Pavel, *Opisanie Gruzii* [Description of Georgia], ed. N Asatiani (Tbilisi, 1973).

Ieromonachos, Gregorios, *A Letter, Relating the Martyrdome of Ketaban, Mother of Teimurases Prince of the Georgia* (Oxford, 1633).

Lamberti, Arcangelo, *Relatione della Colchide hoggi detta Mengrellia: nella quale si trata dell'origine, costumi e cose naturali di quei paesi* (Napoli, 1654).

Lamberti, A., *relac'ia sak'art'veloze*, trans. M. Papashvili and Z. Gamezardashvili (Tbilisi, 2015).

Likhachev, D. (ed.), *puteshestviiā russkikh poslov XVI–XVIII vv.* [Travels of Russian Ambassadors in the sixteenth–eighteenth centuries] (St Petersburg, 2008).

Malingre, Claude, *Histoires tragiques de nostre temps* (Paris, 1635).

Rostovsky, Dimitry, *Zhitiiā Sviātykh* (Kyiv, 2004), 453–77 (repr. of the 1916 edition).

Shelonin, Sergiĭ, *Khronograf*, ed. O. V. Panchenko, in. O. V. Panchenko (ed.), *Knizhnye tsēntry drevneĭ Rusi: Knizhnoe nasledie Solovetskogo monastyriā* (St Petersburg, 2010), 361–512.

Sukhanov, Arseny, *Xozhdenie stroitelja startsā Arseniia Sukhanova v 1649 godu* [The travels of the builder and elder Arseny Sukhanov in 1649] (Kazan, 1870).

Yevlev, Aleksey, *Stateinyĭ spisok o prebyvanii posol'stva v Imeretii 1650–1652* [Notes on the embassy to Imereti 1650–1652], ed. I. Tsintsadze (Tbilisi, 1969).

## Collections of Medieval and Early Modern Documents

Belokurov, S. A., 'Poyezdka starttsā Arseniiā Sukhanova v Gruziu 1637–40', *Khristianskoe chtenie* 3–4 (1884), 438–88.

Belokurov, S. A. (ed.), *Snosheniiā Rosii s Kavkazom 1578–1613* [Russia's Relations with the Caucasus 1578–1613] (Moscow, 1889).

Belokurov, S. A. (ed.), *Delo o prisyl'ke shakhom Abbasom rizy Gospodneĭ tsariū Mikhailu Fëdorovichu v 1625 godu* [Documents Related to the Sending of Christ's chiton to Tsar Mikhail Feodorovich by Shah Abbas in 1625] (Moscow, 1891).
Berzhe, A. (ed.), *Akty sobrannye Kavkaskoĭ Arxeograficheskoĭ Komissieĭ* [Documents collected by the Caucasian archaeographic commission] vol. 2 (Tiflis, 1868), vol. 3 (Tiflis, 1868).
Butkov, P. G. (ed.), *Materialy dliā novoĭ istorii Kavkaza s 1722 po 1803 god* [Materials for the new history of the Caucasus from 1722 to 1803] (St Petersburg, 1869).
Gamakharia, J. (ed.), *Materiali posol'stv Gavriila Gegenava, Fedota Elchina i Pavla Zakhareva, 1636–1640 godi* [Materials of the embassy of Gavriil Gegenava, Fedot Elchin and Pavel Zakharev, 1636–1640] (Tbilisi, 2014).
*Girk' T'łt'oc'* [The Book of Letters], the Armenian text with a Georgian translation, ed. Z. Aleksidze (Tbilisi, 1968).
Shoshiashvili, N. (ed.), *kart'uli carcerebis korpusi 1: aġmosavlet' da samxret' sak'qart'velo (V–X ss.)* [The corpus of Georgian inscriptions 1: East and South Georgia 5th–10th cc.] (Tbilisi, 1980).

## Nineteenth- and Twentieth-Century Sources

Chavchavadze, I., 'St Nino', in R. Siradze (ed.), *Saint Nino 1* (Tbilisi, 2008).
Forsyth, W., *The Martyrdom of Kelavane* (London, 1861).
Kiknadze, P. *siquaruli mamulisa* [The love of the fatherland], ed. T. Kukava (Tbilisi, 1996).
Tsintsadze, K., *sitqva cmidisa moc'ik'ult'ascoris ninos xsenebis dġes* [Discourse on the feast of Saint Nino, equal to the apostles] in M. Ghlonti (ed.), *cmiday nino, embazi k'art'lisay* (Mtskheta, 2015).

## Anthologies of Poetry

Asatiani, L. (ed.), *żveli sak'art'velos poeti k'alebi* [Women poets of old Georgia] (Tbilisi, 1936).
Chikovani, M. (ed.), *K'art'uli xalxuri poezia. Mit'ologiuri lek'sebi 1* [Georgian folk poetry. Mythological poems] (Tbilisi, 1972).

## Online Databases

Dundua, T. *Online English–Georgian Catalogue of Georgian Numismatics.* http://geonumismatics.tsu.ge.
Gippert, J., *TITUS, Thesaurus Indogermanischer Text- und Sprachmaterialien.* https://titus.uni-frankfurt.de.
Ward-Perkins, B., *The Cult of Saints in Late Antiquity: From Its Origins to circa AD 700, across the Entire Christian World.* http://csla.history.ox.ac.uk/.

## Studies

Agamben, G., *State of Exception* (Chicago, 2005).
Ajello, R., 'Armeno *p'aṙk'*, avestico *x̌arənah*', in A. Bausani and G. Scarcia (eds), *Studi iranici: 17 saggi di iranisti italiani* (Rome, 1977), 25–33.

Akinean, N., *Die Einführung des Christentums in Armenien und Georgien* (Vienna, 1949).
Akopyan, A., 'Roman ob albanskom tsare Vachagane Blagochestivom v 'Istorii Albanii' Moiseiā Kalankatuĭskogo' [The tale of the Albanian King Vač'agan the Pious in the History of Albanians by Movsēs Kałankatwac'i], *Kavkaz i Vizantiya* 4 (1984), 159–71.
Aleksidze, N., 'The Disputed Saints of Early Medieval Caucasia', in V. Déroche, B. Ward-Perkins and R. Wiśniewski (eds), *Culte des saints et litterature hagiographique: Accords et desaccords* (Paris, 2020), 77–92.
Aleksidze, N., 'The Murder at Mt Kangar. The Oral Narratives of the Caucasian Schism', in M. Mitrea (ed.), *Tradition and Transformation: Dissent and Consent in the Mediterranean* (Kiel, 2016), 130–49.
Aleksidze, N., 'A Nation among Other Nations: The Political Theology of the Conversion of Georgia', in E. Piazza (ed.), *Qui Est Qui Ligno Pugnat? Missionaries and Evangelization in Late Antique and Medieval Europe (4th–13th centuries)* (Verona, 2016), 227–45.
Aleksidze, N., 'Let Us Not Obstruct the Possible: Dialoguing in Medieval Georgia', in A. Cameron and N. Gaul (eds), *Dialogues and Debates from Late Antiquity to Late Byzantium* (London, 2017), 167–84.
Aleksidze, N., 'Caucasia: Armenia, Albania, Georgia', in J. Lössl and N. Backer-Brian (eds), *A Companion to Religion in Late Antiquity*, Blackwell Companions to the Ancient World (Hoboken, 2018), 135–57.
Aleksidze, N., *Georgia: A Cultural Journey through the Wardrop Collection* (Oxford, 2018).
Aleksidze, N., *The Narrative of the Caucasian Schism: Memory and Forgetting in Medieval Caucasia* (Leuven, 2018).
Aleksidze, N., 'Georgian', in S. Papaioannou (ed.), *The Oxford Handbook of Byzantine Literature* (Oxford, 2021), 620–41.
Aleksidze, N., 'Strangers in a Strange Land: Alienation, Authority, and Powerlessness in Georgian Hagiography (10th–11th c.)', in G. Dabiri (ed.), *Narrating Power and Authority in Late Antique and Medieval Hagiographies from East to West* (Turnhout, 2021), 133–52.
Aleksidze, N., 'Never Have Our Ears Heard the Bane of Heresy: Rewriting Histories in Medieval Caucasia', in E. A. Winkler and C. P. Lewis (eds), *Rewriting History in the Central Middle Ages* (Turnhout, 2022), 101–19.
Aleksidze, N., 'Martyrs, Hunters and Kings: The "Political Theology" of Saints Relics in Late Antique Caucasia', in R. Wiśniewski, R. Van Dam and B. Ward-Perkins (eds), *Interacting with Saints in the Late Antique and Medieval Worlds* (Turnhout, 2023), 249–69.
Aleksidze, Z., 'The New Recensions of the Conversion of Georgia and the Lives of the Thirteen Syrian Fathers Recently Discovered on Mt. Sinai', in O. Capitani (ed.), *Settimane di studio del Centro italiano di studi sull'alto medioevo, XLIII: Il Caucaso: Cerniera fra culture dal Mediterraneo alla Persia (Secoli IV–XI)* (Spoleto, 1996), 409–21.
Aleksidze, Z., 'Four Recensions of the "Conversion of Georgia": A Comparative Study', *Caucasus Christianus: Historical and Philological Studies* 2 (Tbilisi, 2011), 99–106.
Aleksidze, Z., 'użvelesi c'noba bagriont'a dinastiis šesaxeb' [The oldest report on the Bagratid dynasty], *Caucasus Christianus: Historical and Philological Studies* 2 (Tbilisi, 2011), 120–8.
Aleksidze, Z., 'The Visions of Grigor and Sahak Part'ew: Old Georgian Versions and Their Reflection in Georgian Sources', in K. Bardakjian and S. La Porta (eds), *The Armenian Apocalyptic Tradition: A Comparative Perspective* (Leiden, 2014), 326–40.

Aleksidze Z. and Mahé, J.-P., 'Manuscrits Géorgiens découverts à Sainte-Catherine du Sinaï', *Comptes rendus des séances de l'Académie des Inscriptions et Belles-Lettres* 139/2 (1995), 487–94.
Aleksidze Z. and Mahé, J.-P., 'Arsène Sapareli, Sur la séparation des Georgiens et des Arméniens', *Revue des Études Arméniennes* 32 (2010), 59–132.
Allen, W. E. D., 'The March-Lands of Georgia', *The Geographical Journal* 74 (1929), 150–6.
Allen, W. E. D., *Russian Embassies to the Georgian Kings (1589–1605) volume 1* (Cambridge, 1970).
Allsen, T., *The Royal Hunt in Eurasian History* (Philadelphia, 2006).
Alt, P.-A., 'Frauenkörper und Stellvertretung: Frauenkörper und Stellvertretung. Das Martyrium des weiblichen Interregnums in Andreas Gryphius' Trauerspiel Catharina von Georgien (1657)', in S. Horsch und M. Treml (eds), *Grenzgänger der Religionskulturen Kulturwissenschaftliche Beiträge zu Gegenwart und Geschichte der Märtyrer* (München, 2011), 127–49.
Angelova, D., *Sacred Founders: Women, Men, and Gods in the Discourse of Imperial Founding, Rome through Early Byzantium* (Oakland, 2015).
Anisimov, S., *Voenno-Gruzinskaiā doroga* [Georgian military highway] (Moscow, 1925).
Appadurai, A., 'Introduction: Commodities and Politics of Value', A. Appadurai (ed.), *The Social Life of Things: Commodities in Cultural Perspective* (Cambridge: Cambridge University Press, 1986), 3–63.
Baillie, J., *The Prosopography of High Medieval Georgia: A Digital Approach* (doctoral thesis, University of Vienna, 2023).
Bakradze, D., *K'art'veli k'alebi. istoriuli mimoxilva* [Georgian women: A historical overview] (Tbilisi, 1891).
Barker, M., 'Wisdom Imagery and the Mother of God', in L. Brubaker and M. B. Cunningham (eds), *The Cult of the Mother of God in Byzantium: Texts and Images* (London and New York, 2011), 91–109.
Batiashvili, N., 'Between Europeanisation and the Russian-Georgian Brotherhood: Nationalism, Orthodoxy and Geopolitics of the Georgian Church', in T. Köllner (ed.), *Orthodox Religion and Politics in Contemporary Eastern Europe: On Multiple Secularisms and Entanglements* (London and New York, 2018), 157–73.
Batiashvili, N. and Aleksidze, N., 'Symbolic Treasure, Care, and Materiality in Upper Svaneti', in M. Studer-Karlen, M. Bacci and N. Chitishvili (eds), *Medieval Svaneti: Objects, Images, and Bodies in Dialogue with Built and Natural Spaces*, Convivium supplementum 2023/2 (Lausanne, 2023), 208–25.
Beard, M., 'The Sexual Status of Vestal Virgins', *The Journal of Roman Studies* 70 (1980), 12–27.
Beliaevsky, N. (ed.), *Utverzhdenie russkogo vladychestva na Kavkaze* 1 [Establishment of Russian Rule in the Caucasus, vol. 1] (Tbilisi, 1901).
Bezarashvili, K., 'masalebi sak'art'velos ġvt'ismšoblis c'ilxvdomilobis ideisat'vis k'art'ul mcerlobaši' [Materials for the idea of Georgia as the Lot of the Mother of God in Georgian writing], in E. Khintibidze (ed.), *Problems of Old Georgian Literature* (Tbilisi, 2002), 124–39.
Bezarashvili, K., 'Hellenophilism in Georgian Literature as Cultural Orientation towards Byzantine Thought: Ephrem Mtsire's Cultural Orientation, Part 1', *Scripta & e-Scripta* 14–15 (2015), 335–64.
Bezarashvili, K. and Coulie., B., 'On the Understanding of the Word *maqvlovani* in Old Georgian Literature', *Literary Researches* 21 (2000), 56–70.

Bezarashvili K. and Skhirtladze Z., 'The Symbol of the Thorn-Bush in Georgian Narrative and Visual Sources', *Le Muséon* 123/3-4 (2010), 363-85.

Biliarsky, I., 'Old Testament Models and the State in Early Medieval Bulgaria', in P. Magdalino and R. Nelson (eds), *The Old Testament in Byzantium*, Dumbarton Oaks Byzantine Symposia and Colloquia (Washington, DC, 2010), 255-79.

Bíró, M., 'Shushanik's Georgian Vita', *Acta Orientalia* 38 (1984), 187-200.

Bozóky, E., *La politique des reliques, de Constantin à Saint Louis* (Paris, 2006).

Braund, D., *Georgia in Antiquity: A History of Colchis and Transcaucasian Iberia, 550 BC-AD 562* (Oxford, 1994).

Bremmer, J. N. and M. Formisano (eds), *Perpetua's Passions: Multidisciplinary Approaches to the Passio Perpetuae et Felicitatis* (Oxford, 2012).

Brown, P., 'The Rise and Function of the Holy Man in Late Antiquity', *The Journal of Roman Studies* 61 (1971), 80-101.

Brown, P., *The Cult of Saints in Late Antiquity. Its Rise and Function in Latin Christianity* (Chicago, 1981).

Brown, P., *The Body and Society: Men, Women, and Sexual Renunciation in Early Christianity* (New York, 1988).

Bukhrashvili, P., *cminda giorgi didebis mxedari* [St George, the great knight] (Tbilisi, 2014).

Bury, J., 'Iveron and Our Lady of the Gate', *Hermathena* 10 (1897), 71-99.

Calzolari, V., '"Je ferai d'eux mon propre peuple": les Arméniens en tant que peuple élu selon la littérature apocryphe en langue arménienne', *Revue d'Histoire et de Philosophie Religieuses* 90 (2010), 179-97.

Calzolari, V., *Les Apôtres Thaddée et Barthélemy. Aux origines du christianisme arménien. Martyre et Découverte des reliques de Thaddée. Martyre et Découverte des reliques de Barthélemy par Maroutha* (Turnhout, 2011).

Calzolari, V., 'Le sang des femmes et le plan de Dieu. Réflexions à partir de l'historiographie arménienne ancienne (Ve siècle ap. J.-C.)', in F. Prescendi and A. A. Nagy (eds), *Victimes au féminin* (Geneva, 2011), 178-94.

Calzolari, V., 'The Legend of St. Thecla in the Armenian Tradition', in J. W. Barrier, J. N. Bremmer, T. Nicklas and A. Puig i Tàrrech (eds), *Thecla: Paul's Disciple and Saint in the East and West* (Leuven, 2017), 283-304.

Cameron, A., 'Images of Authority: Elites and Icons in Late Sixth-Century Byzantium', *Past & Present* 84 (1979), 3-35.

Canard, M., 'Les reines de Géorgie dans l'histoire et la légende musulmane', *Revue des Études Islamiques* 1 (1969), 3-20.

Casari, M., 'The King Explorer: A Cosmographic Approach to Persian Alexander', in R. Stonemand, K. Erickson and I. Netton (eds), *The Alexander Romance in Persia and the East* (Gronningen, 2012), 178-83.

Castelli, E., 'I Will Make Mary Male: Pieties of the Body and Gender Transformation of Christian Women in Late Antiquity', in J. Epstein, K. Straub (eds), *Body Guards: The Cultural Politics of Gender Ambiguity* (New York, 1991), 29-49.

Charachidzé, G., *Le système religieux de la Géorgie païenne* (Paris, 1968).

Chryssochoidis, K., 'The Portaitissa Icon at the Iveron Monastery and the Cult of the Virgin on Mount Athos', in M. Vassilaki (ed.), *Images of the Mother of God: Perception of the Theotokos in Byzantium* (London and New York, 2004), 133-45.

Chubinashvili, G., *gruzinskoe chekannoe isskustvo* [Georgian repoussé art] (Tbilisi, 1959).

Clark, E., 'Ideology, History, and the Construction of "Woman" in Late Ancient Christianity', *Journal of Early Christian Studies* 2 (1994), 155-84.

Cobb, L., *Dying to Be Men: Gender and Language in Early Christian Martyr Texts* (New York, 2008).
Constas, N., *Proclus of Constantinople and the Cult of the Virgin in Late Antiquity, Homilies 1–5, Texts and Translations* (Leiden and Boston, 2003).
Cooper, K., 'Empress and Theotokos: Gender and Patronage in the Christological Controversy', in R. N. Swanson (ed.), *The Church and Mary*, Studies in Church History 39 (Woodbridge, 2004), 39–51.
Cowe, P. S. 'Armenian Hagiography', in S. Efthymiadis (ed.), *The Ashgate Research Companion to Byzantine Hagiography, vol. 1* (Farnham, 2011), 299–322.
Cronnier, E., *Les inventions de reliques dans l'Empire romain d'Orient (IVe–VIe s.)* (Turnhout, 2016).
Dagron, G., *Emperor and Priest, the Imperial Office in Byzantium* (Cambridge, 2007).
Dagron, G. and Déroche, V., *Juifs et chrétiens en Orient byzantine* (Paris, 2010).
Delierneux, N., 'Virilité physique et sainteté feminine dans l'hagiographie orientale du IVe au VIIe siècle', *Byzantion* 70 (2000), 105–40.
Delierneux, N., 'The Literary Portrait of Byzantine Female Saints', in S. Efthymiadis (ed.), *Ashgate Research Companion to Byzantine Hagiography* 1 (Farnham, 2014), 363–86.
Di Giorgio, T., *San Teodoro. Storia, culto e Iconografia* (Rome, 2016).
Dolakidze, M., *ilarion k'art'velis c'xovrebis żveli redak'c'iebi* [Old Georgian redactions of the Life of Ilarion the Georgian] (Tbilisi, 1974).
Dorfmann-Lazarev, I., *Christ in Armenian Tradition: Doctrine, Apocrypha, Art (Sixth–Tenth Centuries)* (Leuven, 2016).
Doufikar-Aerts, F., *Alexander Magnus Arabicus: A Survey of the Alexander Tradition through Seven Centuries: From Pseudo-Callisthenes to Sūrī* (Paris, 2010), 171–80.
Douglas, M., *Purity and Danger: An Analysis of Concepts of Pollution and Taboo* (London, 2001).
Dović, M. and Helgason, J. K., *National Poets, Cultural Saints* (Leiden and Boston, 2017).
Dunn, S., 'The Female Martyr and the Politics of Death: An Examination of the Martyr Discourses of Vibia Perpetua and Wafa Idris', *Journal of the American Academy of Religion* 71 (2010), 202–25.
Dvornik, F., *The Idea of Apostolicity in Byzantium and the Legend of the Apostle Andrew* (Cambridge, 1958).
Eastmond, A., 'Royal Renewal in Georgia: The Case of Queen Tamar', in P. Magdalino (ed.), *New Constantines: The Rhythm of Imperial Renewal in Byzantium, 4th–13th Centuries* (Cambridge, 1994), 283–95.
Eastmond, A., 'Gender and Orientalism in Georgia in the Age of Queen Tamar', in L. James (ed.), *Women, Men and Eunuchs: Gender in Byzantium* (London, 1997), 100–19.
Eastmond, A., *Royal Imagery in Medieval Georgia* (University Park, PA, 1998).
Eastmond, A., 'Local Saints, Art and Historical Identity in the Orthodox World after the First Crusade', *Speculum* 78 (2003), 707–49.
Eastmond, A., 'Greeks Bearing Gifts: The Icon of Xaxuli and Enamel Diplomacy between Byzantium and Georgia', in I. Foletti and E. Thunø (eds), *The Medieval South Caucasus: Artistic Cultures of Albania, Armenia and Georgia* (Brno-Lausanne, 2016), 88–105.
Eastmond, A., 'Art on the Edge: Church of the Holy Cross, Jvari, Georgia', *The Art Bulletin* 105/1 (2023), 64–92.

Elsner, J., 'From the Culture of Spolia to the Cult of Relics: The Arch of Constantine and the Genesis of Late Antique Forms', *Papers of the British School at Rome* 68 (2000), 149–84.
Eshel, *The Concept of the Elect Nation in Byzantium* (Leiden, 2018).
Esposito, R., *Communitas. The Origin and Destiny of a Community* (Stanford, 2010).
Evans, N., 'Kastron, Rabaḍ and Arḍūn: The Case of Artanuji', in N. Matheou, T. Kampianaki and L. M. Bondioli (eds), *From Constantinople to the Frontier: The City and the Cities* (Leiden, 2016), 343–64.
Fähnrich, H., *Georgische Sagen und Legenden* (Leiden, 1998).
Flannery, J., *The Mission of the Portuguese Augustinians to Persia and Beyond (1602–1747)* (Leiden, 2013).
Frivold, L., *The Incarnation: A Study of the Doctrine of Incarnation in the Armenian Church in the 5th and 6th Centuries according to the Book of Letters* (Oslo, 1981).
Gabidzashvili, E., *cminda giorgi żvel k'art'ul mcerlobaši* [Saint George in old Georgian writing] (Tbilisi, 1991).
Galatariotou, C., 'Holy Women and Witches: Aspects of Byzantine Conception of Gender', *Byzantine and Modern Greek Studies* 9/1 (1984), 55–94.
Garland L., *Byzantine Empresses: Women and Power in Byzantium AD 527–1204* (London, 1999).
Garsoïan, N., 'Prolegomena to a Study of Iranian Aspects in Arsacid Armenia', *Handēs Amsoreay* 90 (1976), 177–234.
Garsoïan, N., 'The Locus of the Death of Kings: Iranian Armenia – The Inverted Image', in R. G. Hovanissian (ed.), *The Armenian Image in History and Literature* (Malibu, 1981), 29–35.
Garsoïan, N., *L'église Arménienne et le grand schisme d'Orient* (Louvain, 1999).
Geary, P., *Furta Sacra: Thefts of Relics in the Central Middle Ages* (Princeton, 1978).
Geary, P., Sacred Commodities: The Circulation of Medieval Relics', in A. Appadurai (ed.), *The Social Life of Things: Commodities in Cultural Perspective* (Cambridge, 1986), 169–91.
Gedevanishvili, E., 'Cult and Image of St George in Medieval Georgian Art', in M. Bacci, T. Kaffenberg and M. Studer-Karlen (eds), *Cultural Interactions in Medieval Georgia* (Wiesbaden, 2018), 143–68.
Gedevanishvili, E., 'The Khakhuli Dome Decoration', in M. Studer-Karlen, I. Foletti, A. Palladino, E. Gedevanishvili, I. Giviashvili, N. Chitishvili, T. Kaffenberger and I. Mamasakhlisi (eds), *Georgia as a Bridge between Cultures: Dynamics of Artistic Exchange* (Turnhout, 2021), 3–21.
Geréby, G., 'The Angels of the Nation: Is a National Christianity Possible?', in T. Bács, A. Bollók and T. Vida (eds), *Across the Mediterranean, along the Nile, vol 2: Studies in Egyptology, Nubiology and Late Antiquity* (Budapest 2018), 819–48.
Gernet, L., *Anthropology of Ancient Greece* (Baltimore, 1981).
Ghaghanidze, M., 'camodga mzet'unaxavi: t'amaris mit'osis literaturuli p'ragmenti akakis lirikidan' [The beauty has risen: A literary fragment of Tamar's myth from the poetry of Akaki Tsereteli], *Literaturuli żiebani* 35 (2014), 141–53.
Gippert, J., 'The Georgian Hagiorites and Their Impact on the Center of Georgian Eruditeness', in D. Muskhelishvili (ed.), *Georgian Athonites and Christian Civilisation* (New York, 2013), 75–83.
Gippert, J. and Dum-Tragut, J. *Caucasian Albania: An International Handbook* (Berlin, 2023).

Gnoli, G., 'Farrah', *Encyclopædia Iranica*, online edition (2012), available at http://www.iranicaonline.org/articles/farrah (accessed 26.07.18).
Goiladze, I., 'Reflection of the Byzantine Oriental Policy in the Georgian Sources', in N. Makharadze and N. Lomouri (eds), *Byzantium in the Georgian Sources* (Tbilisi, 2010), 393–427.
Gordeziani, R., 'amażoni/amażonebi' [Amazon, the Amazons], in R. Gordeziani (ed.), *Encyclopedia Caucasus Antiquus* 2.1 (Tbilisi, 2014), 73–5.
Graeber, D., *Toward an Anthropological Theory of Value: The False Coin of Our Own Dreams* (New York, 2001).
Graeber, D. and Sahlins, M., *On Kings* (Chicago, 2017).
Grant, B., *The Captive and the Gift: Cultural Histories of Sovereignty in Russia and the Caucasus* (Ithaca and London, 2009).
Grdzelidze, T., *Georgian Monks on Mount Athos: Two Eleventh-Century Lives of the Hegoumenoi of Iviron* (London, 2009).
Green, C., 'Holding the Line: Women, Ritual and the Protection of Rome', in S. P. Ahearne-Kroll, P. Holloway and J. A. Kelhoffer (eds), *Women and Gender in Ancient Religions* (Tübingen, 2010), 279–95.
Greenwood, T., 'Sasanian Reflections in Armenian Sources', *E-Sasanika* 5 (2008), https://www.sasanika.org/esasanika/sasanian-reflections-in-armenian-sources-2/.
Gryphius, Andreas, *Catharina von Georgian: Abdruck der Ausgabe von 1663 mit den Lesarten von 1657* (Stuttgart, 2008).
Gvosdev, N., *Imperial Policies and Perspectives towards Georgia, 1760–1819* (London, 2000).
Haas, C., 'Mountain Constantines: The Christianisation of Aksum and Iberia', *Journal of Late Antiquity* 1/1 (2008), 101–26.
Hakobyan, A., 'The Creation of a "Pious" Image of King Vač'agan II (r. c. 485–523) of Caucasian Albania in the Tale of Vač'agan (Early Sixth Century)', in M. Forness, A. Hasse-Ungeheuer and H. Leppin (eds), *The Good Christian Ruler in the First Millenium* (Berlin, 2021), 239–48.
Hanaway, W., 'The Concept of the Hunt in Persian Literature', *Boston Museum Bulletin* 69 (1971), 27–8.
Herrin, J., *Women in Purple: Rulers in Medieval Byzantium* (Princeton, 2001).
Hill, B., 'Imperial Women and the Ideology of Womanhood in the Eleventh and Twelfth Centuries', in L. James (ed.), *Women, Men and Eunuchs: Gender in Byzantium* (London, 1997), 76–100.
Holum, K., *Theodosian Empresses: Women and Imperial Domination in Late Antiquity* (Berkeley, 1982).
Homza, M., *Mulieres Suadentes – Persuasive Women: Female Royal Saints in Medieval East-Central and Eastern Europe* (Leiden, 2017).
Horn, C., 'St. Nino and the Christianisation of Pagan Georgia', *Medieval Encounters* 4/3 (1998), 243–64.
Iamanidze, N., 'The Dragon-Slayer Horseman from Its Origins to the Seljuks: Missing Georgian Archaeological Evidence', in N. Asutay-Effenberger and F. Daim (eds), *Der Doppeladler: Byzanz und die Seldschuken in Anatolien vom späteen 11. Bis zum 13. Jahrhundert* (Mainz, 2014), 97–110.
Iamanidze, N., *Saints cavaliers. Culte et images en Géorgie aux IVe–XIe siècles* (Wiesbaden, 2016).
Ingoroqva, P., *Giorgi merč'ule. k'art'veli mcerali meat'e saukunisa* [Giorgi Merč'ule. Georgian author of the tenth century] (Tbilisi, 1954).

Isachenko, 'Raĭ myslennyĭ' Stefana Sviatogortsa v isdaniiakh i rukopisiiakh RGB' [Mental paradise of Stephen the Hagiorite in the manuscript of RSL], *Polzunovskiĭ Almanakh* (2017), 198–205.
Kalandia, G., *odišis saepiskoebi* [The episcopates of Odishi] (Tbilisi, 2004).
Kantorowicz, E., *The King's Two Bodies: A Study in Medieval Political Theology* (Princeton, 2016).
Karelin, R., *Khristianstvo i Modernizm* [Christianity and Modernism] (Moscow, 1999).
Kauchtschischvili N., 'Santa Nino e la donna a nel mondo bizantino', in G. Shurghaia (ed.), *Santa Nino e la Georgia* (Rome, 2000), 51–60.
Kavtaradze, G., 'The Georgian Chronicles and the Raison d'Être of the Iberian Kingdom', *Orbis Terrarum, Internationale Zeitschrift für Historische Geographie der Alten Welt* 6 (2001), 177–37
Kavtaria, M. (ed.), *Cmiday Nino. embazi k'art'lisay* [Saint Nino, the Baptismal font of Kartli] (Mtskheta, 2015).
Kekelidze, K., 'mok'c'evay k'art'lisays šedgeniloba, cqaroebi da erovnuli tendenc'iebi' [The composition, sources and national tendencies of the Conversion of Kartli], *Etiudebi* 1 (Tbilisi, 1956), 63–83.
Khakhanov, A., 'Iz gruzinskix legend. Novaia versiia skazaniia o tsaritse Tamare' [From Georgian legends: A new tale of Queen Tamar], *Etnograficheskoe obozrenie* 4 (1898), 140.
Khalvashi, T., 'The Horizons of Medea: Economies and Cosmologies of Dispossession in Georgia', *Journal of the Royal Anthropological Institute* 24/4 (2018), 804–25.
Kiknadze Z., 'k'art'lis mok'c'evis andrezuli variantebi' [The andrezi variants of the conversion of K'artli], *Matsne: Language and Literature Series* 1 (1982), 62–71.
Kiknadze Z., *K'art'uli mit'ologia 1: jvari da saqmo* [Georgian mythology 1: The cross and its people] (Kutaisi, 1996).
Kiknadze Z., *Andrezebi* [The foundation stories] (Tbilisi, 2009).
Kiknadze Z., 'Sami etiudi t'amaris mit'osidan' [Three studies in Tamar mythos], *Georgian Source-Studies* 12 (2010), 68–86.
Kiknadze Z., *K'art'uli mit'ologia 2: p'arnavazis sizmari* [Georgian mythology 2: The dream of P'arnavaz] (Tbilisi, 2016).
Kldiashvili, D., 'sinis mt'is xati Davit' Agmašeneblis portretuli gamosaxulebit" [The icon of Mt Sinai with the portrait of David the Builder], *Mravaltavi* 15 (1989), 117–34.
Klein, H., 'Sacred Relics and Imperial Ceremonies at the Great Palace of Constantinople', *Visualisierung von Herrschaft*, ed. F. A. Bauer, *BYZAS* 5 (2006), 79–99.
Kluchevskaia, E. P. and Makhanko, M. A., 'Kazanskaia I Tatarskaia Eparkhia' [The eparchy of Tatarstan and Kazan], *Pravoslavnaia Entsiklopedia* 29 (2017), 134–96.
Krueger, D., 'Mary at the Threshold: The Mother of God Guardian in Seventh-Century Palestinian Miracle Accounts', in L. Brubaker and M. B. Cunningham (eds), *The Cult of the Mother of God in Byzantium: Texts and Images*, Birmingham Byzantine and Ottoman Monographs (Farnham, 2011), 31–8.
Kutateladze, L., *sak'art'velos saxelmcip'o muzeumis k'art'ul xelnacert'a agceriloba* 2 [Description of the Georgian manuscripts of the State Museum of Georgia] (Tbilisi, 1951).
La Porta, S., 'The Vision of St. Grigor Lusaworič' and the Role of Apocalyptic in the Conversion of Armenia', in K. Bardakjian and S. La Porta (eds), *The Armenian Apocalyptic Tradition: A Comparative Perspective* (Leiden, 2014), 296–312.
Lang, D. W., *Lives and Legends of the Georgian Saints* (New York, 1956).

Layton, S., *Russian Literature and Empire: Conquest of the Caucasus from Pushkin to Tolstoy* (Cambridge, 1995).
Leach, E., *Genesis as Myth and Other Essays* (London, 1969).
Lerner, C. B., *The Wellspring of Georgian Historiography: The Early Medieval Historical Chronicle the Conversion of K'artli and the Life of St. Nino* (London, 2004).
Lévi-Strauss, C., *Elementary Structures of Kinship* (Boston, 1969).
Licheli, V., 'St Andrew in Samtskhe: Archaeological Proof?', in T. Mgaloblishvili (ed.), *Ancient Christianity in the Caucasus* (Richmond, 1998), 25–37.
Limberis, V., *Divine Heiress: Virgin Mary and the Creation of Christian Constantinople* (London, 1994).
Lolashvili, I., *żveli k'art'veli mexotbeni 1: c'axruxaże, k'eba mep'isa t'amarisi* [Old Georgian Panegyrists 1: Č'axruxadze, Praise of King Tamar] (Tbilisi, 1957).
Lolashvili, I., *żveli k'art'veli mexotbeni 2: ioane šavt'eli* [Old Georgian Panegyrists: Ioane Šavt'eli, *Abdulmesiani* 2] (Tbilisi, 1964).
Mahé, J.-P., 'Entre Moïse et Mahomet: réflexions sur l'historiographie arménienne', *Revue des Études Arméniennes* 23 (1992), 121–53.
Mahé, J.-P., 'La rupture arméno–géorgienne au début du VIe siècle et les réécritures historiographiques des IX–XI siècles', in O. Capitani (ed.), *Il Caucaso: Cerniera fra culture dal Mediterraneo alla Persia (Secoli IV–XI). Settimane di studio del centro Italiano di studi sull'alto medioevo XLIII*, 2 (Spoletto, 1996), 927–61.
Mahé, J.-P., 'Confession religieuse et identité nationale dans l'église arménienne du VIIe au XIe siècle', in N. Garsoïan and J.-P. Mahé (eds), *Des Parthes au Califat: Quatre leçons sur la formation de l'identité arménienne* (Paris, 1997), 60–78.
Mahé, J.-P., 'Vac'agan III le Pieux et le Culte des Reliques', *Révue des Études Arméniennes* 35 (2007), 13–126.
Mahé, J.-P., 'Le mythe d'Ištar dans l'oralité caucasienne', *Comptes rendus des séances de l'Académie des Inscriptions et Belles-Lettres* 152/1 (2008), 215–30.
Maisuradze G., *mart'lmadidebluri et'ika da arat'avisup'lebis suli* [The Orthodox ethics and the spirit of non-liberty] (Tbilisi, 2013).
Mango, C., 'Constantine's Mausoleum and the Translation of Relics', *Byzantinische Zeitschrift* 83 (1990), 51–62.
Manning, P., *Strangers in a Strange Land: Occidentalist Publics and Orientalist Geographies in Nineteenth-Century Georgian Imaginaries* (Boston, 2012).
Manoukian, A., *New Saints: Canonizing the Victims of the Armenian Genocide* (Geneva, 2015).
Mardirossian, A., *Le Livre des canons arméniens (Kanonagirk' Hayoc') de Yovhannes Awjnec'i. Église, droit et société en Arménie du IV<sup>e</sup> au VIII<sup>e</sup> siècle*, Corpus Scriptorum Christianorum Orientalium 606; Subsidia 116 (Leuven, 2004).
Martin-Hisard, B., 'La pérégrination du moine géorgien Hilarion au XI<sup>e</sup> siècle', *Bedi K'artlisa* 39 (1981), 101–38.
Martin-Hisard, B., 'Le roi géorgien Vakhtang Gorgasal dans l'histoire et dans la légende', in B. Guillemain (ed.), *Temps, mémoire, tradition au Moyen-Âge, Actes du 13<sup>e</sup> congrès de la Société des historiens médiévistes de l'enseignement supérieur public, Aix en Provence, 4–5 juin 1982* (Aix-en-Provence, 1982), 205–42.
Martin-Hisard, B., 'Du T'ao-K'lardzheti à l'Athos: moines géorgiens et réalités sociopolitiques', *Bedi K'artlisa* 61 (1984), 34–46.
Martin-Hisard, B., 'Les "Treize Saints Pères". Formation et évolution d'une tradition hagiographique géorgienne (VI<sup>e</sup>–XII<sup>e</sup> siècles)', *Revue des Études Géorgiennes et Caucasiennes* 1 (1985), 141–68; 2 (1986), 76–111.

Martin-Hisard, B., 'La Vie de Jean et Euthyme et le statut du monastère des Ibères sur l'Athos', *Revue des Études Byzantines* 49 (1991), 67–142.
Martin-Hisard, B., 'Jalons pour une histoire du culte de sainte Nino (fin IV$^e$–XIII$^e$ s.)', in J.-P. Mahé and R. W. Thomson (eds), *From Byzantium to Iran: Armenian Studies in Honour of Nina G. Garsoïan* (Atlanta, 1997), 53–81.
Martin-Hisard, B., 'Moines et monastères géorgiens du IX$^e$ siècle: La Vie de Saint Grigol de Xancta. Deuxième partie: une mise en perspective historique', *Revue des Études Byzantines* 60 (2002), 5–64.
Martin-Hisard, B., 'La Vie de Georges l'Hagiorite (1009/1010–29 Juin 1065). Introduction, traduction du texte Géorgien, notes et éclaircissements', *Revue des Études Byzantines* 64–5 (2006–7), 5–204.
Martin-Hisard, B., 'Georgian Hagiography', in S. Efthymiadis (ed.), *The Ashgate Research Companion to Byzantine Hagiography: Period and Places* 1 (Farnham, 2011), 285–99.
Mauss, M., *The Gift: Forms and Functions of Exchange in Archaic Societies* (London, 1966).
McClintock, A., *Imperial Leather: Race, Gender and Sexuality in the Colonial Contest* (New York, 1995).
McCollum, A., *The Story of Mar Pinḥas*, Persian Martyr Acts in Syriac: Text and Translation 2 (Piscataway, NJ, 2013).
McNamara, 'Imitatio Helenae: Sainthood as an Attribute of Queenship', in S. Sticca (ed.), *Saints: Studies in Hagiography* (New York, 1996), 51–80.
Mergiali-Sahas, S., 'Byzantine Emperors and Holy Relics: Use, and Misuse, of Sanctity and Authority', *Jahrbuch der Österreichischen Byzantinistik* 51 (2001), 41–60.
Mgaloblishvili, T., 'How Mtskheta Turned into the Georgians' New Jerusalem', in B. Kühnel, G. Noga-Banai and H. Vorholt, *Visual Constructs of Jerusalem* (Turnhout, 2014), 59–66.
Mgaloblishvili T. and Gagoshidze, I., 'The Jewish Diaspora and Early Christianity in Georgia', in T. Mgaloblishvili (ed.), *Ancient Christianity in the Caucasus* (London, 1998), 39–59.
Moss, C. R., 'Blood Ties: Martyrdom, Motherhood and Family in the Passion of Perpetua and Felicitas', in S. P. Ahearne-Kroll, P. Holloway and J. A. Kelhoffer (eds), *Women and Gender in Ancient Religions* (Tübingen, 2010), 189–209.
Nachkebia, K., 'Ketevan', *Pravoslavnaia Entsiklopediā* 32 (Moscow, 2017), 566–74.
Nadareishvili, K., 'Medea in the Context of Modern Georgian Culture', *Phasis* 10 (2007), 1–16.
Nikolaishvili, S., *Byzantium and the Georgian World c. 900–1210: Ideology of Kingship and Rhetoric in Byzantine Periphery* (PhD dissertation, Central European University, Budapest, 2019).
Ochiauri, T., *k'art'velta użvelesi sarcmunoebis istoriidan* [From the history of the oldest beliefs of the Georgians] (Tbilisi, 1954).
Ochiauri, T., *Mit'ologiuri gadmoc'emebi aǧmosavlet' sak'art'velos mt'ianet'ši* [Mythological traditions in eastern Georgian highlands] (Tbilisi, 1967).
Okropiridze, A. 'oškis cminda nino' [St Nino of Oški], *Maqvlovani* 2–3 (2014), 43–6.
Paichadze, G., 'masalebi ruset'-sak'art'velos urt'iert'obebis istoriisat'vis 165–1658' [Sources for the Russian–Georgian relations in 1652–1658], *Saistorio moambe* 19–20 (1965), 439–69.
Pancaroǧlu, O., 'The Itinerant Dragon-Slayer: Forging Paths of Image and Identity in Medieval Anatolia', *Gesta* 43/2 (2004), 151–64.
Papamastorakis, T., 'Re-Deconstructing the Khakhuli Triptych', *Deltion tes xristianikes arxeologikes hetaireias* 23 (2002), 225–54.

Peeters, P., 'Ste Shushanik, martyre en Arméno-Géorgie', *Analecta Bollandiana* 53 (1935), 5–48, 245–307.
Pelkmans, M., *Defending the Border, Identity, Religion and Modernity in the Republic of Georgia* (Ithaca, 2006).
Poe, M., 'Moscow, the Third Rome: The Origins and Transformations of a "Pivotal Moment"', *Jahrbücher für Geschichte Osteuropas, Neue Folge* 49/3 (2001), 412–29.
Pogossian, Z., 'Women at the Beginning of Christianity in Armenia', *Orientalia Christiana Periodica* 69 (2003), 355–80.
Preud'homme, N. J., 'Ancient Iberia and the Gatekeepers of the Caucasus', *Iberia-Colchis* 16 (2021), 155–72.
Ram, H. and Shatirishvili, Z., 'Romantic Topography and the Dilemma of Empire: The Caucasus in the Dialogue of Georgian and Russian Poetry', *Russian Review* 63/1 (2004), 1–25.
Rapp, C., 'Old Testament Models for Emperors in Early Byzantium', in P. Magdalino and R. Nelson (eds), *The Old Testament in Byzantium*, Dumbarton Oaks Byzantine Symposia and Colloquia (Washington, DC, 2010), 175–98.
Rapp, S. H., 'Sumbat Davit'is-dze and the Vocabulary of Political Authority in the Era of Georgian Unification', *Journal of the American Oriental Society* 120/4 (2000), 570–6.
Rapp, S. H., *Studies in Medieval Georgian Historiography: Early and Texts and Eurasian Contexts* (Leuven, 2003).
Rapp, S. H., 'Images of Royal Authority in Early Christian Georgia: The Impact of Monotheism?', in A. Al-Azmeh and J. Bak (eds), *Monotheistic Kingship: The Medieval Variants* (Budapest, 2004), 155–72.
Rapp, S. H., 'New Perspectives on "The Land of Heroes and Giants": The Georgian Sources for Sasanian History', *E-Sasanika* 13 (2014), 1–32.
Rapp, S. H., *The Sasanian World through Georgian Eyes: Caucasia and Iranian Commonwealth in Late Antique Georgian Literature* (Farnham, 2016).
Rapp S. and Crego, P., 'The Conversion of K'art'li: The Shatberdi Variant, Kek.Inst. S-1141', *Le Muséon* 119 (2006), 169–225.
Rayfield, D., *The Literature of Georgia: A History* (London, 2000).
Rayfield, D., *Edge of Empires: A History of Georgia* (London, 2012).
Reinink, G. J., *Heraclius, the New Alexander: Apocalyptic Prophecies during the Reign of Heraclius*, in G. J. Reinink and B. Stolte (eds), *The Reign of Heraclius (610–641): Crisis and Confrontation* (Leuven, 2002), 81–94.
Reisner, O., 'Travelling between Two Worlds – The *Tergdaleulebi*, Their Identity Conflict and National Life', *Identity Studies* 1 (2009), 36–50.
Rix, R., *The Barbarian North in Medieval Imagination* (New York, 2015).
Rollason, D., 'Relic-Cults as an Instrument of Royal Policy c.900–1050', *Anglo-Saxon England* 15 (1986), 91–103.
Russell, J., *Zoroastrianism in Armenia* (Cambridge, 1987).
Said, E., *Orientalism* (London, 1977).
Schmidt, A., 'Das armenische "Buch der Briefe". Seine Bedeutung als quellenkundliche Sammlung fur die christologischen Streitigkeiten in Armenien im 6./7. Jh.', in H. C. Brennecke, E. L. Grasmuck and C. Markschies (eds), *Logos. Festschrift fur Luise Abramowski*, BZNW 67 (Berlin and New York, 1993), 511–33.
Schmitt, C., *Political Theology. Four Chapters on the Concept of Sovereignty* (Chicago, 2005).
Serres, M., *Genesis* (Ann Arbor, 1995).

Shaduri, V. (ed.), *Letopis' druzhby grusinskogo i russkogo narodov I* [The chronicle of friendship between the Georgian and the Russian people] (Tbilisi, 1961).
Shoemaker, S., *The First Christian Hymnal: The Songs of the Ancient Jerusalem Church: Parallel Georgian-English Texts* (Chicago, 2019).
Sikharulidze, K., *t'amar mep'e k'art'ul xalxur šemok'medebaši* [Queen Tamar in folklore] (Tbilisi, 1943).
Sikharulidze, K., *k'art'uli xalxuri saistorio sitqviereba* 1. [Georgian historical folklore] (Tbilisi, 1961).
Simmel, G., *The Philosophy of Money* (London, 1978).
Sinitsina, N. V., *Tretiĭ Rim: Istoki i evolutsiia russkoĭ srednevekovoĭ kontseptsii* [Third Rome: History and evolution of a medieval Russian concept] (Moscow, 1998).
Skhirtladze, Z., *iveriis ġvt'ismšoblis xatis močediloba* [The repousse of the Icon of the Mother of God of Iveria] (Tbilisi, 1994).
Skhirtladze, Z., *Ot'xt'a eklesiis p'reskebi* [Frescoes of the church of Otkhta] (Tbilisi, 2009).
Skhirtladze, Z., 'cminda ninos c'xovrebis c'ikli garejis mravalmt'is udabnos monastris mt'avari eklesiis sadiakvnes moxatulobaši' [The cycle of the *Life of Nino* in diaconicon of the main church of the Monastery of Mravalmta of Gareja], *Saistorio Krebuli* 1 (2011), 344–89.
Skhirtladze, Z., 'Apocryphal Cycle of the Virgin in Medieval Georgian Murals: Preliminary Observations', in I. Stević, *ΣΥΜΜΕΙΚΤΑ Collection of Papers Dedicated to the 40th Anniversary of the Institute for Art History, Faculty of Philosophy, University of Belgrade* (Belgrade, 2012), 103–18.
Smith, J., 'Rulers and Relics c.750–c.950: Treasure on Earth, Treasure in Heaven', *Past & Present* 206/5 (2010), 73–96.
Soudavar, A., *The Aura of the Kings: Legitimacy and Divine Sanction in Iranian Kingship* (Costa Mezas, 2003).
Spurr, D., *The Rhetoric of Empire: Colonial Discourse in Journalism, Travel Writing and Imperial Administration* (Durham, 1993).
Steppan, T., 'Überlegungen zur Ikone der Panhagia Portaitissa im Kloster Iwiron am Berg Athos', in P. Naredi Rainer (ed.), *Sinnbild und Abbild. Zur Funktion des Bildes, Kunstgeschichtliche Studien-Innsburg* (Innsbruck, 1994), 23–49.
Strémooukhoff, D., 'Moscow the Third Rome: Sources of the Doctrine', *Speculum* 28/1 (1953), 84–101.
Sulava, N., *XII–XIII saukuneebis k'art'uli himnograp'ia* [Georgian hymnography of the 12th–13th centturies] (Tbilisi, 2003).
Suny, R. G., *The Making of the Georgian Nation* (Bloomington, 1994).
Synek, E. M., 'The Life of St Nino: Georgia's Conversion to its Female Apostle', in G. Armstrong and I. Wood (eds), *Christianizing Peoples and Converting Individuals* (Turnhout, 2000), 3–13.
Tarchnišvili, M., 'Die Legende der heiligen Nino und die Geschichte des georgischen Nationalbewußtseins', *Byzantinische Zeitschrift* 40 (1940), 48–75.
Terian, A., *Patriotism and Piety in Armenian Christianity: The Early Panegyrics on Saint Gregory Crestwood* (New York, 2005).
Thélamon, F., *Païens et chrétiens au IVème siècle. L'apport de 'l'Histoire ecclésiastique' de Rufin d'Aquilée* (Paris, 1981).
Thélamon, F., 'Amazones et Gargaréens: la disjonction des masculins et des féminins au Caucase', in *Mélanges Pierre Lévêque. Tome 7: Anthropologie et société* (Besançon, 1993), 319–38.

Thomson, R. W., 'The Maccabees in Early Armenian Historiography', *Journal of Theological Studies* 26 (1975), 329–41.
Thomson, R. W., *The Teaching of St Gregory* (New York, 2001).
Thomson, R. W., 'The Vision of Saint Gregory and Its Interpretations', in K. Bardakjian and S. La Porta (eds), *The Armenian Apocalyptic Tradition: A Comparative Perspective* (Leiden, 2014), 285–95.
Tinkle, T., *Gender and Power in Medieval Exegesis* (New York, 2010).
Todt, K.-P., 'Die Frau als Selbstherrscher: Kaiserin Theodora, die letzte Angehörige der Makedonischen Dynastie', *Jahrbuch der Österreichischen Byzantinistik* 50 (2000), 139–72.
Tolstaia, T. V., 'Iverskaia Ikona Bozheiei Materi', in *Pravoslavnaia Enciklopedia* 21 (2009), 8–22.
Tolz, V., *Russia's Own Orient, the Politics of Identity and Oriental Studies in the Late Imperial and Early Soviet Periods* (Oxford, 2011).
Toumanoff, C., 'On the Relationship between the Founder of the Empire of Trebizond and the Georgian Queen Thamar', *Speculum* 15 (1940), 299–312.
Toumanoff, C., *Studies in Christian Caucasian History* (Georgteown, 1963).
Troitskaia, T. S. 'Rannie etapy literaturnoĭ istorii povesti o Dinare (XVI v.) [Early stages of the literary tale of Dinara (16th c)], in N. N. Pokrovsy and E. K. Romodonovskaia (eds), *Drevnerusskaiā rukopisnaiiā kniga i eë bytovanie v Sibiri* (Novosibirsk, 1982), 28–45.
Tsintsadze, K., 'sitqua cmidisa moc'ik'ult'ascoris ninos xsenebis dges' [Discourse on the day of the holy equal-to-the-apostles Nino], *Saġvt'ismetqvelo krebuli* 1 (1985), 16–23.
Tuite, K., 'Lightning, Sacrifice and Possession in Traditional Religions of the Caucasus', *Anthropos* 99/1 (2004), 143–59, 481–97.
Tuite, K., 'St George in the Caucasus: Politics, Gender, Mobility', in T. Darieva, T. Kahl and S. Toncheva (eds), *Sakralität und Mobilität im Kaukasus und Südosteuropa* (Wien, 2017), 21–56.
Tuite, K., 'The Old Georgian Version of the Miracle of St George, the Princess and the Dragon: Text, Commentary and Translation', in I. Dorfmann-Lazarev (ed.), *Sharing Myths, Texts and Sanctuaries in the South Caucasus: Apocryphal Themes in Literatures, Arts and Cults from Late Antiquity to the Middle Ages*, Studies on Early Christian Apocrypha 19 (Leuven, 2022), 60–94.
Turner, V., *The Ritual Process: Structure and Anti-Structure* (London, 1995).
Tvaradze, A., *sak'art'velo da kavkasia evropul cqaroebši* [Georgia and Caucasia in European sources] (Tbilisi, 2004).
Van Donzel, E. and Schmidt, A., *Gog and Magog in the Early Syriac and Islamic Sources* (Leiden, 2010).
Van Esbroeck, M., 'Apocryphes géorgiens de la Dormition', *Analecta Bollandiana* 91 (1973), 55–75.
Van Esbroeck, M., 'Généalogie de la Vierge en géorgien', *Analecta Bollandiana* 91 (1973), 347–56.
Van Esbroeck, M., 'La place de Jérusalem dans la "Conversion de la Géorgie"', in T. Mgaloblishvili (ed.), *Ancient Christianity in the Caucasus* (Richmond, 1998), 59–75.
van Lint, Theo M., 'The Formation of Armenian Identity in the First Millenium', *Church History and Religious Culture* 89 (2009), 251–78.
Vashalomidze, S. G., *Die Stellung der Frau im alten Georgien: Georgische Geschlechtverhältnisse insbesondere während der Sasanidenzeit* (Wiesbaden, 2007).

Verdery, K., *The Political Lives of Dead Bodies: Reburial and Postsocialist Change* (New York, 1999).
Vocotopoulos, P., 'Note sur l'icône de la Vierge Portaïtissa', *Zograf* 25 (1996), 27–30.
von Lilienfeld, F., 'Amt und geistliche Vollmacht der heiligen Nino, "Apostel und Evangelist" von Ostgeorgien, nach den ältesten georgischen Quellen', in M. Kohlbacher and M. Lesinski (eds), *Horizonte der Christenheit. Festschrift für Friedrich Heyer zu seinem 85. Geburtstag*, Oikonomia, 34 (Erlangen, 1994), 224–49.
Weiner, A., *Inalienable Possessions: The Paradox of Keeping-While-Giving* (Berkeley, 1992).
Weitbrecht, J., 'Maternity and Sainthood in the Medieval Perpetua Legend', in J. N. Bremmer and M. Formisano (eds), *Perpetua's Passions: Multidisciplinary Approaches to the Passio Perpetuae et Felicitatis* (Oxford, 2012), 150–69.
Wiśniewski, R., *The Beginnings of the Cult of Relics* (Oxford, 2018).
Wortley, J., 'The Earliest Relic-Importations to Constantinople', *Pecia* 8/15 (2005), 207–25.
Yuzbachian, K. N., 'Einige Bemerkungen über die Entwicklung der nationalen Bewusstseinsbildung im kaukasischen Albanien', in W. Seibt (ed.), *Die Christianisierung des Kaukasus: Referate des Internationalen Symposions* (Wien, 1999, 2002), 181–9.
Zakarian, D., *Women, Too, Were Blessed; The Portrayal of Women in Early Christian Armenian Texts* (Leiden, 2020).
Zekiyan, L. B., 'La rupture entre les Églises géorgienne et arménienne au début du VIIe siècle', *Revue des Études Arméniennes* 16 (1982), 155–74.
Zekiyan, L. B., 'Le croisement des cultures dans les régions limitrophes de Géorgie, d'Arménie et de Byzance', Prémisses méthodogiques pour une lecture sociographique', *Annali di Ca' Foscari (Serie orientale 17)* 15/3 (1986), 81–96.
Zekiyan, L. B., 'Die Christianisierung und die Alphabetisierung Armeniens als Vorbilder kultureller Inkarnation, besonders im subkaukasischen Gebiet', in W. Seibt (ed.), *Die Christianisierung des Kaukasus: Referate des Internationalen Symposions* (Wien, 1999, 2002), 189–99.
Zhordania, T., *k'ronikebi da sxva masala sak'art'velos istoriisa 1* [Chronicles and other sources of Georgian history] (Tbilisi, 1892); 2 (Tbilisi, 1897).
Ziadé, R., *Les martyrs Maccabées: de l'histoire juive au culte chrétien: Les homéliees de Grégore de Nazanze et Jean Chrysostome* (Leiden, 2007).
Zuckerman, C., 'The Khazars and Byzantium. The First Encounter', in P. B. Golden, H. Ben Shamai and A. Róna-Tas (eds), *The World of the Khazars: New Perspectives. Selected Papers from the Jerusalem 1999 International Khazar Colloquium* (Leiden and Boston, 2007), 399–432.

# Index of Personal Names

Abashidze, Aslan, 297
Abbas I, shah of Persia, 233–5, 239, 241
Abiat'ar, 74, 84
Abo of Tbilisi, St, 6, 13, 95
Abuserisże Tbeli, 157, 286
Agathangelos, 28, 41–2, 45–52, 57, 67, 75, 80, 84–5, 90, 119–22, 125, 312
Agha Muhammad-Khan, 230–1
Aharon of Vanand, 121–2
Aleksey Yevlev, 186, 173
Alexander I, emperor of Russia, 230–1, 242, 244, 247
Alexander I, king of Kakheti, 230
Alexander, fictional king of Georgia, 252
Alexander the Great, 81–3, 87, 89, 91, 93–6, 152, 269
Alexis I, tsar, 236
Andrew, apostle, 1, 35–6, 71, 137, 141, 149–50, 158, 162–3, 168, 179–82, 185, 187, 209, 224, 301
Antiochos I, king of the Seleucid Empire, 55, 60
Antiochos Strategos, 88
Anton Saġirisże, 201
Antony I, katholikos-patriarch, 103
Antony II, katholikos-patriarch, 231
Archil I, Erismtavari of Kartli, St, 65
Arseni I Sap'areli, katholikos of Kartli, 70, 115
Arseni IV Bulmaisimisże, katholikos-patriarch of Georgia, 211–12
Arseni Beri, presbyter, 149, 164, 169, 187
Arseni Iqalt'oeli, 195

Ašot I, Kouropalates of Tao, 131–3, 142–5, 153
Athenogenes, St, 45–6, 51, 69, 85, 190

Babik, 53, 64–7
Bagrat III, king of Georgia, 133, 135, 147, 154, 158–9
Bagrat IV, king of Georgia, 135–6, 146, 183
Bagrat VI, king of Imereti, 185
Bagrationi, Vakhushti, 78, 100, 155, 185
Bakar, son of Vakhtang VI, 241, 244, 268
Bakradze, Kote, 277–8, 309
Baratashvili, Mamuka, 268–9, 271
Barbara, St, 139–41, 190
Bardas Phokas, 134
Bardas Skleros, 133–4
Bartholomew, apostle, 84, 150, 179
Basil I, emperor, 85, 144
Basil II, emperor, 133–6, 200
Basil Ezosmożġuari, 197, 202, 208, 214–15
Beard, Mary, 17–18
Bezaleel, 173
Brown, Peter, 31
Bughadze, Lasha, 291–2

Chavchavadze, Alexander, 268, 270, 274
Chavchavadze, Ilia, 262–4, 273–9
Constantine I, emperor, 29, 35–7, 39, 56, 66, 82, 85, 94, 123, 148, 154, 201–2, 204, 237, 240–1, 247

## INDEX OF PERSONAL NAMES

Constantine VII, king of Georgia, 229
Constantine VII Porphyrogenitus, emperor, 132, 170
Constantine VIII, emperor, 136, 200
Constantine, martyr saint, 154

Dadiani, Grigol, 248
Dadiani, Nino, 248
Dadiani, Tsotne, 286
David of Israel, 38, 137, 144–6, 153, 158, 166, 170, 192–3, 202, 207, 224, 253
David IV 'the Builder', king of Georgia, 139, 160–1, 171–3, 190, 196, 263–4
David V, king of Georgia, 196
David VI 'Narin', king of Georgia, 216
David VII 'Ulu', king of Georgia 'Ulu', 216
David Kouropalates/Couropalate, king of Tao, 133–5, 147, 158
David, son of Giorgi XIII of Kartli-Kakheti, 248
David-Soslan, 192–3, 197
De Beauvoir, Simone, 10
Deborah, prophetess, 79, 210–11
Demetre I, king of Georgia, 139–40, 171–3, 196, 205
Demetre II, king of Georgia, 262
Demna, prince, 196–7
Dinara, fictional queen of Georgia, 251, 253–4
Diocletian, 43, 45, 51, 141, 159–60, 164
Douglas, Mary, 8, 17

Eastmond, Antony, 99, 139, 141, 160, 200, 204, 206, 212, 265
Elchin, Fedot, 237
Elijah, prophet, 85, 145, 190
Elioz of Mtskheta, St, 84–5, 88
Eliseus, apostle, 50
Ephrem Mc'ire, 72, 134, 150, 186
Epiphanius the Monk, 141, 149–50, 180, 187
Erekle II, king of Kartli-Kakheti, 191, 218, 230–1, 270, 314
Euthymios Hagiorites/Ep't'wime Mt'acmindeli 150, 156, 176–7

Filaret, patriarch of Moscow, 239

Gabriel, archangel, 139
Gabriel, monk, 2, 9, 178
Gagarin, Grigory, 265
Galatariotou, Maria, 19, 198–9
Gamsakhurdia, Zviad, 284–5, 304–6
Gayanē, St, 12, 43–6, 50, 52, 78
Gedevanishvili, Ekaterine, 145, 157–60, 163
George Hagiorites/Giorgi Mt'acmindeli, 71, 134, 150, 177
George, St, 76, 78, 137, 139, 141, 154–67, 179, 190, 207, 220, 224, 234, 307, 309, 313
Giorgi I, king of Georgia, 135–6, 159
Giorgi II, king of Apkhazeti, 156–8
Giorgi III, king of Georgia, 196–7, 201–2, 204, 205, 265
Giorgi III, king of Imereti, 236
Giorgi IV 'Laša', king of Georgia, 193–4, 204, 206, 211, 218, 222, 264–5
Giorgi V, king of Georgia, 183
Giorgi VIII, king of Georgia, 183
Giorgi XIII, king of Kartli-Kakheti, 231, 248, 251
Giorgi Mc'ire, 176
Giorgi Merč'ule, 141, 153, 168, 177, 184
Grant, Bruce, 246
Gregory the Illuminator, St, 14, 28, 30, 42–8, 50, 52, 56, 70, 75–6, 90–1, 93, 113, 119–21, 312
Gregory of Nazianzus, 52, 153
Gregory the Theologian, 98
Grigol Xanc't'eli, 6, 132, 134, 141–6, 153, 168, 184
Grigoris, patriarch of Albania, 30, 50–2, 85

Heraclius, emperor, 30, 65, 81–3, 91, 124, 184, 186, 242
Hr̄ip'simē, St, 12, 43–6, 50, 52, 71, 74–5, 78, 85

Iakhsar, 222
Iakob C'urtaveli, 102, 104, 105, 107
Ilarion the Georgian, St, 174–5

Ilia II, katholikos-patriarch of Georgia, 2, 5, 21, 24, 167, 282–8, 290, 292–3, 297, 301
Ioane Anč'eli, 182
Ioane Bera, 146
Ioane Minč'xi, 155–9
Ioane Mt'acmindeli, 176–7
Ioane Sabanisże, 95
Ioane Šavt'eli, 183, 193–4, 215
Ioane-T'ornik, 133, 177, 262
Ioane Zedazneli, St, 76–7, 94
Ioseliani, Jaba, 305

John the Baptist, 38, 45, 46, 51, 85
John the Evangelist, 169
John Hagiorites/Ioane Mt'acmindeli, 176

Kalistrate I, katholikos-patriarch of Georgia, 279
Karekin II, patriarch and katholikos of all Armenians, 3
Katherine, St, 139–41
Ketevan, princess of Kartli-Kakheti, 270–1
Ketevan, queen of Kartli-Kakheti, 8, 12, 17, 23, 190, 226, 233–6, 251, 256, 259, 278, 290
Khakhanashvili, Alexander, 255
Kiknadze, P'iladelp'os, 271–3, 285
Kiknadze, Zurab, 61, 78–9
Koriwn, 28
Kostanti III, king of Apkhazeti, 156
Kostava, Merab, 284
Kyrion I, katholikos of Kartli, 114, 119

Lazarev, Ivan, 251
Łazar P'arpec'i, 41, 117
Lazarus, 89–90, 175, 196, 240
Leonti Mroveli, 54, 147–8, 180
Levan I Dadiani, 186
Levan V Dadiani, 249
Levi-Strauss, Claude, 18, 22, 115, 125–6
Liparit IV Baġvaši, 183
Longinoz of Karsani, 84–5
Luarsab II, King of Kartli, St, 234–5, 262

Maccabean brothers, 4, 46, 106
Mahé, Jean-Pierre, 52, 187

Maisuradze, Giorgi, 302–3
Manning, Paul, 274
Manoukian, Abel, 5
Mariam Artsruni, 135
Mariam, princess, daughter of Erekle II, 270–1
Mariam, wife of Giorgi XIII, 251
Marušiani, 159
Marwan II 'the Deaf', 131, 154
Mary, Mother of God, 1–3, 9–10, 12, 19, 22–3, 32, 39, 74, 79–80, 84, 103, 115, 128, 137, 145, 167–86, 190, 192–6, 205, 209–12, 221, 224–6, 237–8, 240–3, 248–9, 252–4, 256, 258–97, 299, 301–2, 307–8, 312–15
Maštoc', St, 14, 28, 48, 113, 121
Matthias, apostle, 149
Maximus 'the Greek', 240
Medea, 297–9, 309
Michael I Keroularios, patriarch, 200
Michael I, tsar, 236–40
Michael Psellos, 199, 216
Minani, 69, 73, 79, 83, 100, 125, 162
Mirian III, King of Kartli, 29, 61, 65, 71, 80, 82, 87, 98, 142, 148, 164, 177, 259
Movsēs II, katholikos of Armenia, 113
Movsēs Xorenac'i, 47, 58, 84, 119–20, 122

Nana, queen of Kartli, 74, 80, 82, 279
Nestan-Darejan, princess of India, 63, 213–14, 234
Nicholas I, emperor of Russia, 262
Nikoloz I Gulaberisże, katholikos-patriarch of Georgia, 163, 192, 199, 208–12, 215, 279
Nino, St, 6, 8, 12–16, 20–1, 23, 30, 48, 67–8, 70–103, 110, 113, 119–22, 124–7, 137, 141–2, 146, 148–55, 162–5, 169, 170, 176, 179, 181–3, 185, 187–8, 190–2, 196, 207–12, 223–6, 234, 240, 244–9, 251, 259, 267, 270–2, 275–9, 290–1, 299, 303, 309, 311–13, 315

Odoevsky, Alexander, 250, 256
Orbeliani, Grigol, 265–6
Orbeliani, Maiko, 262

## INDEX OF PERSONAL NAMES

Pantaleon, St, 51–2, 85
P'arnavaz, king of Kartli, 54–61, 65–7, 89, 142, 177
Paul I, Tsar, 231
Paulinus of Nola, 35–6
Perpetua, St, 106–7
Peter I, Tsar, 241, 268
Peter, Apostle, 35, 84, 149
Peter, Bishop, 98, 152
Peter the Iberian, 92, 151
Procopius of Caesarea, 36–7, 51
Pulcheria, empress, 38, 53, 192, 209

Quarquare Jaqeli, 183–4

Romanos III Argyros, emperor, 135
Romanoz of Samtavro, 244
Rostevan, king of Arabia, 213
Rustaveli, 193, 196, 207, 213–15, 219, 234, 314
Rusudan, queen of Georgia, 182, 188, 196, 201, 203, 211, 215–16, 262, 310, 314

Saakashvili, Mikheil, 1, 7, 263, 297
Sabinin, Michael, 258–60, 276, 288
Sahak I, katholikos of Armenia, 28, 121–2
Samżimari, mythological figure, 162–3, 165
Samżivari, fictional queen, 162, 163, 181, 187–8
Sargis I Jaqeli, 183
Schmitt, Karl, 20, 212, 285
Shapur II, Shah, 54, 64
Shevardnadze, Eduard, 269
Shishkov, Alexander, 251
Shota Rustaveli *see* Rustaveli
Shushanik, St, 14, 16–17, 21–2, 102–2, 124–7, 137, 185, 226, 259, 278, 287, 313
Sidonia, daughter of Abiat'ar, 74, 84–7, 94–5, 270–1, 279
Sidonia, St, 74, 85, 259
Siegfried, 63
Simon the Zealot, 149–50, 179, 182
Skhirtladze, Zaza, 145
Socrates Scholasticus, 37, 120

Solomon II of Imereti, 232
Solomon of Israel, 145, 166, 173, 195, 202
Stalin, Joseph, 288, 308
Sukhanov, Arseny, 238–9
Sumbat Davit'isże, 136, 145, 159
Symeon Metaphrastes, 148

Tamar(a), literary/mythological figure, 251, 255
Tamar, queen of Georgia, 8, 12–13, 16–17, 20, 23, 62, 73, 77, 79–80, 128, 138, 163, 182–4, 187–8, 189–208, 211–22, 224–6, 253–4, 259, 262–6, 278, 288, 290–3, 310, 314–15
Taqaishvili, Ekvtime, 283
Tariel, protagonist of the *Knight in the Panther's Skin*, 63, 213–14, 234
Teimuraz I, king of Kartli-Kakheti, 12, 233–6, 239, 241, 256
Tekle, princess, 270
Thaddaeus, apostle, 46–7
Theodora, empress, 198–200, 203, 205
Theodore, St, 139, 141, 159–60, 207
Thomson, Robert, 46
Tinatin, princess of Arabia, 213–14, 315
T'orġva, 63
T'ornik(e), general, 133, 177, 262
T'rdat III, king of Armenia, 27, 42–6, 66, 71
Tsereteli, Akaki, 262, 266, 298
Tuite, Kevin, 155, 161–2, 215

Ukleba, Lia, 289–90
Usupashvili, David, 295–6
Uxtanēs of Sebasteia, 117–20, 127

Vač'agan III, king of Albania, 49–51, 54–8, 61, 65–7, 84–6, 124, 135, 142, 151, 312
Vakhtang I, king of Kartli, 30, 54, 57, 64–5, 82, 96–8, 108, 110, 117, 151–4, 159, 166–8, 177, 179, 184, 191, 202, 224, 269

Vakhtang VI, king of Kartli, 232, 241, 268
Vardan Mamikonean, 4, 28, 104, 108, 117
Varsk'en, 104–10, 114–15
Vrt'anēs K'erdoł, 113

Wardrop, James Oliver, 62
Wardrop, Marjory, 277–8, 309

Yovhannēs Awjnec'i, katholikos of Armenia, 48
Yury Bogolyubsky, 197, 291

Zabylon, 164
Zakharov, Pavel, 237
Zechariah, father of John the Baptist, 51, 52, 85
Zoe, empress, 199–201, 205
Zosimos of Kumurdo, 286–7

# Index of Place Names

Abasgia, 132, 149
Achara, 7, 148, 157, 180–1, 286, 297–8
Acquri, 1–2, 9, 168, 179, 181–5, 209, 226
Alania, 150
Alaverdi, 156, 235
Amaras, 66
Ananuri, 244–5, 255, 267
Anč'i, 9, 182
Ani, 208
Antioch, 134, 150, 168, 185
Apkhazeti, 147–8, 154, 156–8, 168, 179–80, 182, 185, 249, 298, 304
Artanuji, 131–2, 153
Artsakh, 52
Artvin, 62
Athos, Mt., 1–2, 73, 134, 149, 156, 176–8, 208, 210, 240–2, 254, 262
Avarayr, 5, 28, 108

Baghdad, 82, 192
Bodbe, 247–8
Betania, 264–5
Bočorma, 160–1

Caesarea, 45
Cappadocia, 71, 155, 163–4, 313
Caucasian Albania, 21, 27–31, 49–52, 55, 65–7, 117, 124, 131, 142, 252
Constantinople, 128, 133–7, 140, 149, 153, 159–60, 171, 184, 186, 197, 200, 237, 248, 300, 307, 311
Chorokhi, 182
C'urtaw *see* Tsurtavi

Darial, 95–7, 100, 112, 245, 254–5, 270
Dighomi, 59
Dwin, 31

Elbrus/Ialbuzi, Mt, 98, 218

Gelati, 170–3, 192
Gergeti, 97, 100–1, 267
Gugareti/Gogarene/Gugark', 104, 108–12, 114–17, 119, 127, 185

Hadishi, 161

Iberia *see* Kartli, late antique kingdom
Iberia, Theme, 135
Ispahan, 59, 233
Iveria, 1–2, 9, 177, 230, 236, 240–4, 253–4, 271–2, 308

Javakheti, 131, 135, 286–7
Jerusalem, 1, 22, 29, 38, 71, 84–5, 88, 91–2, 125, 128, 134, 142, 153, 169–71, 173, 203, 208, 310
Jvari of Mtskheta, 77, 91, 99, 112, 113–14, 119, 121, 127

Kakheti, 76, 147, 156–7, 160–1, 229–31, 233–5, 248
Karati, 68, 78–9, 162
Kartli-Kakheti, 230, 233, 239, 242–3, 248, 251

Kartli, late antique kingdom, 21, 27–31, 54–5, 61, 65, 67–8, 70, 73–7, 80–99, 110–11, 119–20, 124–5, 132, 137, 150–4, 165, 170, 177, 209, 247, 259, 279
Kartli, late medieval kingdom, 185–6, 229–36, 238, 241, 244, 273
Kartli, medieval principality, 131–3, 141–8, 156–7, 167, 176, 179, 181–6, 207–8, 223–4
Kazbegi, 100–1, 244–5, 267
Khakhmati, 162
Khakhuli, 133, 145, 146, 172–3, 192–3
Khevi, 97, 100–1
Khevsureti, 68–9, 79, 100, 162, 222
Khobi, 186, 286
Klarjeti, 71, 131–5, 142, 145–9, 156
Kumurdo, 286–7
Kutaisi, 147, 154, 170, 201
Kyiv, 8, 242

Lašaris Jvari, 193, 220–1
Latali, 139–40
Lazica/Lazeti, 27, 149–50, 287–8

Martvili, 156, 159
Meskheti, 148, 182–7, 301
Moscow, 236–42, 244, 247, 253, 308
Mtkvari, 99, 131
Mtskheta, 30–1, 73–4, 77, 82, 84–8, 91–4, 99–104, 119, 121, 127, 132, 145–8, 169–71, 178–9, 182, 208, 212, 223, 238–9, 245, 255–6, 267, 271
Muscovy, 13, 23, 173, 229–30, 234–8, 252, 308

Odishi, 185, 186, 229, 238
Oshki, 72, 145–6, 177, 207

Pankisi, 63
Pontus, 149, 153
Pshavi, 68

Rkinis Jvari, 181

Saint Petersburg, 256, 274
Samegrelo, 186, 226, 237–8, 248–9, 286
Samtskhe, 162, 168, 181–8, 229
Sevan, 64
Shatberdi, 71, 80, 99, 146, 148, 164
Sinai, Mt, 160–1, 164
Siwnikʿ, 64, 74
Sokhumi, 167, 182
Sousania, 150, 180, 187
Svaneti, 139–41, 158–9, 162, 182, 186–7, 190, 217, 315

Tabakhmela, 194
Tao, 71, 73, 116, 131–3, 135, 142, 145–8, 153, 156, 158, 172, 180
Tbilisi, 133, 194, 223, 230, 244, 246, 261, 264–5, 267, 271, 282–3, 303–6
Tergi/Terek, 254–5, 267–9
Tskhinvali, 304
Tsurtavi, 104–5, 112–13, 108–18

Ukraine, 242
Urekan, 50–1
Urtʾxva, 157–8

Vardzia, 183, 194, 205–6, 208
Vladikavkaz, 245, 267, 274

Zadeni, 89. 181–2
Zedazeni, 76–7

EU representative:
Easy Access System Europe
Mustamäe tee 50, 10621 Tallinn, Estonia
Gpsr.requests@easproject.com